D1565942

Emotion, Development, and Self-Organization

In the last twenty to thirty years, a new way to understand complex systems has emerged in the natural sciences – an approach often called nonlinear dynamics, dynamical systems theory, or chaos theory. This perspective has allowed scientists to trace the emergence of order from disorder, and in particular the emergence of complex, higher-order forms from interactions among lower-order constituents. This process is called self-organization, and it is thought to be responsible for both change and continuity in physical, biological, and social systems.

Recently, principles of self-organizing dynamic systems have been imported into psychology, and especially developmental psychology, where they have helped us reconceptualize basic processes of motor and cognitive development. *Emotion, Development, and Self-Organization* is the first book to apply these principles to emotional development. The contributors address such fundamental issues as the biological bases of emotion and emotional development, relations between cognition and emotion in real time and development, personality development and individual differences, interpersonal processes, and clinical implications. The result is a comprehensive and innovative volume that includes the most recent work of recognized leaders in the field as well as contributions by a new generation of theorists who take principles of self-organization as their starting point.

Marc D. Lewis is associate professor of developmental psychology at the University of Toronto.

Isabela Granic is a doctoral candidate in developmental psychology at the University of Toronto.

Cambridge Studies in Social and Emotional Development

General Editors: Martin L. Hoffman, *New York University*
Carolyn Shantz, *Wayne State University*

Advisory Board: Nancy Eisenberg, Robert N. Emde,
Willard W. Hartup, Lois W. Hoffman, Eleanor E. Maccoby,
Franz J. Mönks, Paul Mussen, Ross D. Parke,
Michael Rutter, and Carolyn Zahn-Waxler

Emotion, Development, and Self-Organization

Dynamic Systems Approaches to Emotional Development

Edited by

MARC D. LEWIS
University of Toronto

ISABELA GRANIC
University of Toronto

PUBLISHED BY THE PRESS SYNDICATE OF THE UNIVERSITY OF CAMBRIDGE
The Pitt Building, Trumpington Street, Cambridge, United Kingdom

CAMBRIDGE UNIVERSITY PRESS
The Edinburgh Building, Cambridge CB2 2RU, UK   http://www.cup.cam.ac.uk
40 West 20th Street, New York, NY 10011-4211, USA   http://www.cup.org
10 Stamford Road, Oakleigh, Melbourne 3166, Australia
Ruiz de Alarcón 13, 28014 Madrid, Spain

First published 2000

Printed in the United States of America

Typeface Times Roman 10.25/13 pt.   *System* DeskTopPro$_{/UX}$ [BV]

A catalog record for this book is available from the British Library.

Library of Congress Cataloging in Publication data

Emotion, development, and self-organization : dynamic systems approaches to emotional
development / edited by Marc D. Lewis, Isabela Granic.
p. cm. – (Cambridge studies in social and emotional development)
ISBN 0-521-64089-X (hb)
1. Emotions.   2. Self-organizing systems.   I. Lewis, Marc D.   II. Granic,
Isabela.   III. Series.
BF531 E484 2000
152.4 – dc21   99-048061

ISBN 0 521 64089 X hardback

Contents

Contributors

Linda A. Camras
Department of Psychology
DePaul University
2219 N. Kenmore Ave.
Chicago, IL 60614

**Carolina de Weerth and
  Paul van Geert**
Department of Psychology
University of Groningen
Grote Kruisstraat 2/1
9712 TS Groningen
The Netherlands

Walter J. Freeman
Department of Molecular and Cell
  Biology
129 LSA, Neurobiology Division
University of California, Berkeley
Berkeley, CA 94720

Isabela Granic
Department of Human Development
  and Applied Psychology
Ontario Institute for Studies in
  Education
University of Toronto
252 Bloor Street West
Toronto, Ontario M5S 1V6
Canada

**Debra Harkins and
  Thomas Harakal**
Department of Psychology
Suffolk University
Beacon Hill
Boston, MA 02115

Kate L. Harkness
Western Psychiatric Institute and
  Clinic
University of Pittsburgh
3811 O'Hara Street
Pittsburgh, PA 15213

**Carroll E. Izard, Brian P.
  Ackerman, Kristen M. Schoff,
  and Sarah E. Fine**
Department of Psychology
University of Delaware
Newark, DE 19716

**Daniel P. Keating and
  Fiona K. Miller**
Department of Human Development
  and Applied Psychology
Ontario Institute for Studies in
  Education
University of Toronto
252 Bloor Street West
Toronto, Ontario M5S 1V6
Canada

**Deborah J. Laible and
Ross A. Thompson**
Department of Psychology
University of Nebraska
209 Burnett Hall
Lincoln, NE 68588-0308

Marc D. Lewis
Department of Human Development
and Applied Psychology
Ontario Institute for Studies in
Education
University of Toronto
252 Bloor Street West
Toronto, Ontario M5S 1V6
Canada

Michael F. Mascolo
Department of Psychology
Merrimack College
North Andover, MA 01845

Jaak Panksepp
Department of Psychology
Bowling Green State University
Bowling Green, OH 43403

**Kimberly D. Ryan, John M.
Gottman, James D. Murray,
Sybil Carrère, and
Catherine Swanson**
Department of Psychology
University of Washington
Box 351525
Seattle, WA 98195-1525

Klaus R. Scherer
Université de Genève
F.P.S.E.
9, route de Drize
CH-1227 Carouge
Switzerland

Allan N. Schore
UCLA School of Medicine
9817 Sylvia Avenue
Northridge, CA 91324

Don M. Tucker
Department of Psychology
University of Oregon
Eugene, OR 97403

Foreword

This book offers a paradigm shift in the way emotion is conceptualized. There is, at a minimum, the paradigm shift from seventeenth-century Newtonian models of cause and effect, antecedents and outcomes, toward twentieth-century dynamic systems models. The latter are characterized by self-organization through iterative feedback processes that afford the possibility of both stability and change, dynamic pattern formation and emergent innovation, order and chaos, determinism and indeterminism. Dynamic systems models generalize to supernovas, insect communication, the growth of cities, and economic cycles. This should be plenty of paradigm possibilities for anyone.

When dynamic systems ideas are used in psychology, however, scientists get more than just the principled application of those ideas. All the other disciplines that partake of dynamic systems thinking deal with concrete and measurable entities. The pulsing of stars and insect wings, the disposition of shopping malls and market swings have two things in common: (1) they can be counted, quantified, and reduced to numbers, and (2) they are substantiated in actual entities of flesh and stone. The psyche – the complexity of human experience – is none of that, neither commensurate nor substantial. Psyche coexists with matter, lives in bodies and ecosystems, but it is fundamentally nonmaterial. Psyche is emergent at the very core of its ontology whether we have dynamic systems ideas about it or not.

Every spiritual discipline in human history has been created to account for the mysterious transcendence of the psyche. The works of spiritual leaders are narrative accounts based on direct observation of psychological experience. Read the descriptions of Moses, Christ, Augustine, Buddha, and Gandhi. You'll find compelling testimonies of developmental transformations, of unpredictable and unprecedented psychological processes, woven together by agonies and ecstasies. It is not by chance that spirituality is connected with the deepest of human emotions: facing one's most dreaded fears, dealing with profound loss, or being transported by boundless joy.

I beckon the reader of this scientifically groundbreaking book on emotional development with a reminder about the connection between emotion and spirituality, not because it appears as a major theme in the subsequent chapters, but rather to help frame the work reported here in the entirety of the paradigm shift to which, at least implicitly, it speaks. Emotion is grounded in the matrix of the body, affecting and being affected dynamically by every part of it. Heat and color come into the cheeks and neck, the breath betrays pain and passion, the heart pounds or flutters, genitals stiffen and slacken, legs quiver or run like hell. Emotion is visceral like nothing else. If you didn't get the message of your subversive thoughts just wait until your stomach clenches or your heart breaks to find out what is really going on.

Read the chapters of this book to get a state-of-the-art rendering of the codynamics of the brain and body, the person and context, in the formation and development of the emotions. If you haven't been fortunate enough to let the dynamic systems perspective reinvent your way of looking at the physical and psychological universe, this book is a great place to start. The science of dynamic systems is already captivating, and its application to emotions is, well, compelling and provocative. Enjoy!

Sure, you are invited to do the academic thing – raise questions, challenge the authors, pick friendly fights – if you want. All these notable and accomplished scholars can take care of themselves. But I urge you not to stop there. Pay attention to what is happening to you emotionally as you read and as new ideas are created in your dialogues with the authors. Check your whole body. While your thoughts are ticking away with the logic of ifs and thens, notice if your feet want to dance or to kick or if your breath is shallow or full. Can you pinpoint a single, specific location of the emotion in your body? As you stockpile reasons for believing in your own views or evidence for the author's point in your own data or experience, notice how those feelings of agreement and disagreement are connected to what you might want to say to the author, or to your colleagues about the author. Can you separate your "own" emotion from the process of communication generated between you and the imagined other? Can you distinguish intention from desire?

I want to tell you that emotion transcends the body even though it is of the body, but I know that such knowledge can come only from the testimony of your own experience. I want to say that everyone can appreciate how emotion connects us to all things, but I know that the psyche has reasons to select congenial evidence without homage to the dynamic system from which it derives its nourishment and existence. I want to tell you that emotions are available to navigate in a vast network of relationships, ways of experiencing communion and estrangement, a seventh sense: intense as red and soft as a caress. I want to state that claiming ownership of emotion has no moral warrant, any more than coveting the air we breathe or the earth on which we walk. All I can really tell you is that all this wanting hurts, that words are inadequate, and that explanations are poor substitutes for the living truth of emotional experience.

So read, yes. This book takes a huge, meritorious step toward encompassing the dynamic system of emotional experience. Read and discover what can happen when scientists collect the immeasurably raw data from their own hearts.

Rome, Italy   ALAN FOGEL
June 1999

INTRODUCTION

A New Approach to the Study of Emotional Development

Marc D. Lewis and Isabela Granic

Emotional development traces a detailed pattern across the lifespan. This pattern is comprised of periods of rapid change alternating with periods of consolidation and stability, self-amplifying individual variations on universal developmental themes, and progressive complexity in feelings, thoughts, personality, behavior, and self-regulation. We know that the patterning of emotional development is not a direct expression of some species-specific or genetic program. Nor is it simply a readout of socialization practices, family experience, or any other set of environmental contingencies. Despite our attempts to predict it, emotional development is indeterminate and malleable at almost any age. Despite our normative classifications, it is characterized by idiosyncratic and unique trajectories. In short, emotional development is organized and orderly without being prespecified or programmed. How do we account for its intrinsic organization? How does emotional development achieve its coherence, complexity, and patterning without design or instruction?

As in other developmental domains, the best answer to this question seems to depend on principles that extend well beyond developmental psychology. These principles express a new approach to change and novelty across the natural sciences, an approach variously called nonlinear dynamical systems theory (or dynamic systems theory, for short), complex systems theory, or chaos theory. At the heart of this perspective is the idea that natural systems behave very differently than the simple, idealized systems so well described by Newtonian mechanics. Systems in nature are characterized by interactions among many components, whether molecules in a fluid, cells in a body or brain, organisms in an ecosystem, or individuals in a society. This complexity is not just a detail. The interactions among the elements of complex systems are reciprocal, with constituents influencing each other simultaneously, and they recur over time, as systems

1

continue to evolve or perpetuate their own stability. Thus, cause-effect relations take the form of feedback loops. Effects grow or shrink due to the activity of the system itself, and change does not rely on information received from the environment. The most important and dramatic result of this kind of system dynamics is the emergence of novel forms at higher levels of organization. This process is called self-organization.

In the sciences at large, self-organization refers to the emergence of order from disorder, and in particular the emergence of coherent, higher-order forms from the interactions of many lower-order components. Prigogine and Stengers (1984) explain how recurring chemical reactions give rise to global patterns of molecular coherence. Haken (1977) describes how the movements of atoms in a laser synchronize spontaneously to produce light of a uniform frequency. Haken's theory has been extended to living systems in which coherent actions arise from the automatic cooperation of muscular and sensory components (Kelso, 1984; Turvey, 1990). The cybernetic scientists Ashby (1952) and von Neumann (1958) discovered the emergence of recurrent patterns in electronic circuits, providing the first glimpse of cognitive self-organization. Today's neural networks are descendants of these efforts. Biologists such as Eigen (1992) and Kauffman (1993) have explored self-organizing patterns in networks of organic molecules such as DNA strands, leading to models of molecular evolution, gene expression, and the origins of life. Finally, Maturana and Varela (e.g., 1987), spanning cell biology, immunology, and perception, have coined the term "autopoiesis" to describe the self-organization and self-maintenance of living and cognitive systems. These and other contributions have collectively changed scientific thinking and practice in the last twenty years, leading to talk of a paradigm shift to a "science of complexity" (e.g., Lewin, 1992).

Self-organizational approaches have recently been imported into the social sciences as well, where they are used to model growth and stabilization in economics, anthropology, social organization, and psychology. In psychology, they have proliferated so quickly that it is difficult to trace their path, but at least two broad routes of theoretical progress can be delineated. The first is the study of self-organizing cognitive systems, first introduced in the 1960s and currently expressed in biological and connectionist approaches to cognitive science (e.g., Elman et al., 1996; Varela, Thompson, and Rosch, 1991) and neuroscience (Freeman, 1995; Tucker, 1992) as well as in dynamic models of basic cognitive processes (Port and van Gelder, 1995). The second is the study of self-organizing developmental systems, beginning with Piaget's model of equilibration (Chapman, 1991) and recently elaborated in dynamic systems models of motor, cognitive, social, and neural development (e.g., Fogel, 1993; Thatcher, 1991; Thelen and Smith, 1994; van Geert, 1991). These pathways, like the boughs of a tree, support a proliferating network of branches that extend to clinical, physiological, social, abnormal, and personality psychology.

In the midst of all this proliferation, the study of emotion and its development has been slow to incorporate principles of self-organization; but movement in this direction is now gaining momentum. By looking at emotional development as self-organization, investigators are beginning to view its intrinsic orderliness as an emergent form, accruing from recurrent, self-perpetuating emotional processes in real time. This approach links emotion and emotional development in a single field of inquiry, and it demands detailed attention to the elements and interactive mechanisms that contribute to emerging structure. In order to encourage this trend, help give it shape, and suggest new directions for its growth, the present volume gathers together the ideas of developmentalists, other psychologists, and neurobiologists who have started to look at emotion and emotional development as self-organizing processes. But before going on to introduce these contributions in detail, we start by asking why the study of emotional processes has lagged behind other domains in embracing principles of self-organization, and we show how recent work in emotion theory, developmental theory, and particularly emotional development has set the stage for renewal.

Theoretical progress in emotion theory has been constricted by traditional cognitivist approaches (Lewis and Granic, 1999a). In particular, much of emotion theory derives from cognitive psychology, where linear (i.e., step-by-step, incremental) information processing has been the dominant metaphor for decades. This computationalist dictum is clearly evident in appraisal theories of emotion. These theories propose that cognitive activities compute the significance of events and thereby give rise to emotional reactions. Much of the work on mood-congruent cognition has also reflected this orientation, with its depiction of moods as control signals or stable belief states. Such linear thinking may have slowed theoretical progress by perpetuating the debate over cognitive versus emotional primacy in one form or another, hampering our ability to model relations between goals, emotions, and emotion regulation in a convincing way, and supporting an overly reductionist approach to clinical and personality processes. It is interesting to note that many cognitive psychologists are starting to embrace nonlinear dynamic ideas, and traditional emotion theory may be one of the last strongholds of orthodox cognitivism.

In the last few years, however, some emotion theorists have begun to circumvent traditional cognitivism or openly criticize its implications. Some make explicit use of constructs such as graded influences, nonlinearity, feedback, emergence, and context-sensitivity, which are antithetical to computationalism and suggestive, instead, of emergent emotional processes. The mood models of Teasdale and Mathews have important feedback components, and context-sensitivity in the work of Parkinson and Manstead is congenial with self-organization. Frijda and Scherer have advocated nonlinear models of appraisal-emotion processes, and Scherer has begun to explicitly model emotions as episodes of synchronization in a nonlinear dynamic system. Some of these emerging directions were voiced at an invited symposium at the 1996 convention of the International Society for Research on Emotions. Alan Fogel, Klaus Scherer, Linda Camras, and Marc Lewis presented papers on emotional self-organization, and Carroll Izard acted as discussant. The symposium generated considerable debate and excitement, and the present volume includes contributions from all of these participants.

The field of emotional development has also been dominated by traditional theoretical agendas. Nativist theories, with their emphasis on hard-wired or prespecified emotions, have a difficult time dealing with the emergence of new emotional forms in development and, in particular, with the contribution of cognition to complex emotional outcomes (from secondary emotions to personality styles). Constructivist approaches suggest that cognitive schemas are the vehicles of emotional development, and that emotions and their elicitors become more sophisticated as these schemas increase in complexity. But emotion itself gets lost in this portrayal and is treated as merely another component of an essentially cognitive process. Functionalist approaches see emotional development as a result of individual adaptations to social, cognitive, and biological circumstances. However, their view of adaptation is based on learning models, with their implication of ''best choices'' or optimal solutions, and they cannot easily explain developmental paths that are idiosyncratic and illogical. Critics have argued that developmental psychology cannot progress further without a scientific explanation for novelty, increasing complexity, and emerging coherence, free of innate programs, generic rules, and specific instructions from the environment (e.g., Elman et al., 1996; Molenaar, 1986). This certainly rings true for emotional development, where novel forms arise unpredictably and coherent outcomes are both complex and idiosyncratic.

In response to this challenge, theorists from across developmental disciplines have begun to focus on nonlinear, dynamical, self-organizing processes. These efforts are typified by developmentalists who refer to themselves as dynamic systems (DS) theorists (e.g., Fogel and Thelen, 1987; Lewis, 1995; Thelen and Smith, 1994; van Geert, 1991), but they are joined by other contemporary systemic thinkers (e.g., Elman et al., 1996; Keating, 1990; Oyama, 1989; Sameroff, 1995; Sroufe, 1995; van der Maas and Molenaar, 1992). From a dynamic systems perspective, novel forms arise in development through the spontaneous coordination of system constituents that interact with each other recursively in the service of a particular function, task, or goal. In motor development, for example, recurring interactions among muscular and perceptual activities give rise to patterns of coordination underlying coherent skills such as walking (Thelen and Smith, 1994). In communicative development, consensual frames or rituals emerge within dyads through reciprocal coordination of actions, gestures, speech, and emotional expressions (Fogel, 1993). In cognitive development, new capabilities arise from the coordination (or, cooperation versus competition) of attentional, conceptual, and linguistic components (Smith, 1995; van Geert, 1991). DS theorists emphasize that these and other developmental phenomena can all be explained by a common set of principles concerning nonlinear causation and self-organization (Lewis, 2000).

Whereas DS approaches to motor and cognitive development have gained considerable attention, a DS literature on emotional development is just beginning to emerge. A few years ago, Fogel and colleagues (1992) proposed that emotions are self-organizing products of psychological and bodily processes that arise and develop within interpersonal transactions. Camras (1992) examined developing emotions as dynamic assemblies of hedonic, motor, appraisal, and expressive constituents. More recently, Lewis (1995, 1997) modeled emotional and personality development as the consolidation of cognition-emotion interactions that self-organize across occasions. Other theorists have proposed DS approaches to personality formation (Cloninger, Svrakic, and Svrakic, 1997), adult personality change (Magai and Nusbaum, 1996), identity development (Haviland and Kalbaugh, 1993), and self-referential emotions (Mascolo and Harkins, 1998). The development of the self (Schore, 1997) and the consolidation of temperament (Derryberry and Rothbart, 1997) have also been modeled as self-organizing coordinations of biological and social subsystems. Over a decade ago, Campos, Campos, and Barrett (1989) encouraged emotional developmentalists to seriously explore the DS perspective, as did Sroufe (1995) more recently. Theorists and researchers are finally beginning to take up this call in earnest.

In summary, emotion theorists have begun to turn away from cognitivist conceptions of mind and explore notions of nonlinearity and emergence.

At the same time, developmentalists have started applying DS ideas, established in other domains, to the study of emotional, personality, interpersonal, and self development. Yet these contributions are still so few and so new that theorists of different persuasions are often unaware of the conceptual links among them. The present volume attempts to tie these strands together, highlight their common features, help guide their rapid and chaotic growth, and look toward future directions.

Most of the chapters in this volume take a developmental perspective, but some are concerned with real-time processes instead. This mix is intended to highlight theoretical links between emotional processes in real time and development, and it makes up for an unfortunate schism between emotion theory and emotional development. This schism becomes untenable when we view emotional processes as self-organizing, because the causal interdependence of different time scales is a critical assumption of the dynamic systems approach. Emerging emotions in real time forge links across occasions that give rise to developmental patterns. Conversely, developmental patterns strongly constrain real-time emotions and related processes such as regulation and action. Good explanations of the connections between emotional development and real-time emotional processes have long eluded psychologists in general and developmentalists in particular, but these explanations may finally be available through the study of self-organization.

Contents of the Volume

The first section of the book deals with emotional processes that are primarily studied within rather than between individuals. The contributions in this section are theoretically diverse, but they share an emphasis on subsystem coordination or coupling as the basis for the emergence of global emotional forms (e.g., emotions themselves, emotion expressions, emotional amalgams, moods, cognitive-emotional structures, and personality). In Chapter 1, Izard and his colleagues use dynamic systems principles to elaborate and complement key aspects of their longstanding *differential emotions theory*. They then provide a thoughtful analysis of matches and mismatches between dynamic systems and differential emotions perspectives. In the second chapter, Lewis models the relations among self-organizing cognition-emotion interactions at three time scales – emotions, moods, and personality development. At each of these scales, global intentional forms are proposed to arise from and entrain lower-order cognition-emotion interactions. Next, Scherer models emotions as episodes of synchronization among bodily subsystems, driven by appraisal, and falling into short-term attractor states. He then examines abrupt emotional transitions with an elegant application of catastrophe theory to appraisal processes. The fourth chapter presents Camras's research on the spontaneous coordination of muscular movements in global emotion expressions. Her depiction of muscular coupling and recruitment is one of the few empirically grounded models of self-organization in an emotion-related system. Finally, Mascolo and his colleagues look at emotional development from a social constructivist perspective incorporating both neo-Piagetian and self-organizational assumptions. Their picture of context-specific emotional constellations assembled from component subsystems is similar to Scherer's, but drawn in development rather than real time.

The second section concerns neurobiological perspectives, and it reveals a consensus on the self-organizing character of brain processes involved in emotion. In particular, the four chapters in this section point toward the biological underpinnings of the psychological coordinations that were the subject of the first section. In Chapter 6, Schore maps out the neural bases of appraisal, emotional experience, self-regulation, and interpersonal attunement in a detailed model of developmental self-organization. He shows how appraisals in the right orbitofrontal cortex emerge and how they regulate individual differences in early self-development. In the next chapter, Harkness and Tucker look at the impact of early abuse and neglect on neural organizations that later give rise to depression and other pathologies. Their model crisply explicates developmental self-organization as a cascade of neural outcomes that become more intransigent as the brain loses its plasticity. In Chapter 8, Freeman sketches a remarkable synthesis of a decade and a half of research into brain self-organization, and he examines the role of emotion in this process. According to Freeman, all brain activities become synchronized around self-organizing intentions or goals, and emotion is felt as both the anticipation of intentional action and the control of action in the service of rationality. Finally, in the ninth chapter, Panksepp provides an overview of theoretical and measurement issues related to the neurobiology of emotion, and he emphasizes the need for models and methods that examine nonlinear phenomena. Panksepp explains that all brain processes, and emotional processes in particular, are inherently nonlinear and self-organizing, but the means for studying them are still largely undeveloped.

The third and final section deals with socioemotional processes that can only be examined at the interpersonal level. Despite diversity in content and time scales, the chapters in this section demonstrate that emotional outcomes in relationships self-organize in much the same way as psychological and neural outcomes within individuals. This suggests a picture of nested systemic relations spanning biological, psychological, and social dimensions. In Chapter 10, Granic reviews contemporary models of bidirectional effects in parent-child relationships as a springboard toward the application of DS principles. For her, bidirectionality implies reciprocity and recursion, which in turn account for the self-organization of particular parent-child relationships and dyadic trajectories. Laible and Thompson view attachment theory through a self-organizational lens in the next chapter. They examine the emergence of attachment styles, their enactment in real-time exchanges, and their effects on subsequent development by applying key DS concepts such as phase transitions, attractors, and control parameters. In Chapter 12, de Weerth and van Geert provide theoretical and empirical strategies for studying the convergence of socioemotional stability from initial variability in infant development. Their approach grounds the study of developmental self-organization in new statistical methods for comparing developmental periods. The final chapter, by Ryan and her colleagues, reviews Gottman's theory of marital satisfaction, with emphasis on the affective processes central to this particular form of dyadic development. The authors demonstrate how theoretical predictions about the course of a marriage can be tied to nonlinear mathematical techniques for studying dyadic interactions.

A Word on Terminology

There is still a great deal of variability and dissonance in the terminology used to convey these new ideas (Lewis and Granic, 1999b). This seems to be the fate of any new paradigm before it stabilizes and becomes more broadly familiar. The authors in this volume have tried to achieve some consistency in their terminology, but even here disparities will appear. To help the reader through, we provide a brief synopsis of some generally agreed-on definitions.

Dynamic systems theory is a mathematical theory that predicts the future state of a system based on its present state. It does this by solving coupled equations (for different values of the variables defining the system) or by mapping out a spatial depiction of the tendencies of the system as a whole. Nonmathematical DS approaches, like most of those featured in this volume, rely on spatial depictions or on qualitative descriptions of how these tendencies might appear.

Spatial depictions often take the form of a *state space*, a map of all the possible states a system can assume, with paths or trajectories indicating its tendencies over time. Such a map is often shown as a topographical surface pocked by wells or valleys that stand for *attractors* and hills that stand for *repellors*. Attractors are defined as stable, recurrent, or resilient states in which systems tend to settle or get stuck. Attractors are surrounded on the state space by *basins* – regions of states that gravitate to the attractor. Repellors are states the system tends to move away from or avoid.

In *nonlinear dynamic systems*, the state of the system changes disproportionately (nonlinearly) with the values of the variables that define it. Nonlinear systems are extremely sensitive to interactions (or feedback) among these variables, and complex systems tend to show a high degree of nonlinearity. As a result, only complex nonlinear dynamic systems show the dramatic characteristics that are of interest to developmentalists.

The sensitivity of nonlinear dynamic systems often leads to abrupt shifts in the state of the system despite incremental change in external or internal conditions. These shifts, or *phase transitions*, have become key constructs for modeling developmental discontinuities (e.g., van Geert, 1994). A phase transition denotes a change in the state space of the system, whereby new states (and new attractors) may become available while old ones become inaccessible. The term is often used more loosely to describe any discontinuous change in the organization of a dynamic system.

Chaos theory describes a unique class of nonlinear systems whose future cannot be predicted, even approximately. But chaos also refers to instabilities (e.g., during phase transitions) in systems that usually behave in an orderly fashion. While chaos theory is sometimes substituted for self-organization theory and nonlinear dynamics, we avoid this usage. Here, chaos refers to noisy, unstable, or turbulent states.

Self-organization refers to a set of related principles (or a paradigm – Dalenoort, 1989) concerning the spontaneous emergence of order from the interaction of components of a (nonlinear dynamic) system. Self-organization is particularly useful for modeling the coming-into-existence of new forms or properties, not through prior programming or present instruction, but through processes intrinsic to the system itself. Models of self-organization describe the emergence of order, coherence, organized complexity, and true novelty in all natural systems.

Self-organization in psychological systems is generally described at two time scales, *real time* and *development*. Real-time self-organization refers to the convergence of a system to its attractor, or a shift from one attractor to another when that shift is indeterminate and self-propagating. Developmental self-organization describes the emergence of developmental forms, properties, or constraints through recurrent real-time interactions. Phase transitions and other DS phenomena can be demonstrated at both of these scales.

Intended Audience

This volume is intended to provide developmentalists working in this area with an anchor point for their emerging ideas and an inducement to explore new empirical methods. The volume offers researchers in the larger arena of emotional development, as well as those in related areas such as emotion theory, attachment, personality development, and developmental psychopathology, a package of self-organizational approaches that can resonate with their interests. Finally, this book provides psychologists outside these areas, and other developmentalists in particular, with a unique picture of the conceptual tool kit offered by DS approaches and models of self-organization.

References

Ashby, W. R. (1952). *Design for a brain*. New York: Wiley.
Campos, J. J., Campos, R. G., and Barrett, K. C. (1989). Emergent themes in the study of emotional development and emotion regulation. *Developmental Psychology, 25*, 394–402.
Camras, L. A. (1992). Expressive development and basic emotions. *Cognition and Emotion, 6*, 269–283.
Chapman, M. (1991). Self-organization as developmental process: Beyond the organismic and mechanistic models? In P. van Geert and L. P. Mos (Eds.), *Annals of theoretical psychology* (vol. 7, pp. 335–348). New York: Plenum.
Cloninger, C. R., Svrakic, N. M., and Svrakic, D. M. (1997). Role of personality self-organization in development of mental order and disorder. *Development and Psychopathology, 9*, 881–906.
Dalenoort, G. J. (1989). *The paradigm of self-organization: Studies of autonomous systems*. London: Gordon and Breach.
Derryberry, D., and Rothbart, M. K. (1997). Reactive and effortful processes in the organization of temperament. *Development and Psychopathology, 9*, 633–652.
Eigen, M. (1992). *Steps toward life*. Oxford: Oxford University Press.
Elman, J. L., Bates, E. A., Johnson, M. H., Karmiloff-Smith, A., Parisi, D., and Plunkett, K. (1996). *Rethinking innateness: A connectionist perspective on development*. Cambridge, MA: Bradford/MIT Press.
Fogel, A. (1993). *Developing through relationships: Origins of communication, self, and culture*. Chicago: University of Chicago Press.
Fogel, A., Nwokah, E., Dedo, J. Y., Messinger, D., Dickson, K. L., Matusov, E., and

Holt, S. A. (1992). Social process theory of emotion: A dynamic systems approach. *Social Development, 1*, 122–142.

Fogel, A., and Thelen, E. (1987). Development of early expressive and communicative action: Reinterpreting the evidence from a dynamic systems perspective. *Developmental Psychology, 23*, 747–761.

Freeman, W. J. (1995). *Societies of brains*. Hillsdale, NJ: Erlbaum.

Haken, H. (1977). *Synergetics – An introduction: Nonequilibrium phase transitions and self-organization in physics, chemistry and biology*. Berlin: Springer-Verlag.

Haviland, J. M., and Kalbaugh, P. (1993). Emotion and identity processes. In M. Lewis and J. Haviland (Eds.), *The handbook of emotion* (pp. 327–338). New York: Guilford.

Kauffman, S. A. (1993). *The origins of order: Self-organization and selection in evolution*. New York: Oxford University Press.

Keating, D. P. (1990). Charting pathways to the development of expertise. *Educational Psychologist, 25*, 243–267.

Kelso, J. A. (1984). Phase transitions and critical behavior in human bimanual co-ordination. *American Journal of Physiology, 15*, A1000–A1004.

Lewin, R. (1992). *Complexity: Life at the edge of chaos*. New York: Macmillan.

Lewis, M. D. (1995). Cognition-emotion feedback and the self-organization of developmental paths. *Human Development, 38*, 71–102.

Lewis, M. D. (1997). Personality self-organization: Cascading constraints on cognition-emotion interaction. In A. Fogel, M. C. Lyra, and J. Valsiner (Eds.), *Dynamics and indeterminism in developmental and social processes* (pp. 193–216). Mahwah, NJ: Erlbaum.

Lewis, M. D. (2000). The promise of dynamic systems approaches for an integrated account of human development. *Child Development* (special millennial issue), *71*, 1–23.

Lewis, M. D., and Granic, I. (1999a). Self-organization of cognition-emotion interactions. In T. Dalgleish and M. Power (Eds.), *Handbook of cognition and emotion* (pp. 683–701). Chichester: Wiley.

Lewis, M. D., and Granic, I. (1999b). Who put the self in self-organization? A clarification of terms and concepts for developmental psychopathology. *Development and Psychopathology, 11*, 365–374.

Magai, C., and Nusbaum, B. (1996). Personality change in adulthood: Dynamic systems, emotions, and the transformed self. In C. Magai and S. H. McFadden (Eds.), *Handbook of emotion, adult development, and aging* (pp. 403–420). San Diego, CA: Academic Press.

Mascolo, M. F., and Harkins, D. (1998). Toward a component systems approach to emotional development. In M. F. Mascolo and S. Griffin (Eds.), *What develops in emotional development?* (pp. 189–217). New York: Plenum.

Maturana, H. R., and Varela, F. J. (1987). *The tree of knowledge: The biological roots of human understanding*. Boston: New Science Library.

Molenaar, P. C. (1986). On the impossibility of acquiring more powerful structures: A neglected alternative. *Human Development, 29*, 245–251.

Oyama, S. (1989). Ontogeny and the central dogma: Do we need the concept of genetic programming in order to have an evolutionary perspective? In M. R. Gunnar and E. Thelen (Eds.), *Minnesota Symposium on Child Psychology: Vol. 22. Systems and development* (pp. 1–34). Hillsdale, NJ: Erlbaum.

Port, R. F., and van Gelder, T. (1995). *Mind as motion: Explorations in the dynamics of cognition*. Cambridge, MA: Bradford/MIT Press.

Prigogine, I., and Stengers, I. (1984). *Order out of chaos*. New York: Bantam.

Sameroff, A. J. (1995). General systems theories and developmental psychopathology. In D. Cicchetti and D. J. Cohen (Eds.), *Developmental psychopathology* (vol. 1, pp. 659–695). New York: Wiley.

Schore, A. N. (1997). Early organization of the nonlinear right brain and development of a predisposition to psychiatric disorders. *Development and Psychopathology, 9*, 595–631.

Smith, L. B. (1995). Self-organizing processes in learning to learn words: Development is not induction. In C. A. Nelson (Ed.), *Minnesota Symposium on Child Psychology: Vol. 28. New perspectives on learning and development* (pp. 1–32). New York: Academic Press.

Sroufe, L. A. (1995). *Emotional development: The organization of emotional life in the early years*. New York: Cambridge University Press.

Thatcher, R. W. (1991). Maturation of the human frontal lobes: Physiological evidence for staging. *Developmental Neuropsychology, 7*, 397–419.

Thelen, E., and Smith, L. B. (1994). *A dynamic systems approach to the development of cognition and action*. Cambridge, MA: Bradford/MIT Press.

Tucker, D. M. (1992). Developing emotions and cortical networks. In M. R. Gunnar and C. Nelson (Eds.), *Minnesota Symposium on Child Psychology: Vol. 24. Developmental behavioral neuroscience* (pp. 75–128). Hillsdale, NJ: Erlbaum.

Turvey, M. T. (1990). Coordination. *American Psychologist, 45*, 938–953.

van der Maas, H. L., and Molenaar, P. C. (1992). Stagewise cognitive development: An application of catastrophe theory. *Psychological Review, 99*, 395–417.

van Geert, P. (1991). A dynamic systems model of cognitive and language growth. *Psychological Review, 98*, 3–53.

van Geert, P. (1994). *Dynamic systems of development: Change between complexity and chaos*. New York: Harvester Wheatsheaf.

Varela, F. J., Thompson, E., and Rosch, E. (1991). *The embodied mind: Cognitive science and human experience*. Cambridge, MA: Bradford/MIT Press.

von Neumann, J. (1958). *The computer and the brain*. New Haven, CT: Yale University Press.

PART I

Intrapersonal Processes

1 Self-Organization of Discrete Emotions, Emotion Patterns, and Emotion-Cognition Relations

Carroll E. Izard, Brian P. Ackerman,
Kristen M. Schoff, and Sarah E. Fine

A core principle of differential emotions theory (DET) is that emotions operate as systems (Izard, 1971; Izard et al., 1965). An emotion is a complex system in the sense that it emerges from interactions of constituent neurohormonal, motoric, and experiential processes. Although person-environment transactions play a role in the development of healthy emotions, the potential for each component of each discrete emotion system self-organized in phylogeny and emerged as an evolutionary adaptation. Individual emotions also coassemble with other emotions to form contingent emotion patterns that stabilize over repetitions and time. Thus, discrete emotions are both the product and stuff of system organization. The systems are self-organizing in the sense that recursive interactions among component processes generate emergent properties.

This system perspective of DET fits well with the general emphasis of dynamic systems (DS) theories of development on the self-organization of the structure of behavior. Both DS theories of development and DET have the central theoretical goal of understanding organization and pattern in complex systems, without recourse to some deus ex machina (Izard, 1977; Smith and Thelen, 1993; Thelen, 1989). For both theories, structure and complexity emerge from constituent processes to yield behavioral performances that vary among individuals and within individuals over time. Understanding the individual variation is a main theoretical concern of both DET and DS theories of development.

Given these commonalities, is there anything to be gained by translating DET into the language of dynamic systems? Does the DS framework add body to DET, or is it simply a new bottle for old wine? We explore this issue in this chapter in several ways. First, we apply core dynamic concepts in describing the generation and operation of discrete emotions and emotion patterns from the perspective of DET. That is, we explore the "fit" of the theories. Next we discuss the emotion of shame and shame patterns as specific examples of self-organizing systems. Finally, we discuss aspects of DET that distinguish it from a dynamic systems perspective.

The Emotion Systems

Differential emotions theory describes each discrete emotion as a system. Sets or patterns of co-occurring emotions constitute higher-level systems. All the discrete emotions and patterns of emotions operate within the more inclusive emotions system. Finally, the emotions system functions as the primary motivational system within the superordinate self-system or personality. Personality development emerges through interactions of emotions and cognition and their linkage in affective-cognitive structures. The flexibility in relations among components of any system in this systems hierarchy derives from its complexity. A discrete emotion system is the simplest in the hierarchy and has the least flexibility in relations among its components (Izard, 1992). The contribution of innate structure and hardwiring to system assembly is greatest for a discrete emotion.

This section describes the assembly of this hierarchy of systems and relations. First, we identify and explain core processes of dynamic models and note their equivalents or approximations in DET. Then we apply the processes as an aid in understanding the self-organization of discrete emotions systems, systems of emotion patterns, and affective-cognitive structures. Finally, we consider individual variability in emotion systems.

Core Processes

Each of the emotion systems and their interrelations with the cognitive system derive from constituent processes that form the core of the dynamic systems approach to emotion (M. D. Lewis and Granic, 1999). These processes constitute the self-organization of a dynamic system. For our purposes, the processes include: (a) recursion among system elements, (b) emergence of unique forms and patterns, (c) consolidation of the forms over repetition and time, and (d) constraints on system formation.

In framing DET with DS concepts, *recursion* describes reciprocal interactions among the elements of a system in the form of positive and negative feedback that affects the element interrelations. *Emergence* concerns the generation of unique and idiosyncratic emotion patterns (e.g., systems) and affective-cognitive structures from nonlinear recursive cycles. Emergent forms and patterns represent ''attractors'' for the emotions system as a whole. Attractors are unique configurations or organizations of simpler elements that represent preferred solutions to organismic, environmental, and historical influences (i.e., previous solutions). The preference becomes stronger, and the "attraction" deepens and broadens, as similar solutions repeat over time. Emergent forms such as emotion patterns and affective-cognitive structures *consolidate*, stabilize, and become more accessible as the couplings among the elements strengthen. Consolidation increases the predictability and determinacy of emotion experiences and emotion-cognition-action sequences. Though determinacy increases over repetition, the set of possible attractors is never infinite. Instead, the set of preferred solutions is always *constrained* by organismic variables (e.g., physiological reactivity), initial organizations of system elements, the extent to which attractors are developmentally embedded, and task demands. These constraints contribute to individual differences in system emergence and organization.

In DET, this framework applies to the development of psychopathology as well as to the development of healthy personality. Given a low threshold for anger activation in frustrating situations, for example, child-environment interactions may foster the emergence of an "attractor" that represents maladaptive "solutions" to environmental challenges. Similarly, the principles that apply to the development of adaptive attractors also apply to the development of maladaptive attractors. For example, high-stress situations, inadequate parental guidance, and proneness to negative emotionality contribute to the repetition and consolidation of deviant emotion-cognition-action sequences. Once consolidated, these sequences may occur rapidly and with little opportunity for cognitive interpretation of the context and modification of action.

Discrete Emotion Systems

A discrete emotion consists of a system of interacting neural, expressive-behavioral, and experiential components. These components influence each other reciprocally through feedback loops. The basic structure of each discrete emotion system self-organized phylogenetically through evolution, is hard-wired ontogenetically, and its biological roots constrain the relations among its components.

The innate organization of individual emotion systems provides numerous adaptive advantages (Izard and Malatesta, 1987). Emotion systems are highly sensitive to changes in the internal and external environments. They have the capacity to respond rapidly, automatically, and unconsciously to

imminent threat and, more moderately, to higher-order cognitive evaluations of complex situations (cf. M. D. Lewis and Douglas, 1998). Although
each discrete emotion has innate structure and function, a degree of flexibility characterizes the relations among its components. For example, an
emotion expression can be dissociated from the emotion feeling. Each
emotion operates as a system that participates in the self-organization of
patterns of emotions and emotion-cognition relations.

An emotion begins when a noncognitive or cognitive process activates
certain neural evaluative processes (Izard, 1993). In fear, for example,
the activating information or impulse travels from sense organs to thalamus, neocortex, and amygdala. The amygdala determines the emotional
significance (fear-worthiness) of the stimulus. If the neural evaluation indicates danger, impulses travel from the amygdala to the hypothalamus,
which triggers autonomic nervous system activity, such as increased
heart rate, and to the brain stem central grey, which triggers behavioral
responses such as freezing (Bechara et al., 1997; LeDoux, 1996). Feedback from either the expressive-behavioral activity or the subjective state
can influence subsequent neural evaluative processes. Changes in the latter can, in turn, moderate the expressive and experiential components of
emotion.

Several types of interactions characterize the relations between the expressive and experiential components of emotion. Since Darwin (1872/
1965) and James (1890/1990), we have known that regulating emotion
expression has a regulatory effect on emotion feeling. In the past twenty
years, numerous experiments have confirmed an expression feedback effect
that is probably recursive in nature (Izard, 1990; Laird, 1974; Matsumoto,
1987; cf. Zajonc, Murphy, and Inglehart, 1989).

Emotion Patterns as Higher-Level Systems

A situation activates a discrete emotion that organizes and motivates
behavior. Simultaneously, the activated emotion, in concert with contextual
variables, typically recruits other emotions. In effect, the individual responds to many conditions and situations with multiple emotions. These
emotions self-organize as a coherent set or pattern of interacting emotions
(Ackerman et al., 1997; Izard, 1972; Izard and Youngstrom, 1996). Thus
the first discrete emotion activated by a new situation may have minimal
effects before other emotions come into play. The set as a whole emerges
as a pattern of emotions or motivational complex. Organization as a pattern
means that the emotions interact freely and influence each other recipro-

cally. Each emotion in the pattern has the capacity to moderate (attenuate, amplify) the others. Thus, the pattern that emerges and the resulting emotion experiences are unique to the person and situation.

The concurrent activation of two or more emotions in complex situations provides an adaptive advantage. A single emotion fosters a limited number of behavioral alternatives. For example, a person cannot effectively explore a situation when fear is the dominant emotion. Fear greatly narrows the field of perception and attention to the threatening object and possible escape routes (Derryberry and Tucker, 1994; Easterbrook, 1959). This narrowing dramatically inhibits curiosity and exploration. The activation of another emotion (e.g., interest) increases the available options. Thus, multiple emotions yield a greater variety of choices and an increased capacity to confront a complex situation.

A core principle of DET is that each discrete emotion retains its inherent organizational and motivational properties even while it operates within a self-organized set of interacting emotions. The behavioral effects of each emotion, however, may be moderated by the motivational effects of other discrete emotions in the pattern. For example, in the sad-mad component of the depressive pattern, anger mobilizes energy that attenuates the slowing function of sadness and increases the likelihood of active coping. In general, the complexity of cause-effect or emotion-behavior relations increases as each emotion in a pattern recruits its own cognitive accompaniments. Thoughts associated with anger are different from those associated with contempt.

Frustration or the presence of a barrier blocking the goal path provide other examples of situations that elicit multiple emotions. These conditions usually elicit anger, but they can invoke other emotions as well. The activation of the other emotions in an anger-eliciting situation follows from their lawful relations with anger and the cognition and behavior associated with it. The resulting pattern of emotions is not a random set. The emotions that co-occur in situations of frustration and restraint have privileged relations with the emotion of anger. These interemotion relations constrain the emerging pattern. Here the privileged status results from some similarity in the goals of the emotions in the pattern.

Similarity of goals among emotions is one factor that fosters their sequential activation, interaction, and self-organization as a pattern. Thus anger, disgust, and contempt co-occur and assemble as a pattern because each represents a type of hostile motivation designed to overcome (anger), reject (disgust), or dismiss or disdain (contempt) the stimulus. The emotions share the hostile motivation of overcoming (or rejecting or dismissing) the stimulus. The frequent co-occurrence of the anger-disgust-contempt pattern in situations that initially elicit any one of the individual emotions supports the notion that they form a hostility triad (Izard, 1972, 1977). The form of a rapid or impulsive response to a frustrating or goal-blocking event might be determined solely by anger. In other cases, however, all three of the emotions in the hostility triad may influence the form of the response.

In addition to the effects of similarity of goals, dynamic relations among emotions influence their self-organization into coherent patterns. Thus anger may coassemble with fear because the former can attenuate the latter. The attenuating effect results partly from the incompatibility of the two emotions. In a situation that has already activated fear, the activation of anger can reverse cognitive and behavioral processes. Fear activates cognition and action designed to avoid or escape the threatening situation. Anger, on the other hand, fosters approach tendencies and confrontation. Fear may energize flight or reduce energy to the point that the individual feels shaky and jittery or even experiences momentary freezing. Anger reliably has the opposite effect. Anger increases blood flow to the striate muscles, the voluntarily controlled muscles of action (Cannon, 1929).

Finally, socialization processes create links between emotions and help explain the co-occurrence and patterning of emotions. Socialization processes create links between emotions. The child whose anger repeatedly results in the loss of her favorite toy or game may eventually enable anger experience to activate sadness. We return to these principles in the section on emotion patterning.

Affective-Cognitive Structures

An emotion links to an image or thought to form an affective-cognitive structure (Izard, 1977, 1992; Tomkins, 1962). The information in emotion provides a key to understanding the linkages between emotion and cognition. The conscious component of an emotion, the motivational or feeling state, contains information. In keeping with the way we have defined emotion, this is noncognitive information. Put another way, emotion feeling produces cues for cognition and action (Izard, 1971). Information in emotion is noncognitive in that it derives from the evolutionary-biological characteristics of the emotion itself. The felt action tendency in anger and the withdrawal tendency in sadness exemplify a type of emotion information or behavioral cue (Izard, 1991; cf. Frijda, 1986; Lang, 1979).

Thus we propose that emotions contain cues for perceptual and cognitive processes as well as action tendencies. With positive emotions, perceptual and cognitive tendencies may be more characteristic than action tendencies. In many adults, the emotion of interest leads to intellectual pursuits more frequently than to physical activities (Renninger, Hidi, and Krapp, 1992). Several experiments have demonstrated associations between positive emotion and particular types of thought or information processing (Fredrickson, 1998; Isen, 1984).

Thus the information inherent in the emotion itself plays a major role in determining the nature of an affective-cognitive structure. Nevertheless, the information in emotion is broad-gauged and cues only a type or category of thought. Joy spawns expansive and free-ranging cognition whereas fear has virtually the opposite effect. The specific content of the cognition that links to an emotion has determinants in culture, socialization, and idiosyncratic experience.

Single and more often multiple occurrences of an emotion-thought sequence may lead to the stabilization of an affective-cognitive structure. The recurring thought component in the sequence does not need to be identical. Development of the structure requires only recurring thoughts of the same type that are congruent with the goal associated with the emotion.

Once stabilized, an affective-cognitive structure attracts similar structures to form a related set. These coupled sets of affective-cognitive structures further consolidate and stabilize as traits of personality. A complex set of such structures that relate to each other at varying strengths forms a broad dimension of personality (e.g., extroversion). A more limited and tightly bonded set of strongly related thought-feeling structures emerges as a specific trait (affiliation, nurturance).

Our concept of affective-cognitive structure is similar to Tomkins's (1962) concept of ideoaffective organization and to Lewis's (Lewis and Douglas, 1998) construct of emotional interpretation. Lewis gives an elegant and detailed description of the self-organization of cognition in relation to emotion, a process that produces emotional interpretations. The latter assemble as characteristics of personality, and the processes of assembly constitute the processes of personality development.

Individual Differences

Individual differences in behavioral performance comprise a key feature of DS approaches to development. Such differences represent robust evidence against a priori instructions for structuring behavior or hard-wired programming of the structure, and for the emergence of a novel structure contingent on task and context. The central focus of DET also concerns the contingency of discrete emotions and emotion patterns and the variability of emotion experiences and affective-cognitive structures across and within individuals. Although the set of discrete emotion solutions to the organismic-environmental press is finite, similar objective situations may be associated with discretely different emotions in different individuals. Furthermore, similar situations may be associated with different emotions at one time or another for a particular individual. Thus, the set of possible variations in patterns of emotions, affective-cognitive structures, and intensity of emotions is large.

The individual differences are rooted in neurohormonal, sensorimotor, affective, and cognitive systems that activate and regulate discrete emotions (Izard, 1993). Each of these general systems constitutes a source of individual differences in the self-organization of emotions patterns and emotion-cognition relations. The noncognitive systems, in particular, establish the sensitive dependence of emotion systems on initial conditions within individuals, a key feature of chaotic and dynamic systems. Neurohormonal and affective processes, for instance, influence thresholds, levels of arousal, and energy levels and flows that condition the nature and intensity of emotion experiences. Fatigue and negative mood, for example, limit joy experiences. The cognitive system, by contrast, may play a particularly strong role in the consolidation and stabilization of particular emotion system attractors. The repeated coupling of affective and cognitive elements stabilizes affective-cognitive structures. Because the cognitive story is developed elsewhere in this book, we focus on noncognitive systems here.

Genetic processes operate through the neurohormonal system to determine the initial settings of the thresholds for each of the discrete emotions (cf. Rothbart and Derryberry, 1981). Robust evidence testifies to the existence of individual differences in the activation thresholds of discrete emotions (Izard, Hembree, and Huebner, 1987; Kagan, Reznick, and Snidman, 1988; Tangney, 1990). A given emotion threshold controls the individual's proneness to experience that emotion and consequently influences the likelihood of its inclusion in a pattern (cf. H. Lewis, 1971; Tangney et al., 1992). A person's profile of emotion thresholds sets the stage for the self-organization of a particular pattern of emotions in a personally significant situation. This concept of an emotion threshold profile may provide a precise way of thinking about an individual's emotional reactivity or emotion-based dimensions of temperament or personality.

A second source of individual variation is the recursive feedback loop linking emotion expression and emotion experience (see Izard, 1990; Matsumoto, 1987; Winton, 1986; and Zajonc et al., 1989, for reviews). Although researchers disagree as to the mechanism of action, many agree that even experimenter-directed contractions of the facial muscles of emotion expression have real effects on emotion feelings. The effects suggest that the motor mimicry that occurs in infant-mother face-to-face play, social referencing, and empathy may automatically and unconsciously initiate the emergence or amplification of an emotion feeling and the formation of a new pattern of emotions.

A third source of individual differences concerns affective processes. Affects include physiological drive states and emotions, and both types of motivational processes play a role in the organization of patterns of emotions and emotion-cognition relations. In some circumstances, affects exert their effects through noncognitive processes. For example, unanticipated pain in young infants elicits expressions of anger and sadness (Izard et al., 1987). This pain-anger-sadness sequence occurs well before infants have any conception of the agent of harm and before they show any signs of pain anticipation. In contrast, when a child forms an association between an agent and an aversive experience, anticipation of pain produces fear and the emotions of the anxiety pattern (Izard and Youngstrom, 1996).

Other drive states, particularly when occurring at high intensity, also influence the self-Organization of patterns of emotions. The sex drive and sexual pleasure recruit interest and joy. Intense or chronic hunger may elicit the irritability characteristic of low-level anger.

Individual differences in emotion thresholds affect the processes of interemotion regulation (one emotion influencing another), processes that may occur independent of cognition. Joy may occur spontaneously to provide a respite from a long period of intense play in the child or intellectual activity in the adult. Anger may emerge to prevent the sadness of depression from totally disengaging an individual from the social surround. Shame as a strong motivation to repair the self-image may also emerge in the depression pattern and break the cycle of withdrawal and loneliness. The person's thresholds for joy, anger, and shame will determine the timing of these interemotion regulatory processes.

The Shame Systems

In this section, we develop an account of the emotion of shame as a specific example of a self-organizing system that can be nested within other systems. Shame is a particularly interesting emotion system for these purposes because it emerges developmentally and because its prevalence varies so widely across individuals and cultures (Izard, 1971). Developmental and individual variability establishes shame as an emergent phenomenon organized from constituent elements but not reducible to those elements.

Shame as a Self-Organizing System

Shame is a dependent emotion in the sense that its activation (but not its inherent motivational properties) depends on cognitive development (i.e., self-representations) and appraisal processes. Although shame depends on cognition for its activation, it has status as a discrete emotion system for DET. The strong hard-wired potential for the components of shame (neural, behavioral, and experiential) resulted from evolutionary processes that account for its universality. Unlike the independent emotions, such as anger and fear, shame does not have a consistent and specific expressive signature (Ackerman, Abe, and Izard, 1998). Tomkins (1963) described shame as an emotion involving indignity, defeat, and alienation. An individual feeling shame views herself as an object of contempt and thus feels belittled (H. Lewis, 1971). In shame, the individual experiences a sudden loss of control (Erikson, 1950, 1956) coupled with a heightened state of self-awareness (Izard, 1991).

In contrast to the early onset of the independent emotions, shame develops in late toddlerhood and early childhood. Shame cannot emerge until the child has developed a sense of self. This sense of self includes the ability to distinguish self from others and to identify and compare self and others as potential causal agents. Both cognitive and noncognitive processes activate shame and trigger neural processes that evaluate a stimulus and generate a behavioral response.

In the shame experience, recursive feedback from expressive-behavioral activity influences further evaluative processes, initiating a cycle. The influence of this recursive cycle of elements is particularly evident in the emergence of shame because the shame experience requires self-referential activity. For example, blushing may occur as an immediate, automatic physiological response to shame, which can trigger more shame (Tomkins, 1963). The external evidence of shame, the blushing face, brings attention to the person and often heightens self-consciousness and the feeling of shame. This self-reflective attention to the feeling is critical to the shame experience. Shame is, therefore, an emerging discrete emotion system, self-organized by recursive interactions among constituent elements and processes.

As with other discrete emotions, the experience of shame serves adaptive functions. In particular, shame may enhance adaptation by motivating the acquisition of knowledge or skills that strengthen the self and decrease its vulnerability to future shame experiences (Izard, 1977; Tomkins, 1963). Shame may also contribute to social order and the preservation or regulation of social relationships (Retzinger, 1995). Indeed, Gilbert and colleagues (1994) compared the human experience of shame to the submissive behavior of an animal confronting a more powerful predator. In this interpretation, shame relates to rank and power and serves the protective function of initiating submission to more powerful beings (cf. Öhman, 1986). Something similar may be involved when a parent or teacher uses harsh shaming techniques in the socialization process.

These ideas about the universality and evolutionary roots of shame suggest that the structural elements that allow shame experiences (e.g., neurohormonal systems) are innate, though the emerging network of representations of shame-activating events organizes itself over time. Thus, the developmental onset and frequency of shame experiences are likely to vary, and are contingent on experiential, social (e.g., parenting), and personal variables. These variables encourage the consolidation, stabilization, and strengthening of the affective-cognitive structures (i.e., attractors) that include the emotion of shame.

For example, shame may arise initially in early parent-child interactions where the child feels belittled by the parent in some way (Schore, 1991). Given the onset of a particular shamelike reaction by a child to a social violation, parents may shape shame experiences as a socializing tool. Parental linking of affective reactions with cognitive attributions (e.g., self as inept) and appraisals construct shame-cognition links that act as attractors in response to the affective uncertainty induced by perceived social rule violations. Although shame is usually experienced in interpersonal relationships, some researchers suggest that shame also can be experienced even when a person is alone. Here, the individual feels shame simply by thinking about the violation of certain social norms and expectations (Miller and Tangney, 1994).

The behavioral outcomes of shame depend on cognitive appraisals of the context and on traits of personality. Individuals who have a low sense of self-worth, for example, are likely to react to shame by withdrawing (Harter and Jackson, 1993). By contrast, individuals who have unrealistically high self-concepts often react to shame experiences with aggressive behavior (Baumeister, Smart, and Boden, 1996). We develop these points further in the context of higher-level patterns.

In the three subsections that follow, we provide examples of higher-level systems involving shame. Such systems are patterns or assemblies of emotions that self-organize according to principles described earlier.

Patterning Processes Involving Shame

A recursive feedback cycle involving cognitive appraisal, neural-evaluative processes, and expressive behavior generates shame. The shame, in interaction with appraisals and traitlike affective-cognitive structures (e.g., self-concepts), can trigger additional discrete emotion systems. The emotions interact with shame through feedback loops. Through repetition of activity in such feedback loops, an emotion pattern self-organizes and stabilizes as an attractor that represents a consistent and robust response to particular situations.

Emotions theorists have long recognized the patterning of shame and other discrete emotions. Tomkins (1963) suggests, for example, that examination of a facial expression enables prediction of the behavioral outcome (i.e., withdrawal or aggression) of a shame-fear or shame-anger pattern. The facial expression can reveal whether the emotion experienced along with shame is anger, fear, or sadness. Thus, facial expressions may signal the emotions that recursively magnify or attenuate shame.

The process of pairing shame with other emotions begins with the emergence of self-awareness, when shame first develops as a discrete emotion. One mechanism that couples shame with other emotions involves parental shaping and socialization of emotion displays through shaming practices. If a child is frequently shamed for displaying a certain emotion, shame and the other emotion become coupled. The child's unsuccessful attempts to inhibit the forbidden emotion open the door to shame. This socialization-based mechanism is central in the development of shame-fear and shame-anger patterns.

Patterns Involving Fear and Shame

A prime example of two emotions that couple easily is fear plus shame. Many boys, for example, are taught to feel ashamed of being afraid. This coupling is particularly likely in environments where masculinity and pride in physical prowess are highly valued. Consistent shaping of the *fear-shame* link by parenting practices and other social influences consolidates the pattern.

Consolidation of a pattern changes the dynamics of emotion activation. In the present case, the pattern consists of the focal or event-related emotion of fear and the linked emotion of shame. The *perception* of threat or danger activates the fear. By contrast, the *feeling* of fear activates the shame. The consolidation of the pattern automatizes the activation of the shame element of the pattern. This means that any situation of uncertainty, ambiguity, or perceived harm that elicits fear in the child may automatically elicit shame. Thus, in pattern dynamics, shame may lose its dependence on cognition. It remains a dependent emotion, but its dependence becomes affective instead of cognitive.

The automatic, affectively activated shame in the fear-shame pattern has several consequences. For example, the shame feedback can shift the locus of concern from external to internal, from situational context to self. This shift in attention and concern can attenuate the fear as the fear-shame system and its cognitive and behavioral accompaniments self-organize. The automaticity in the pattern and the shift or oscillation in locus of concern minimize the role of cognitive appraisals in interpreting the significance of the fear stimulus and experience.

In addition to parenting practices, situations that elicit social and evaluation anxiety may also forge a link between fear and shame. Everyone experiences heightened self-awareness and embarrassment from time to time, and everyone occasionally feels humiliated or ashamed. Because shame is primarily a ''social'' emotion, such instances usually occur in social and interpersonal situations. Given the considerable unpleasantness of the shame experience, the experience invites fear and avoidance of social interaction. For shame-prone individuals, the fear of negative evaluation and failure (cf. Beck, Emery, and Greenberg, 1996) may be overwhelming.

In such cases, the fear-shame pattern becomes a *shame-fear* pattern. The distinction has implications for understanding such phenomena as social anxiety and social phobia. In the fear-shame pattern, perception of danger activates fear, and the fear feeling, in turn, activates shame. The child is ashamed of being afraid. In the shame-fear pattern, shame activates fear. In a child who has concepts of self as inept or inadequate, the self-exposure and increased vulnerability resulting from the shame experience may be perceived as self-in-danger. The child is afraid of being ashamed. As the shame-fear pattern consolidates and stabilizes over time, it becomes an attractor for social situations fraught with ambiguity or uncertainty. Support for our interpretation of social anxiety as fear generated by shame and shame anticipation comes from clinical investigations that discuss the prevalence of shame in these fear-centered disorders (American Psychiatric Association, 1994).

The Shame-Anger Pattern

Shame frequently pairs with anger. Individuals characterized by a trait-like shame-anger pattern often behave aggressively (Tangney et al., 1996). In the recursive processes of the pattern, shame both activates and amplifies anger. By contrast, anger may diminish the shame experience and protect the individual against what shame brings to light (Retzinger, 1995). The intensity of the angry reaction to shame depends on several factors. These include: (a) the significance of the person who caused the shame experience and of the others who witnessed it, (b) whether the rejection concerned one aspect of the individual or the entire self, and (c) whether the rejection came as a surprise or not. When social criticism activates shame in a person with an unrealistically inflated self-concept, the violence serves to refute the criticism and prevent further rejection. Insofar as the violence increases dominance over others, it decreases the sources of shame (cf. Baumeister et al., 1996).

As with shame experiences, the frequency of shame-anger patterns varies among and within individuals. Childhood experiences play a strong role in the consolidation of the pattern, and these as well as genetically set thresholds for the component emotions help determine the child's proneness to experience the pattern. Early emotional abuse, for example, is associated with shame-anger patterns in college students (Hoglund and Nicholas, 1995). In addition, type A personality profiles are associated with the shame-anger pattern. Malatesta-Magai and colleagues (1992) suggest that the source of this experience is the early socialization of shame paired with anger. Other research suggests that individuals with unrealistically positive self-concepts that are unstable and dependent on external validation are especially prone to the shame-anger emotion pattern.

As with shame-fear, consolidation and stabilization of the shame-anger pattern increase the automaticity of the activation of the anger component in the pattern. The automatic activation of anger minimizes the role of cognitive appraisals in interpreting the anger activators, and it may thereby increase the probability of impulsive behavior, including aggression. Although the concept of automatic activation of anger in the shame-anger pattern requires further validation, a few empirical and clinical investigations lend some support. Retzinger (1987, 1991), for example, recorded rapidly alternating cycles of shame and anger at five-second intervals. These results confirm and extend earlier clinical investigations of H. Lewis (1971, 1987), who found that the occurrence of anger frequently followed shame activated by a real or perceived rejection. Lewis suggests that, once shame is evoked, anger is quick to follow.

The co-occurrence and patterning of shame and anger have a strong tendency to become self-perpetuating. Retzinger (1995) suggests that un-acknowledged shame may act as both an inhibitor and generator of anger, rendering the individual incapable of expressing anger but intensifying the feeling of anger. This pattern may escalate and lead to aggressive behavior.

In a study of shame and anger by Tangney and her colleagues (1992), shame related to indirect aggression, suggesting that the spiral often relates to a seething and resentful type of anger. However, Tangney and colleagues (1996) also found a relation between shame and more direct forms of aggression, including both physical and verbal attacks. Other specific examples of the aggressive outcomes of the shame-anger pattern concern borderline personality disorder and spousal abuse. Fisher (1985) describes the former as a shame-based pathology whereby the individual is prone to humiliation and reacts to the humiliation with anger. In incidents of spousal abuse, the abuser may feel shamed by a spouse's criticism and may react with violence (Lansky, 1987) as a form of self-defense against the criticism.

Conclusion

These second-order systems or emotion patterns acquire a network of representations of activating events. This network of representations and linked emotion patterns consolidates and stabilizes as dimensions or traits of personality. Variations in emotion thresholds, behavioral goals, socialization, and other person-environment transactions account for individual differences in these traits.

Theoretical Distinctions

In the previous sections, we discussed the core DET constructs of discrete emotions, emotion patterns, and affective-cognitive structures in the language of dynamic systems theories of development. We found that the core dynamic principles of recursion, emergence, consolidation, and constraint are useful in describing aspects of DET, including processes that generate and constitute emotion systems. Application of DS principles also contributed to our theoretical emphasis on recursion in the amplification and attenuation of discrete emotions in patterns. Finally, we found that the theoretical thrust of DS theories of development on individual variability is consistent with a main thrust of DET. Application of DS principles to specific discrete emotions and patterns and the identification of specific processes and structures that constitute local reactions to emotionally evocative stimuli will undoubtedly enhance DET. Nonetheless, at this point, the primary benefit of the intertheoretical discussion in itself has been to redescribe metaphors and constructs that have been enduring staples of DET.

A more productive strategy might be to focus on theoretical boundary conditions. Perhaps the most interesting and potentially informative use of DS theories of development in understanding emotions is in focusing on the theoretical differences and clashes with DET, rather than on the similarities. Some of these differences are just in emphasis, but others may reveal fundamental issues to be resolved and perhaps reconciled – or not. Some differences address the theoretical spirit of DET and DS theories of development, while others address more local applications of DS principles to emotion theory (cf. M. D. Lewis and Douglas, 1998).

Five theoretical distinctions seem important. These distinctions bear on limitations of both theories, and the correct direction of modification is uncertain. First, a number of dynamic systems theories of development (e.g., Fogel, 1993; Thelen, 1989) reject the notion of prior instructions and the influence of hard-wired programming that yield fixed and universal products (for an exception, see M. D. Lewis, 1995; Lewis and Douglas, 1998). Indeed, a prime motivation for applying dynamic systems modeling to developmental processes has been to reconceptualize development as the emergence of behavioral structure as a function of local contingencies. In DS theories of development, structure is a product of local processes rather than a prior cause of behavioral process.

DET, by contrast, requires a set of biogenetic primitives termed discrete emotions that reflect evolutionary adaptations. These emotions, therefore, are universal across the human species and both reflect and constitute innate structure. DS theories of development also require primitives to the extent that elements compose systems. For DET, however, a strong potential for each component of a discrete emotion system and for its self-organization is hard-wired. Relations among components and their activation are sensitive to local contingencies, and an extremely harsh environment may produce deviant emotion systems. However, the cross-individual and cross-cultural invariance of discrete emotion system products (e.g., anger feeling per se) testify to their origins in evolutionary and biogenetic processes. The complement of this principle bears repetition:

Emotion-cognition relations and emotion-action sequences *do* change over time and vary across individuals and cultures.

DET and DS theories of development differ in conceptualizing a specific emotion per se. For some proponents of DS approaches to development (cf. Fogel, 1993), the discrete emotions are simply the ones that are named, and these appear among many other emotions in a child's life that are inchoate, unnamed, and perhaps less frequent. From this perspective, naming conventions privilege some emotions over others. For DET, the primitives reflect a small and predetermined set of hard-wired emotions. They have dedicated neural substrates and are named across most cultures. The individual varieties of emotion experiences reflect differences in emotion-thought linkages and varying patterns of co-occurring discrete emotions.

Second, in a dynamic system, the elements lose individuality, more or less. Emergence means that the system product is not predictable or reducible to the constituent elements. Element functions are amplified or attenuated in recursive interactions with other elements, but elements also assume qualitatively new and different functions in a system configuration. By contrast, in DET, elements in discrete emotions and emotion patterns do not lose individuality. Even in multiple-emotion patterns the elements, at the level of discrete emotions, retain their qualitatively distinct functions.

Third, dynamic systems theorists refer to behavioral products as representing *relations* among processes rather than as *things* with an ontogenetic trajectory. Thus emotions are processes rather than states. For DET, discrete emotions and perhaps stable emotion patterns reflect relations among constituent processes, but they also have statelike characteristics. As already noted, the phenomenological experience (feeling component of a given emotion) does not vary qualitatively across episodes. Anger feeling does vary, however, in intensity, as do its cognitive accompaniments, across individuals and situations.

Similarly, fourth, emotion feelings do not vary developmentally. This point is important because the causa belli for many systems theorists is to understand developmental change. For DET, however, change in the basic structure and function *within* discrete emotion systems is minimal (cf. Ackerman et al., 1998). Higher-level systems or patterns of emotions emerge and vary, and the predominance of some patterns may vary across contexts and time. Yet the emergence of higher-order complexity and change is not related in any principled way to *qualitative* changes in organismic variables.

There is an area of theoretical overlap in conceptualizing developmental processes in the cognitive-dependent emotions, such as shame and guilt.

These emotion systems emerge after the infancy period and the processes that activate them reflect clear developmental acquisitions. Nevertheless, the products of these emotion systems (shame feelings, guilt feelings) remain constant over the life span. What develop robustly for DET are the linkages between the emotional and cognitive systems or the affective-cognitive structures that emerge and consolidate. But consolidation and stabilization reflect classical principles of contiguity, similarity, repetition, observational learning, and reinforcement, and emergence may not often reflect any coherent developmental logic. The interesting exception here may concern attachment-related processes (cf. Sroufe, 1996).

Our notion of affective-cognitive structures also overlaps with similar constructs in dynamic systems approaches to emotion, in particular with Lewis and Douglas's (1998) concept of emotional interpretations. Both constructs describe the structures that emerge out of self-organizing couplings of elements of the emotions system and the cognitive system. For Lewis, however, the contribution of the cognitive system (as the seat of self-organization) seemingly has more causal weight than the contributions of the emotions system, and he does not treat the concept of emotion patterns that interact with the cognitive system. Both we and Lewis recognize that linking emotions to the cognitive system introduces immense flexibility and variability in emerging structures. We also agree with Lewis on the principle of reciprocal causation between the emotions and cognitive systems. We may differ a bit from Lewis in preferring to think of the emotion systems per se, particularly discrete emotions, as more modular and less malleable and as the motivational roots of personality.

The fifth distinction concerns the construct of skill. For some systems theorists (Thelen and Ulrich, 1991), skill acquisition in a particular context is sometimes a substitute for the conception of development as a goal-directed progression of qualitatively different stages or structures. Skill reflects behavioral structure emerging out of qualitatively different organizations of constituent elements. Sometimes theorists apply the honorific descriptors of "efficient" and "complex" to these novel structures, but skill per se simply reflects a relation among temporally organized structures assembled by task demands and unique local contingencies. In this sense, skill often reflects automatized attractors. Given a constant environment, behavioral skill is what emerges developmentally.

For DET, skill, as it relates to emotion, is an ambiguous concept. The metaphor of emotional intelligence is consistent with a skill-based perspective on emotional development, and the conception that emotion regulation increases over childhood fits with a skill-acquisition perspective. Both ideas have a place in DET as reflecting emerging affective-cognitive structures. The problem, however, is that the concept of skill has no referent in describing the functions of the discrete emotion systems and emotion patterns. Though automaticity may change for particular systems, the changes do not reflect skill. The changes are not directional in terms of local contingencies, even in the sense that patterns of emotions are higher-level systems. "Higher-level" simply describes the nature of relations among elements.

Conclusion

We are strongly attracted to aspects of dynamic systems theories of development as powerful metaphors for conceptualizing the processes constituting emotions and emotion patterns. The "systems" metaphor has always played a key role in differential emotions theory in describing discrete emotions and stable patterns of emotions, but dynamic systems approaches have provided new ways of thinking about what "system" means, and about the what, how, and why of development. For us, however, the most provocative and informative aspect of "fitting" differential emotions theory and dynamic systems theories of development is that not all the parts fit well. Pouring old wine from a new bottle sometimes invites formulation of a new wine, but it may also inspire another look at the old bottle.

Acknowledgment

This work was supported by the William T. Grant Foundation, award no. 93-1548-93.

References

Ackerman, B. P., Abe, J. A., and Izard, C. E. (1998). Differential emotions theory and emotional development: Mindful of modularity. In M. Mascolo and S. Griffin (Eds.), *What develops in emotional development?* (pp. 85–106). New York: Plenum.

Ackerman, B. P., Izard, C. E., Schoff, K., Youngstrom, E. A., and Kogos, J. (1997). *Cumulative risk, caregiver emotionality, and the aggressive behavior of 6- and 7-year-old children from economically disadvantaged families.* Manuscript submitted for publication.

American Psychiatric Association (1994). *Diagnostic and statistical manual of mental disorders* (4th ed.). Washington, DC: American Psychiatric Association.

Baumeister, R. F., Smart, L., and Boden, J. M. (1996). Relation of threatened egotism to violence and aggression: The dark side of high self-esteem. *Psychological Review, 103*, 5–33.

Bechara, A., Damasio, H., Tranel, D., and Damasio, A. R. (1997). Deciding advantageously before knowing the advantageous strategy. *Science, 275*, 1293–1294.

Beck, A. T., Emery, G., and Greenberg, R. L. (1996). Cognitive therapy for evaluation anxieties. In C. G. Lindemann (Ed.), *Handbook of the treatment of the anxiety disorders* (2nd ed., pp. 235–260). Northvale, NJ: Jason Aronson.

Cannon, W. B. (1929). *Bodily changes in pain, hunger, fear and rage: An account of recent researches into the function of emotional excitement.* New York: Appleton-Century-Crofts.

Darwin, C. (1965). *The expression of the emotions in man and animals.* Chicago: University of Chicago Press. (Original work published 1872.)

Derryberry, D., and Tucker, D. M. (1994). Motivating the focus of attention. In P. M. Niedenthal and S. Kitayama (Eds.), *The heart's eye: Emotional influences in perception and attention* (pp. 167–196). San Diego, CA: Academic Press.

Easterbrook, J. A. (1959). The effect of emotion on cue utilization and the organization of behavior. *Psychological Bulletin, 66*, 183–201.

Erickson, E. H. (1950). *Childhood and society.* New York: Norton.

Erickson, E. H. (1956). Growth and crises of the healthy personality. In C. Kluckhohn, H. A. Murray, and D. M. Schneider (Eds.), *Personality in nature, society and culture* (pp. 185–225). New York: Knopf.

Fisher, S. F. (1985). Identity of two: The phenomenology of shame in borderline development and treatment. *Psychotherapy, 22*, 101–109.

Fredrickson, B. L (1998). What good are positive emotions? *Review of General Psycholgy, 2,* 300–319.

Frijda, N. H. (1986). *The emotions.* New York: Cambridge University Press.

Fogel, A. (1993). *Developing through relationships: Origins of communication, self, and culture.* Chicago: University of Chicago Press.

Gilbert, P., Pehl, J., and Allan, S. (1994). The phenomenology of shame and guilt: An empirical investigation. *British Journal of Medical Psychology, 67*, 23–36.

Harter, S., and Jackson, B. K. (1993). Young adolescents' perceptions of the link between low self-worth and depressed affect. *Journal of Early Adolescence, 13*, 383–407.

Hoglund, C. L. , and Nicholas, K. B. (1995). Shame, guilt, and anger in college students exposed to abusive family environments. *Journal of Family Violence, 10,* 141–157.

Isen, A. (1984). Toward understanding the role of affect in cognition. In R. Wyer and T. Srull (Ed.), *Handbook of social cognition* (vol. 3, pp. 179–236). Hillsdale, NJ: Erlbaum.

Izard, C. E. (1971). *The face of emotion.* New York: Appleton-Century-Crofts.

Izard, C. E. (1972). *Patterns of emotions: A new analysis of anxiety and depression.* New York: Academic Press.

Izard, C. E. (1977). *Human emotions.* New York: Plenum.

Izard, C. E. (1990). Facial expressions and the regulation of emotions. *Journal of Personality and Social Psychology, 58*, 487–498.

Izard, C. E. (1991). *Psychology of emotions.* New York: Plenum.

Izard, C. E. (1992). Basic emotions, relations among emotions, and emotion-cognition relations. *Psychological Review, 99*, 561–565.

Izard, C. E. (1993). Four systems for emotion activation: Cognitive and noncognitive processes. *Psychological Review, 100*, 68–90.

Izard, C. E., Hembree, E. A., and Huebner, R. R. (1987). Infants' emotion expressions to acute pain: Developmental change and stability of individual differences. *Developmental Psychology, 23*, 105–113.

Izard, C. E., and Malatesta, C. Z. (1987). Perspectives on emotional development: I. Differential emotions theory of early emotional development. In J. D. Osofsky (Ed.), *Handbook of infant development* (2nd ed., pp. 494–554). New York: Wiley.

Izard, C. E., Wehmer, C. M., Livsey, W., and Jennings, I. R. (1965). Affect awareness and performance. In S. S. Tomkins and C. E. Izard (Eds.), *Affect, cognition, and personality* (pp. 2–41). New York: Springer.

Izard, C. E., and Youngstrom, E. A. (1996). The activation and regulation of fear and anxiety. In D. A. Hope (Ed.), *Nebraska Symposium on Motivation: Vol. 43. Perspectives in anxiety, panic, and fear* (pp. 2–59). Lincoln: University of Nebraska Press.

James, W. (1990). *The principles of emotion.* New York: Dover. (Original work published 1890.)

Kagan, J., Reznick, J. S., and Snidman, N. (1988). Biological bases of childhood shyness. *Science, 240*, 167–171.

Laird, J. D. (1974). Self-attribution of emotion: The effects of expressive behavior on the quality of emotional experience. *Journal of Personality and Social Psychology, 29*, 475–486.

Lang, P. J. (1979). A bio-informational theory of emotional imagery. *Psychophysiology, 16*, 495–512.

Lansky, M. R. (1987). Shame and domestic violence. In D. L. Nathanson (Ed.), *The many faces of shame* (pp. 335–362). New York: Guilford.

LeDoux, J. E. (1996). *The emotional brain.* New York: Simon and Schuster.

Lewis, H. (1971). Shame and guilt in neurosis. *Psychoanalytic Review, 58*, 419–438.

Lewis, H. (Ed.) (1987). *The role of shame in symptom formation.* Hillsdale, NJ: Erlbaum.

Lewis, M. D. (1995). Cognition-emotion feedback and the self-organization of developmental paths. *Human Development, 38*, 72–102.

Lewis, M. D., and Douglas, L. (1998). A dynamic systems approach to cognition-emotion interactions in development. In M. F. Mascolo and S. Griffin (Eds.), *What develops in emotional development?* (pp. 159–188). New York: Plenum.

Lewis, M. D., and Granic, I. (1999). Self-organization of cognition-emotion interactions. In T. Dalgleish and M. Power (Eds.), *Handbook of cognition and emotion* (pp. 683–701). Chichester: Wiley.

Malatesta-Magai, C., Jonas, R., Shepard, B., and Culver, L. C. (1992). Type A behavior pattern and emotion expression in younger and older adults. *Psychology and Aging, 7*, 551–561.

Matsumoto, D. (1987). The role of facial response in the experience of emotion: More methodological problems and a meta-analysis. *Journal of Personality and Social Psychology, 52*, 769–774.

Miller, R. S., and Tangney, J. P. (1994). Differentiating embarrassment and shame. *Journal of Social and Clinical Psychology, 13*, 273–287.

Öhman, A. (1986). Face the beast and fear the face: Animal and social fears as prototypes for evolutionary analyses of emotion. *Psychophysiology, 23*, 123–145.

Renninger, K. A., Hidi, S., and Krapp, A. (Eds.) (1992). *The role of interest in learning and development*. Hillsdale, NJ: Erlbaum.

Retzinger, S. M. (1987). Resentment and laughter: Video studies of the shame-rage spiral. In H. B. Lewis (Ed.), *The role of shame in symptom formation* (pp. 151–181). Hillsdale, NJ: Erlbaum.

Retzinger, S. M. (1991). Shame, anger, and conflict: Case study of emotional violence. *Journal of Family Violence, 6*, 37–59.

Retzinger, S. M. (1995). Shame and anger in personal relationships. In S. Duck and J. T. Wood (Eds.), *Confronting relationship challenges* (vol. 5, pp. 22–42). Thousand Oaks, CA: Sage.

Rothbart, M. K., and Derryberry, D. (1981). Development of individual differences in temperament. In M. E. Lamb and A. L. Brown (Eds.), *Advances in developmental psychology* (vol. 1, pp. 37–86). Hillsdale, NJ: Erlbaum.

Schore, A. N. (1991). Early superego development: The emergence of shame and narcissistic affect regulation in the practicing period. *Psychoanalysis and Contemporary Thought, 14*, 187–250.

Smith, L. B., and Thelen, E. (Eds.). (1993). *A dynamic systems approach to development: Applications*. Cambridge, MA: MIT Press.

Sroufe, L. A. (1996). *Emotional development: The organization of emotional life in the early years*. New York: Cambridge University Press.

Tangney, J. P. (1990). Assessing individual differences in proneness to shame and guilt: Development of the self-conscious affect and attribution inventory. *Journal of Personality and Social Psychology, 59*, 102–111.

Tangney, J. P., Wagner, P., Fletcher, C., and Gramzow, R. (1992). Shamed into anger? The relation of shame and guilt to anger and self-report aggression. *Journal of Personality and Social Psychology, 62*, 669–675.

Tangney, J. P., Wagner, P. E., Barlow, D. H., Marschall, D. E., and Gramzow, R. (1996). Relation of shame and guilt to constructive versus destructive responses to anger across the lifespan. *Journal of Personality and Social Psychology, 70*, 797–809.

Thelen, E. (1989). Self-organization in developmental processes: Can systems approaches work? In M. R. Gunnar and E. Thelen (Eds.), *Minnesota Symposium on Child Psycholgy: Vol. 22. Systems and development* (pp. 77–117). Hillsdale, NJ: Erlbaum.

Thelen, E., and Ulrich, B. D. (1991). Hidden skills: A dynamic systems analysis of treadmill stepping during the first year of life. *Monographs of the Society for Research in Child Development, 56* (serial no. 223).

Tomkins, S. S. (1962). *Affect, imagery, consciousness: Vol I. The positive affects*. New York: Springer.

Tomkins, S. S. (1963). *Affect, imagery, consciousness: Vol. II. The negative affects*. New York: Springer.

Winton, W. M. (1986). The role of facial response in self-reports of emotion: A critique of Laird. *Journal of Personality and Social Psychology, 50*, 808–812.

Zajonc, R. B., Murphy, S. T., and Inglehart, M. (1989). Feeling and facial efference: Implications of the vascular theory of emotion. *Psychological Review, 96*, 395–416.

2 Emotional Self-Organization at Three Time Scales

Marc D. Lewis

Theories of emotion and theories of emotional development have remained largely insulated from each other. As a result, important interactions between emotional processes in real time (moment-to-moment) and emotional patterning over development are rarely examined in detail. This split is particularly troublesome for the study of individual differences. For example, appraisal theories claim that cognitive interpretations give rise to emotions, and individual differences in interpretations are what make this claim interesting (Frijda and Zeelenberg, in press). However, without exposure to models of individual development, appraisal theorists have been unable to explain individual differences and have largely ignored them instead. Conversely, the study of personality development assumes that individual pathways emerge from recurrent real-time emotional processes (e.g., cognition-emotion interactions). But without theoretical insights into the nature of these processes, it is difficult to specify how they create long-lasting structure. As in other psychological domains, nobody doubts the importance of interscale relations, but the means for studying them remain elusive.

The premise of this chapter is that principles of self-organization provide the necessary tools for bridging emotional time scales. All self-organizing systems are characterized by the interdependence of processes at different scales, and complex, nested, multiscale patterns are ubiquitous in the natural world. In general, large-scale or macroscopic patterns (e.g., the contours of a coastline) set the conditions for small-scale or microscopic processes (e.g., the erosion of rocks by waves), and these microscopic processes contribute to macroscopic patterning in turn. With temporal scales, longstanding forms guide ongoing structuration, while such structuration is the leading edge of longstanding forms. Dynamic systems (DS) approaches to psychology and cognition often specify reciprocal influences between time scales (e.g., van Gelder and Port, 1995). Developmentalists with a DS orientation are particularly interested in how developmental self-organization constrains real-time emergent processes while real-time self-organization lays down the path of development (Fogel and Thelen, 1987; Thelen and Ulrich, 1991). Thus, the study of self-organization brings interscale relations to the foreground of psychological theorizing and suggests principles by which they can be explained.

Most of the chapters in this volume look at emotional processes in either real time or development. However, many hint at relations between the two scales, and a few model these relations explicitly (e.g., Granic, Izard et al., Laible and Thompson, Schore). In the present chapter, I propose the first rendition of a multiscale theory of emotional development, linking real-time and developmental time scales with a third, intermediate time scale. The three kinds of emotional phenomena most often studied are single emotion episodes lasting for seconds or minutes, moods lasting for hours or days, and personality patterns that persist for years. The vastly different time parameters of these phenomena can be neatly accommodated by nested scales of microdevelopment, mesodevelopment, and macrodevelopment. Examining these scales through a single theoretical lens can reveal multiple causal connections among them and point toward an eventual unity in the study of emotion and its development.

In the first part of the chapter, I introduce general principles of self-organization that apply at any scale. Next, emotional self-organization is discussed at each of three scales: the microdevelopment of emotion episodes, the mesodevelopment of moods, and the macrodevelopment of personality (summarized in Table 2.1 on page 59). Emotional self-organization at each scale is modeled as an *emergent cognition-emotion interaction*, using the following format. First, conventional approaches to cognition-emotion interactions at that scale are summarized; second, these approaches are critiqued from current psychological and neurobiological perspectives; third, principles of self-organization are used to fashion an alternative model; and fourth, preliminary support for this model is drawn from contemporary theory and research. In the final section, I outline principles by which scales of self-organization act upon each other and propose paths of influence between cognitive-emotional processes at each scale. By way of conclusion, I speculate on features of self-similarity across the three scales of emotional development, emphasizing the superordinate role of intentionality at each scale.

Principles of Self-Organization for Developmental Modeling

Before proceeding to model emotional development at different time scales, it is useful to review some general principles of self-organization. These principles are derived from the physical, biological, and cognitive sciences, and they apply to self-organizing processes at any scale.

Self-organizing systems become more ordered over time, and their orderliness arises spontaneously (i.e., without programming or instruction). At the same time, they become more deterministic, starting off with many degrees of freedom but becoming more fully specified, with fewer degrees of freedom, as they develop. For example, the temperament characteristics of an individual are indeterminate during embryogenesis until neural and humoral systems knit together before or after birth (Derryberry and Rothbart, 1997). Once established, some of these characteristics endure for a lifetime. In addition, self-organizing systems are much more sensitive to perturbations early in their histories than later, an axiom known as "sensitive dependence on initial conditions." The more order that has accumulated over time, the greater the push that is necessary to shift the system's trajectory. Thus, a consolidating pattern of activation in a neural network can shift more easily after a few iterations than after many. Exceptions to this rule are found at transition points, when coherence diminishes and indeterminism increases temporarily. These are discussed later.

Self-organizing systems become more complex. Their increasing orderliness allows them to maintain a more intricate arrangement of interacting parts or processes. For example, cortical self-organization over development gives rise to more complex concepts and perceptions than could be supported by a less organized (developmentally earlier) cortex. In the same way, the attachment system of an older infant supports a more articulated set of expectancies, contingencies, or tendencies than that of a younger infant. Both increasing order and increasing complexity rely on a basic mechanism of self-organization, the coordination or coupling of interacting system elements. This coupling can be described as ongoing reciprocal interaction (or entrainment) among elements. Coupling is demonstrated by the tendency for neurons firing at the same time to maintain each other's activation, or simply by conversants maintaining their conversation. Through coupling, elements team up to form ensembles, and ensembles of ensembles, providing an overarching orderliness that supports complex structuration.

The specific characteristics that emerge in self-organization influence the path of subsequent self-organization. In other words, the products of a growth process constrain the conditions for further growth. I have called this axiom *cascading constraints*, because each node of converging order constrains or narrows the possibilities for the system's subsequent path, and later assemblies must be compatible with the orderliness already laid down by earlier ones (Lewis, 1997). In embryogenesis, for example, cell adhesion processes fashion cellular assemblies which then modify gene expression in a cascading sequence (Thelen and Smith, 1994). Note that certain coherences or cooperativities are so powerful that they dominate all downstream activity as with the QWERTY keyboard (the one we all type on) that has sculpted a hundred-year lineage through the many possibilities of communicative artifacts (Papert, 1980).

The outcomes of self-organization are fixed or periodic organizational patterns that endure for some period of time. These states are called *attractors* in dynamic systems theory, because they attract the trajectory of the system. A living system is characterized by many coexisting attractors, a condition called *multistability* (Kelso, 1995), and it rapidly moves or "evolves" into one or another of these attractors when perturbed in real time. Living systems end up with far fewer attractors than were technically possible at the outset of development, an expression of the increasing determinism intrinsic to all self-organizing processes. But they also end up with predictable attractors, suggesting that prespecified organizing principles, and not just bottom-up chance, guide organic self-organization (Goodwin, 1987). An example is the small number of basic designs to which all life forms adhere, despite the infinite diversity available through natural selection (Goodwin, 1993).

A unique form of causation typifies self-organizing systems. This has been termed *circular causality* (Haken, 1987), by which a higher-order form *causes* a particular pattern of coupling among lower-order elements, while this pattern simultaneously *causes* the higher-order form. (Note that this is different from reciprocal causality, another characteristic of nonlinear systems, by which elements at the same level influence each other.) Circular causality is seen when the life of a cell maintains the chemical interactions of its molecular constituents, while those interactions maintain the life of the cell. In behavioral systems, functions such as walking or reaching maintain the coordinations of perceptual and muscular constituents, while those coordinations maintain that particular function (Thelen and Smith, 1994). The higher-order form or function is coupled, in turn, with events in the environment, with which it exchanges the energy that fuels the coordination of its components. For example, a living cell moves toward targets to seek nourishment by which it maintains the biochemical interactions that constitute it. Metaphorically, the higher-order form is hooked into the flow of time (at a particular scale).

Because orderliness is limited to a small number of stable states, the system crosses *thresholds* of instability in its journey from one orderly pattern to the next. That is, rather than exhibiting gradual or linear change, self-organizing systems jump abruptly to new stabilities, and they do so at all scales. These jumps, often called *phase transitions*, occur when system orderliness breaks down, sensitivity to perturbations increases, and new patterns of organization rapidly self-amplify. Phase transitions are exemplified by Gould's (1980) punctuated equilibria, rapid changes in species evolution sandwiched between long periods of stability. At a smaller (developmental) scale, phase transitions can be used to model shifts between cognitive-developmental stages (van Geert, 1994), and, at an even smaller (real-time) scale, they describe rapid switches in patterns of muscular coordination (Kelso, 1995).

Microdevelopment: Self-Organization of Emotion Episodes

Conventional Models

One of the most prolific lines of investigation into the relationship between cognition and emotion has been appraisal theory. According to this approach, cognitive evaluation of the significance of a situation is constructed along several appraisal dimensions (e.g., conduciveness to goals, agency, coping potential). This construction is the basis for an emotional response that fits the situation and directs behavior for the duration of an emotion episode. In some theories, appraisal proceeds in a series of steps which may or may not be repeated. For example, Lazarus (1991) postulates a primary appraisal of general relevance and a secondary appraisal of coping potential, whereas Scherer (1984) posits a set of five stimulus checks of increasing specificity that recycle rapidly over time. For nearly all appraisal approaches, however, multiple appraisal components are combined into a single composite evaluation that generates the emotional response (e.g., Smith and Lazarus, 1993). Appraisals are taken to be necessary for emotions and to precede them in emotion episodes. Individual differences are acknowledged, as when individuals regard the same objective situation in very different ways; but the sequence of appraisal steps or the dimensions being evaluated are usually considered to be universal and invariable (Smith and Ellsworth, 1985).

The findings of appraisal research provide an elegant inroad to our understanding of emotion in real time, but some premises of appraisal theory clash with cognitive psychology and everyday experience. First, research suggests that cognitive evaluations in real-world settings rely on rapid gistlike information processing (Brainerd and Reyna, 1990) and contextual highlighting of events (Barsalou, 1987). Interpretations of emotion-eliciting events should also be capriciously affected by situational context. Instead of taking stock of set categories of meaning, they should be captivated by particular features while ignoring much else of potential relevance (cf. Ellsworth, 1991). Moreover, reasoning about global preferences taps only the coarsest level of processing (Brainerd and Reyna, 1990), a level one might refer to as "quick and dirty." Emotion-related appraisals have similarly been found to be thematic and lacking in detail (Christianson and Loftus, 1991), giving them a distinctly noncomputational flavor. In addition, the additive or combinatorial assumption of appraisal theory is incompatible with evidence that earlier perceptual events bias later ones in concept formation and decision making (Barsalou, 1987; Brooks, 1987). This may explain why appraisals, once formed, are so hard to change – at least for a while. Finally, it is not at all clear that appraisals actually precede emotion (Buck, 1985; Frijda, 1993b; Izard, 1993). Emotion may well be the driver of appraisal even as appraisal drives emotion (Izard, 1993).

Conventional models of appraisal have trouble with neurobiological evidence as well. First, LeDoux's (e.g., 1993) studies of pathways between the thalamus and the amygdala reveal rapid emergence of an emotional response based on coarse sensory information. Emotion is triggered before the perception of the event is complete, and it is not until roughly half a second later that the hippocampus has a chance to distill its conceptual meaning. Hence, not only is cognitive appraisal not necessary to elicit emotion, full-scale appraisals are impossible until after emotion has been activated (cf. Frijda, 1993b). This challenge to the fundamental premise of appraisal theory points to continuity and co-emergence, not to antecedent-consequent relations between cognition and emotion (Lewis, 1996). Contemporary brain research suggests, further, that organized mental activity is always co-emergent and always globally distributed across conceptual, emotional, and perceptual subsystems (Damasio, 1994; Freeman, 1995). Cortical activity evolves in rapidly updated cycles, through continuous feedback with the limbic and lower brain systems. Global meanings converge together with emotion at the corticolimbic interface in a seamless progression (Freeman, this volume; Tucker, 1992). Thus, the rational computation of meaning, free of motivational backwash, is as unlikely in neural terms as it is in psychological terms.

Self-Organizing Emotional Interpretations

Propositions. Based on the principles of self-organization listed above, appraisal processes can be reconceptualized as emergent order in the cognitive system corresponding to, but not preceding, emotion. The beginning of an emotion episode can be any fluctuation in the integrated stream of perception, cognition, action, and emotion. Attention is shaken loose from its attractor and drawn toward aspects of the world that *seem* important (coarse processing). Emotion shifts correspondingly, increasing in intensity and converging toward a specific state (e.g., surprise with attention to change, fear at the approach of something dangerous, anger as attention moves to an obstruction). Appraisal does not precede this emotional swelling, it self-organizes as emotional and cognitive changes become synchronized, arriving at an attractor when the new situation is subjectively understood and an action tendency has formed to deal with it. Attention and emotion modify one another continuously during this process, such that discrepancies disappear quickly (negative feedback) while global synchronies are enhanced and elaborated (positive feedback). For example, an angry appraisal minimizes attention to threat and maximizes attention to goal blockage while an angry feeling and sense of power consolidate. We (e.g., Lewis and Granic, 1999) have referred to these appraisal-emotion amalgams as *emotional interpretations* (EIs). They are similar to Izard's (1984) affective-cognitive structures, except that we construe them as emerging states of global coherence, not static states of local coherence. Thus, appraisals are a major component of self-organizing EIs: they consolidate as part of a larger self-organizing process involving cognition *and* emotion.

How does this model incorporate the principles listed previously? EIs rapidly increase in orderliness. Early in the emergence of an EI there are many degrees of freedom and high sensitivity to small differences. Seeing one's lover unexpectedly can lead to happiness, suspicion, desire, or shame, depending on the associations, words, or gestures that occupy attention in the first second or so. Then the appraisal stabilizes, the event or situation is felt to be understood, a dominant emotional state converges, and a path of action consolidates. Once a shame EI emerges, for example, it is soon insensitive to further perturbation because attention to one's own faults holds shame in place, shame maintains attention to self, and action is directed toward hiding or shielding the self. As well, EIs rapidly grow in complexity. The convergence of an orderly appraisal supports a highly articulated network of thoughts, expectancies, rehearsed behaviors, and anticipated outcomes. From the first flash of rage to the intricate ordering of a planned retaliation, the cognitive system rapidly complexifies under the guidance of an emerging EI. It is in this sense that real-time emotion episodes *develop*.

The vehicle for self-organization is coupling of system elements or of whole subsystems. In the case of appraisal, I have emphasized the coupling of cognitive elements (Lewis, 1995, 1996). Other authors have stressed synchronization among other subsystems, including perception, arousal, and action (Mascolo et al., this volume; Scherer, 1984, this volume). Indeed, any state of coherent attention implies massive coupling among all these systems (Freeman, 1995). But appraisal relies, at the very least, on coupling among percepts, concepts, associations, expectancies, plans, and rehearsed actions – all broadly subsumed under *cognition*. Most important from the present perspective, this cognitive coupling stabilizes only as it becomes entrained with emotion, establishing a more comprehensive coupling between the cognitive and emotional subsystems (Lewis, 1995). The resulting form is an emotional state coupled with a detailed appraisal of a situation, including plans for acting upon it. This evolution may be progressively refined by *cascading constraints* in real time, leading in several seconds to an action and an expectancy regarding its consequences.

As in all self-organizing processes, a circular causality can be imputed between a global, higher-order form and the coupling of its lower-order constituents. An EI (or appraisal) is one description of this higher-order form. The term ''emotional interpretation'' is somewhat problematic, however, because it simply joins two terms that each applies to a lower level of description. Perhaps a better depiction of the higher-order form, and one that truly captures its qualitative distinctness, is Freeman's (1995) notion of a global *intention* for acting on the world. Freeman (1995, this volume) argues that a seamless intentional unity arises from and entrains coordinations among all sensory and motor cortices. This emergent unity is centered at the corticolimbic (roughly, cognitive-emotional) interface, specifically in the hippocampus or in the loop between hippocampus and prefrontal cortex. The idea that an intentional state is superordinate to emotion fits surprisingly well with the centrality of *goals* in most models of emotional elicitation (e.g., Oatley and Johnson-Laird, 1987) and with the centrality of *action readiness* in Frijda's (1986) model. Emotions are generally assumed to serve goals through appraisals that lead to action. Thus, if intentions or goal states are viewed as emergent (in real time), they could be said to *cause* the lower-order coordination of cognitive and affective elements that (circularly) cause those intentions. In fact, it seems to be this emergent intentionality that locks onto the stream of events in real time, exchanging energy with the world and thereby fueling its underlying coordinations.

What sort of attractors are available for self-organizing EIs (or their corresponding intentions)? The principles listed earlier stipulate that there are far fewer orderly outcomes than degrees of freedom along the way. This fits the observation that appraisals fall into a small number of types (Scherer, 1994; Smith and Lazarus, 1993). Categories of appraisal (e.g., threat, obstacle, loss) may be dictated by ordering principles inherent in modes of interacting with the world (e.g., escape, acquire, overcome) while they, in turn, correlate with biologically specified features of basic emotions (Ekman, 1984; Izard, 1977). These limiting factors on psychological organization are analogical to the constraints on biological organization discovered by Goodwin (1993). However, many possibilities exist at the early stages of an EI, when small variations in attention and context can lead down drastically different paths. It may only be when one starts to formulate an action that one's interpretation of an event can crystallize to an attractor, perhaps several seconds after the initial swell of emotionality.

Finally, movement from one EI to another can be modeled as a phase transition in microdevelopment (Lewis, 1995). Scherer (this volume) also models emotional shifts as sudden jumps or *catastrophes*. The variability and indeterminacy that exist early in the evolution of an EI are precisely what characterize phase transitions, when orderliness is minimal and the system can evolve in a number of directions. In other words, each self-organizing EI can be considered an epoch in an ongoing trajectory of branching and stabilizing microdevelopmental paths. The available resting points for this trajectory are represented by attractors on the psychological state space. Thus, branching paths in microdevelopment remain bounded by the contours of the state space even though they continue to evolve in time.

Support. This conception of self-organizing emotion episodes is consistent with research in cognitive psychology, cited earlier, showing that context, previous events, and superficial appearances strongly influence interpretation and judgment. From this perspective, the orderliness of appraisal is not dependent on the computation of situational dimensions; it is a consequence of how cognition, emotion, and action fit together in a working relationship with each other and with a changing, capricious world. The notion of self-organizing EIs has much in common with Scherer's (1984, this volume) concept of synchronization among organismic subsystems in emotional processes. It is also supported by evidence that attention tends to "get stuck," showing a longer latency for disengagement when processing emotion-related cues (Derryberry and Tucker, 1994; Mathews and MacLeod, 1985). Yet it is perhaps most congenial with the ideas of Izard (1984, 1993), Buck (1985), and Frijda (1993b), who assign no causal priority to cognition in cognition-emotion interactions.

The present approach is consistent with neurobiological theory and findings as well. According to Tucker (1992) and Schore (1994), coherence across cortical subsystems is mediated by the paralimbic cortex, where gistlike meanings are fashioned and entrained with emotion-mediating limbic circuits. The cortical convergence feeding this coherence has been located in the ventromedial prefrontal or orbitofrontal cortex (Damasio, 1994; Schore, 1994) and in the entorhinal cortex that receives its outputs (Freeman, 1995). Schore (this volume) refers to this region as the locus of "orbitofrontal appraisals." These appraisals are continuously entrained with emotional circuitry in the limbic system in a co-emergent wholeness. The epicenter of this co-emergence is characterized by Freeman (1995, this volume) as a global intentional state self-organizing in the hippocampus (Freeman, this volume). I view emotional interpretations as the psychological correlate of the resonance between orbitofrontal (appraisal) and limbic (emotional) activity. Freeman's global intentions may both emerge from this resonance and maintain it in a circular causality. In addition, global changes in these patterns of resonance have been modeled as phase transitions in neural activity, and they can be triggered by small stimulus changes (Freeman, 1995; Schore, this volume). Finally, bursts of emotion early in appraisal may strongly influence its direction. According to the axiom of sensitive dependence on initial conditions, LeDoux's (1993) thalamus-to-amygdala pathway, activating emotional change prior to conceptual elaboration, would skew appraisal toward habitual EIs. Thus, not only could appraisals not precede emotions, but familiar evaluations would unavoidably follow emotions (Power and Dalgleish, 1997).

Mesodevelopment: Emotional Self-Organization in Moods

Conventional Models

Emotion theorists have devoted far less attention to modeling the middle time scale of emotional phenomena: that most often referred to as mood. Some existing models view moods as extended affective states based on extended cognitive configurations. Mood states such as depression may arise from recurrent or stable attitudes or beliefs about the self or others, perhaps triggered by negative life events (Beck, Epstein, and Harrison, 1983). Or they may result from the activation of cognitive networks by emotional associations, biasing memory, judgment, and learning for extended periods (Bower, 1981). Conversely, mood states may be maintained by emotion rather than cognition. Frijda (1993a) has described moods as long-lasting affective states resulting from events that are no longer in awareness. Because they have lost their "aboutness" in relation to a specific causal antecedent, moods have a diffuse character (cf. Forgas, 1995), yet they maintain a propensity for appraisals biased toward certain themes. Frijda specifies no causal link between emotions and appraisals in moods, but we can assume that the affective state biases cognition, as has been well documented (e.g., Keltner, Ellsworth, and Edwards, 1993; Mathews and MacLeod, 1985). A third kind of model explains mood continuity on the basis of a feedback relation in which negative thoughts perpetuate an affective state (e.g., depressed or anxious mood) which is one of several factors that generate ongoing negative thoughts (Teasdale and Barnard, 1993). For this kind of model, the causal basis of mood is an interaction effect, not cognition or emotion per se.

While these models ring true to some extent, they share a number of potential shortcomings, particularly with respect to emotion. First, whether viewed as patterns of network activation, stable belief states, or enduring emotional states, moods are defined as static constructions independent of any goal-directed activity. In contrast, emotions, and the action tendencies associated with them, are viewed as being specifically directed toward goal acquisition through action (Frijda, 1986; Oatley and Johnson-Laird, 1987; Stein and Trabasso, 1992). The presence of emotions in moods may be impossible to model successfully without considering the role of goals and actions. Second, biased (e.g., mood-congruent) cognition has received more empirical attention than any other aspect of mood, yet such bias is not specifically tied to emotion in most of these models. In fact, cognitive research reveals lasting biases unrelated to mood or emotion (e.g., Markovits and Nantel, 1989). How, then, is mood-congruent bias an emotional phenomenon? Finally, describing moods as the maintenance of a particular state does little to explain them. In a constantly changing world, stable states must be maintained by something, and in the case of moods that something is likely to be emotional. Teasdale and Barnard (1993) do offer a mechanism of maintenance that is intrinsic to cognition-emotion interactions – a self-sustaining feedback loop – suggesting a useful direction for further modeling.

Neurobiological models may explain aspects of mood that cognitive models do not. Consistent with the effects of mood-altering drugs and the chemical by-products of stress reactions (e.g., corticosteroids), moods have been strongly linked to the slow-acting effects of neurohormones (e.g., Panksepp, 1998, this volume). Could neurohormones explain Frijda's enduring emotional states? They might; but Frijda and others emphasize the diffuse character of such states. In contrast, neurohormones affect cognition by entraining cortical synapses in preparation for specific classes of activity (e.g., aggression, mating, nurturance). This implies moods with specific perceptual and cognitive content, not just a vague feeling. It also implies that goal states are central to moods, contrary to present cognitive models.

Self-Organizing Moods

Propositions. The phase transition marking the onset of a mood involves more than movement from one attractor to another: the entire state space becomes modified for a period of hours, days, or weeks. Metaphorically, the surface of the state space is altered, increasing the slope toward some attractors, decreasing it toward others, changing hills (repellors) into valleys (new attractors), or fashioning deep attractors out of shallow wells. Thus, following Globus (1995), one can say that the contour of the state space has been retuned. Trajectories may get stuck in regions that they used to pass through easily, now that anxiety, anger, depression, or shame dominates the emotional landscape. Like all phase transitions, mood change involves fluctuations, characterized as a chaotic buckling of the state space until an enduring mood finally settles in and state space variability is suppressed once again. For example, angry, sentimental, and guilty states may fluctuate prior to the onset of depression. This progression from fluctuation to entrenchment is what characterizes moods as *developmental* processes.

Self-organizing emotional interpretations (EIs) were described as interpretive coherences arising through the entrainment of cognition and emotion in microdevelopment. Self-organizing moods – at least negative moods – may arise through the entrainment of an interpretive bias with a narrow range of emotional states. This entrainment may evolve over occasions from the coupling of components in recurrent EIs, augmenting cooperativities that favor particular emotions and interpretations. Once a mood is triggered, the orderliness of this entrainment does not dissipate, and interpretations of events no longer start from "zero." In fact, this orderliness seems to crystallize, and interpretive and emotional tendencies become more entrenched, as moods develop over minutes, hours, and even days.

If appraisal and emotion are inseparable in EIs, as suggested earlier, then the causal basis for mood could never be assigned to one or the other. Rather, emotional continuity and prolonged cognitive organization must cause one another in moods. This view is consistent with Teasdale and Barnard's (1993) feedback model. But the principle of circular causality demands that feedback processes give rise to some higher-order form that maintains them. What might this form be?

Consistent with Freeman's emphasis on the wholeness of intentionality, mood might be dominated by an enduring *intentional orientation*. According to this definition, moods are different from EIs because intentional states in moods persist, and I suggest that they persist *because no action can be taken to resolve them* (cf. Scheff, 1987). Intentions (or real-time goals) prepare for actions, and actions dissipate intentions. But if actions are not attempted or are not effective, then emotional engagement with goal-relevant associations and plans may keep the goal alive, not as an immediate prospect but as a need or wish extending over time. Thus, an intentional orientation may maintain feedback or resonance between a subset of emotions and interpretations related to achieving something that is too difficult to achieve or that cannot be achieved immediately. Moreover, enduring intentions would flood the mind with very specific expectancies – those corresponding to actions that are continually rehearsed but not executed. Not only would these expectancies be impossible to "turn off" while the intentions that produce them persisted, but expectancies of negative outcomes would very effectively block action and thereby maintain moods, as commonly reported in the clinical literature (e.g., Horowitz, 1998; Polivy, 1998).

What evidence is there for a link between nonaction and enduring psychological orderliness? In Freeman's studies of the perception-action cycle in animals, EEG coherence during the perception phase *dissipates* when action is initiated. This leaves the brain in a chaotic "background" state from which new coherences can emerge in the next cycle (Skarda and Freeman, 1987). Thus, action breaks down the organization that has converged in perception, and the organism's brain returns to a state of disorganization (literally, chaos) in preparation for new goals. But what happens if action is blocked? If the goal cannot be abandoned (as is typical of humans, with their advanced symbolic and memory capacities), then the orderliness of appraisal and emotion may persist. Goal-related behaviors may be rehearsed, expected responses monitored, and contingencies checked and rechecked. Thus, angry moods persist when one cannot get rid of the obstruction to one's plans, as with an impasse in a marriage or a dead-end job. Depressed moods may be maintained by an inability to demand closeness or nurturance from others due to their unavailability or to fear of rejection. In these cases, a global intentional orientation maintains a real-time attentional bias toward emotionally relevant perceptions and expectancies as well as action plans that can neither be executed nor abandoned.

Then why do moods seem diffuse (Forgas, 1995; Frijda, 1993a)? Moods are sometimes very specific. One can feel grumpy and resentful toward one's boss or anxious about one's health for days or weeks at a time. But moods sometimes are impenetrable and seemingly disconnected from present circumstances. One reason for this blurring of "aboutness" may be that long-term intentional orientations become highly generalized, as exemplified by the search for safety in anxiety and the commitment to hide or devalue the self in a shameful or depressed mood. Moreover, from a psychodynamic perspective, unattainable goals refer back to unresolved but highly compelling issues from earlier in development. Our inability to "let go" of goals in mood states makes sense from this perspective. Thus, appraisals, emotions, and expectancies in moods may refer to distant events, displacing if not blurring the aboutness of moods in what psychoanalysts call *transference*. As well, persistent goals in moods may come in mutually inhibitory pairs or groupings, expressing the clashing contingencies so common to human interactions. For example, goals for demanding nurturance yet avoiding rejection, punishing others yet avoiding punishment, or hiding the self yet asserting one's power, may forge the mixtures of anger, sadness, shame, and anxiety that persist in depressive moods. Thus, contradictory goals may blur the aboutness of moods while maintaining emotional blends for long periods. Finally, defenses, or habitual and unconscious regulating strategies, may have evolved to deal with the painfulness of recurrent, unattainable goals and wishes (Horowitz, 1998), and such defenses could also be responsible for dimming the aboutness of moods.

Support. Unlike other models, this account stipulates a place in moods for the goal-oriented nature of emotions. Moreover, the role suggested is sufficient to constrain cognitive-emotional feedback in a coherent fashion. Feedback between cognitive biases and emotional highlighting has been demonstrated in mood states by Teasdale and Barnard (1993). In the present model, such feedback disposes the individual to particular expectancies that guide perception and limit action, consistent with cognitive accounts of the role of anticipation in the perception-action cycle (Neisser, 1976).

The proposed relation between negative expectancies, mental rehearsal, and prolonged emotionality is known to characterize rumination in mood states such as depression, and reliable correlations have been found between the tendency to ruminate and the endurance of such states (Nolen-Hoeksema and Morrow, 1991; Teasdale and Barnard, 1993).

The present definition of mood ignores positive affective states. A good deal of evidence points to asymmetry between the impacts of positive and negative affective states on cognition, with positive affect defocusing attention and negative affect narrowing it (Isen, 1990). Only negative moods are hypothesized to constrain cognitive organization in the present account. Yet, as noted by Davidson (1994, p. 52), some degree of mood may always be present as an ''affective background,'' and positive states such as excitement could also persist through nonaction when attainable goals are simply delayed. When moods do change, I suggest that new goal states and associated biases emerge through a phase transition. Vallacher and Nowak (1997) also view change in the structure of goals as a phase transition in psychological systems.

The proposed overorderliness of moods is consistent with research on chaotic dynamics in human systems. Self-Organizing trajectories from heart rates to psychotherapy are most healthy and most adaptive when they are somewhat random or chaotic (e.g., Goldstein, 1997). In fact, overorderliness has been empirically related to affective disorders including depression (Kreindler and Lumsden, 1998). The correspondence between inhibited action and prolonged negative (or maladaptive) psychological states was a cornerstone of Freud's theory and has been verified empirically (Polivy, 1998). The present approach folds this insight into a general model of overorderliness.

There is also neurobiological evidence that intentions or goals shape perception, action plans, and anticipations, all of which constrain one another reciprocally. Freeman (1995, this volume) discusses circuits from the hippocampus to all sensory cortices as a ''preafference loop'' that strongly influences perception before it happens, and does so on the basis of goal-related expectancies entrained with motor rehearsal. Thus, extended goal states would necessarily maintain sensory-motor-affective patterns for long periods. Such extended states are also likely to involve neurohormones. These chemicals act diffusely on large regions of cortex, enhancing particular synaptic connections and inhibiting others over long periods (Freeman, 1995; Panksepp, 1998). They also directly promote the growth and intensification of emotional states, specifically those related to aggression, abandonment, caretaking, and other mammalian themes (Panksepp,

1998). Most important, neurohormones are released from the brain stem consequent to limbic activity mediating the construction of plans in frontal and motor cortex (Freeman, 1995; Panksepp, 1998). Thus, neurohormonal modulation could not be independent of specific *intentions* (Freeman, this volume). This adds credence to the idea that moods are fashioned around enduring goal states. By linking limbic, lower brain, bodily, and cortical states, neurohormones can maintain goal-specific resonances among wishes, emotions, and expectancies.

Macrodevelopment: Self-Organizing Personality Patterns

Conventional Models

Theories of personality development going back to Freud view personality as a crystallizing pattern of goals, behaviors, emotions, and interpretations based on the accumulation of experience interacting with innate dispositions. Theories of attachment and emotional development provide a contemporary framework for looking at personality development in terms of emotion-cognition relations. Attachment theory attributes personality stability to the construction of an internal working model of one's own actions, expected parental reactions, and associated emotions. Change in working models stems from major environmental shifts or alternate caregiving arrangements (e.g., Lamb, 1987), but attachment continuity from infancy onward is still the default assumption (Laible and Thompson, this volume). Emotional developmentalists in the biological tradition are more specific about the psychological underpinnings of this process. For them, stable personality habits form around affective-cognitive structures (Izard, 1984). These linkages between emotion and interpretation derive from recurrent experiences and lead to the establishment of lifelong emotion traits (Malatesta and Wilson, 1988). According to the organizational perspective on emotional development, such styles or habits also reflect hierarchical integration of earlier cognitive and emotional constituents (Cicchetti and Sroufe, 1978).

Critics have long pointed to an unresolved tension between change and stability in models of personality development (Block and Robins, 1993). For example, evidence for low continuity in attachment style challenges the notion of internal working models as templates of stability (e.g., Thompson, Lamb, and Estes, 1982). In addition, mechanisms for change after infancy (environmental discontinuity) are incommensurate with those for the initial establishment of an attachment style (maternal sensitivity).

The notion of affective-cognitive structures is more versatile. There is no critical period for their construction, and they are experience-dependent at any age. However, emotion traits cannot easily accommodate changes in behaviors and goals due to varying situational parameters, as highlighted by some personality theorists (McAdams, 1994; Wright and Mischel, 1987). Moreover, it is not clear how emotion traits could be malleable enough to be fashioned through experience yet stable enough to endure over a lifespan. Perhaps they do not endure, and developmental discontinuities deserve a much more prominent role in models of personality growth (Hinde, 1982; Rutter, 1984). Magai and Hunziker's (1993) recent emphasis on personality transitions represents a move in this direction, and Magai and Nusbaum (1996) touch on dynamic systems constructs that help explain such transitions. Similarly, Michael Lewis (1997) suggests that individual determinism is contradicted by evidence for abrupt and unpredictable changes, and he recommends looking to chaos and catastrophe theories to model these changes.

Neurobiological findings also demand a synthesis of individual continuity and developmental reorganization. Many neurodevelopmentalists agree that individual continuity crystallizes in development through the experience-driven selection of cortical pathways, the pruning of nonfunctional connections, and self-perpetuating links between cortical and limbic structures (Derryberry and Rothbart, 1997; Schore, 1994; Tucker, 1992). However, they also point to major discontinuities, including critical periods, nonlinear developmental effects, and neural reorganizations based on traumatic life events. An example is the sudden onset of depressive patterns due to interactions between early corticolimbic sensitization and later precipitating experiences (Harkness and Tucker, this volume). More global discontinuities may be linked with age-specific changes in cortical connectivity (Thatcher, 1991), and these may be the basis for socioemotional transitions related to shifts in cognitive development (Case, 1991; Fischer and Ayoub, 1996).

Personality Development as Emotional Self-Organization

Propositions. Recently, a few theorists have begun to model personality development as a process of self-organization (Cloninger, Svrakic, and Svrakic, 1997; Derryberry and Rothbart, 1997; Lewis, 1995, 1997; Magai and Nusbaum, 1996; Schore, 1997). Most of these approaches see personality as knit together from constituents over developmental time (macrodevelopment), with early patterns setting the course for the subsequent channeling of learning and experience. Some of these models are also quite explicit about developmental transitions at which the personality system goes through qualitative reorganizations. Yet only a few (e.g., Lewis, 1995; Schore, 1997) emphasize resonances between cognitive appraisals and emotional states as the mechanism by which personality self-organizes in the first place and becomes progressively refined and entrenched with development.

Personality development can be described as change and stabilization in the state space of cognition-emotion interactions. As discussed earlier, emotional interpretations (EIs) gravitate to attractor locations on this state space, and moods constitute temporary modifications to the contour of the state space itself. However, both of these time scales of emotional phenomena do not alter the basic shape of the state space permanently. Personality development can be modeled as permanent (or very long-lasting) changes in the structure of the state space. These include the initial establishment of attractors for recurrent EIs in infancy and the reconfiguration or replacement of those attractors during periods of personality transition (Lewis and Douglas, 1998; Lewis and Junyk, 1997). How can such changes be explained?

As discussed earlier, the entrainment of emotion and attention in microdevelopment relies on coupling between cognitive and perceptual elements, forming a coherent appraisal, and on the resonance of that appraisal with an emotional state. In order for this to occur, self-organizing processes must take advantage of complementarities (or cooperativities) within and between the cognitive and emotional systems. For many parents, the sight of a distressed child looking down enlists (cognitive) complementarities between the child's distress and helplessness, attributions of harm and parental responsibility, and anticipations of being a "good parent." Real-time coupling among these elements, resonating with an emerging emotional state, might produce an EI of empathy, remorse, or guilt. A distressed child running away might enlist additional complementarities with a script for a transgression, such that concern for the child competes with concern for a broken dish. Interacting cognitive elements are "ready" to resolve into ensembles supporting sensible interpretations, based on complementarities among them and on coupling with ongoing perception. But to converge to an EI such ensembles must couple with emotions, and they therefore rely on superordinate complementarities with the emotion system as well. Where do complementarities at each of these levels come from?

At the subordinate level, complementarities among conceptual and perceptual elements arise through experience or learning. As argued by Izard and his colleagues (this volume), complementarities between emotions themselves may also emerge through experience. At the superordinate level, complementarities between the cognitive and emotional systems derive from biologically specified links between emotions and appraisals, such as the link between anger and perceived obstruction (Ekman, 1984; Izard, 1993). But these appraisal-emotion complementarities are extended and elaborated through learning as well (Izard, 1984). Thus, all these complementarities are updated if not originally fashioned through experience, specifically emotional experience, and therefore derive from the *coupling of elements* in EIs and moods.

Through recurrent patterns of coupling, early complementarities are strengthened and entrenched. The situations that induce them come to be experienced as similar whether or not they have much in common objectively. Perceptual associations and conceptual generalizations extend this stamp of meaningfulness to other situations with shared features (Lewis, 1995, 1997). These situations are then appraised and reacted to in the same way. Thus, personality stability comes to be reflected in interpretive and behavioral consistencies within broad classes of situations (Mischel and Shoda, 1995). As tacitly assumed by appraisal theories, it is these consistencies rather than the objective features of situations that shape emotional reactions (Ellsworth, 1991).

In summary, the vehicle of personality is a network of complementarities that evolves over macrodevelopment with recurrent experiences, and these complementarities both arise from and constrain coupling in EIs and moods. The stabilization of this network seems to mark the consolidation of personality in infancy. Sensitive dependence on initial conditions characterizes this early stage, as when a communicative mismatch between mother and infant diminishes the infant's sense of effectance and leads to habitual withdrawal and avoidance (Tronick, Ricks, and Cohn, 1982). Developmental phase transitions take place when the personality state space becomes reorganized, as occurs for example at about eighteen months, marked by emotional turbulence and new patterns of interpersonal behavior and self-regulation (Mahler, Pine, and Bergman, 1975; Schore, 1994). At these junctures, cognitive and emotional complementarities become reshuffled, such that predictable EIs and moods no longer converge and new ones take their place. Such changes may be extremely rapid, as when traumatic events such as a hospitalization refashion or revalence a small but pivotal set of links. Or they can be slower but still discontinuous, as when cognitive development updates the global structure of interpersonal understanding (Case, 1988) or new emotions such as shame reshuffle the balance of appraisal and regulation (Schore, 1994).

Cascading constraints epitomize the growth of complementarities over personality development. At the most basic level, coupling on one occasion strengthens complementarities that end up constraining coupling on a later occasion, creating a sequence of increasing refinements (Lewis, 1997). Cascading constraints are evident within periods, as complementarities reinforce themselves through recurring appraisals. But cascading constraints can also be seen across periods, over the lifespan, as when the resolution of each developmental passage constrains the negotiation of the next one (Erikson, 1963). It is in this way that early patterns of self- and other-regulation fashion long-standing interpersonal and cognitive habits (Keating, 1990). Through these processes, personality self-organizes over many years, evolving from a set of potentials, through self-propagating patterns of experience and interpretation, to an entrenched set of cognitive-emotional tendencies in adulthood.

Although every individual is truly unique, personality patterns can be grouped into a small number of types (York and John, 1992). These types are reminiscent of the basic designs found in biological organisms as a function of the intrinsic principles constraining their dynamics (Goodwin, 1993). What principles of psychological orderliness might constrain self-organizing personality patterns? We might expect to find intrinsic principles for emotion regulation and temperament structure, for the semantic coherence of interpretations, self-narratives, and identity configurations, and for achieving predictable reactions from other people. Cognitive-developmental stages may also shape personality styles (Case, 1991), which seem to settle down into stage-specific equilibria following developmental transitions (Lewis, 1997). The interacting constraints of these and other principles might some day explain personality types as meta-attractors on the state space of psychological design.

Finally, in keeping with the assumption of circular causality, some higher-order form should function to maintain the cognitive and emotional complementarities that constitute this form in turn. This higher-order form would have to be consistent over changing EIs and moods, and over the ebb and flow of intentions and goals, thus maintaining the continuity of complementarities in a personality system. If immediate intentions subsume cognition-emotion coordination in microdevelopment, and intentional orientations subsume the coordination of emotional-interpretive biases in mesodevelopment, then perhaps the superordinate form in macrodevelopment can also be portrayed as a subjective, intentional, thrusting forward into the world – this time lasting for months and years. A *sense of self* (i.e., the "I-self," not the "me-self") seems to fit this description. Continuity in a sense of self lasts for years, but it breaks down at personality transitions just as the continuity of immediate intentions breaks down between EIs. For example, adolescents report that their selves are different than they were before puberty, and indeed their overarching strivings have changed substantially in content and orientation (Harter, 1998).

Moreover, the sense of self can be construed as a long-standing orderliness that is built up around the nonresolution (or partial resolution) of emotionally valenced goals over a period of years. These goals may include achieving basic needs for love and admiration, hiding weakness or aggressiveness, and punishing others out of envy or vengeance. This proposition implies that personality is not *just* a product of recurrent cognitive-emotional interactions (or EIs), as argued by emotion theorists such as Izard (1984) and Malatesta and Wilson (1988). Rather, it is built up from episodes at the middle scale of cognition-emotion resonance, described here as moods. Mood states lock interpretive and affective biases together in an ongoing resonance that cannot be relieved by action. I am suggesting that these resonances not only modify the cognitive-emotional state space temporarily but lay down permanent changes if they recur sufficiently often. The young child who often feels angry and excluded, and who cannot maintain his parents' attention, dreams of dominance and revenge when alone in his room, and eventually becomes dominating and vengeful as a person. On a more positive note, long-lasting play sessions characterized by excited anticipation seem to create the sense of a responsive world where others are ready to be engaged. Overorderliness in macrodevelopment thus derives from overorderliness in mesodevelopment and comes to constitute a sense of self.

Support. Adult personality has been described as a cognitive-affective system that is differentially activated in different situations, as reflected by situation-specific consistencies (Mischel and Shoda, 1995). These consistencies suggest that "stability resides in the internal mechanisms producing behavior" rather than in some central schema that interprets events uniformly, and this is consistent with dynamic systems principles (Vallacher and Nowak, 1997, p. 77). Indeed, Mischel's patterns could be mapped as attractors on a cognition-emotion state space, reflecting system complementarities that consolidate through enduring affective experiences. This resonates with Goldsmith's (1994) definition of temperamental traits as "tendencies to enter into an emotional state or perhaps to remain in an emotional mood" (p. 70).

The idea that personality is centred around unfulfilled wishes or long-standing goals has an illustrious history, extending from Freud to contemporary personality theorists (e.g., Higgins, 1987; Horowitz, 1998). Many of these theorists also emphasize the role of self-continuity. From the present perspective, the "perpetually unfinished business" manifested by a cohesive personality (Thorne and Klohnen, 1993, p. 226) is, once again, a special case of overorderliness, consistent with the work in chaos theory cited earlier (Goldstein, 1997; Kreindler and Lumsden, 1998).

The assumption that personality crystallizes early in life is shared by attachment, psychodynamic, and neurodevelopmental theories. However, personality can also become reconfigured when complementarities among cognitive and emotional elements break down and reorganize. Such reorganizations fit Magai and McFadden's (1995) criteria for personality transitions: abrupt changes in appraisal structures accompanied by emotional upheavals. They also fit with Goldsmith's (1994) definition of personality transitions as periods of sensitivity to fluctuations sandwiched between stages of temperamental continuity. Such reorganizations might explain the generally weak correlations between early measures of attachment (and temperament) and later indices of interpersonal functioning (Laible and Thompson, this volume).

The present account is also consistent with recent neurobiological perspectives. First, psychological states perpetuate themselves across occasions through a variety of neuronal selection mechanisms (e.g., Greenough and Schwark, 1984; Tucker, 1992). Second, developmentalists assume that individual differences are reflected in the organization of the infant brain (Fox, 1989; Rothbart and Derryberry, 1981) and that they guide the selection and strengthening of cortical connections by constraining experience, thus further refining individual styles (Derryberry and Rothbart, 1997). Third, the selective mechanisms underlying this process of crystallization appear to be centered in corticolimbic areas where cognitive appraisal and emotional states resonate with each other (Freeman, this volume; Schore, 1994, this volume; Tucker, 1992). This suggests a site for personality crystallization that specializes in cognition-emotion complementarities. Fourth, the impact of moods on personality may be mediated by the effects of neurohormones on the cortex. Neurohormones enhance the selection of particular synaptic connections and the inhibition of others over long periods, thus promoting Hebbian learning for emotion-relevant associations

Table 2.1. *Three scales of emotional self-organization, showing parallels and distinctions across scales and hypothesized psychological and neurobiological mechanisms*

	Emotional interpretation	Mood	Personality
Developmental scale	Micro	Meso	Macro
Duration	Seconds–minutes	Hours–days	Months–years
Description	Rapid convergence of cognitive interpretation with emotional state	Lasting entrainment of interpretive bias with narrow emotional range	Lasting interpretive-emotional habits specific to classes of situations
Dynamic systems formalism	Attractor	Temporary modification of state space	Permanent structure of state space
Psychological mechanism	Cognition-emotion coupling or resonance, successful goal-directed action	Cognition-emotion coupling, goal preoccupation, inhibited or unsuccessful action	Cognition-emotion complementarities that arise from and constrain coupling in EIs and moods
Possible neurobiological mechanism	Cortical coherence mediated by orbitofrontal organization entrained with limbic circuits	Orbitofrontal-corticolimbic entrainment, motor rehearsal and preafference, sustained neurohormone release	Selection and strengthening of some corticocortical and corticolimbic connections, pruning of others, loss of plasticity
Higher-order form in circular causality	Intention, goal	Intentional orientation	Sense of self

(Freeman, 1995; Panksepp, 1998). Finally, developmental reorganizations have been observed at the neural level. In Thatcher's (1991) model, mye-lination spurts underlie age-specific advances in cortical connectivity within and across hemispheres. Schore (1994) has argued that Thatcher's growth spurts, alternating between left and right hemispheres, underlie distinct stages in the development of the self.

Interactions between Scales of Emotional Self-Organization

There are two directions of influence between scales of self-organization. First, small-scale self-organizing processes, repeated over many iterations, influence large-scale self-organizing processes. There are many examples. The sculpting of a riverbed, through recursive patterns of carving and silt transportation, fashions the course of the whole river system (cf. Iberall, 1987). In neural networks, temporary patterns of activation influence the attractor characteristics of the entire network over long periods. A general principle of structural change seems to underlie such effects in living systems: coupling among components strengthens their connections with each other, increasing the probability of their coupling in the future. This is exemplified in neurobiology by Hebbian cell assemblies, where neurons that are activated simultaneously increase their connectivity for future interactions.

   Self-organizing EIs have been argued to emerge in microdevelopment through the coupling of cognitive and affective constituents. How would this process affect development at longer scales? First, the coupling of cognitive constituents within appraisals would enhance their connectedness on future occasions. This is evident at the psychological level, where making sense of a situation on one occasion facilitates a similar interpreta-tion on the next occasion. At the neural level, the activation of cortical synapses within an appraisal increases the probability of their coparticipa-tion in a similar appraisal in the future. Thus, coupling within EIs strength-ens interpretive habits, laying down characteristic appraisals, models, or schemas over macrodevelopment. It also predisposes an individual toward interpretive biases that forge moods in mesodevelopment. Second, cogni-tive couplings within EIs are nested in cognition-emotion couplings. Thus, scale-to-scale influences are transmitted only through emotional events. These influences include the facilitation of particular emotions over longer scales (cf. Malatesta and Wilson, 1988). For example, a three-year-old child whose interpretation of an approaching stranger couples with fear on one occasion reexperiences both the interpretation (e.g., tall, male) and the fear on future occasions (K. Runions, personal communication, September 1998). Their coselection over development is thus already facilitated by a single EI. Third, longer interpretive configurations resonating in mesodevelopment should have a greater capacity to adjust complementarities over macrodevelopment. EIs embedded in moods should therefore have the greatest impact on personality.

At the neural level, corticolimbic resonance, which holds appraisals and emotions in synchrony in real time, maintains the coupling responsible for stable EIs. This establishes long-lasting tendencies for the feeling, expression, and regulation of habitual emotions linked with habitual appraisals (Schore, 1994; Tucker, 1992). Whereas any EI can influence personality in this manner, moods (and the EIs embedded in them) are hypothesized to have the greatest impact. Neurohormonal activation in moods extends intentional states, maintains cortical configurations for longer periods, and promotes "long-lasting changes in synaptic gains" (Freeman, this volume). Moods thus have the potential to guide synaptic learning as well as emotional conditioning over long periods, fashioning permanent modifications to global attractors for emotional development (Panksepp, this volume). Schore (this volume) relates neuromodulator action to the creation of neural circuits and the pruning of early plasticity in cortical development. Thus, the mesodevelopment of mood and the macrodevelopment of personality should be especially interconnected in early childhood. When intense emotions and moods are reexperienced over many occasions, such effects may be greatly magnified, as when the recurrence of traumatic events early in life "kindles" limbic sensitivity to depression or anxiety with increasing predictability over the lifespan (Harkness and Tucker, this volume).

The converse direction of influence is from larger scales to the smaller scales embedded within them. This theme is ubiquitous in the natural world, in which the structure of the tree guides the growth of the branch, twig, and leaf, the ecosystem constrains the patterning of its resident populations, and the self-organizing biosphere constrains speciation in evolution. The emergence of large-scale patterns always stipulates the parameters of self-organization at smaller scales, by fashioning the structures, contingencies, and constraints by which order is created.

Personality self-organization has been argued to influence the content of moods and EIs. In other words, the complementarities that have been laid down over months, years, and decades should strongly constrain the possibilities for feeling and thinking in the moment. The notion of EIs moving to attractors on a personality state space expresses this principle. Attractors represent habitual end points to which EIs tend in real time. Moreover, the retuning of the state space in moods is obviously constrained by the structure of that state space. There is only so much variance available for making sense of and feeling about the world, and the scope of moods to alter experience is bound by this variance. Nevertheless, within the range defined by personality as a whole, moods strongly influence EIs. Frijda (1993a) notes that moods dispose one to ongoing affective states and interpretive themes. Only EIs that are compatible with these states and themes can cohere within moods. I suggest that EIs grow out of system orderliness maintained in moods by an inability to achieve present goals. In a parallel fashion, moods may grow out of the orderliness maintained in personality by an inability to achieve more permanent goals. In fact, I speculate that the content of a given mood necessarily taps an important theme in the content of personality, and the inability to relinquish goals in moods reflects their entrenchment over longer periods.

At the neural level, personality self-organization constrains moods and EIs in a surprisingly severe fashion. The cognition-emotion complementarities that solidify in personality development constitute lasting structural changes in the brain. While neural assemblies are becoming more organized with development, there is also a selective loss of connections, including neural cell death, by which activity-dependent pruning shapes the developing brain (Schore, 1994; Tucker, 1992). From this perspective, the limited options for self-organizing EIs in microdevelopment can be traced to the sculpting of neural tissue in macrodevelopment. The loss of plasticity in the cortex resulting from lifelong learning (Harkness and Tucker, this volume) thus confines degrees of freedom for moods and EIs. However, evidence for neural replenishment in adulthood suggests that the brain does not close down all its opportunities for change (Greenough and Schwark, 1984). The embedding of EIs in moods is also constrained at the neural level. As described earlier, neurohormonal backwash from limbic output to the brain stem floods the cortex with excitatory and inhibitory biases (Freeman, 1995; Panksepp, 1998). EIs that converge within moods are constrained by the intersection of these cortical biases with limbic activity patterns subserving emotional and behavioral tendencies.

As a final note, *reciprocal* influences between scales are an important causal mechanism in complex developing systems (Gottlieb, 1991). An EI can grow into or trigger a mood, which may then set the occasion for more of the same EI. Reciprocal influence between moods and associated EIs can then enhance the frequency of those EIs while strengthening and perpetuating the mood. Similarly, moods in infancy and childhood can forge personality configurations that go on to constrain subsequent moods

(Demos, 1986). Temperamental tendencies may become consolidated through such an interactive process (cf. Goldsmith, 1994). These interscale effects can be viewed as causal, but they can also be seen as different rates of crystallization in a multiscale self-organizing system that functions as an integrated whole. What seems certain is that no theory of emotion or emotional development at any scale can be complete without consideration of processes at other scales.

Conclusion: Self-Similarity across Time Scales

Complex systems in nature – whether clouds, capillaries, or cauliflowers – often display a beautiful symmetry that cannot be captured by Euclidean geometry: self-similarity. This is the appearance of similar forms at different scales of time or space. The previous section suggested ways in which different time scales of emotional self-organization influence each other. By way of conclusion, this section presents a speculative glimpse of self-similarity across these scales. Parallels across scales serve at least to summarize the common characteristics of emotional self-organization at each scale. At most, they point toward a branching, treelike structure of emotional development that may soon be specified empirically.

Self-similarity can be seen in four related parallels. First, at each scale, some sort of perturbation triggers fluctuations in cognition-emotion stability, bringing on a phase transition. In microdevelopment, this is the occasion for an emerging EI; in mesodevelopment it is the occasion for a mood change; and in macrodevelopment it is the beginning of a personality transition. Second, after a period of system turbulence or disorganization, a new pattern coheres in cognition-emotion relations. This pattern represents one of a number of options, but as it stabilizes other options become less accessible. In microdevelopment, a coherent appraisal-emotion state converges rapidly. In mesodevelopment, a coherent interpretive bias locks together with an emotional tendency. In macrodevelopment, a way of understanding the world becomes entrained with an emotional repertoire. This process of selection and consolidation, repeated over several phase transitions, gives rise to a branching pattern of emotional development in which each of these scales participates. Thus, the branching pathway image used to depict developmental differentiation may have a fractal-like structure. A third type of self-similarity resides in a temporal path of cascading constraints, crystallizing stability in the present period and narrowing variability over future periods. This is witnessed in increasingly refined EIs, moods, and personality configurations across their respective time scales.

Finally, a fourth expression of self-similarity is in the nature of the higher-order form that interacts with its lower-order constituents in a circular causality. This higher-order form, at all scales, is a type of intentionality. According to Freeman (this volume), the human brain is always goal-directed. Goals are not just future states to pursue; they are ways for the brain to stay organized, and they are the necessary condition for emotion. In microdevelopment, a superordinate intentionality is realized in immediate intentions or goals, pursued with little hesitation. In mesodevelopment, it is realized in an intentional orientation or commitment to ongoing goals, not immediately attainable, and pursued more through wishes than actions. In macrodevelopment, it is realized in a sense of self that retains coherence across changing goals and that harnesses attention, appraisal, mood, and emotion in a path of continual striving. This analysis suggests that the sense of self in personality maintains consistency across moods in the same way that an intentional orientation in mood maintains consistency across emotion episodes, and an intention in an EI maintains consistency within emotion episodes. These parallels may express deep principles by which order arises through intentional processes that cause emotion at all scales.

References

Barsalou, L. W. (1987). The instability of graded structure: Implications for the nature of concepts. In U. Neisser (Ed.), *Concepts and conceptual development: Ecological and intellectual factors in categorization* (pp. 101–140). Cambridge: Cambridge University Press.

Beck, A. T., Epstein, N., and Harrison, R. (1983). Cognitions, attitudes and personality dimensions in depression. *British Journal of Cognitive Psychotherapy, 1*, 1–16.

Block, J., and Robins, R. W. (1993). A longitudinal study of consistency and change in self-esteem from early adolescence to early adulthood. *Child Development, 64*, 909–923.

Bower, G. H. (1981). Mood and memory. *American Psychologist, 36*, 129–148.

Brainerd, C. J., and Reyna, V. F. (1990). Gist is the grist: Fuzzy-trace theory and the new intuitionism. *Developmental Review, 10*, 3–47.

Brooks, L. R. (1987). Decentralized control of categorization: The role of prior processing episodes. In U. Neisser (Ed.), *Concepts and conceptual development: Ecological and intellectual factors in categorization* (pp. 141–174). Cambridge: Cambridge University Press.

Buck, R. (1985). Prime theory: An integrated view of motivation and emotion. *Psychological Review, 92*, 389–413.

Case, R. (1988). The whole child: Toward an integrated view of young children's cognitive, social, and emotional development. In A. D. Pellegrini (Ed.), *Psychological bases for early education* (pp. 155–184). New York: Wiley.

Case, R. (1991). Stages in the development of the young child's first sense of self. *Developmental Review, 11*, 210–230.

Christianson, S. A., and Loftus, E. F. (1991). Remembering emotional events: The fate of detail information. *Cognition and Emotion, 5*, 81–108.

Cicchetti, D., and Sroufe, L. A. (1978). An organizational view of affect: Illustration from the study of Down's Syndrome infants. In M. Lewis and L. Rosenblum (Eds.), *The development of affect* (pp. 309–350). New York: Plenum.

Cloninger, C. R., Svrakic, N. M., and Svrakic, D. M. (1997). Role of personality self-organization in development of mental order and disorder. *Development and Psychopathology, 9*, 881–906.

Damasio, A. R. (1994). *Descartes' error: Emotion, reason, and the human brain.* New York: Avon.

Davidson, R. J. (1994). On emotion, mood, and related affective constructs. In P. Ekman and R. J. Davidson (Eds.), *The nature of emotion: Fundamental questions* (pp. 51–55). New York: Oxford University Press.

Demos, V. (1986). Crying in early infancy: An illustration of the motivational function of affect. In T. B. Brazelton and M. W. Yogman (Eds.), *Affective development in infancy* (pp. 39–73). Norwood, NJ: Ablex.

Derryberry, D., and Rothbart, M. K. (1997). Reactive and effortful processes in the organization of temperament. *Development and Psychopathology, 9*, 633–652.

Derryberry, D., and Tucker, D. M. (1994). Motivating the focus of attention. In P. M. Niedenthal and S. Kitayama (Eds.), *The heart's eye: Emotional influences in perception and attention* (pp. 167–196). San Diego, CA: Academic Press.

Ekman, P. (1984). Expression and the nature of emotion. In K. Scherer & P. Ekman (Eds.), *Approaches to emotion* (pp. 319–344). Hillsdale, NJ: Erlbaum.

Ellsworth, P. C. (1991). Some implications of cognitive appraisal theories of emotion. In K. T. Strongman (Ed.), *International review of studies on emotion* (pp. 143–161). Chichester: Wiley.

Erikson, E. H. (1963). *Childhood and society.* New York: Norton.

Fischer, K. W., and Ayoub, C. (1996). Analyzing development of working models of close relationships: Illustration with a case of vulnerability and violence. In G. G. Noam and K. W. Fischer (Eds.), *Development and vulnerability in close relationships* (pp. 173–199). Mahwah, NJ: Erlbaum.

Fogel, A., and Thelen, E. (1987). The development of early expressive and communicative action: Re-interpreting the evidence from a dynamic systems perspective. *Developmental Psychology, 23*, 747–761.

Forgas, J. P. (1995). Mood and judgment: The affect infusion model (AIM). *Psychological Bulletin, 117*, 39–66.

Fox, N. A. (1989). Physiological correlates of emotional reactivity during the first year of life. *Developmental Psychology, 25*, 364–372.

Freeman, W. J. (1995). *Societies of brains.* Hillsdale, NJ: Erlbaum.

Frijda, N. H. (1986). *The emotions.* Cambridge: Cambridge University Press.

Frijda, N. H. (1993a). Moods, emotion episodes, and emotions. In M. Lewis and J. M. Haviland (Eds.), *Handbook of emotions* (pp. 381–403). New York: Guilford.

Frijda, N. H. (1993b). The place of appraisal in emotion. *Cognition and Emotion, 7*, 357–387.

Frijda, N. H., and Zeelenberg, M. (in press). Appraisal: What is the dependent? In

K. R. Scherer, A. Schorr, and T. Johnstone (Eds.), *Appraisal processes in emotion: Theory, methods, research*. Oxford: Oxford University Press.

Globus, G. (1995). *The postmodern brain*. Philadelphia: John Benjamins.

Goldsmith, H. H. (1994). Parsing the emotional domain from a developmental perspective. In P. Ekman & R. J. Davidson (Eds.), *The nature of emotion: Fundamental questions* (pp. 68–73). New York: Oxford University Press.

Goldstein, J. (1997). Embracing the random in the self-organizing psyche. *Nonlinear Dynamics, Psychology, and Life Sciences, 1*, 181–202.

Goodwin, B. C. (1987). Developing organisms as self-organizing fields. In F. E. Yates (Ed.), *Self-organizing systems: The emergence of order* (pp. 167–180). New York: Plenum.

Goodwin, B. C. (1993). Development as a robust natural process. In W. Stein and F. J. Varela (Eds.), *Thinking about biology* (pp. 123–148). Reading, MA: Addison-Wesley.

Gottlieb, G. (1991). Experiential canalization of behavioral development: Theory. *Developmental Psychology, 27*, 4–13.

Gould, S. J. (1980). *The panda's thumb*. New York: Norton.

Greenough, W. T., and Schwark, H. D. (1984). Age-related aspects of experience effects upon brain structure. In R. N. Emde and R. J. Harmon (Eds.), *Continuities and discontinuities in development* (pp. 69–91). New York: Plenum.

Haken, H. (1987). Synergetics: An approach to self-organization. In F. E. Yates (Ed.), *Self-organizing systems: The emergence of order* (pp. 417–434). New York: Plenum.

Harter, S. (1998). The development of self-representations. In W. Damon (series ed.) and N. Eisenberg (vol. ed.), *Handbook of child psychology: Vol. 3. Social, emotional, and personality development* (5th ed., pp. 553–617). New York: Wiley.

Higgins, E. T. (1987). Self-discrepancy: A theory relating self and affect. *Psychological Review, 94*, 319–340.

Hinde, R. A. (1982). *Ethology*. London: Fontana.

Horowitz, M. J. (1998). *Cognitive psychodynamics: From conflict to character*. New York: Wiley.

Iberall, A. S. (1987). On rivers. In F. E. Yates (Ed.), *Self-organizing systems: The emergence of order* (pp. 33–47). New York: Plenum.

Isen, A. M. (1990). The influence of positive and negative affect on cognitive organization: Some implications for development. In N. Stein, B. Leventhal, and T. Trabasso (Eds.), *Psychological and biological processes in the development of emotion* (pp. 75–94). Hillsdale, NJ: Erlbaum.

Izard, C. E. (1977). *Human emotions*. New York: Plenum.

Izard, C. E. (1984). Emotion-cognition relationships and human development. In C. E. Izard, J. Kagan, and R. B. Zajonc (Eds.), *Emotions, cognition and behavior* (pp. 17–37). Cambridge: Cambridge University Press.

Izard, C. E. (1993). Four systems for emotion activation: Cognitive and noncognitive processes. *Psychological Review, 100*, 68–90.

Keating, D. P. (1990). Charting pathways to the development of expertise. *Educational Psychologist, 25*, 243–267.

Kelso, J. A. (1995). *Dynamic patterns: The self-organization of brain and behavior*. Cambridge, MA: Bradford/MIT Press.

Keltner, D., Ellsworth, P. C., and Edwards, K. (1993). Beyond simple pessimism: Effects of sadness and anger on social perception. *Journal of Personality and Social Psychology, 64*, 740–752.

Kreindler, D. M., and Lumsden, C. J. (1998). *Depression as temporal pathology: Mood scaling via self-organized criticality.* Paper presented at the meeting of the Society for Chaos Theory in Psychology and the Life Sciences, Boston, August.

Lamb, M. E. (1987). Predictive implications of individual differences in attachment. *Journal of Consulting and Clinical Psychology, 55*, 817–824.

Lazarus, R. S. (1991). *Emotion and adaptation.* New York: Oxford University Press.

LeDoux, J. E. (1993). Emotional networks in the brain. In M. Lewis & J. M. Haviland (Eds.), *Handbook of emotions* (pp. 109–118). New York: Guilford.

Lewis, M. (1997). *Altering fate: Why the past does not predict the future.* New York: Guilford.

Lewis, M. D. (1995). Cognition-emotion feedback and the self-organization of developmental paths. *Human Development, 38*, 71–102.

Lewis, M. D. (1996). Self-organising cognitive appraisals. *Cognition and Emotion, 10*, 1–25.

Lewis, M. D. (1997). Personality self-organization: Cascading constraints on cognition-emotion interaction. In A. Fogel, M. C. Lyra, and J. Valsiner (Eds.), *Dynamics and indeterminism in developmental and social processes* (pp. 193–216). Mahwah, NJ: Erlbaum.

Lewis, M. D., and Douglas, L. (1998). A dynamic systems approach to cognition-emotion interactions in development. In M. F. Mascolo and S. Griffin (Eds.), *What develops in emotional development?* (pp. 159–188). New York: Plenum.

Lewis, M. D., and Granic, I. (1999). Self-organization of cognition-emotion interactions. In T. Dalgleish and M. Power (Eds.), *Handbook of cognition and emotion* (pp. 683–701). Chichester: Wiley.

Lewis, M. D., and Junyk, N. (1997). The self-organization of psychological defenses. In F. Masterpasqua and P. Perna (Eds.), *The psychological meaning of chaos: Translating theory into practice* (pp. 41–73). Washington, DC: American Psychological Association.

Magai, C., and Hunziker, J. (1993). Tolstoy and the riddle of developmental transformation: A lifespan analysis of the role of emotions in personality development. In M. Lewis and J. M. Haviland (Eds.), *Handbook of emotions* (pp. 247–259). New York: Guilford.

Magai, C., and McFadden, S. H. (1995). *The role of emotions in social and personality development: History, theory, and research.* New York: Plenum.

Magai, C., and Nusbaum, B. (1996). Personality change in adulthood: Dynamic systems, emotions, and the transformed self. In C. Magai and S. H. McFadden (Eds.), *Handbook of emotion, adult development, and aging* (pp. 403–420). San Diego, CA: Academic Press.

Mahler, M. S., Pine, F., and Bergman, A. (1975). *The psychological birth of the human infant.* New York: Basic Books.

Malatesta, C. Z., and Wilson, A. (1988). Emotion/cognition interaction in personality development: A discrete emotions, functionalist analysis. *British Journal of Social Psychology, 27*, 91–112.

Markovits, H., and Nantel, G. (1989). The belief-bias effect in the production and evaluation of logical conclusions. *Memory and Cognition, 17*, 11–17.

Mathews, A., and MacLeod, C. (1985). Selective processing of threat cues in anxiety states. *Behaviour Research and Therapy, 23*, 563–569.

McAdams, D. P. (1994). Can personality change? Levels of stability and growth in personality across the life span. In T. F. Heatherton and J. W. Weinberger (Eds.), *Can personality change?* (pp. 299–313). Washington, DC: American Psychological Association.

Mischel, W., and Shoda, Y. (1995). A cognitive-affective system theory of personality: Reconceptualizing situations, dispositions, dynamics, and invariance in personality structure. *Psychological Review, 102*, 246–268.

Neisser, U. (1976). *Cognition and reality: Principles and implications of cognitive psychology*. New York: Freeman.

Nolen-Hoeksema, S., and Morrow, J. (1991). A prospective study of depression and distress following a natural disaster: The 1989 Loma Prieta earthquake. *Journal of Personality and Social Psychology, 61*, 115–121.

Oatley, K., and Johnson-Laird, P. N. (1987). Towards a cognitive theory of emotions. *Cognition and Emotion, 1*, 29–50.

Panksepp, J. (1998). *Affective neuroscience: The foundations of human and animal emotions*. New York: Oxford University Press.

Papert, S. (1980). *Mindstorms, children, computers and powerful ideas*. New York: Basic Books.

Polivy, J. (1998). The effects of behavioral inhibition: Integrating internal cues, cognition, behavior, and affect. *Psychological Inquiry, 9*, 181–204.

Power, M. J., and Dalgleish, T. (1997). *Cognition and emotion: From order to disorder*. Hove: Psychology Press.

Rothbart, M. K., and Derryberry, D. (1981). Development of individual differences in temperament. In M. E. Lamb and A. L. Brown (Eds.), *Advances in developmental psychology* (pp. 37–86). Hillsdale, NJ: Erlbaum.

Rutter, M. (1984). Continuities and discontinuities in socioemotional development. In R. N. Emde and R. J. Harmon (Eds.), *Continuities and discontinuities in development* (pp. 41–68). New York: Plenum.

Scheff, T. J. (1987). Creativity and repetition: A theory of the coarse emotions. In J. Rabow, G. Platt, and M. Goldman (Eds.), *Advances in psychoanalytic sociology* (pp. 70–100). Malabar, FL: Krieger.

Scherer, K. R. (1984). On the nature and function of emotion: A component process approach. In K. R. Scherer and P. Ekman (Eds.), *Approaches to emotion* (pp. 293–318). Hillsdale, NJ: Erlbaum.

Scherer, K. R. (1994). Affect bursts. In S. H. van Goozen, N. E. van de Poll, and J. A. Sergeant (Eds.), *Emotions: Essays on emotion theory* (pp. 161–193). Mahwah, NJ: Erlbaum.

Schore, A. N. (1994). *Affect regulation and the origin of the self: The neurobiology of emotional development*. Mahwah, NJ: Erlbaum.

Schore, A. N. (1997). Early organization of the nonlinear right brain and development of a predisposition to psychiatric disorders. *Development and Psychopathology, 9*, 595–631.

Skarda, C. A., and Freeman, W. J. (1987). How brains make chaos in order to make sense of the world. *Behavioral and Brain Sciences, 10*, 161–195.

Smith, C. A., and Ellsworth, P. C. (1985). Patterns of cognitive appraisal in emotion. *Journal of Personality and Social Psychology, 48*, 813–838.

Smith, C. A., and Lazarus, R. S. (1993). Appraisal components, core relational themes, and the emotions. *Cognition and Emotion, 7*, 233–269.

Stein, N. L., and Trabasso, T. (1992). The organisation of emotional experience: Creating links among emotion, thinking, language, and intentional action. *Cognition and Emotion, 6*, 225–244.

Teasdale, J. D., and Barnard, P. J. (1993). *Affect, cognition, and change: Re-modelling depressive thought*. Hillsdale, NJ: Erlbaum.

Thatcher, R. W. (1991). Maturation of the human frontal lobes: Physiological evidence for staging. *Developmental Neuropsychology, 7*, 397–419.

Thelen, E., and Smith, L. B. (1994). *A dynamic systems approach to the development of cognition and action*. Cambridge, MA: Bradford/MIT Press.

Thelen, E., and Ulrich, B. D. (1991). Hidden skills: A dynamic systems analysis of treadmill stepping during the first year of life. *Monographs of the Society for Research in Child Development, 56* (serial no. 223).

Thompson, R. A., Lamb, M. E., and Estes, D. (1982). Stability of infant-mother attachment and its relationship to changing life circumstances in an unselected middle-class sample. *Child Development, 53*, 144–148.

Thorne, A., and Klohnen, E. (1993). Interpersonal memories as maps for personality consistency. In D. C. Funder, R. D. Parke, C. Tomlinson-Keasey, and K. Widaman (Eds.), *Studying lives through time: Personality and development* (pp. 223–253). Washington, DC: American Psychological Association.

Tronick, E. Z., Ricks, M., and Cohn, J. F. (1982). Maternal and infant affective exchange: Patterns of adaptation. In T. Field and A. Fogel (Eds.), *Emotion and early interaction* (pp. 83–100). Hillsdale, NJ: Erlbaum.

Tucker, D. M. (1992). Developing emotions and cortical networks. In M. R. Gunnar and C. Nelson (Eds.), *Minnesota Symposium on Child Psychology: Vol. 24. Developmental behavioral neuroscience* (pp. 75–128). Hillsdale, NJ: Erlbaum.

Vallacher, R. R., and Nowak, A. (1997). The emergence of dynamical social psychology. *Psychological Inquiry, 8*, 73–99.

van Geert, P. (1994). *Dynamic systems of development: Change between complexity and chaos*. New York: Harvester Wheatsheaf.

van Gelder, T., and Port, R. F. (1995). It's about time: An overview of the dynamical approach to cognition. In R. F. Port and T. van Gelder (Eds.), *Mind as motion: Explorations in the dynamics of cognition* (pp. 1–43). Cambridge, MA: MIT Press.

Wright, J. C., and Mischel, W. (1987). A conditional approach to dispositional constructs: The local predictability of social behavior. *Journal of Personality and Social Psychology, 53*, 1159–1177.

York, K., and John, O. P. (1992). The four faces of Eve: A typological analysis of women's personality at midlife. *Journal of Personality and Social Psychology, 63*, 494–508.

3 Emotions as Episodes of Subsystem Synchronization Driven by Nonlinear Appraisal Processes

Klaus R. Scherer

Introduction

This chapter argues for a radical departure from the classic paradigms of emotion psychology. It emphasizes the *emotion process*, that is, the dynamic time course of constantly changing affective tuning of organisms as based on continuous evaluative monitoring of their environment. Whereas many emotion psychologists have theoretically endorsed the notion of emotion as a process, most research has been firmly wedded to the notion of *emotional state* and its assessment via verbal labels. This situation has led to a theoretical and empirical impasse that only a paradigm shift can remedy. The *component process model* of emotion (Scherer, 1981, 1984, 1986, 1987) is used to illustrate the type of theoretical approach that, by providing an open architecture for process modeling, might be more germane to the dynamic nature of emotion processes. Most importantly, it is suggested that researchers go beyond classic linear process models and evaluate the potential of recently developed nonlinear dynamic modeling notions vis-à-vis the emotion phenomenon. Particular emphasis is given to the notions of *coupled oscillators*, as used in dynamic systems theory, and of *hysteresis*, a central concept in catastrophe theory.

The Need for a Paradigm Shift

According to Kuhn (1981) one of the telltale signs of an imminent paradigm shift in a discipline is the existence of *incommensurable* approaches. In such cases, the dissension among researchers seems to concern concepts, definitions, or research procedures, but in reality it masks fundamental differences in viewing the nature of the phenomenon. This stage may have been reached in the psychology of emotion, where there seems to be an increasing polarization of approaches to the conceptualization and empirical study of the emotions.

While, as always, one would need to distinguish many subtle differences, for the sake of argument I distinguish two major pairs of competing approaches: (1) psychobiological versus sociopsychological approaches, and (2) structural-modular versus componential-dynamic approaches.

1. *Psychobiologically oriented theories* (Ekman, 1984, 1992; Izard, 1977, 1993; Panksepp, 1982; Tomkins, 1984; to name some major examples) highlight aspects such as the functions of emotion for biological adaptation, insisting on their neural basis and phylogenetic continuity. They underline the central importance of emotional action tendencies and the specificity of response patterning in such domains as facial and vocal expression as well as physiological symptoms. In particular, discrete or basic emotion theories suggest the existence of a limited number of pre-wired emotion categories in the form of neuromotor programs or circuits. In terms of ontogeny, these theories postulate developmental preformation and view the influence of culture mostly as modulating or controlling the underlying psychobiological mechanisms. *Sociopsychological theories* (Averill, 1980; see also Oatley, 1993; Shweder, 1993; and contributions in Harré, 1986; again to name but a representative sample), on the other hand, highlight the central role of culture and language for the constitution and elicitation of emotion, often adopting a constructivist approach. They assume that emotions convey meaning in specific cultural contexts and emphasize the communicative function of emotion. They often claim nonspecificity of response patterning and developmental plasticity.

2. *Structural-modular approaches* to the conceptualization of emotion (Zajonc, 1980) often implicitly espouse Plato's classic notion of a tripartite structure of the soul, insisting on a strict separation between independent systems of cognition, emotion, and motivation. *Componential-dynamic approaches* (Ellsworth, 1991; Frijda, 1986; Lazarus, 1991; Scherer, 1984, 1986; Smith, 1989; Smith and Ellsworth, 1985), on the other hand, assume emotion to consist of continuously changing configurations of component states *including* cognitive and motivational processes. Some of these theories lean toward what one might call *fuzzy set* approaches, postulating a large variety of different emotional processes, with the more frequently occurring configurations amenable to identification and labeling (see Scherer, 1994).

Needless to say, the sharpening of the distinctions between these competing paradigms is a rhetorical device to better illustrate what I consider to be some of the fundamentally different tenets that underlie these theoretical proposals. Not all of the theorists mentioned explicitly espouse all of the prototypical claims postulated above. Yet, by exaggerating the differences between the respective approaches, it is hoped to identify the specific thrusts of certain classes of theory more clearly.

I believe that the incommensurability of these competing paradigms can be traced to the fact that the protagonists in each of the debates start from verbal emotion labels that are ostensibly identical – anger, fear, sadness, joy, disgust, pride, shame, and so on. However, it becomes increasingly obvious that each camp means something quite different by the very same terms. For example, a word like anger can denote (and more importantly still, connote) a neurophysiological program, a subjective feeling state, an interactive stance, or a value instantiation, depending on the theoretical framework of the respective scholar. Such fundamental dissension clearly goes beyond the normal disagreements, found in any field, on details of definitions or operationalizations of concepts. Rather, such disputes concern, as mapped out by Kuhn, fundamental disagreements about the nature of the phenomena to be studied.

Furthermore, many researchers seem to ascribe explanatory or reifying functions to the verbal emotion labels that exist in natural languages. However, it can easily be demonstrated that not only the specific labels for individual emotions (i.e., the mapping of semantic domains) but even the existence of overarching terms for ''emotion'' vary among languages and cultures (van Brakel, 1994). Thus, a true science of emotion (or ''affective science'') needs to keep its distance from the cherished habit of anchoring all thinking and research about emotion around a convenient set of apparently natural categories of affective states as provided by the respective languages (with an increasingly dominant position for English). It is a valid, even fascinating exercise in semantics to unpack the meaning structures of emotion terms in a language (including their cultural and historical ramifications). However, this should be but one facet in the multifaceted enterprise of understanding the nature of emotion, not the royal road.

A paradigm shift is imperative, not only because of the incommensurability of the respective approaches but also because many of the established, paradigm-driven research traditions use concepts or research procedures that are inconsistent with the evidence that is accumulating with respect to the phenomena. This is particularly true with respect to treating, despite occasional verbal declarations to the contrary, emotions as steady states rather than processes. Again, this problem has its roots in the domination of emotion research by verbal labels that, by their very nature, refer to stable states. In consequence, in many studies subjects are asked to describe their emotions by using one or more verbal labels for a given, often extensive, period of time. In reality, as some of the actuarial studies have shown (see Scherer and Tannenbaum, 1986), emotional reactions change very rapidly with changes in events and/or their evaluation by the person. In consequence, the phenomena to be studied by the affective sciences consist of incredibly complex, multicomponential processes that cannot be captured and described by verbal labels. The writer Robert Musil has captured this admirably in his monumental novel *The Man without Qualities*: ''. . . the self-conscious word renders the invisible movements of our inner life in but an arbitrary and poor fashion'' (1930/1978, p. 504; my translation). The ways in which people under certain circumstances have recourse to verbal labels or statements to describe such processes – in an incomplete, approximate fashion – is an object of study in itself.

I submit that the two tendencies described previously (state orientation and reifying of verbal labels) are responsible for the difficulties in designing and executing critical empirical tests of contradictory theoretical claims, because (1) the time dimension, essential for the description of dynamic phenomena, is lost, and (2) there is no determinate mapping from socio-psychobiological phenomena, which tend to vary in a continuous fashion in multidimensional spaces, to discrete language labels. I further submit that in order to design research that can elucidate the nature of emotion, we need models with an architecture that can handle the complex-process nature of the phenomenon under study. I next describe a type of model that attempts to accommodate the design features of the emotion process. I will focus on my own theoretical model for the purpose of argument (other theorists have presented similar ideas: Ellsworth, 1991; Frijda, 1986; Lazarus, 1991; Smith, 1989; Smith and Ellsworth, 1985; Smith and Lazarus, 1993).

The Component Process Model of Emotion

The fundamental problem of any emotion theory is to explain – within a single model – (a) *both* the dynamic, continuously fluctuating nature of emotion processes *and* the existence of discrete language labels referring to steady states; (b) *both* the psychobiological nature, including phylogenetic continuity, of emotion *and* its cultural constitution and significance; (c) *both* the phenomenological distinctiveness *and* the intricate interweaving of cognition and emotion.

The *component process model* of emotion was developed to cope with this difficulty. In this model, emotion is defined as a sequence of state changes in each of five – functionally defined – organismic subsystems:

- the cognitive system (appraisal)
- the autonomic nervous system (arousal)
- the motor system (expression)
- the motivational system (action tendencies)
- the monitor system (feeling)

occurring in an *interdependent and interrelated* fashion (as compared to normal, more independent functioning of these subsystems) in response to the evaluation of a stimulus, an event, or intraorganismic changes of central importance to the major needs and goals of the organism (Scherer, 1981, 1984, 1986, 1987). I have postulated that a certain degree of *synchronization* of the subsystems should be considered as a *necessary condition* for an emotion episode *sensu strictu* to occur (see also Scherer, 1993).

The model predicts a *component patterning process* in which:

(a) the organism appraises events on the basis of a series of sequential stimulus evaluation checks (novelty, intrinsic pleasantness, goal significance, coping potential, and norm compatibility),

(b) the result of each individual check modifies the state of each organismic subsystem in the direction of adaptation to the event, and

(c) the pattern of emotional reaction is the cumulative result of all these appraisal-driven state modifications and the ensuing feedback and feedforward interactions between the subsystems (see Scherer, 1984, 1986, 1987).

This model is illustrated in Figure 3.1. The figure shows changes in the five organismic subsystems during a time slice following an event of major importance to the organism. The period of synchronization of these subsystems is considered to be an emotion episode. In consequence, the responses in the five subsystems are seen as the *components* of emotion. The elicitation and the differentiation of the synchronization is determined by five major stimulus evaluation (or appraisal) checks (not to be confused with the five component subsystems) that are part of the cognitive component.

As demonstrated by the parallel bands in the figure, the information processing underlying the appraisal of these five criteria (which comprise a number of more differentiated subchecks; see Scherer, 1984, 1988) is expected to occur in parallel fashion. However, it is expected that an efferent effect on other components (the vertical arrows in the figure) will occur only at a point when the status of the criterion has been resolved, that is, when a decision has been reached (although further processing may

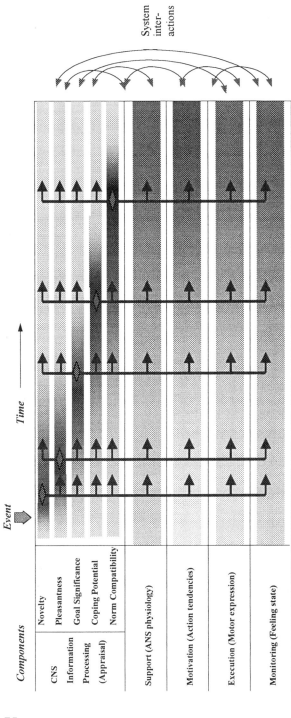

Figure 3.1. The component process model of emotions.

change this preliminary result). In Figure 3.1, the region in the respective bands showing increasing and decreasing grayscale coloration is supposed to indicate a decision process, with the lozenge marking the apex, at the point when efferent information and commands are sent to other subsystems. As shown by the bundle of rounded arrows to the right of the figure, the interactions between the subsystems will also affect the synchronization of the changes.

The processing times to reach a decision leading to efferent effects are expected to be different for the five stimulus evaluation checks. This is due to both processing constraints and logical requirements. With respect to processing constraints, it is expected that novelty and intrinsic pleasantness can be processed on the level of sensorimotor or schematic processing (possibly using structures comparable to the direct pathways from sensory thalamic regions to the amygdala empirically demonstrated by LeDoux, 1989), whereas the remaining checks will require processing via cortical association regions (see Leventhal and Scherer, 1987; Scherer, 1993). With respect to logical requirements, it can be shown, for example, that the determination of coping potential requires information about the degree of goal obstructiveness and the urgency of a reaction as an input (see Scherer, 1987, 1993). Given the differential delay of the decision points due to processing requirements, the efferent effects of the stimulus evaluation checks are *sequential*.

In this fashion, the synchronization of the subsystems that constitute the emotion episode is driven by the results of the appraisal checks. Yet, at the same time, these checks are being themselves affected in a recursive fashion by the changes in the overall organization of the macro system. For example, feedback of increasing arousal from the physiological system or changes in the motivational system can affect attention deployment or change perception and judgment thresholds.

One of the major arguments that critics have leveled against the notion of synchronization, driven by appraisal, concerns the apparent lack of empirically demonstrable covariation between different modalities of emotional responses. This argument rests mostly on the difficulty experienced by psychophysiologists in finding reliable intercorrelations between different physiological indicators for specific emotions. However, simple linear Pearson correlations between physiological parameters (often integrated over fairly long periods of time) may not be the appropriate yardstick to measure synchronization. We do know from extensive work in physiology that the various subsystems of the nervous system (e.g., central, somatic, autonomous), and even functional submechanisms within any one of these,

do not respond in a uniform manner to stimulation. The response characteristics (attack and decay) and the regulation mechanisms can be very
different. In consequence, rather than expecting physiological signals to
correlate in a direct, linear fashion, we need to look for lagged synchronization, nonlinearity, differential damping, and many other aspects of complex covariation.

As an example, I provide a case illustration from one of the recent
studies conducted in our laboratory. Figure 3.2 shows a single subject's
physiological response, using several indicators, to losing a spaceship in a
computer game designed to induce emotions on the basis of manipulated
appraisals (Banse et al., 1999; van Reekum, Johnstone, and Scherer, 1997).
The figure shows the raw, nonaveraged signals for the different response
domains for a period of 15 secs. The gray vertical line shows the moment
in time when the spaceship was lost – a major setback to advancing in the
game. Visual inspection of the waveforms clearly suggests (a) that most of
the respective physiological response domains seem to react to the event
by changes in level or direction (sometimes in an anticipatory fashion), and
(b) that while these changes are triggered by the same event, there are
major differences in the onset, intensity, and time course (e.g., damping)
of the change. Subtle changes and lagged synchronization might well
completely disappear if one were to integrate the signals over longer periods of time – that is, several seconds – as is often done in the psychophysiological emotion literature. Clearly, simple Pearson correlations over
integrated segments would not reveal much of interest about the complex
covariations between these different signals. The importance given to the
synchronization process in the component process model requires a methodological approach different from what has been the customary data-
analytic routine in this area.

Admittedly, the operationalization of the component process model is
yet to be accomplished. How exactly is synchronization defined? What are
the criteria for the beginning and the ending of synchronization? Do all
subsystems need to be involved? How does the model deal with continuous
input into the system? How does it explain sudden changes in the type of
emotion elicited? How can it predict the differentiation of emotion by a
limited set of antecedents (e.g., appraisal processes)? So far, there are no
ready answers to these questions.

Unfortunately, neither our conceptual nor our methodological tool kits
are adapted to dealing with systems of the degree of complexity exhibited
by emotion processes. There is little hope of "repairing" our concepts and
methods in a piecemeal fashion in order to do justice to the phenomenon

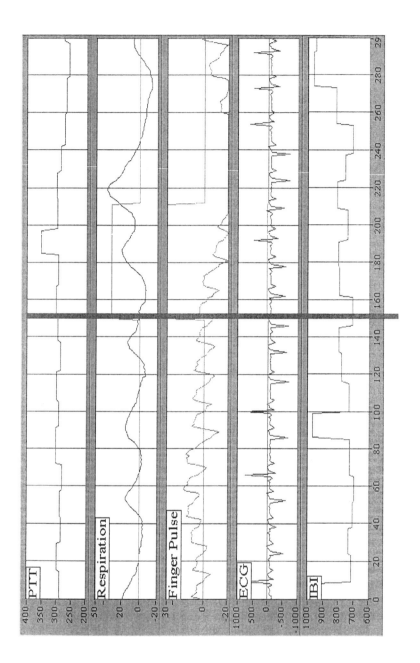

78

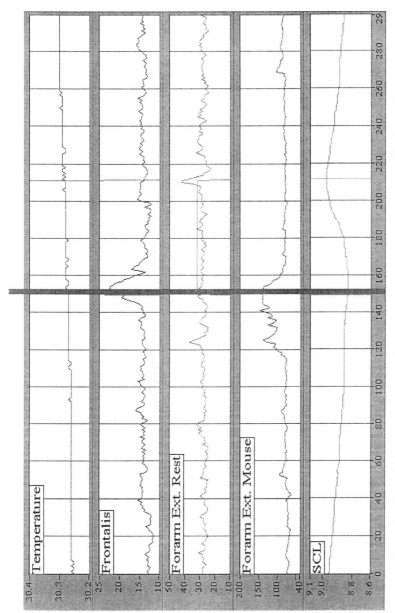

Figure 3.2. Physiological responses to the loss of a spaceship in a computer game. The figure shows a number of physiological parameters for an episode of 15 secs: (in order from top to bottom) pulse transit time, respiration, finger pulse amplitude, electrocardiogram, interbeat interval, finger temperature, electromyographic activity of frontalis muscle, of forearm extender muscle of resting arm, and of forearm extender muscle of mouse-operating arm. The gray vertical line shows the moment of the explosion of the space ship.

79

under study. Rather, we need a complete revolution in our thinking about the nature of emotion, comparable to other paradigm shifts in the history of science. In particular, we need to move from thinking in terms of discrete boxes, labels, or even neural programs to a *nonlinear dynamic systems perspective of emotion*.

In following the impact of nonlinear dynamic systems theory on a number of sciences, I have been fascinated by the idea that emotion episodes might be considered as processes of self-organization among neurophysiological systems that are mapped onto cultural meaning structures. Such a conceptualization, adopting many of the nonlinear dynamic characteristics described by self-organization theory, chaos theory, and catastrophe theory, and the mathematical-statistical tools that are being elaborated in this domain, might be just what we need to pursue a new process-oriented paradigm in the affective sciences. In particular, such models may help to develop an operationalization of and measurement procedures for *synchronization*, which I see as a central concept in defining and measuring emotions. In the remainder of the chapter, I will outline some very speculative leads in this direction. In particular, I will emphasize the analogy with *coupled oscillators* and the potential role of *hysteresis* in affective response functions.

The Promise of Theories Describing System Self-Organization, Chaos, and Catastrophes

These theories, admittedly far too fashionable, provide models that seem to have the characteristics necessary to solve some of the problems raised earlier: discreteness within continuity, order within chaos, simplicity within complexity, nonlinear dynamics, emergence of structure, self-organization, complex coupling, synchronization, entrainment of subsystems, sensitivity to initial values, sudden change (see Gleick, 1987; Haken, 1991; Zeeman, 1976). In the interest of facilitating a paradigm shift, we need, in the Kuhnian sense, a translation, a mapping of these paradigms onto our problem domain. This is not the place to discuss details of this process, but in what follows I attempt to give a brief introduction to the kind of argument one could construct.

In the natural sciences, these new approaches have brought about a major paradigm shift in disciplines in which the classic paradigms had ceased to work (e.g., the understanding of turbulence in physics). Increasingly, concepts from nonlinear dynamic systems theory are used in disciplines close to psychology, such as physiology and medicine, to help understand the complex regulation in time of a large set of biological oscillators (Glass, 1991; Haken, 1991). The same logic can be applied to emotion. As will be argued in more detail later, I propose to operationalize my theoretical emotion construct of *synchronization driven by appraisal* as *synchronization of coupled neurophysiological oscillators due to entrainment by patterns of CNS activity*.

Before going further, it may be useful to review the notion of coupled oscillators and related concepts. Much of the world around us is based on more or less orderly periodic vibrations or oscillations of particles or changes in electrical charge. This is the case with regard to light waves, sound waves, ultrasound waves, flow phenomena in liquids, and all of electricity. It is also true of beating hearts, clocks, motors, and similar devices based on rhythmical output. In all of these cases, the respective systems are based on oscillation, that is, a more or less regular change in a quantity over time, varying in amplitude, frequency, and/or phase. If you take an old-fashioned grandfather clock with a large, free-swinging pendulum, wind it up, connect a pen to the pendulum, give the latter a starting push, and then slowly and continuously draw a long piece of paper across the path of the swinging pendulum, you get one of the most basic forms of oscillation – something that approaches a sine wave form. The wider the pendulum swings, the stronger the amplitude of the resulting wave. The faster it swings back and forth, the higher the frequency of the wave. The phase of the wave depends on where the pendulum happens to be in its excursion when you start drawing the paper across.

Much of linear dynamic systems theory has to do with phenomena like grandfather clocks. While the regularity of a pendulum's swinging behavior is the norm in such clocks, the normal state in many physical and biological systems seems to be characterized by chaotic, irregular oscillations. They become more regular, or orderly, in special cases, due to specific state changes (for example, the freezing of liquids) or the need for adaptation (such as changes in heart rate under exercise). The explanation of such shifts of systems between more or less ordered and chaotic states has been at the root of the recent popularity of *nonlinear* dynamic systems theory.

Herrmann Haken, one of the pioneers of the interdisciplinary field of *synergetics* – the science of complex, self-organizing systems, based on dynamic systems theory and related to chaos theory – provides an intriguing rationale for why biological systems, in particular, make ample use of oscillators. Caught in the dilemma of having to maintain the stability of organismic parameters while at the same time allowing for rapid adaptation, biological systems regulate oscillators by keeping the amplitude relatively stable while varying phase (Haken, 1991). Most importantly, most biological systems are incredibly complex assemblies of a large number of very diverse but coordinated oscillators. Typically, in cases of adaptation to internal or external change the degree of coordination or synchronization of the different system oscillators is boosted in order to respond optimally to the emergency. This synchronization can occur in two rather distinct ways (Anishchenko et al., 1992): (a) synchronization forced by external actions, or (b) mutual synchronization of auto-oscillatory systems. External synchronization is often achieved by a central "master oscillator" (or pacemaker) that *enslaves, drives*, or *entrains* other oscillators by imposing its own rhythm (with more or less constraining force). The authors, using spectral displays of waveforms, illustrate the phenomenon of forced synchronization by showing examples of different degrees of entrainment or enslavement of a "slave oscillator" by a "master oscillator," depending on the degree of coupling and the constraining force.

Haken (1991) has used the example of a laser to illustrate this kind of synchronization or entrainment. In a normal gas lamp, the electricity that passes through the gas-filled tube excites atoms that will then emit light wave trains. This occurs in a rather irregular fashion, with different atoms emitting light at different times. In the case of a laser, however, the excitation of the atoms is regulated (or "ordered") by the driving frequency of the laser, thereby emitting light in a well-regulated fashion. A less technologically advanced example might be provided by a little boy who amuses himself by imposing the same rhythm on two different grandfather clocks by manually forcing the swinging of the pendula. The enforced rhythm can be considered a forced "attractor space" for the oscillation of the enslaved systems, since the central pacemaker keeps them within particular limit cycles. Another example might be the coupling of the marching steps of a group of soldiers by means of a military march.

As shown earlier, a different form of synchronization of coupled oscillators consists of "mutual" synchronization of interactive subsystems in the absence of a central pacemaker. Experimental research shows that in the case of mutual synchronization many families of attractors exist and that the region of synchronization for each of these has its own boundaries (see Anishchenko et al., 1992). For both the externally driven and the mutually interactive synchronization of subsystems, the notion of attractor implies that the synchronized subsystems or oscillators are "drawn into" specific synchronized modes that have a tendency to be more stable than other, continuously changing states.

As mentioned previously, the "normal" state of many biological oscillator systems seems to be close to chaotic organization, whereas specific states of adaptation are characterized by more regular or ordered, synchronized attractors. Haken (1991) suggests the interesting hypothesis that physiological systems, in their normal functioning, are close to instability points, as this allows the system to adapt to new situations rapidly (by transiting to more synchronized attractor states). As we shall see, this kind of system characteristic is ideally suited to modeling emotions as attractor states of limited duration in the service of rapid adaptation to changed conditions. Before developing this idea, it seems useful to briefly review some examples of psychobiological systems for which chaotic organization and synchronized attractor states, involving coupled oscillation, have been demonstrated.

For example, Mahowald, Schenk, and O'Connor (1991) have shown that the predictable oscillations of REM and NREM sleep are driven by presumed neural pacemakers that are entrained to the twenty-four-hour wake/sleep cycle within the geophysical twenty-four-hour cycle. The authors suggest that the neuronal/humoral oscillators once entrained by external pacemakers or central pattern generators may in turn entrain other systems. Zwiener, Bauer, and Lüthke (1992) have shown attractor states of rhythm synchronization between respiration and cardiovascular parameters due to a mutual reinforcement of the coupling of the rhythmic activities in the different systems (see also Kaplan and Talajic, 1991).

Such increased forms of synchronization through entrainment are found not only for mental load and other types of sympathetic arousal but also in the case of somatic, psychosomatic, and neurotic disturbances (Zwiener et al., 1992). Much current attention in cardiovascular medicine is devoted to understanding the role of differential degrees of coupling between these different systems in various syndromes of illness (Goldberger, Rigney, and West, 1990; Kaplan and Talajic, 1991). It has been suggested (Glass, 1991) that some forms of human disease can be associated with bifurcations in the dynamics of physiological systems, due to changes in control parameters.

Most of the work to date on the dynamics of oscillatory biological systems and the role of forced synchronizations in coupled systems has been performed on fairly automatic adaptive or regulatory systems in animal and human physiology, especially on cardiovascular fluctuations and neural recruitment in CNS functioning. However, this dynamic approach can also be extended to the role of psychological factors that may serve as pacemakers or drivers of underlying biological oscillators (being careful to avoid the mixing of different levels of analysis). For example,

Redington and Reidbord (1992) examined spontaneously occurring autonomic activity of a patient during one hour of psychotherapy. Their data suggest that the patient's cardiac responses associated with psychologically meaningful events possess nonlinear characteristics and may be indicative of chaos. They identify four types of clusters or trajectories in heart rate state space that are seen as representing psychophysiological attractors. Some of these are also seen as complex chaotic attractors in phase space, likely to be related to relatively healthy psychological functioning, whereas others correspond to more stable attractors, which may be typical of "incarceration" within disturbed psychological states such as regression. Other trajectories are seen as chaotic bifurcations, related in time to psychologically meaningful events. This is similar to the notion that normality may be close to chaotic organization, while emotions may be represented as ordered attractors of short duration, and stress or pathology as long-term confinement in stable attractors.

Redington and Reidbord's (1992) claim that psychological states (defined as coherent packages of cognitions, affects, and behaviors) can serve to entrain physiological oscillators into a specific attractor, is close to what I have suggested for the emotions. I propose to view the synchronization of all organismic subsystems that constitutes the basis for my definition of emotional episodes as the entrainment of normally more or less chaotic neurophysiological oscillators to one of a number of limit cycle attractors that are characteristic of the respective adaptive functions. The driving force for this transition from more or less chaotic oscillations, characterizing low affect or "normal" states, to more regular or ordered excursions, in the sense of emotion attractor spaces, is expected to be provided by the outcome of the emotion-driving appraisal process.

One could object that this model might be applicable to physiological reactions in emotion but rather unsuitable for cognitive appraisal, expressive motor movement, or the verbalization of feeling state – all of which are considered to be components of emotion. However, adopting a neurophysiological approach, one can view cognition as coupled oscillation of spatiotemporal CNS excitation and motor movement as coordinated efferent output to various muscle systems – again characterized by coupled oscillation. The basic idea is that to conceptualize the emotions as an increase in coupling or entrainment of several organismic oscillators, including the neurophysiological activities in the brain, might help us to finally study emotion as a process rather than as a state.

While readers may find it quite acceptable to conceive of pulsing lasers enslaving gas atoms or respiration cycles entraining cardiac rhythms, they may balk at the idea of discrete appraisal check results serving as pacemakers for the forced synchronization of psychophysiological oscillators. Similarly, it seems more convincing to assume *oscillation* with respect to the autonomic nervous or the somatic (striated muscle) system than with respect to motivation or subjective feeling components of emotion. Yet, one can make an argument that even seemingly discrete changes in global systems can, at some level, be conceived of as dynamic oscillations. To begin with, in many cases the brain or central nervous system acts as either the generator or the modulator of the complex rhythms in many of the neurophysiological oscillators mentioned above (Glass, 1991; Haken, 1991). Furthermore, there is little doubt that cognitive processes at different levels of processing in the CNS (see van Reekum and Scherer, 1997) can affect or control a variety of physiological processes (Jennings, 1986; Redington and Reidbord, 1992; Zwiener et al., 1992). Finally, it is not necessary to conceive of a constantly active external pacemaker in order to explain synchronization. As shown earlier, mutual synchronization often occurs under certain conditions in coupled, interactive auto-oscillatory systems. In consequence, one might conceive of appraisal as an input to dynamic psychophysiological systems that serves to trigger mutual synchronizations and to direct these entrainment processes in the direction of specific attractors by specifying order parameters. I will use the example of the perception of odors to illustrate the system architecture that might be involved.

Freeman and his collaborators have presented an extremely elegant dynamic systems account of the processing of odor perception in the rabbit (Freeman, 1992; Skarda and Freeman, 1987). These authors start from the assumption that chaotic dynamics provides an essential interface between the infinite complexity of the environment and the finite capacity of the brain in its function as a multidimensional pattern generator. The brain is seen as basing its selective action on its sensitivity to initial conditions and its ability to amplify microscopic events into macroscopic patterns that allow rapid adaptations to fast-changing environments (Freeman, 1992, p. 480). Essentially this is how the function of the appraisal-emotion mechanism could be defined. How does the odor-processing apparatus in the rabbit do it?

The work by Freeman and his associates shows that when the olfactory system is given a step input by an inhalation that excites the olfactory receptors in the nose, the olfactory bulb is excited by a surge of receptor firing. The olfactory bulb's response to this excitation can be shown by a slow wave in the EEG that accompanies inhalation. Superimposed on this respiration-based oscillation is a brief burst of oscillation near the characteristic frequency of the olfactory bulb. This burst is transmitted to coupled oscillators, where the burst appears at the carrier frequency of the olfactory bulb (which serves as pacemaker). These bursts are interpreted as a destabilization of the basic chaotic state of the olfactory system – a phase transition to an attractor state. Most importantly, this process does not require continuous input from an external pacemaker. The carrier wave in the olfactory system is not imposed by external input; rather, it merges as a cooperative activity that is self-organized by the neural masses (Freeman, 1992, p. 468).

While it is difficult to generalize from the olfactory system in rats and rabbits to emotion-driving appraisal in humans, we can conceive of a similar architecture. In other words, the assumption is that appraisal results serve as input to massively coupled psychophysiological oscillators that, upon triggering by this input, undergo a state transition from previously chaotic behavior to synchronization through the process of increased coupling and mutual entrainment. As mentioned above, one would have to postulate that different patterns of appraisal results produce different sets of order parameters that ''push'' the synchronization process in the direction of specific attractor states. The end of the emotion episode would be characterized by a steady weakening of the synchronization, a decrease in the degree of coupling of the component systems, and a transition back to a more or less chaotic state (or, in some cases, because of new appraisal input, by an abrupt transition to a new attractor state).

I have proposed to limit the use of the term *emotion* to episodes in time during which the degree of coupling or synchronization of *all* organismic subsystems exceeds a threshold of normal covariation. (By arguing for a synchronization of all subsystems, I am taking a strong stand that may well need to be modified in the future to allow for a synchronization of a majority rather than all of the subsystems.) Thus a certain degree of entrainment is the *conditio sine qua non* to speak of emotion in the sense defined here. Of course, the threshold beyond which subsystem synchronization warrants the use of the term emotion remains to be defined. In order to do this, we first need preliminary data for the range of coupling under different emotional and nonemotional circumstances, allowing us to specify order parameters. It is possible that there will be strong individual differences with respect to where this threshold is situated.

At this point it may be appropriate to discuss the underlying notion of causality implicit in the concepts presented here. Appraisal is a process in time with constantly changing results and, in turn, constantly changing driving effects on subsystem synchronization (and, consequently, type of emotion). The assumption is that the specific appraisal profile that moves subsystem synchronization into an attractor space, that characterizes a modal emotion episode, is the end result (in terms of a time slice) of accumulation and refinement of sequential information. Appraisal is seen as the initiator and driver of the synchronization process but *also* as being *driven by it*. As is usually the case in self-organizing systems, there is no simple, unidirectional sense of causality (see Lewis, 1996, for an extensive discussion of such reciprocal effects). Furthermore, in the sense of Haken (1977), we have to conceive of a circular causality between the macro organization and the microelements of a system.

So far, I have not dealt with the subjective feeling component of emotion. Phenomenologically oriented readers might draw the line here, insisting that *qualia* are the last bastion against oscillatory imperialism. I would like to argue for the contrary. I believe that a dynamic systems account of emotion actually helps us to focus some of the questions concerning the intractable mysteries of subjective feeling and the role of consciousness. Concretely, I have suggested that *feeling* (to be sharply distinguished from ''emotion,'' of which it is only one component) should be viewed as a reflection of all ongoing changes in the different organismic subsystems. Using the language of nonlinear dynamic systems theory, I suggest that it consists of a qualitative change in a monitor system that reacts to a degree of coupling or synchronization of the subsystems that surpasses the normal baseline fluctuations. Speculatively, one might assume that this is also the point when unconscious reflections of component subsystem changes become conscious.

I strongly insist on treating the colloquial use of emotion labels as a separate phenomenon, related to emotional communication and the representation of cultural knowledge structures. These processes cannot be understood in the sense of oscillating systems but instead require categorical approaches. Obviously, the results of categorization and labeling, once having occurred, can and will influence appraisal and emotional regulation, and thus constitute an important input to the synchronization process. One of the major issues for the future is to understand the relationship between continuous time series or oscillations, on the one hand, and more stable, discrete states amenable or accessible only through categorization, on the other. The notion of ''attractors'' – describing relatively stable patterns of repeated coupled oscillations with similar characteristics – may be useful in this context. In consequence, I propose to view what I have called ''modal emotions'' (as discussed earlier) – in contrast to basic or fundamental emotions – as attractors in this sense.

So far, I have dealt with appraisal as the *driver* of the emotion-constituting synchronization process in a rather superficial manner. However, many of the most intriguing aspects of emotional arousal are difficult to explain by standard appraisal theory notions (see Scherer, 1999, for a review). For example, we need to account for complex blends or mixtures of emotion as well as for sudden shifts in emotional processes. I will now turn to another nonlinear modeling approach that may help us to model many of the specific characteristics of the emotion process in a more appropriate manner – *catastrophe theory*.

Nonlinear Shifts in the Driving Function: Contributions from Catastrophe Theory

Catastrophe theory, originally developed by the French mathematician René Thom, has become quite fashionable in the social and behavioral sciences, and there are now a number of very suggestive catastrophe theory explanations for behavioral phenomena (Flay, 1978; Stewart and Peregoy, 1983; van der Maas and Molenaar, 1992; Zeeman, 1976). One of the concepts popularized by catastrophe theory that is of particular interest to emotion theorists is *hysteresis*. This term refers to the property of a function with a nonlinear part that is inaccessible and that doubles back in its course. Let us take the example shown in Figure 3.3. The figure plots the relationship between the degree of frustration and the anger elicited by it. Whereas a linear function would predict steadily rising anger with increasing frustration, the hysteresis function, containing a folded-back, nonacces-

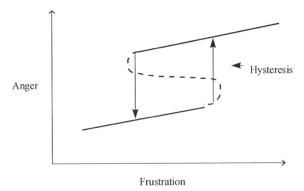

Figure 3.3. An illustration of hysteresis in the frustration-anger relationship.

sible region, suggests that the intensity of anger will change abruptly for specific degrees of frustration. This explains two important phenomena.

The first is that with increasing frustration there may be a point where anger will, in a dramatic fashion, jump to a considerably higher level rather than continue to increase in a linear fashion. In many languages, we have colloquial expressions for this kind of sudden flaring up of anger. We say things like "I felt like I'd explode" or "hot under the collar" and similar phrases (see also Lakoff, 1987, on emotion metaphors). What is referred to here is the sudden jump in anger at a certain point in frustration intensity, which is not predicted by the shape of a linear function. Similar phenomena observed in fear, boredom, and many other emotions may also require modeling by nonlinear functions.

The second phenomenon that is well explained by the hysteresis function is the importance of the departure point. For example, if I start out with little frustration, and consequently little anger, there is a point where rising frustration will make my anger jump to a much higher level without going through any intermediate stages (which make up the nonaccessible parts of the function). However, when starting from a high level of anger, produced by high frustration, and calming down because of a diminution of frustration, it is not at the same point (as in the other direction) that my anger will suddenly drop. Rather, it will take much less frustration before a drop to the lower level will occur. This is explained by partial overlapping due to the fold in the function.

These characteristics of emotional responses are phenomenologically well known to us, and most emotion psychologists are likely to confirm their existence. However, our current conceptualization and modeling of emotion does not allow us to predict the occurrence of such phenomena. We need concepts like hysteresis as tools for modeling these rather special effects. Obviously, the modeling of such a nonlinear function will require more sophisticated mathematics and statistics than what is offered by standard analysis of variance or regression approaches, all of which are based on the assumption of linearity.

Hysteresis, which as we have seen can be explained quite simply, is at the basis of even the most complex catastrophe models. The difference is that the more complex models contain more dimensions that need to be taken into account in predicting the underlying phenomenon. Figure 3.4 presents a three-dimensional model reproduced from Zeeman (1976), one of the pioneers of the utilization of catastrophe theory in the social and behavioral sciences. This figure shows a famous example of the application

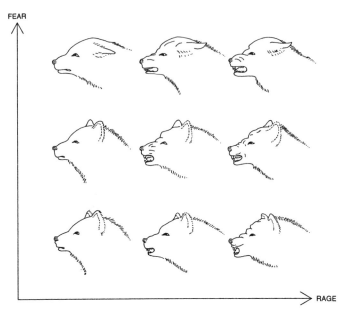

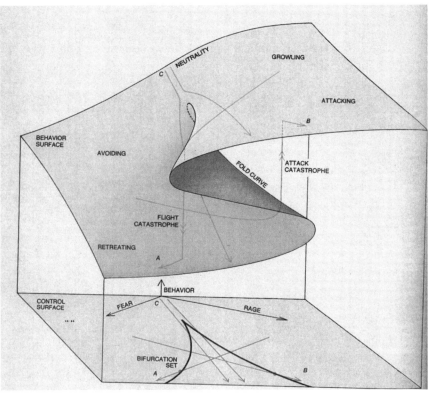

of catastrophe theory to a classic behavioral phenomenon in ethology – the response conflict between attack and flight in a dog faced with an adversary of unknown strength (Lorenz, 1965). The catastrophe conceptualization of this phenomenon consists in postulating a *control space* (at the bottom of the graph) that maps the dimensions or factors controlling the behavior of the animal. The upper level of the graph shows the *behavior or response surface* upon which the respective values of the variables in the control space are projected. In the dog example, it is the relative strength of the opposing tendencies to fight or flee which represent the two orthogonal factors in the control space determining the respective positions of the behavior on the response surface. As the relative strength of the opposing behavior tendencies of the dog change constantly – that is, the respective values of the two control factors vary in relation to each other – the change in behavior of the dog can be plotted as a path on the response surface.

The twist that makes the catastrophe theory model superior to what would seem otherwise a pretty straightforward account of the underlying processes is the introduction of hysteresis in the form of a *fold* in the response surface. This nonlinearity in the response surface accounts for a number of well-known characteristics of emotional behavior – the fact, already illustrated, that emotions can abruptly change from one moment to another. This is modeled by the arrows labeled "abrupt change" at the front edge of the fold. Furthermore, the fold in the behavior surface accounts for the fact that the change over time and the nature of the change in emotion processes will depend on the origin of the path. As shown earlier, this is one of the major features of hysteresis in a nonlinear function. It accounts for the fact that increases in one underlying dimension will have different effects than decreases. In the two-dimensional system shown in Figure 3.4, with hysteresis involved only at one end of the

Figure 3.4 (*facing page*). Catastrophe modeling of the flight-attack dilemma in dogs. Aggression in dogs can be described by a model based on one of the elementary catastrophes. The model assumes that aggressive behavior is controlled by two conflicting factors, rage and fear, which are plotted as axes on a horizontal plane – the control surface (see top panel). Control factors in the model of aggression are rage and fear, which in dogs can be measured by facial expression. The behavioral expressions as projected onto the behavioral plane are shown in the lower panel, showing mixtures of the two control factors. Rage is reflected by the extent to which the mouth is opened, and fear is revealed by the degree to which the ears are flattened back. From these indicators it is possible to judge the dog's emotional state, and through the model to predict its behavior (adapted from Zeeman, 1976).

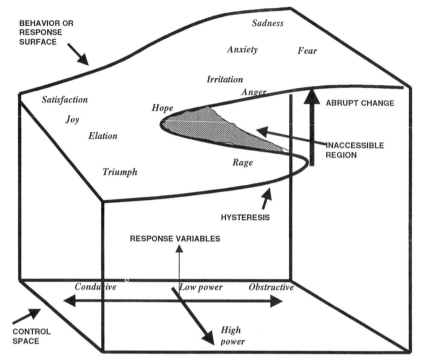

Figure 3.5. A preliminary catastrophe model of appraisal.

continuum, complex paths involving abrupt or smooth changes (depending on the location on the behavior surface) are possible.

The projection of the inaccessible region represented by the folded part of the behavior surface onto the control surface yields what is known as the *bifurcation set* or *cusp*, which is one of the distinguishing features of catastrophe theory (see Zeeman, 1976).

It seems to me that catastrophe theory modeling (using the projection of control space changes onto a behavior or response surface characterized by hysteresis) can be profitably employed to model emotion responses as based on appraisal processes. Figure 3.5 shows a two-dimensional model, as proposed by Zeeman (1976), where I have introduced, in an illustrative fashion, two of the major dimensions postulated by all appraisal theorists into the control space. Concretely, I have called Factor A the *goal conduciveness gradient*, characterized by the appraisal of the probability of reaching one's goal (to the left) or not reaching one's goal (to the right). I have called Factor B, orthogonal to Factor A, *control* or *power*, representing the appraisal of the degree of coping potential available to the organism to deal with a given situation (ranging from very little power toward the back, to high power toward the front). Using the highly convergent predictions of appraisal theorists (see Scherer, 1988, 1999) one can project various positions of this two-dimensional control space onto the behavior or response surface and describe specific regions on this surface using emotion labels. Thus, as predicted by most appraisal theorists, anger is predicted to occur in conditions where the organism perceives a goal to be obstructed but considers itself to have sufficient coping potential to deal with the block. What catastrophe modeling can add to the straightforward appraisal theoretical account is again due to the hysteresis fold in the behavior surface. Using the model, one can imagine how someone faced with adversity – that is, seeing goal attainment increasingly threatened but perceiving a fairly high degree of coping potential or power – will move through states of hope and increasing determination to a point where a sudden switch to anger or even rage will occur. The fact that only a very small change in perceived obstructiveness and power needs to precede the sudden change is explained by the hysteresis fold in the behavior surface. Another example might be someone who appraises goal conduciveness as fairly low but evaluates coping potential as increasing. This person moves from anxiety to resentment and then, following a sudden change due to hysteresis, to determination. Again, while the increment in perceived coping potential is relatively small, the change in the resulting emotion quality is quite dramatic.

Appraisal theorists postulate many more than two underlying control factors, and the locations of the emotion labels on the behavior surface are in consequence quite approximate. In order to model additional control factors, one needs to move to complex, higher-order catastrophe models, as described by René Thom and other catastrophe theorists (Stewart and Peregoy, 1983; Thom, 1982; Zeeman, 1976). Obviously, the introduction of higher-order bifurcation sets in several dimensions allows an enormous variety of outcomes based on a fairly simple control structure.

This theoretical modeling of the dynamic processes involved in the sequence of appraisal changes may help appraisal theory to move beyond a rather static prediction of the semantic meanings of particular emotional terms to a more dynamic approach, highlighting the changes that occur upon incremental changes of the appraisal on particular dimensions. Most importantly, the effects of these changes may be nonlinear. In other words, depending on the region involved and on the combination of the underlying appraisal dimensions, relatively small changes may produce dramatic consequences. Obviously, an empirical investigation of theoretical models of this sort requires a much finer measurement of the appraisal dimensions (for example, the use of interval scales) as well as a process measurement of appraisal in time (see Edwards, 1998) rather than retrospective one-point measurement, as has been the case in most appraisal research to date. This is an example of how modeling based on catastrophe theory can guide theoretical and empirical development in one of the central areas of current emotion research. In addition, such modeling promises to do a better job in explaining a number of intuitively obvious characteristics of emotional responses (such as abrupt changes that are difficult to explain by linear functions, and dependency of the response on the origin or departure point).

It must be stressed that the nonlinear dynamics approaches described earlier in the chapter *complement* the catastrophe modeling as described later. For example, the regions labeled by emotion terms on the response surface in Figure 3.5 can be seen as attractors with auto-organizational properties. Thus, attractor spaces on the surface represent multidimensional vectors that are differentially affected by changes in the control structure. As mentioned previously, the coupling of normally independent oscillating systems is explained by the need for adaptation that results from certain appraisals (represented as positions in the underlying control space in the model). Thus, it is the current state of the control structure that couples the independent oscillators. Of course, changes of position in the control space must also explain the decoupling of oscillators underlying the movement of the organism along a path on the response surface over time. However, most physical and biological systems have some degree of inertness built in, requiring a relaxation of prior constraints over some period of time before uncoupling can occur. This characteristic explains how attractors maintain the persistence of a particular state for some time.

Conclusions

Much of what I have suggested here is extremely speculative, and I would be hard pressed to expand on the presumed processes in greater detail or to specify the paradigms for empirical study. It would be premature to attempt to provide a blueprint for further work in this area, a task better left to experts in the area of nonlinear dynamic modeling. My aim as an emotion psychologist, worrying about the further development of the field, has been mainly to show the promise of some of the ideas that are inherent in nonlinear dynamic theory and catastrophe theory for conceptual and theoretical development in emotion psychology that may ultimately lead to new paradigms for empirical research. I would be happy if I have succeeded in showing that some of the particular characteristics of nonlinear systems modeling seem to provide very powerful tools to model aspects of emotional phenomena that classic approaches have found difficult. Even more importantly, it would seem that the effort to model emotion within such a framework raises issues that so far have rarely been attacked directly, particularly with respect to the dynamic unfolding of emotion processes or paths on the response surface and to the relationships between an appraisal control structure and the ensuing changes in multiple response modalities. I hope to have sketched out an approach to conceptualizing the dynamics of the emotion process that might help to bring about a paradigm shift in the Kuhnian sense.

In suggesting a nonlinear dynamic systems approach, I feel comforted by the zeitgeist. In a recent review, Lewis and Granic (1999) have highlighted the important contributions made by a number of emotion theorists – without formally endorsing the conceptual framework of self-organizing systems theory – to the understanding of recursion, emergence, and consolidation of cognition-emotion relations. Fogel (1993; Fogel et al., 1992) and Lewis (1996) have been among the first authors to propose explicit self-organization models of cognition-emotion relationships, particularly with respect to developmental processes. There is some hope that this movement will gain momentum and, in fact, eventually lead to the paradigm shift advocated in the introduction to this chapter.

Is the nonlinear dynamic systems approach yet another *Sprachspiel* for psychologists – with little or no real consequence for theorizing or research design? It depends on how seriously we want to adapt our practices to the phenomena we are studying. Some of the consequences of the paradigm shift suggested here are obvious: They involve the need to (a) study ongoing processes over time, (b) study multiple systems and their interactions (cognition, physiology, expression), (c) adopt experimental approaches using well-controlled manipulations, and (d) formalize predictions. These are tall orders. The current landscape of emotion research does not look encouraging in this respect, given that the bulk of the work is devoted to verbal descriptions of emotional *states*. Nevertheless, it is to be hoped that a growing realization that emotion research is falling behind the conceptual and methodological advances in other areas of the cognitive and behavioral sciences will, in hysteresis-like fashion, produce a sudden jump in the direction advocated here.

This chapter might do something to blaze alternative trails that help theory and research on emotion escape from the impasse that we seem to have reached. Then again, it might not. However, I believe that it is worth trying. We have little to lose but much to gain.

Acknowledgments

Most of the points in this piece were first presented in the context of keynote addresses at meetings of the Société Psychologique de Québec, Québec, 1993, and the Assoziatione Italiana de la Psicologia delle Emozioni, Milan, 1994. A preliminary version was presented at the 1996 ISRE meeting in Toronto.

The preparation of this chapter was greatly aided by expert advice from Thomas Wehrle. The author also gratefully acknowledges comments by Marc Lewis and Isabel Granic.

References

Anishchenko, V. S., Vadivasova, T. E., Postnov, D. E., and Safonova, M. A. (1992). Synchronization of chaos. *International Journal of Bifurcation and Chaos, 2,* 633–644.

Averill, J. R. (1980). A constructivist view of emotion. In R. Plutchik and H. Kellerman (Eds.), *Emotion: Theory, research, and experience* (vol. 1, pp. 305–340). New York: Academic Press.

Banse, R., van Reekum, C. M., Johnstone, T., Scherer, K. R., Etter, A., and Wehrle, T. (1999). *Psychophysiological responses to emotion-antecedent appraisal in a computer game.* Manuscript submitted for publication.

Edwards, P. (1998). *Étude empirique de déterminants de la différenciation des émotions et de leur intensité* [An empirical study of the determinants of the differentiation of emotions and of their intensity]. Unpublished doctoral dissertation, University of Geneva, Geneva.

Ekman, P. (1984). Expression and the nature of emotion. In K. R. Scherer and P. Ekman (Eds.), *Approaches to emotion* (pp. 319–344). Hillsdale, NJ: Erlbaum.

Ekman, P. (1992). An argument for basic emotions. *Cognition and Emotion, 6,* 169–200.

Ellsworth, P. C. (1991). Some implications of cognitive appraisal theories of emotion. In K. Strongman (Ed.), *International review of studies on emotion* (pp. 143–161). New York: Wiley.

Flay, B. R. (1978). Catastrophe theory in social psychology: Some applications to attitudes and social behavior. *Behavioral Science, 23,* 335–350.

Fogel, A. (1993). *Developing through relationships: Origins of communication, self, and culture.* Chicago: University of Chicago Press.

Fogel, A., Nwokah, E., Dedo, J. Y., Messinger, D., Dickson, K. L., Matusov, E., and Holt, S. A. (1992). Social process theory of emotion: A dynamic systems approach. *Social Development, 1,* 122–142.

Freeman, W. J. (1992). Tutorial on neurobiology: From single neurons to brain chaos. *International Journal of Bifurcation and Chaos, 2,* 451–482.

Frijda, N. H. (1986). *The emotions*. Cambridge: Cambridge University Press.

Glass, L. (1991). Nonlinear dynamics of physiological function and control. *Chaos, 1*, 247–250.

Gleick, J. (1987). *Chaos: Making a new science*. New York: Penguin Books.

Goldberger, A. L., Rigney, D. R., and West, B. J. (1990). Chaos and fractals in human physiology. *Scientific American* (February), 43–49.

Haken, H. (1977). *Synergetics: An introduction*. Heidelberg: Springer.

Haken, H. (1991). Synergetics – Can it help physiology? In H. Haken and H. P. Koepchen (Eds.), *Rhythms in physiological systems* (pp. 21–31). Heidelberg: Springer.

Harré, R. M. (1986). *The social construction of emotions*. Oxford: Blackwell.

Izard, C. E. (1977). *Human emotions*. New York: Plenum.

Izard, C. E. (1993). Four systems for emotion activation: Cognitive and noncognitive processes. *Psychological Review, 100*, 68–90.

Jennings, J. R. (1986). Memory, thought and bodily response. In M. G. Coles, E. Donchin, and S. W. Porges (Eds.), *Psychophysiology: Systems, processes, and applications* (pp. 290–308). New York: Guilford.

Kaplan, D. T., and Talajic, M. (1991). Dynamics of heart rate. *Chaos, 1*, 251–256.

Kuhn, T. (1981). *The structure of scientific revolutions*. Chicago: University of Chicago Press.

Lakoff, G. (1987). *Women, fire, and dangerous things: What categories reveal about the mind*. Chicago: University of Chicago Press.

Lazarus, R. S. (1991). *Emotion and adaptation*. New York: Oxford University Press.

LeDoux, J. E. (1989). Cognitive-emotional interactions in the brain. *Cognition and Emotion, 3*, 267–289.

Leventhal, H., and Scherer, K. R. (1987). The relationship of emotion to cognition: A functional approach to a semantic controversy. *Cognition and Emotion, 1*, 3–28.

Lewis, M. D. (1996). Self-organizing cognitive appraisals. *Cognition and Emotion, 10*, 1–25.

Lewis, M. D., and Granic, I. (1999). The self-organization of cognition-emotion interactions. In T. Dalgleish and M. Power (Eds.), *Handbook of cognition and emotion* (pp. 683–701). Chichester: Wiley.

Lorenz, K. (1965). *Evolution and modification of behavior*. Chicago: University of Chicago Press.

Mahowald, M. W., Schenk, C. H., and O'Connor, K. A. (1991). Dynamics of sleep/wake determination – Normal and abnormal. *CHAOS, 1*, 287–298.

Musil, R. (1978). *Der Mann ohne Eigenschaften* [The man without qualities]. Reinbek, Germany: Rowohlt. (Original work published 1930.)

Oatley, K. (1993). Social construction in emotions. In M. Lewis and J. M. Haviland (Eds.), *Handbook of emotions* (pp. 341–352). New York: Guilford.

Panksepp, J. (1982). Toward a general psychobiological theory of emotions. *Behavioral and Brain Sciences, 5*, 407–467.

Redington, D. J., and Reidbord, S. P. (1992). Chaotic dynamics in autonomic nervous system activity of a patient during a psychotherapy session. *Biological Psychiatry, 31*, 993–1007.

Scherer, K. R. (1981). Wider die Vernachlässigung der Emotion in der Psychologie. [Against the neglect of emotion in psychology]. In W. Michaelis (Ed.), *Bericht über den 32. Kongress der Deutschen Gesellschaft für Psychologie in Zürich 1980* [Report of the thirty-second congress of the German Psychological Association, Zurich, 1980] (pp. 304–317). Göttingen: Hogrefe.

Scherer, K. R. (1984). On the nature and function of emotion: A component process approach. In K. R. Scherer and P. Ekman (Eds.), *Approaches to emotion* (pp. 293–318). Hillsdale, NJ: Erlbaum.

Scherer, K. R. (1986). Vocal affect expression: A review and a model for future research. *Psychological Bulletin, 99*, 143–165.

Scherer, K. R. (1987). Toward a dynamic theory of emotion: The component process model of affective states. *Geneva Studies in Emotion and Communication, 1*, 1–98.

Scherer, K. R. (1988). Criteria for emotion-antecedent appraisal: A review. In V. Hamilton, G. H. Bower, and N. H. Frijda (Eds.), *Cognitive perspectives on emotion and motivation. NATO ASI series D: Behavioural and social sciences* (vol. 44, pp. 89–126). Dordrecht: Kluwer.

Scherer, K. R. (1993). Neuroscience projections to current debates in emotion psychology. *Cognition and Emotion, 7*, 1–41.

Scherer, K. R. (1994). Toward a concept of "modal emotions." In P. Ekman and R. J. Davidson (Eds.), *The nature of emotion: Fundamental questions* (pp. 25–31). Oxford: Oxford University Press.

Scherer, K. R. (1999). Appraisal theories. In T. Dalgleish and M. Power (Eds.), *Handbook of cognition and emotion* (pp. 637–663). Chichester: Wiley.

Scherer, K. R., and Tannenbaum, P. H. (1986). Emotional experiences in everyday life: A survey approach. *Motivation and Emotion, 10*, 295–314.

Shweder, R. A. (1993). The cultural psychology of the emotions. In M. Lewis and J. M. Haviland (Eds.), *Handbook of emotions* (pp. 417–434). New York: Guilford.

Skarda, C. A., and Freeman, W. J. (1987). How brains make chaos in order to make sense of the world. *Behavioral and Brain Sciences, 10*, 161–195.

Smith, C. A. (1989). Dimensions of appraisal and physiological response in emotion. *Journal of Personality and Social Psychology, 56*, 339–353.

Smith, C. A., and Ellsworth, P. C. (1985). Patterns of cognitive appraisal in emotion. *Journal of Personality and Social Psychology, 48*, 813–838.

Smith, C. A., and Lazarus, R. S. (1993). Appraisal components, core relational themes, and the emotions. *Cognition and Emotion, 7*, 233–269.

Stewart, I. N., and Peregoy, P. L. (1983). Catastrophe theory modeling in psychology. *Psychological Bulletin, 94*, 336–362.

Thom, R. (1982). *Structural stability and catastrophes – Science and engineering.* New York: Wiley.

Tomkins, S. S. (1984). Affect theory. In K. R. Scherer and P. Ekman (Eds.), *Approaches to emotion* (pp. 163–196). Hillsdale, NJ: Erlbaum.

van Brakel, J. (1994). Emotions: A cross-cultural perspective on forms of life. In W. M. Wentworth and J. Ryan (Eds.), *Social perspectives on emotion* (vol. 2, pp. 179–237). Greenwich, CT: JAI Press.

van der Maas, H. L., and Molenaar, P. C. (1992). Stagewise cognitive development: An application of catastrophe theory. *Psychological Review, 99*, 395–417.

van Reekum, C. M., Johnstone, T., and Scherer, K. R. (1997). *Multimodal measurement of emotion induced by the manipulation of appraisals in a computer game.*

Paper presented at the Third European Conference of Psychophysiology, Konstanz, Germany.

van Reekum, C. M., and Scherer, K. R. (1997). Levels of processing for emotion-antecedent appraisal. In G. Matthews (Ed.), *Cognitive science perspectives on personality and emotion* (pp. 259–300). Amsterdam: Elsevier.

Zajonc, R. B. (1980). Feeling and thinking: Preferences need no inferences. *American Psychologist, 2*, 151–176.

Zeeman, E. C. (1976). Catastrophe theory. *Scientific American, 234*, 65–83.

Zwiener, U., Bauer, R., and Lüthke, B. (1992). Pathophysiologische Aspekte in der Dynamik kardiovaskolärer Kurzzeitfluktuationen [Pathophysiological aspects of the dynamics in short-term cardiovascular fluctuations]. *Wissenschaftliche Zeitschrift der Humboldt Universität zu Berlin, 41*, 77–81.

4 Surprise! Facial Expressions Can be Coordinative Motor Structures

Linda A. Camras

This chapter presents a dynamical systems perspective on both facial expression specifically and emotion communication more generally. I have been developing this perspective in response to several interesting problems that have recently emerged in attempts to verify one currently popular theory of infant emotional expression. In this chapter, I will review these problems and discuss the limitations of extant theory. The dynamical systems view I will present is not a fully articulated alternative proposal. Instead, it is intended to represent a new direction for theoretical and empirical exploration in which solutions to the problems with the current theory may be found.

A Theory of Infant Emotional Expression

The currently popular view of infant emotional expression is most fully embodied in Izard's (1977, 1991) differential emotions theory. According to this theory, there is a species-specific set of human emotions that emerge during development according to a maturational timetable. In its original formulation (Izard, 1971; Izard and Malatesta, 1987; Izard et al., 1995), the theory proposes an innate concordance between infant emotions and a specified set of infant facial expressions (Izard, Dougherty, and Hembree, 1983). These expressions are direct readouts of their corresponding emotions, that is, they are automatically produced when the emotion is experienced and are not produced in other circumstances. Thus, facial expressions serve as veridical indices of infant affects and can be simply "read" by observers to determine the infant's emotional state. In recent years, Izard (1997; this volume) has begun to qualify his early assertions about the invariant relationship between infant affect and facial expression, adopting a position more consistent with empirical demonstrations of nonconcord-

100

ance (e.g., Camras, 1992). Nonetheless, the original view is currently represented in many developmental psychology textbooks, probably because of its straightforward nature and the simple solution it offers to the problem of understanding nonverbal infants.

Within the community of infant emotion researchers, challenges of two different types have been raised with respect to Izard's original "strong" formulation. First, some researchers (Camras, 1991, 1992; Lewis and Michalson, 1983; Oster, Hegley, and Nagel, 1992; Sroufe, 1996) have challenged the view that infant emotions correspond to the same set of discrete affects described for adults. For example, Camras (1992) has proposed that young infants may experience not discrete adultlike "anger" and "sadness," but instead a less differentiated state of "distress." Second, some researchers (Barrett and Campos, 1987; Camras, 1991; Matias and Cohn, 1993) have questioned the assertion that certain specified facial expressions are invariantly produced to accompany their corresponding emotions in early infancy. As part of their functionalist theory of emotion, Barrett and Campos (1987) have argued that emotional facial expressions may be expected to occur or not occur depending upon their utility in a particular emotion situation. Along similar lines, my colleagues and I (Camras, 1991, 1992; Camras, Lambrecht, and Michel, 1996; Michel, Camras, and Sullivan, 1992) have previously described several specific examples of noncorrespondence between emotions and emotional facial expressions and discussed their possible causal basis within the context of a dynamical systems framework.

The Relationship between Emotions and Emotional Facial Expressions

Three anomalous phenomena can be identified that challenge the direct-readout hypothesis with respect to infant emotional expression. First, some expressions have rarely been observed in situations that are commonly believed to elicit their corresponding emotion. For example, Hiatt, Campos, and Emde (1979) failed to find fear expressions in infants who showed other indications of fear when confronted by a stranger or placed on the "visual cliff." Second, facial configurations that meet coding criteria for some emotions have been observed in situations where the emotion is unlikely to occur. For example, codeable "surprise" expressions are often produced when infants open their mouths in anticipation of mouthing a nonsurprising object (Camras et al., 1996, to be described further here). Third, more than one "prototypic" expression has been described for some emotions (e.g., interest; Izard et al., 1983). Yet causal factors underlying the production of one of these variant expressions rather than another have not yet been proposed.

It is important to point out that similar phenomena have also been observed for adult emotional expressions. In fact, noncorrespondences of the first two types just described are acknowledged in virtually all contemporary discrete emotion theories (e.g., Buck, 1988; Ekman, 1972, 1992; Frijda, 1986; Izard, 1997; Plutchik, 1980; Tomkins, 1982). Such disjunctions are accounted for primarily by the notion of "display rules" (Ekman and Friesen, 1969). That is, spontaneously produced emotional expressions may be subjected to voluntary control such that an expression may be minimized, completely inhibited, or masked through substitution of a different (perhaps more socially appropriate) facial expression. In addition, adults may falsify their facial behavior by voluntarily producing an emotional expression when no genuine emotion is being experienced.

Display-rule-governed dissociations between emotion and emotional expression are thought to occur as the result of socialization processes. During the course of development, the individual comes to exert control over his or her expressive behavior in conformity with personal standards and/ or sociocultural norms. In these cases, variation in expressive behavior involves altering the "natural course of events," that is, the spontaneous production of species-specific emotional facial expression. However, such alterations would not be expected in young infants because traditionally infants have not been thought to engage in intentional communicative behavior, at least during the first eight months. Even in older infants, it is often difficult to envision circumstances under which inhibition or nongenuine expression of some emotions (e.g., surprise) would be expected to occur.

Regarding the third anomalous phenomenon described earlier, current systems for identifying emotional expressions include a number of variant expressions for each emotion. For example, the FACSAID database (Ekman et al., 1998) used to interpret facial behavior coded using Ekman and Friesen's (1978) Facial Action Coding System currently contains over ten configurations identified as "surprise" expressions and over fifteen additional configurations identified as possible expressions of surprise. However, as for infants, the causal basis for such variability has not been fully explicated (but see Ekman, 1979, for some proposals).

Coordinative Motor Structures

The problem of variability among facial expressions in the same emotional category is interesting because it resembles a classic dilemma in movement science known as "Bernstein's problem" (Bernstein, 1967; Turvey, 1990). Movement scientists have long been confronted with the challenge of accounting for the fact that functionally equivalent actions are never completely equivalent topographically (e.g., one never walks twice from point A to point B in exactly the same way). Minor variability inevitably occurs due to numerous contextual particularities, such as initial position when starting out, slight unevenness in the surface underfoot, and so forth. One way of accounting for such variability is to posit a central planning agent who continually monitors the details of the organism's activity and makes continual adjustments to compensate for minor variations in the environmental context in which the activity takes place. However, movement scientists have deemed this solution inadequate because it places too great a burden on the central controlling agent. Instead, they have proposed that contextually sensitive adjustments are made at lower levels through synergistic relationships among neuromuscular action components (Kelso and Scholz, 1986; Kugler, Kelso, and Turvey, 1980; Michel, 1991). That is, groups of muscles are proposed to be synergistically linked such that the action of one member of the group may recruit the action of other members. These synergistically related groups of muscles are called "coordinative motor structures." Via such neuromuscular linkages, minor perturbations in a planned action sequence (due to contextual factors, such as occur when walking over slightly uneven ground) may be automatically compensated for via recruitment of compensatory movements. In addition, performance of some activities may be made more efficient because executive control can be implemented at the level of the grouping rather than at the level of the individual muscles themselves.

A Dynamical Systems Framework

Coordinative motor structures are a class of patterned activities that have been proposed to fall within the explanatory framework of dynamical systems (Kelso, 1995). The dynamical systems approach attempts to account for the organization of complex systems of various sorts, many of which involve a large number of components that might potentially be combined in a nearly infinite number of possible ways (Fogel et al., 1992; Fogel and Thelen, 1987; Kelso, 1981, 1995; Schoner and Kelso, 1988;

Thelen, 1989a). Despite this potential for infinite variability, such systems (e.g., human motor action) tend to assume a limited number of states or patterns (termed "attractor states"; Abraham and Shaw, 1982), although some degree of variability within these patterns often occurs. According to the dynamical systems perspective, these states are self-organized (Fogel et al., 1992; Kugler, Kelso, and Turvey, 1982; Thelen, 1989b; Turvey, 1990), for example, they may involve constrained coordinative relationships among lower-order components rather than being fully dictated in detail by a higher-order command program. The system assumes one or another of its attractor states depending upon a number of factors. These include the value of some identified "control" parameter as well as the initial condition of the system when the control parameter changes value. For example, in an elegant set of experiments, Kelso and his colleagues (Kelso, 1995) have demonstrated that rhythmic multijoint arm movements (involving flexions and extensions of the elbow and wrist) will assume different patterns depending upon the initial position of the arm and the speed at which the arm is moved. Shifts from one pattern to another (termed "phase shifts") tend to occur relatively abruptly at the point at which the control parameter reaches its critical value. For example, when wrist and elbow movements accelerate beyond a certain velocity, they may switch from a pattern involving simultaneous wrist flexion and elbow extension to a pattern in which the wrist and elbow are constrained to flex (and extend) simultaneously. As the control variable (e.g., movement velocity) approaches its critical value, increasing fluctuations in the current pattern may occur, indicating loss of stability. Furthermore, when the system is perturbed (by some outside factor such as tapping the arm or an uneven spot on the ground), pattern recovery is slower if a control variable is near the critical value at which a change from one organized pattern to another will be catalyzed. Within this framework, the coordinative structures proposed as a solution to Bernstein's problem of motor coordination may be considered a class of dynamical systems "attractor states."

Dynamical systems models offer an attractive alternative to theories that attempt to explain systems that involve considerable variability solely by means of a central controlling agent (Fogel and Thelen, 1987; Kugler, Kelso, and Turvey, 1980; Oyama, 1989). According to the dynamical systems perspective, a system's activity takes place within a larger context that critically influences its component structure and thus produces such variability (Fogel et al., 1992; Thelen, 1989a). This important idea is expressed in the popular dynamical systems dictum: the task dictates the behavior.

Although its applications in psychology have been limited thus far, a dynamical systems perspective potentially might successfully explain the organization of any type of complex system. Furthermore, it might be applied to several different behavioral systems that operate at different levels of behavioral analysis, that is, microsystems embedded within macrosystems (see Vallacher and Nowak, 1994, for examples in social psychology). Herein, I will explore the possibility that a dynamical systems approach might be used to explain the anomalies of infant facial expression described earlier. To do this, I will argue that human emotions and human facial expressions may constitute overlapping but partly separate dynamical systems. To explain emotional facial expression, both systems must be examined as well as their points of overlap and integration. My approach shares considerable common ground with recent work by Fogel, Messinger, Dickson, and their colleagues (e.g., Fogel, 1985; Messinger, Fogel, and Dickson, 1997), who have primarily focused on infant smiling. Much of my discussion will be speculative in nature, but I will also review and present new data to support the ideas proposed herein.

Emotions, Expressions, and Dynamical Systems

Within this volume, the several chapter authors are applying dynamical systems approaches to the study of emotion in a variety of creative and productive ways (see also Fogel et al., 1992). Emotions are obvious candidates for explanation in terms of dynamical systems because they are highly complex and involve the coordination of multiple components. Furthermore, emotion-related behavior is patterned and yet variable across emotion episodes.

As applied to infant emotional facial expressions, a dynamical systems approach might be used to account for the first anomalous phenomenon described earlier, that is, the absence of emotional facial expressions in some emotion situations. This noncorrespondence might be expected to occur if emotional expressions are recruited for display in a selective task-specific manner. Facial expressions are viewed as being similar to other emotion-related behaviors (i.e., instrumental responses) whose occurrence within an emotion episode is dictated by the situational context rather than being automatically mandated by a central control system. Interestingly, this perspective is gaining some prominence within the area of animal communication. For example, Marler and Evans (1997) have recently found that several avian species may or may not produce vocal communication signals depending upon contextual factors, rather than upon presumed alterations in their own internal state. Of significance, Marler interprets his findings as requiring a revision of traditional theories in which animal communication signals have been viewed as direct readouts of the animal's motivational tendencies. However, consistent with the perspective proposed herein (and in contrast to other proposed alternatives, e.g., Fridlund, 1994), Marler does not relinquish the notion that animal communication signals may be considered to be expressions of emotion.

Related to this last idea, the dynamical systems perspective might also be used to account for the second anomalous phenomenon of infant facial expression described here: production of a codeable "emotional" expression in circumstances where it is unlikely that emotion is being experienced. This phenomenon might be explained by incorporating nonemotional (as well as emotional) facial expressions into the dynamical systems framework. Even discrete emotion theorists acknowledge that many facial expressions are not manifestations of emotion. Starting from this acknowledgment, facial expression itself may be viewed as a complex behavioral system presenting just those sorts of problems for which dynamical systems approaches attempt to provide a solution. The face can produce numerous muscle actions that potentially occur in a nearly infinite number of combinations. Nonetheless, only a limited number of combinations appear to occur (although these do exceed the number described as being emotional expressions). Dynamical systems proponents might propose that the face can assume only a limited number of patterned states due to constraints imposed by lower-order synergistic relationships among muscle actions (i.e., coordinative motor structures). Such coordinative structures might be activated in several different ways. One source of activation might be the experience of an emotion itself (e.g., surprise). However, the same facial action ensemble might also be activated if one of its components were produced as an instrumental action (e.g., opening the mouth widely to incorporate an object). In this case, the activated component (mouth opening) might recruit other facial actions (e.g., brow raising) that are elements of a common coordinative motor structure. Such recruitment would take place via lower-order synergistic relationships among facial muscle actions. As a consequence, the emotion-relevant facial configuration might sometimes be produced when no emotion is being experienced.

A dynamical systems model might also be used to account for the third anomalous facial expression phenomenon: variability among the several facial configurations that are all considered to be expressions of a particular emotion. First, particular components of a complete prototypic expression might occur or not occur depending upon their functional utility within the situational context in which the emotion is being experienced. This argument is similar to that advanced when discussing the first anomaly. Going back as far as Darwin (1872/1998), the functional value of certain facial actions has been recognized (e.g., widening the eyes and raising the brows increases the visual field). However, both Darwin and later ethologists have argued that such movements may become divorced from their functional origins (e.g., when they become "ritualized" or specialized as communicative signals; Tinbergen, 1952, but also see Andrew, 1963). Nonetheless, to account for the presence or absence of a particular facial action in an instance of emotional expression, perhaps its utilitarian instrumental value within a particular expressive context should be reconsidered and empirically investigated (see Ekman, 1979, for some examples).

Nevertheless, utility alone probably could not fully account for variability among emotional expressions within the same emotional category. This is because the instrumental value of many facial movements involved in emotional expression is not clear. However, it may also be the case that some components of the prototypic emotional expression may or may not occur because of their involvement in certain coordinative motor structures relevant to aspects of the situation other than the emotion in and of itself. For example, as I will elaborate later, muscle actions involved in raising the head, gaze, and brows may be part of a coordinative motor structure such that deliberately raising the head and/or gaze may recruit brow raising, a component of surprise and interest expressions. Thus brow raising might occur in surprise or interest episodes in which lifting the head and/or gaze takes place but might not occur in other instances of these emotions.

Commentary

Developmental scholars have been reluctant to acknowledge these anomalies of emotional expression because their existence might appear to make it impossible for us to understand and adaptively respond to nonverbal infants. However, I will argue that accurate emotion communication does not require an innate concordance hypothesis for infants. Just as we are capable of understanding adult emotion despite the operation of display rules, so are we able to understand infants' emotion even if there is no unique one-to-one relationship between specific facial expressions and specific affects. Toward the end of this chapter, I will tentatively suggest how a dynamical systems perspective might provide a framework in which we might account for such a communicative phenomenon. For now, I will simply suggest that, by the same token, if subsequent research with adults demonstrates disjunctions between expression and emotion beyond those attributable to display rules, a dynamical systems perspective might also help us account for the preservation of effective emotion communication among adults.

Empirical Observations of Infant Brow Raises and Surprise Expressions

In the remainder of the chapter, I will further pursue a dynamical systems approach with respect to two forms of infant facial expressions: brow raises and surprise expressions. Brow raising is a facial action that may occur alone or in combination with other facial movements. Within Izard's AF-FEX coding system (Izard et al., 1983) it is included as a component of both the expression of interest and the expression of surprise. More specifically, according to AFFEX, interest expressions may involve either raised brows or horizontally knit brows, and either slightly pursed lips or slightly parted lips. The expression of surprise involves raised brows, widened eyes, and an open, rounded mouth. However, in using AFFEX, surprise may be coded if only two of the three surprise components are present (i.e., open mouth accompanied by raised brows or widened eyes). Thus, variability in the expression of both emotions is acknowledged within the AFFEX system, although a causal basis for this variability is not presented.

Beyond this acknowledged variability, previous observations and several empirical studies have indicated that mismatches between emotion and these expressions may occur during infancy. My original observations of these disjunctions were made during a systematic study of my own daughter's expressive behavior in her first two and a half months (Camras, 1992). During this time, I observed a striking association between her looking upward and raising her brows. Sometimes this occurred with slightly parted lips, producing a codeable "interest expression." While the association between looking up and brow raises might be attributed to a common emotional basis (i.e., the emotion of interest underlying both the facial movement and head/gaze lifting), the appropriateness of such an attribution seemed uncertain because visual regard in the upward direction was often fleeting rather than sustained. Thus, if anything, the raised brow movement appeared more closely related to visual searching than to the kind of sustained attention usually considered characteristic of interest as an emotion.

With respect to surprise, an initially important observation was merely that surprise expressions indeed occurred quite often during the course of the study. This observation was striking because very few surprise expressions had previously been observed in laboratory investigations in which the emotion of surprise has been assumed to be evoked. For example, studies of object permanence and other investigations utilizing expectancy-violation procedures (e.g., Baillargeon, 1986) evoke surprise expressions so infrequently that such expressions cannot be used as indices of a surprise response. By contrast, my daughter Justine often produced prototypic surprise expressions, but she produced them in familiar rather than surprising circumstances. For example, when placed beneath the familiar softly glowing kitchen lamp, she would invariably look upward at the light, become visibly excited, wave her arms in the direction of the lamp, raise her brows, widen her eyes, and open her mouth. Rather than as an indication of surprise in this context, her expression might be more reasonably interpreted as an example of a spreading appetitive sensory reaction described by the Austrian physiologist Albrecht Peiper (1963). As proposed by Peiper, Justine's facial reactions appeared to occur in the service of facilitating desirable sensory input. Similarly, Justine often showed the surprise expression as she opened her mouth in preparation for nursing. Taken together, these observations suggested that facial configurations codeable as interest and surprise expressions might occur in infants when these emotions were not actually present and that alternative systemic factors underlying their production might be identified.

Further empirical support for these ideas was produced in two systematic follow-up studies involving a larger number of infants. In one study (Michel, Camras, and Sullivan, 1992), five- and seven-month-old infants were presented with attractive toys at either above or below eye level. Raised brow movements significantly co-occurred with head-up and/or eyes-up movements at both ages. Presumably infants were equally interested in the toys irrespective of their presentation trajectory. Nonetheless, raised brows (a key component of the interest expression) occurred more often when looking at the toys required raising the head and/or gaze. Based on these findings, we proposed that raised brows is part of a coordinative motor structure involving actions of the head, eyes, and brows. The operation of this coordinative motor structure may determine whether infants produce a variant of the interest expression involving raised brows when they are displaying their emotion. Furthermore, we suggested that raised brows may sometimes be produced when head and/or gaze are lifted but the emotion of interest is not present. Thus, converging sources of evidence may be required before emotion can be inferred from the brow actions of infants.

With respect to surprise facial configurations, we reached similar conclusions in a study examining the facial actions of five- to seven-month-old infants as they carried nonsurprising objects toward their mouths in order to orally explore them (Camras, Lambrecht, and Michel, 1996). This study found that the facial action of moderately or widely opening the mouth was accompanied by brow raising and trace levels of eye widening. Thus, infants produced codeable "surprise" expressions in a nonsurprise situation. Again, these results suggest that coordinative motor structures are available for recruitment for a variety of purposes and that unique and exclusive ties may not be formed between some emotions and their corresponding facial expressions.

Surprise and Interest Expressions in Two Expectancy-Violation Procedures

More recently, my colleagues and I have begun to examine infants' facial behavior during procedures designed to elicit the emotion of surprise by means of expectancy violation. These procedures were administered as part of a collaborative cross-cultural investigation of infant expressive behavior. In this project, we studied eleven-month-old infants from the United States, Japan, and mainland China in stimulus situations designed to elicit mild anger/frustration and fear as well as surprise (see Camras et al., 1998, for a report of the anger and fear situations). Herein, I will present some preliminary analyses of the surprise-eliciting procedures.

We employed two different procedures in order to assess the situational specificity of infants' surprise reactions. Both procedures have been previously employed in other investigations and are expected to evoke surprise in infants of the age we studied. Both procedures involve violating notions of object permanence and constancy that are believed to develop well before eleven months.

In the first procedure, *vanishing object*, a small barking toy dog that the infant is watching suddenly appears to vanish instantaneously. This illusion is created with a large two-field tachistoscope having a one-way mirror in the center. The dog is placed behind the mirror. When the light is changed from one wing to the other, the dog appears to vanish while its barking can still be heard. In the second procedure, *toy switch*, the infant sees a toy covered by a cloth during a series of trials. After removing the cover and finding the same toy during the first four trials, the infant inexplicably finds a different toy on the fifth trial. This illusion is created by utilizing a table with a shallow well in which the toy is placed before covering. The well contains two compartments that can be rotated from under the table during the fifth trial so that the second compartment holding a different toy is exposed when the infant removes the cover.

The infants' facial behavior was coded using a modified version of BabyFACS (Oster and Rosenstein, 1995), an anatomically based scoring system for infant facial behavior based on Ekman and Friesen's (1978) adult-oriented Facial Action Coding System (FACS). In both BabyFACS and FACS, the basic scoring units are discrete, minimally distinguishable actions of the facial muscles (termed action units or AUs). One virtue of BabyFACS is that facial behavior is objectively described without making a priori assumptions about its emotional meaning. However, using this system, we were able to identify facial configurations that are interpreted as expressing surprise within Izard and colleagues' (1983) AFFEX system as well as in Ekman and colleagues' (1998) FACSAID (FACS Affect Interpretation Database).

Because facial coding is extremely labor-intensive, we selected a ten-second baseline episode and a ten-second stimulus episode to be coded for each procedure. For the vanishing object procedure, the baseline episode was the ten-second period preceding the first disappearance of the barking dog, while the stimulus episode was the ten-second period initiated by the disappearance. For the toy switch procedure, the baseline episode was the ten-second period preceding the baby's uncovering the unexpected object, while the stimulus episode was the ten-second period initiated by the baby's uncovering the unexpected object.

In addition to coding movements of the facial musculature, we also coded head and gaze movements. This allowed us to follow up on our previous studies examining relationships between these movements and the infants' production of raised brows. Since surprise expressions involve a raised brow movement, we wished to determine whether surprise expressions might also be selectively related to upward head and gaze movements occurring during our surprise procedures. Our coding categories were: (a) head/gaze – UP45 (i.e., head and/or gaze direction shifts upward from its initial position by at least 45 degrees), (b) head/gaze – control (i.e., head and/or gaze direction shifts horizontally or shifts upward but by less than 10 degrees), and (c) other head/gaze movements (e.g., downward movements or upward shifts of less than 45 degrees but more than 9 degrees). Because head and gaze movements for the Japanese babies have not yet been coded, our data analyses include only the American and Chinese infants whose faces were visible (not facing away from the camera or obscured by their hands) during some part of the coding interval. This produced a sample size of 24 American infants and 23 Chinese infants for the vanishing object procedure, and 24 American infants and 16 Chinese infants for the toy switch procedure.

We identified surprise expressions based on the criteria found in FAC-SAID (the FACS-based database for emotion interpretations) and AFFEX (Izard and colleagues' emotion-oriented coding system for infants). Only four infants showed a facial configuration identified with certainty as "surprise" by FACSAID. These configurations involved raised brows (AU 1+2), eyes widened via raising of the upper eyelid (AU 5), and moderately to widely open mouth (AU 26b/27). However, substantially more infants (n = 46; 53%) produced a facial configuration identified as "hypothesized" or "questionable" surprise by FACSAID. This expression involved raised brows and moderately open mouth but did not include a codeable raising of the eyelid. Instead, the eyes were slightly widened by the pulling of the skin below the brows, or the lids were lifted only to a "trace" level, that is, not enough to be coded with certainty. Nonetheless, based on the movements of the brows and mouth, this facial configuration would be codeable as "surprise" by the AFFEX system. Herein, I will refer to this facial configuration as the BROM (brow raise open mouth) configuration.

We compared the number of infants who produced the BROM configuration during baseline versus stimulus episodes for each procedure. Surprisingly, almost as many infants showed the configuration during baseline as during stimulus episodes (40 percent during baseline and 49 percent during stimulus for vanishing object; 28 percent for baseline and 33 percent for stimulus for toy switch; see Table 4.1). Chi-square analyses failed to show that more infants produced the BROM configuration during stimulus than during baseline episodes for all infants combined into a single group or for

Table 4.1. *Percent of infants producing BROM configurations in baseline and stimulus episodes*

		Episode	
Procedure	Culture	Baseline	Stimulus
Vanishing object	American (*N* = 24)	37.5	45.8
	Chinese (*N* = 23)	43.5	52.2
Toy switch	American (*N* = 24)	37.5	37.5
	Chinese (*N* = 16)	12.5	25.0

Note: N = number of infants

the American and Chinese infants examined separately. These results suggested that the BROM configurations were not selectively produced when the infants were presumably experiencing the emotion of surprise during the particular experimental procedures we examined.

Based on our earlier research on relationships among brow, head, and gaze lifting, we hypothesized that if BROM configurations were not serving as surprise expressions during our procedures, they might instead be selectively related to the infants' raising of their head and gaze. To assess this possibility in a preliminary fashion, we conducted several analyses. In these analyses, we treated individual instances of facial, head, and gaze movements as independent scores, irrespective of which or how many movements came from each individual infant. This decision was made in order to generate a larger sample size. Consequently, the results of these analyses must be viewed with some caution, although we believe that they have produced an interesting pattern of results that can be pursued more rigorously in future studies.

For the first analysis, we identified all BROM configurations in each of our two procedures as well as all facial configurations that did not involve brow raising (no-brow-raise configurations; henceforth NBRO configurations). For each configuration, we examined the infant's accompanying head and gaze direction (see Table 4.2). Combining across infants from both cultures and across the baseline and stimulus procedures, we conducted chi-square analyses comparing the distribution of BROM versus NBRO configurations across two categories of head/gaze movements: HG–UP45 and HG–control. Results showed that BROM configurations were more likely to be accompanied by HG–UP45 than were NBRO configurations, $\chi^2 = 5.95$, $df = 1$, $p < .02$, for the vanishing object procedure, and $\chi^2 = 6.38$, $df = 1$, $p < .02$ in the toy switch procedure. We also conducted follow-up chi-square analyses comparing American and Chinese infants' distribution of BROM configurations across the two head/gaze positions and comparing these distributions in the baseline versus stimulus episodes. No significant results were obtained in these analyses, suggesting that the relationship between BROM configurations and HG–UP45 holds for infants in both cultures and during both episodes of each procedure. These data suggested that BROM expressions (or some components thereof) may be part of a coordinative motor structure involving upward head and/or gaze movements. While BROM configurations may express the emotion of surprise in some situations, in our procedures they appeared to be components of a larger motoric ensemble that operated during both the baseline and stimulus episodes.

Table 4.2. *Number of BROM, BRO, and NBRO configurations accompanied by head/gaze up or control position*

			Facial configuration and head/gaze position					
Procedure	Episode	Culture	BROM HG–UP45	BROM HG–CON	BRO HG–UP45	BRO HG–CON	NBRO HG–UP45	NBRO HG–CON
Vanishing object	Baseline	American	1	5	4	11	6	36
		Chinese	6	12	4	18	3	37
		Total	7	17	8	29	9	73
	Stimulus	American	9	4	12	6	15	24
		Chinese	6	9	15	1	11	18
		Total	15	13	27	7	26	42
Toy switch	Baseline	American	4	6	17	0	8	27
		Chinese	1	0	14	4	6	17
		Total	5	6	31	4	14	44
	Stimulus	American	6	4	13	6	15	35
		Chinese	3	1	5	6	1	12
		Total	9	5	18	12	16	47

Note: BROM = Brow raised + open mouth configuration (AU26B/27)

BRO = Brow raised + other = raised brow ± any facial actions other than open mouth

NBRO = No brow raised + other configuration = any facial configuration without raised brows

HG–UP45 = Head and/or gaze raised at least 45°

HG–CON = Head and/or gaze control position (10° or less above horizontal)

In addition to examining the surprise-related BROM configuration, the present study afforded the opportunity of replicating previous findings (Michel et al., 1992) regarding the relationship between the raised brows action itself and raised head and/or gaze. To do so, we began by identifying all brow raise (BR) configurations. These included both BROM configurations and BR configurations (defined as configurations involving brow raise that were not BROM configurations). Conducting analyses similar to those already described, we found that BR configurations were accompanied more often by HG–UP45 than were NBRO configurations, $\chi^2 = 14.99$, *df* = 1, *p* < .001 for the vanishing object procedure, and $\chi^2 = 35.21$, *df* = 1, *p* < .001 for the toy switch procedure. Again, we conducted follow-up chi square analyses comparing American and Chinese infants' distribution of BR configurations across the two head/gaze positions and comparing these distributions in the baseline versus stimulus episodes. For the vanishing object procedure, results indicated that BR configurations occur with HG–UP45 more often in the stimulus episode than in the baseline episode. Informal inspection of the videotapes showed that at the onset of the baseline coding interval for this procedure, infants often were already looking intently at the visible barking dog with raised brows and unmoving level head/gaze. Thus their BR configurations may have resulted from previous encoded HG–UP45 movements or may be related to some other factor (see further discussion to follow). Overall, however, the analyses replicated the results of Michel and colleagues (1992), who also found a relationship between raised brows and raised head/gaze occurring during a (nonsurprising) toy presentation procedure.

In interpreting their findings, Michel and colleagues (1992) proposed a recruitment hypothesis, suggesting that the instrumental actions of lifting head and gaze recruited the accompanying brow raise movement. To assess this possibility more directly in our study, we conducted additional chi square analyses in which we began by identifying the onset of all HG–UP45 and all HG–control movements. We then determined whether each head/gaze movement was accompanied by or followed (within .5 second) by the onset of a BR configuration. Head/gaze movements occurring when the brows were already raised were eliminated from the data analysis. Results showed that HG–UP45 was accompanied (or followed) by raised brow significantly more often than were HG–control movements, $\chi^2 = 14.67$, *df* = 1, *p* < .001 for vanishing object, $\chi^2 = 84.54$, *df* = 1, *p* < .001 for toy switch. Follow-up analyses failed to show differences between the American and Chinese infants or between the baseline and stimulus episodes for either of the two procedures. The results provide stronger evidence supporting the hypothesis that brow raises can be recruited by raising the head and/or gaze and are part of a coordinative motor structure.

We also conducted similar analyses in which we looked only at the BROM configurations to determine whether HG–UP45 recruited these specific surprise-related configurations more often than did the HG–control movements. Significant results were not obtained for the vanishing object procedure. However, in the toy switch procedure, HG–UP45 was accompanied or followed by BROM configurations significantly more than HG–control movements, $\chi^2 = 13.05$, $df = 1$, $p < .001$. Thus there was some weak evidence that head/gaze raises selectively recruited BROM configurations, but only in the toy switch procedures. This further suggests that BROM configurations may sometimes be produced by causal factors other than the emotion of surprise.

Discussion

The results of these analyses revealed statistically significant associations between BROM and BR configurations and HG–UP45 movements in infants. Both facial configurations were accompanied by HG–UP45 movements more often than by HG-control movements. Conversely, HG–UP45 movements were accompanied or followed by brow raise configurations more often than were HG–control movements. In addition, HG–UP45 movements were accompanied or followed by BROM configurations more often than were HG–control movements in the toy switch procedure, but this did not occur statistically more often in the vanishing object procedure. How strongly do these data suggest that raised brows, head, and gaze are components of a coordinative motor structure in which upward movement of the head and/or gaze will tend to recruit brow raising and/or BROM expressions?

Brow Raise Configurations

Despite their tendency to co-occur with HG–UP45, data inspection (see Table 4.2) showed that many BR expressions were produced with HG–control and that many HG–UP45 movements were produced without recruiting (i.e., being accompanied or followed by) BR expressions. However, the fact that these movements did not *always* co-occur does not itself disprove the coordinative motor structure hypothesis. According to a dynamical systems perspective, components of a coordinative motor structure do not always operate in unison. Individual motor actions are multifunctional, available for a variety of tasks. Furthermore, the operation of a CMS depends upon a variety of factors, including the initial state of the organism and the values of other "control" parameters.

Viewed conservatively, our data suggest that further investigation is required to confirm the hypothesis that upward movements of the head, gaze, and brows constitute a coordinative motor structure in which raising the head and/or gaze may recruit brow lifting. Such investigations might involve procedures similar to those employed in studies of nonfacial coordinative structures (see Kelso, 1995). In investigations of this type, candidate control parameters are varied experimentally in order to determine whether a phase shift (i.e., an abrupt switch from one coordinative pattern to another) occurs when a parameter assumes some critical value.

In the present study, initial position of the head/gaze and speed of upward head/gaze movement might be proposed as control parameters. Regarding initial head/gaze position, we observed that this variable tended to differ across the two procedures, with the infant initially looking down at the object during toy switch and across at the display apparatus during vanishing object. Correspondingly, 82% of HG–UP45 movements were accompanied or followed by brow raises in the toy switch procedure, while 41% of the HG–UP45 movements were accompanied or followed by brow raises in the vanishing object procedure. Possibly the difference in initial head/gaze position produced the stronger recruitment of brow raising by HG–UP45 in the toy switch procedure. Velocity of head/gaze lifting may also have differed between the procedures and may be related to the recruitment of brow raising. In several studies of nonfacial movements (summarized in Kelso, 1995), movement velocity has been found to be an important control parameter underlying phase shifting. Further investigation is necessary to determine if movement velocity is a control variable determining whether HG–UP45 recruits brow raising. This might be achieved by experimentally inducing head/gaze movements of different speeds (e.g., in the context of a visual "following" task) and determining whether brow raising begins to occur when movement velocity reaches a particular value. Further tests might also examine other dynamical systems characteristics such as the changing effects of perturbing the system (e.g., gently touching the forehead) as the control parameter approaches its critical value.

While the discussion thus far has focused on possible factors determining whether brow raising is recruited by HG–UP45, we must also consider instances in which brow raising may occur with HG–control movements. Brow raising occurred with 12% of HG–control movements in the vanishing object condition and 3% of the control movements in the toy switch condition. Although these figures are low, they suggest that brow raises are sometimes produced by factors other than the coordinative motor structures we have identified. This possibility is again consistent with a dynamical systems interpretation of facial behavior positing that individual facial actions are available for recruitment by a variety of structures in a task-specific manner.

BROM Configurations

Regarding the surprise-related BROM configurations, when these occurred, the infant's head tended to be in the HG–UP45 position significantly more often than when other (NBR) expressions occurred. However, BROM expressions occurred relatively infrequently following HG–UP45 (11% of the time in the vanishing object and 16% in the toy switch procedures, respectively). Finally, in the vanishing object procedure, BROM expressions were not produced significantly more often after HG–UP45 than after HG–control movements.

Overall, these data do not strongly suggest that BROM expressions themselves are recruited by raising the head and/or gaze. More likely, when HG–UP45 movements recruit brow raising, the infant's mouth may sometimes open for other reasons. In the toy switch procedure, mouth opening and BROM configurations may occur as the infant brings the toy to his or her mouth for oral exploration (as was found by Camras et al., 1996). In the vanishing object procedure, mouth opening may occur as the jaw is relaxed while the infant sustains attention to the stimulus. This proposal is similar to one presented by Darwin (1872/1998) in his discussion of surprise and astonishment. However, it might also be used to account for the occurrence of BROM configurations in the nonsurprise baseline episodes of our procedures.

BROM Configurations as Surprise Expressions

Earlier in the chapter, I rejected the possibility that BROM configurations are invariably expressions of the emotion of surprise because they occurred equally often in the nonsurprise baseline and surprise-inducing stimulus episodes. However, possibly BROM configurations are *sometimes* produced when the infant is surprised, and in these cases the emotion itself is the underlying causal factor. If BROM configurations sometimes express surprise and sometimes do not, how would an observer be able to use these facial configurations to read emotion?

One possibility is that our codeable BROM configurations differ in some crucial way depending upon whether or not they are expressions of surprise. This line of argument is similar to Frank, Ekman, and Friesen's (1993; Frank, 1997) proposal that genuine and nongenuine smiling may differ in their temporal profiles (e.g., smoothness of onset, duration of apex). Although the BROM configurations did not vary in terms of their action-unit components, possibly these configurations varied in some dynamic feature (e.g., intensity of mouth opening, speed of facial action onset) depending upon whether they reflected surprise or merely the operation of a coordinative motor structure (cf. Scherer, this volume). We are currently attempting to examine this possibility by comparing dynamic features of BROM configurations occurring in the nonsurprise baseline episodes to those occurring in the surprise-producing stimulus episodes.

A second possibility is that surprise and nonsurprise BROM configurations are identical morphologically and can be distinguished only by their context of occurrence. For example, BROM configurations occurring in a context where surprise is plausible will be interpreted as expressing surprise, while BROM configurations occurring when surprise is not plausible will be discounted or attributed to something other than genuine emotion. Theories of social cognition (e.g., Kelly, 1973) propose that such discounting processes routinely take place when observers attempt to make causal attributions regarding other persons' behavior. Such processes are also implicated in attempts to explain children's and adults' understanding of display-rule-dictated facial behavior. From a dynamical systems perspective, identical facial configurations might sometimes be expected to flow from different causal bases because (as indicated earlier) motoric actions may be recruited for a variety of purposes. Furthermore, this need not interfere with accurate emotion perception on the part of the observer. Within a dynamical systems framework, perception itself is viewed as a "synergetic pattern forming process" (Kelso, 1995, p. 187) in which observers will "sort a continuously changing signal into an appropriate category, whether it be of objects, emotions, or events" (Kelso, 1995, p. 201).

A third possibility is that none of our codeable BROM configurations are legitimate expressions of emotion and that this is why their frequency of occurrence did not differ in the baseline and stimulus episodes. As indicated above, according to FACSAID, the status of this configuration is questionable, that is, the BROM configuration has not been strongly confirmed as a surprise expression in adult recognition or production studies. Future investigations may show that only facial expressions that include more distinct raising of the eyelids are genuine expressions of this emotion. However, I believe it is equally plausible that some – but not all – BROM configurations are genuine expressions of surprise and that these are not morphologically distinguishable from BROM configurations produced via other causal pathways. Although such inconsistency in their causal basis may appear to threaten the ability of these configurations to serve as effective communication signals, as I have indicated previously, this need not be the case. According to a dynamical systems perspective, emotion communication should involve a process of pattern formation in terms of perception as well as expression production. Thus observers read emotion from the entire pattern of received information rather than from the presence of any one component.

Conclusion

In this chapter, I have described three phenomena of infant facial expression that are difficult to accommodate within theories that assume an invariant concordance between discrete emotions and specific infant facial expressions. As an alternative, I proposed that infant facial expressions may be viewed as patterned activities available for recruitment by either emotional or nonemotional dynamic behavioral systems. This alternative perspective differs importantly from other critiques recently launched against traditional discrete emotion theories. Such critiques (e.g., Fridlund, 1994; Ortony and Turner, 1990; Russell, 1997) attempt to dethrone discrete emotions as the causal basis for human facial expressions but replace discrete emotions with other unitary causal systems (e.g., social motives or emotional dimensions). That is, they still propose an invariant concordance between facial expressions (or facial expression components) and some underlying state, thus merely substituting one type of unitary controlling agent for another. Furthermore, these componential models fail to consider self-organizing anatomical synergies as an important factor determining the assemblage of facial components into both emotional and nonemotional facial configurations. Adopting a dynamical systems perspective, by contrast, allows us to retain the idea that facial behavior may express discrete emotions but to view these emotions as a "softly assembled" dynamic system in which no one component is required. According to the dynamical systems approach, facial expression may serve many masters, both affective and nonaffective, but this in no way jeopardizes our capacity to engage in effective interpersonal emotion communication.

Acknowledgments

Data reported in this chapter were obtained from a collaborative project (with J. Campos, H. Oster, K. Miyake, T. Ujiie, Z. Meng, and L. Wang) supported by National Institute of Mental Health Grant MH-47543. I thank the mothers and infants who participated in this study. I also wish to express particular appreciation to Amy Calla-Murdoch and Sawako Suzuki for their devoted coding of the infants' facial, head, and gaze movements.

References

Abraham, R., and Shaw, C. (1982). *Dynamics: The geometry of behavior*. Santa Cruz, CA: Aerial Press.

Andrew, R. J. (1963). The origins and evolution of the calls and facial expressions of the primates. *Behavior, 20*, 1–109.

Baillargeon, R. (1986). Representing the existence and the location of hidden objects: Object permanence in 6- and 8-month-old infants. *Cognition, 23*, 21–41.

Barrett, K., and Campos, J. (1987). Perspectives on emotional development: II. A functionalist approach to emotions. In J. Osofsky (Ed.), *Handbook of infant development* (2nd ed., pp. 555–578). New York: Wiley.

Bernstein, N. (1967). *Coordination and regulation of movements*. New York: Pergamon.

Buck, R. (1988). *Human motivation and emotion* (2nd ed.). New York: Wiley.

Camras, L. A. (1991). Conceptualizing early infant affect: View II and reply. In K. Strongman (Ed.), *International review of studies on emotion* (pp. 16–28, 33–36). New York: Wiley.

Camras, L. A. (1992). Expressive development and basic emotions. *Cognition and Emotion, 6*, 269–284.

Camras, L. A., Lambrecht, L., and Michel, G. (1996). Infant "surprise" expressions as coordinative motor structures. *Journal of Nonverbal Behavior, 20*, 183–195.

Camras, L. A, Oster, H., Campos, J., Campos, R., Ujiie, T., Miyake, K., Lei, W., and Meng, Z. (1998). Production of emotional facial expressions in American, Japanese and Chinese infants. *Developmental Psychology, 34*, 616–628.

Darwin, C. (1998). *The expression of the emotions in man and animals* (reprinted with introduction, afterword, and commentary by P. Ekman). New York: Oxford University Press. (Original work published 1872.)

Ekman, P. (1972). Universals and cultural differences in facial expressions of emotion. In J. Cole (Ed.), *Nebraska Symposium on Motivation: Vol. 19. Current theory and research in motivation* (pp. 207–283). Lincoln: University of Nebraska Press.

Ekman, P. (1979). About brows: Emotional and conversational signals. In M. von Cranach, K. Foppa, W. Lepenies, and D. Ploog (Eds.), *Human ethology* (pp. 169–248). Cambridge: Cambridge University Press.

Ekman, P. (1992). An argument for basic emotions. *Cognition and Emotion, 6,* 169–200.

Ekman, P., and Friesen, W. V. (1969). The repertoire of nonverbal behavior: Categories, origins, usage, and coding. *Semiotica, 1,* 49–98.

Ekman, P., and Friesen, W. V. (1978). *The facial action coding system.* Palo Alto, CA: Consulting Psychologists Press.

Ekman, P., Hager, J., Irwin, W., and Rosenberg, E. (1998). *FACSAID: Facial Action Coding System Affect Information Database* [on-line]. Available: http://nirc.com (by subscription).

Fogel, A. (1985). Coordinative structures in the development of expressive behavior in early infancy. In G. Zivin (Ed.), *The development of expressive behavior* (pp. 249–267). New York: Academic Press.

Fogel, A., Nwokah, E., Dedo, J., Messinger, D., Dickson, K., Matusov, E., and Holt, S. (1992). Social process theory of emotion: A dynamic systems approach. *Social Development, 1,* 122–142.

Fogel, A., and Thelen, E. (1987). The development of early expressive and communicative action. *Developmental Psychology, 23,* 747–761.

Frank, M. (1997). Some thoughts on FACS, dynamic markers of emotion and baseball. In P. Ekman and E. Rosenberg (Eds.), *What the face reveals* (pp. 239–242). New York: Oxford University Press.

Frank, M., Ekman, P., and Friesen, W. (1993). Behavioral markers and recognizability of the smile of enjoyment. *Journal of Personality and Social Psychology, 64,* 83–93.

Fridlund, A. (1994). *Human facial expression: An evolutionary view.* New York: Academic Press.

Frijda, N. (1986). *The emotions.* Cambridge: Cambridge University Press.

Hiatt, S., Campos, J., and Emde, R. (1979). Facial patterning and infant emotional expression: Happiness, surprise, and fear. *Child Development, 50,* 1020–1035.

Izard, C. (1971). *The face of emotion.* New York: Appleton-Century-Crofts.

Izard, C. (1977). *Human emotions.* New York: Plenum.

Izard, C. (1991). *The psychology of emotions.* New York: Plenum.

Izard, C. (1997). Emotions and facial expressions: A perspective from differential emotions theory. In J. Russell and J. M. Fernandez-Dols (Eds.), *The psychology of facial expression* (pp. 57–77). Cambridge: Cambridge University Press.

Izard, C., Dougherty, L., and Hembree, E. (1983). *A system for identifying affect expressions by holistic judgments (AFFEX).* Newark, DE: Instructional Resources Center, University of Delaware.

Izard, C., Fantauzzo, C., Castle, J., Haynes, M., Rayias, M., and Putnam, P. (1995). The ontogeny and significance of infants' facial expressions in the first 9 months of life. *Developmental Psychology, 31,* 997–1015.

Izard, C., and Malatesta, C. (1987). Perspectives on emotional development: I. Differential emotions theory of early emotional development. In J. D. Osofsky (Ed.), *Handbook of infant development* (pp. 494–554). New York: Wiley.

Kelly, H. (1973). The process of causal attribution. *American Psychologist, 28*, 107–128.

Kelso, J. (1981). Contrasting perspectives on order and regulation. In J. Long and A. Baddeley (Eds.), *Attention and performance* (vol. 9, pp. 437–457). Hillsdale, NJ: Erlbaum.

Kelso, J. (1995). *Dynamic patterns.* Cambridge, MA: MIT Press.

Kelso, J., and Scholz, J. (1986). Cooperative phenomenon in biological motion. In H. Haken (Ed.), *Synergetics of complex systems in physics, chemistry, and biology* (pp. 124–149). New York: Springer-Verlag.

Kugler, P., Kelso, J., and Turvey, M. (1980). On the concept of coordinative structures as dissipative structures: I. Theoretical line. In G. Stelmach and J. Requin (Eds.), *Tutorials in motor behavior* (pp. 3–48). Amsterdam: North-Holland.

Kugler, P., Kelso, J., and Turvey, M. (1982). On the control and co-ordination of naturally developing systems. In J. Kelso and J. Clark (Eds.), *The development of movement control and coordination* (pp. 5–78). New York: Wiley.

Lewis, M., and Michalson, L. (1983). *Children's emotions and moods.* New York: Plenum.

Marler, P., and Evans, C. (1997). Animal sounds and human faces: Do they have anything in common? In J. Russell and J. M. Fernandez-Dols (Eds.), *The psychology of facial expression* (pp. 133–157). Cambridge: Cambridge University Press.

Matias, R., and Cohn, J. (1993). Are MAX-specified infant facial expressions during face-to-face interaction consistent with differential emotions theory? *Developmental Psychology, 29*, 524–531.

Messinger, D., Fogel, A., and Dickson, K. (1997). A dynamic systems approach to infant facial action. In J. Russell and J. M. Fernandez-Dols (Eds.), *The psychology of facial expression* (pp. 205–226). Cambridge: Cambridge University Press.

Michel, G. (1991). Development of infant manual skills: Motor programs, schemata or dynamic systems? In J. Fagard & P. Wolff (Eds), *The development of timing control and temporal organization in coordinated action* (pp. 175–199). New York: Elsevier.

Michel, G., Camras, L., and Sullivan, J. (1992). Infant interest expressions as coordinative motor structures. *Infant Behavior and Development, 15*, 347–358.

Ortony, A., and Turner, T. (1990). What's basic about basic emotions? *Psychological Review, 97*, 315–331.

Oster, H., Hegley, D., and Nagel, L. (1992). Adult judgements and fine-grained analysis of infant facial expressions. *Developmental Psychology, 28*, 1115–1131.

Oster, H., and Rosenstein, D. (1995). *Baby FACS: Analyzing facial movement in infants.* Unpublished manuscript.

Oyama, S. (1989). Ontogeny and the control dogma: Do we need the concept of genetic programming in order to have an evolutionary perspective? In M. R. Gunnar and E. Thelen (Eds.), *Minnesota Symposium on Child Psychology: Vol. 22. Systems and development* (pp. 1–34). Hillsdale, NJ: Erlbaum.

Peiper, A. (1963). *Cerebral function in infancy and childhood* (B. Nagler and H. Nagler, trans.). New York: Consultants Bureau. (Original work published 1963.)

Plutchik, R. (1980). *Emotion: A psychoevolutionary synthesis.* New York: Harper and Row.

Russell, J. (1997). Reading emotions from and into faces: Resurrecting a dimensional-contextual approach. In J. Russell and J. M. Fernandez-Dols (Eds.), *The psychology of facial expression* (pp. 295–320). Cambridge: Cambridge University Press.

Schoner, G., and Kelso, J. (1988). Dynamic pattern generation in behavioral and neural systems. *Science, 239*, 1513–1520.

Sroufe, L. A. (1996). *Emotional development.* Cambridge: Cambridge University Press.

Thelen, E. (1989a). Conceptualizing development from a dynamical systems perspective. In B. Bertenthal, A. Fogel, L. Smith, and E. Thelen (chairs), *Dynamical systems in development.* Preconference workshop conducted at the meeting of the Society for Research in Child Development, Kansas City, MO, April.

Thelen, E. (1989b). Self-organization in developmental processes: Can systems approaches work? In M. R. Gunnar and E. Thelen (Eds.), *Minnesota Symposium on Child Psychology: Vol. 22. Systems and development* (pp. 77–118). Hillsdale, NJ: Erlbaum.

Tinbergen, N. (1952). Derived activities: Their causation, biological significance, origin, and emancipation during evolution. *Quarterly Review of Biology, 27*, 1–32.

Tomkins, S. S. (1982). Affect theory. In P. Ekman (Ed.), *Emotion in the human face* (2nd ed., pp. 353–395). Cambridge: Cambridge University Press.

Turvey, M. (1990). Coordination. *American Psychologist, 45*, 938–953.

Vallacher, R., and Nowak, A. (Eds.). (1994). *Dynamical systems in social psychology.* New York: Academic Press.

5 The Dynamic Construction of Emotion: Varieties in Anger

Michael F. Mascolo, Debra Harkins,
and Thomas Harakal

Within psychology and other disciplines, discussions of emotion have traditionally drawn upon a series of dualisms. Theorists and researchers debate the extent to which emotions are best understood as universal or context-dependent, innate or acquired, dependent or independent of cognition, and so on. Current systems approaches in the social and physical sciences provide innovative frameworks that may enable theorists to break out of such polarizing dichotomies (Barton, 1994; Fischer and Bidell, 1998; Fogel, Lyra, and Valsiner, 1997; Fogel and Thelen, 1987; M. D. Lewis, 1996; Thelen and Smith, 1994; van Geert, 1994). In what follows, we outline a component systems approach to emotional development (Mascolo and Harkins, 1998; Mascolo, Pollack, and Fischer, 1997). At its most basic level, a component systems view holds that although individuals are composed of multiple distinct subsystems (e.g., affective, cognitive, overt action), component systems necessarily modulate each other in the production of emotional action and experience. An analysis of how component systems coregulate each other within social contexts can reveal both striking order and emergent variability in the production of emotional states.

Contemporary Approaches to Emotion

In recent decades, models that depict basic emotions as discrete and innate neuromuscular responses have been highly influential (Ekman, 1984; Izard, 1977, 1991; Tomkins, 1962). In their *differential emotions theory*, Izard and Malatesta (1987) define emotions as "a particular set of neural processes that lead to a specific expression and a corresponding specific feeling" (p. 496). As such, emotions consist of discrete states that are distinct from other psychological processes (e.g., cognition and instrumental action). Izard and his colleagues have proposed ten discrete emotions,

125

each with a distinct neurophysiological state that organizes cognition and action. These include interest-excitement, enjoyment-joy, startle-surprise, distress-anguish, rage-anger, disgust-revulsion, contempt-scorn, fear-terror, shame-shyness-humiliation, and guilt-remorse (Izard, 1991; Izard and Malatesta, 1987). Researchers have reported evidence suggesting that emotions emerge according to a genetic timetable and show stability across ontogenesis and culture (Ackerman, Abe, and Izard, 1998; Ekman and Friesen, 1971; Izard and Malatesta, 1987).

Whereas discrete emotion theorists define emotions in terms of encapsulated neurophysiological states, others define emotion more broadly. *Appraisal theorists* maintain that different emotional reactions rely upon different ways of interpreting relations between events and one's goals, motives, and concerns (Frijda, 1986; Lazarus, 1991; Roseman, Spindel, and Jose, 1990; Scherer, 1994; Smith and Ellsworth, 1985). Researchers have reported evidence demonstrating that patterned assessment of events along a variety of different dimensions of event appraisal is systematically related to reports of different emotional experiences. Similarly, *functionalist theorists* suggest that emotions consist of organized configurations of multiple processes (e.g., physiological, experiential, appraisal, internal reaction, motivational, overt action, expressive, and social display) that serve adaptive functions relative to personally significant events (Barrett, 1998; Barrett and Campos, 1987; Frijda and Mesquita, 1998). According to this view, particular emotional states are defined in terms of how individuals respond to significant events. As such, there are as many different emotional experiences as there are ways of adapting to events, and no single process provides an essential condition for the attribution of emotion (Barrett and Campos, 1987). As the capacity to appreciate the significance of some events is pre-wired, emotions can be observed in early infancy; as such capacities grow, new ways of experiencing emotion arise.

Social constructionist (Gergen, 1985; Harré and Gillett, 1994) and *sociocultural theorists* (Lutz, 1988; Shweder, 1994) warn that it is inappropriate to assume that the events we call emotions refer to real or bounded entities. Social constructionists argue that it is important to understand that the term *emotion* represents a socially constructed *concept*. The meaning of this concept cannot be seen as a simple reflection of inner experience. Like all events, inner experience must be understood in terms of existing category systems, which themselves are products of the ways in which communities use language to solve human problems. As such, word meanings are derived from social relations and cannot be seen to reflect the essential nature of their assumed referents (Gergen, 1985). Thus, social constructionist scholars analyze the meanings and uses of emotion words within different communities (Harré and Gillett, 1994; Lutz, 1988; Shweder, 1994). In so doing, they argue that emotional experiences are products of locally created interpretive systems. For example, Harré and Finlay-Jones (1986) note that the medieval emotion of *accidie*, which refers to a sense of boredom or dejection in fulfilling religious duty, was founded in social rules about the need to perform religious duties with joy rather than indolence. As an obsolete emotion, *accidie* illustrates how emotions can be founded upon judgments shaped by sociohistorical and moral circumstances.

These approaches to emotion differ in the extent to which they view emotions as basic or derived, innate or constructed, and whether affect or cognition is primary in the determination of emotional states. In an attempt to transcend these polarizing dichotomies, we offer a component systems approach to emotion. From this perspective, emotional experiences consist of the coordination of multiple component systems and processes (e.g., appraisal-affect-action ensembles). Although component systems are *distinct* from one another, they mutually regulate each other and are thus *inseparable* as causal processes in the formation of any given experience. The idea that component systems can be distinct but not independent can provide a framework for constructing an integrative model of emotional development.

A Component Systems Approach to Emotional Development

A component systems approach to emotional development (Mascolo and Fischer, 1998; Mascolo and Harkins, 1998; Mascolo, Pollack, and Fischer, 1997) proceeds from four basic assertions. The first is that emotional states and experiences are composed of *multiple component processes* (Scherer, 1994). Second, emotional experiences emerge through the *mutual regulation* (Fischer and Bidell, 1998; Fogel, 1993; M. D. Lewis, 1996) of component systems over time and within particular social contexts. Third, component systems are *context-sensitive*, meaning they not only adjust themselves to each other but also to continuous changes in social context. As such, emotional experiences *self-organize* (Fogel, 1993; M. D. Lewis, 1996) into a series of more or less stable patterns or *attractors* that yield a large number of minor variations (Camras, 1992).

Components of Emotional States and Experiences

The first assertion of a component systems view is that emotional episodes are composed of multiple component processes. This is an assumption that is common to functionalist (Barrett, 1998; Campos, 1994; Frijda and Mesquita, 1998) and social process (Dickson, Fogel, and Messinger, 1998; Fogel et al., 1992) approaches to emotion. Figure 5.1 depicts a hierarchical representation of a series of partially distinct systems that contribute to the production of emotional experiences. One important component is *appraisal*. Appraisals refer to assessments of relations between perceived events and one's goals, motives, and concerns (Frijda, 1986; Lazarus, 1991). Appraisals themselves arise from coordinations among partially distinct sensory-perceptual, cognitive-representational, and motivational systems. Assessments that events are consistent with one's motives and goals contribute to the experience of positively valenced emotional reactions; assessments that events are motive-inconsistent accompany negatively valenced reactions. Distinctions among experiences can be attributed in part to textured differences in event appraisals (Roseman, Spindel, and Jose, 1990).

Emotional episodes also involve changes in the central nervous system (CNS), autonomic nervous system (ANS), and other *affective systems* that contribute to the *feeling tone* (Kagan, 1978; LeDoux, 1994; Levenson, 1994) of a given experience. Event appraisals and affect influence the production of different types of *motive-action tendencies*, which include the propensity to want something and to do something in the service of changes in significant events. Action tendencies themselves are composed of a series of interlocking systems, including both voluntary and involuntary overt action systems (e.g., facial and vocal activity). Coordinated feedback from all classes of systems (appraisal, affective, action systems, etc.) together provide the broad experience of emotion.

A component systems approach differentiates between the concepts of *emotional state* and *emotional experience* (M. Lewis, 1998). An emotional *state* refers to the specific patterning of all component systems (appraisal, affective, action, etc.) as they mutually regulate each other in the context of notable changes in one's environment. An emotional *experience* refers to the phenomenal aspects of an emotional state. For example, an experience of *anger* among Western adults often involves appraisals that an accountable other has violated conditions that one asserts ought to exist (de Rivera, 1981; Fischer, Shaver, and Carnochan, 1990). Such appraisals may be accompanied by patterned bodily changes, including CNS and ANS activity, which produces fluctuating heart rate, perspiration, and bodily temperature (Barrett and Campos, 1987; Ekman, Levenson, and Friesen, 1983). The phenomenal experience of anger often involves angry feeling tone as well as experiences of "heat," "pressure," or "tension." Persons

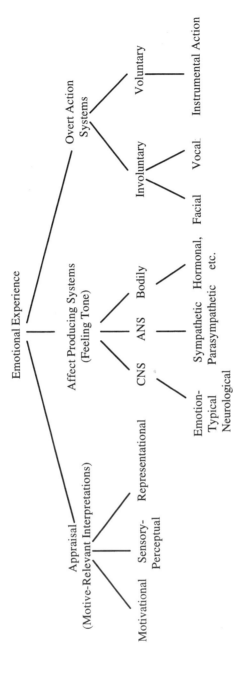

Figure 5.1. A hierarchy of emotion-related component systems.

often experience a strengthening of will that supports one's motive-action tendency to remove the conditions judged as contrary to what should exist (de Rivera, 1981; Shaver et al., 1987).

The Mutual Regulation of Component Emotion Systems

A second principle is that component systems *mutually regulate* each other within a social context (Fogel, 1993; M. D. Lewis, 1995, 1996; M. D. Lewis and Douglas, 1998; Mascolo and Harkins, 1998). The concept of mutual regulation implies that although the emotion components have integrity as *distinct* systems, individual systems are *not independent* or autonomous. Mutual regulation refers to the processes by which component systems adjust themselves to each other's ongoing (and anticipated) outputs and activities (Fogel, 1993). We use the concept of mutual regulation broadly to refer to both positive and negative feedback processes. Through mutual regulation, component systems and processes jointly organize, modulate, and otherwise influence each other. Thus, when component systems mutually regulate each other, they become part of the very process of each other's functioning.

To illustrate the concept of mutual regulation in emotional processes, consider the relations between appraisal, affective, and overt action systems (see Figure 5.2, top panel). At any given time, appraisal processes monitor a multiplicity of different classes of event-related inputs in parallel. This includes nonconscious monitoring of the relation between all classes of sensory changes and a person's goals and motives. Throughout activity, motive-relevant appraisals continuously modulate ongoing affect-producing systems (CNS, ANS, and other bodily processes). Simultaneously, affective feeling tone provides continuous feedback to appraisal (and action) systems. In so doing, affect functions to *amplify and select for conscious awareness and further action the very appraisals that helped initiate the affective reactions in the first place* (Brown, 1994; Brown and Kozak, 1998; M. D. Lewis, 1996; Mascolo and Harkins, 1998). As appraisals are selected, they continue to evolve, producing further affective changes, and so forth. Neither appraisal nor affect has priority in the process, and one cannot ordinarily function without the other. Although appraisals precipitate feeling tone, feeling tone biases and organizes the construction of event appraisals from their very inception.

For example, imagine that an individual hurries from work to prepare dinner for guests. Entering a queue at the market, the desire to get home directs appraisal processes (perhaps nonconscious) to the line's progress.

Mutual Regulation Between Two Component Systems

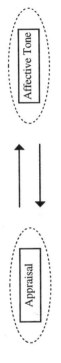

Mutual Regulation Within and Between Persons

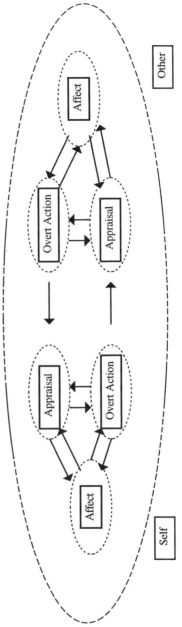

Figure 5.2. Mutual regulation among component systems.

131

As the line moves slowly, she begins to sense a delay. This appraisal modifies her affective state, which thereupon amplifies and selects this very same appraisal for conscious attention and action. Further coregulation over time results in an affectively charged appraisal that the clerk is working too slowly – an appraisal of blame to a responsible agent. Thus, in this example, the experience of anger takes on a variety of nuanced forms as it evolves continuously over time through the mutual regulation of affect and appraisal.

Of course, as represented in the bottom panel of Figure 5.2 (in either the "self" or "other" pole of the diagram), mutual regulation is not restricted to appraisal and affect, but includes systems of overt action as well. Appraisals not only modulate affect, but also activate overt actions in ways relevant to the appraised fate of one's motives; affective tone not only selects appraisal, but organizes and intensifies action as well. Over time, overt actions (including, for example, facial feedback to affective systems – see Izard, 1977; Laird, 1984) and their social effects provide continuous feedback to affective and appraisal systems, which can modulate, transform, or even terminate a given experience.

Context-Sensitivity in the Continuous Coordination of Emotion Systems

Thus far, we have discussed the coregulation of components of the emotion process as they occur within individuals. However, emotional episodes are not simply products of processes that occur within individuals. Just as component systems adjust to each other within persons, they also continuously adjust themselves to inputs and meanings that arise *between* individuals. The proposition that activity and experience are mutually regulated between individuals follows from a *continuous process* rather than a *discrete state* conception of human communication (Fogel, 1993). In discrete state communication (e.g., mail, e-mail, fax), only a single individual is active at any given time. A fixed message originates within a single individual (the sender) and is passed along a fixed communication channel; the message remains fixed until it is received, at which point a new message can be formed and sent back to the original sender. By contrast, in continuous process communication (e.g., face-to-face interaction), both partners are simultaneously active. Information and meanings are continuously modified and negotiated through the very process of communicating. As such, meanings, actions, and experiences are jointly constructed between individuals. Because both partners are simultaneously active, neither can properly be regarded as the single sender, receiver, or originator of a message. Partners *coregulate* each other as they adjust their actions to the ongoing and anticipated actions of the other (Fogel, 1993).

The coregulation of emotion-relevant systems both within and between individuals is represented in the bottom panel of Figure 5.2. In social interaction, an individual's appraisal-affect-action systems change continuously as they adjust to each other as well as to the ongoing and anticipated actions of her or his social partner(s). In face-to-face interaction, on-line changes in the facial and vocal activities of mothers have a direct influence on an infant's ongoing and subsequent emotion-related facial actions (Fogel et al., 1992; Trevarthen, 1984). Similarly, we suggest that both marked and subtle changes in one's appraisals of another's ongoing actions are accompanied by continuous modification of affective and action systems. For example, in the shopper-clerk example described previously, any one of a number or continuously evolving processes (e.g., the clerk's degree of awareness of the problem, his attention to the problem or to the shopper, his own changing affective state, or the simple passage of time) might be sufficient to prompt a transition in the particular quality of the shopper's appraisal-affect-action systems. It might be helpful to describe changes in such anger-related states using terms like *frustration, annoyance, anger, indignation*, or even *outrage*.

Self-Organization in the Dynamic Construction of Emotional Episodes

Although appraisal, affect, and action constitute distinct integral systems, they nonetheless interpenetrate each other in the formation of emotional episodes. No single component system is primary in the generation of an emotional episode, and there is no single, prescribed, or generalized sequence to the generation or constitution of any particular class of emotional episodes or experiences. Thus, *emotional episodes self-organize through the mutual regulation of component systems within a given social context*. Emotional episodes self-organize both in ontogenesis as well as in real time within particular contexts (M. D. Lewis, 1996). The concept of self-organization stipulates that there is no single plan that directs the formation of any particular emotional reaction. Different emotional episodes arise not from any particular genetic or cultural plan, but instead from differences in the specific ways in which component systems coact (Gottlieb, 1992) with each other in a given context (Fogel, 1993).

In theory, the number of particular ways that component systems can combine to produce different emotional states is extremely large. However, when component systems mutually regulate each other, they place constraints on each other's functioning. Any change in one system's function-ing reduces the degrees of freedom that other component systems have to operate (Fogel, 1993). This especially follows if we assume that emotional processes function in the service of salient motives and concerns. As such, an individual's salient concerns within a context constrain the emergent organization of any given emotional pattern. Thus, even though component systems can combine in an almost infinite number of ways, emotional processes have a tendency to settle into a finite number of stable patterns, sometimes called *attractors* (Fogel, 1993; M. D. Lewis, 1995). Such gen-eral patterns may correspond to emotional states labeled by basic emotion terms (e.g., anger, joy, sadness, love). It is also possible, even likely, that emotional processes self-organize into stable patterns that are not indexed clearly by our existing emotion lexicon.

Although emotional episodes self-organize into general attractors, within any given class of emotional attractors there are numerous minor variations in the pattern of the particular components produced. In part, this is a product of what dynamic systems theorists call *sensitive dependence on initial conditions* (Barton, 1994; Thelen, 1990). In real time, emotional reactions begin to evolve from different starting points. For any two expe-riences of, say, anger, there will be subtle differences in the initial state of appraisal-affect-action systems, as well as in the demands of the local social context. As component systems begin to coact, even small differ-ences in conditions under which different emotional experiences arise can lead to increasingly large differences in their organization.

Merits of a Component Systems Approach

Thus, from a component systems view, (a) emotional episodes consist of the coordination of appraisal, affective, and action systems as they continuously adjust themselves to each other within any given social con-text. As such, (b) emotional experiences and episodes emerge on-line and in development through the mutual regulation of embedded and component systems that exist both within and between individuals. In so doing, (c) emotional experiences self-organize into a series of stable forms (attractors) that themselves exhibit a large number of local variations in different social contexts. Thus, (d) there is no single plan for the organization of any given class of emotion, and no single component system is primary in the genesis and constitution of emotion.

A component systems view holds out the promise of offering an integra-tive approach for understanding emotion and its development. Like differential emotions theory (Ackerman, Abe, and Izard, 1998; Izard, 1991) and biologically oriented approaches (Panksepp, Knutson, and Pruitt, 1998), component systems theory maintains that it is useful to speak of distinct yet interacting affective and cognitive subsystems.[1] However, unlike these approaches, the proper unit of analysis in thinking about emotion in the component systems view is the entire emotional episode, not the activation of an encapsulated emotion system. This follows for several reasons. First, component systems theory takes seriously the idea that emotions consist of intentional states – that is, that emotions are *about* something (Solomon, 1976). I am not simply angry or proud, I am angry *that* or proud *of*. Intentionality implies that emotions are like appraisals or involve judgments as an important element of their constitution. Second, while differential emotions theory maintains that distinct affective and cognitive systems interact, they are viewed as doing so only in the sense that invariant feelings become attached to changing cognitive structures (Ackerman, Abe, and Izard, 1998). The idea of mutual regulation, however, implies that affect, appraisal, and other component systems modulate each other. Thus, affect does not simply organize appraisal, and it is possible that subtle differences in appraisal (and action) can result in changes that produce subtle differences in feeling tone and phenomenal experience for a given emotion category.

Third, unlike approaches that postulate a set of innate basic emotions, a component systems view builds on an epigenetic systems view of human development. In this view, any psychological process *emerges* in development through the *inseparable* interplay among biogenetic, organismic, and sociocultural processes (Gottlieb, 1992; Mascolo, Pollack, and Fischer, 1997). To be sure, different classes of emotional experience build on epigenetically canalized biological substrates (Panksepp et al., 1998), and biogenetic changes pave the way for emotional changes. However, biogenetic processes necessarily coact with organismic and sociocultural systems to produce such changes. As the brain grows and develops, individuals gain the capacity to construct higher-order event appraisals in a given context. As they do so, emotional experiences change in development as individuals seize cultural meanings to construct novel appraisals of their relations to their culturally created environments.

Like appraisal (Lazarus, 1991; Roseman, 1984) and functionalist approaches to emotion (Barrett, 1998; Campos, 1994; Frijda and Mesquita, 1998), a component systems view embraces the idea that emotional experiences consist of multicomponent processes. In so doing, it extends functionalist approaches by invoking the concepts of *self-organization* and *mutual regulation* to explain the processes by which emotional syndromes take shape. Further, unlike functionalist theory (Barrett, 1998), a component systems view embraces the idea that it is possible to speak of developmental transformations or levels in the organization of emotional experiences (see Sroufe, 1996).

A component systems approach also draws upon social constructionist (Lutz, 1988) and social process models (Dickson, Fogel, and Messinger, 1998; Fogel et al., 1992) of emotion. Like social process theory, a component systems approach holds that any given emotional experience arises on-line in coregulated interaction *between* people. Further, like social constructionist approaches, component process theory maintains that as children develop the capacity to appropriate cultural meanings from their social interactions, appraisals involved in emotional experiences undergo developmental change. As a result, with increased development, emotional experiences develop in the direction of culturally valued endpoints. However, unlike social constructionist approaches, from a component systems view emotional experiences cannot simply be seen as social or cultural constructions. Emotional experience emerges not only as a product of processes that occur *between* people, but also as a result of coactions that occur *within* individuals. Further, although culture is necessary for the development of higher-order emotions, cultural systems work together with epigenetically canalized biological systems to prompt changes in emotion.

Varieties in the Self-Organization of Anger

From a component systems perspective, laypersons and scientists alike use the term anger to refer to a family of emotional episodes and experiences that are defined by an idealized pattern or prototype (Russell, 1991; Shaver et al., 1987). Earlier, we described one idealized episode of the experience of anger among Western adults. However, there are many variations in the experiences that are commonly categorized as anger. The English language contains many terms referring to varieties of anger. These include terms like anger, rage, outrage, frustration, fury, annoyance, moral indignation, irritation, and so forth (Russell and Fehr, 1994). These terms not only index variations in intensity, but also in the dynamic organization of angry episodes. Despite the variability codified by these common terms, it is also likely that there are meaningful and systematic variations in anger that are not codified by such lay terms. In what follows, we examine variation in the organization of anger episodes that results from changes in social context and development.

Social Context and Variability in Anger Episodes

To illustrate how particular classes of emotional states self-organize into different attractor patterns, we examine the intersystemic origins of two attractors that we tentatively label *frustration* and *interpersonal anger.* Theorists and researchers have long debated the distinction between frustration and anger. For example, M. Lewis (1993) has used the term *frustration* to refer to a set of eliciting conditions (e.g., goal-frustration) and the term *anger* to refer to the resulting affective state. Other theorists use the terms *anger* and *frustration* to refer to different emotional states. Some theorists suggest that anger and frustration can be differentiated in terms of whether or not motive-inconsistent events are appraised as human-caused or circumstance-caused (Roseman, 1984; Roseman, Antoniou, and Jose, 1996; Roseman, Spindel, and Jose, 1990; Smith and Ellsworth, 1985).

We use the term *frustration* to refer to episodes that involve goal blockage and an appraisal that one cannot attain a still-wanted goal. Regardless of whether the event is seen as circumstance-caused or human-caused, the focus in frustration is on one's inability to obtain the wanted goal. Among the action tendencies involved in frustration, persons can become more aggressive in their pursuit of the wanted goal, a phenomenon we call *energized frustration.* By contrast, they may evince what might be called *frustrated discharge* (e.g., flailing arms accompanied by gritted teeth, growling, etc.), which consists of a discharge of emotional energy as a result of inability to attain a wanted goal. *Interpersonal anger* involves appraisals that a responsible other has acted contrary to the way one *should* act. We refer to such appraisals as *ought violations.* Interpersonal anger is directed toward another person (or personified entity) in an attempt to remove the violation of what one believes ought to exist. Each of these attractor patterns self-organize over time within a given social context.

To illustrate, we performed an in-depth analysis of a single child's emotional reactions to a variety of goal-violating situations. A thirty-nine-month-old Caucasian female toddler (Nina) of an upper-educated two-parent family from a suburban town in eastern Massachusetts was the subject of this analysis. Nina is the oldest of two girls; her sibling is an eighteen-month-old female. Nina's mother is a thirty-two-year-old psychologist, and her peer is a forty-two-month-old female cousin (Karrie) who visits on a weekly basis. Videotaped sessions took place every other week for a total of five sessions ending when Nina was forty-two months of age. All sessions took place in the participant's home. The mother was asked to prompt Nina to engage in independent activities that might pose a challenge to her, to ask Nina to engage in unenjoyable activities that generally occur in their daily routines, and to interrupt or forbid Nina from engaging in prohibited activities. In addition, the mother was asked to involve Nina in competitive tasks with her cousin Karrie (e.g., a competitive game; providing the dyad with one desirable toy for play).

A rich set of data emerged. We observed fourteen scenarios (e.g., tasks or settings) in which at least one negative emotional reaction occurred. These scenarios ranged from forty seconds to eight minutes in length for a total of forty minutes and included the following activities: abruptly ending an enjoyable activity (e.g., putting together a new, age-appropriate puzzle); forbidding an enjoyable activity (e.g., watching television); encouraging an activity that was physically challenging (e.g., riding a heavy tricycle; combining two Playdough colors into one); asking Nina to engage in an unenjoyable task (e.g., washing dishes); encouraging participation in a competitive game with a peer (e.g., playing a board game); making available one desirable toy in the presence of two children (e.g., a large stuffed Minnie Mouse doll); and sibling interference in an enjoyable task (e.g., toddler tries to grab string and beads when Nina and the peer are making ''jewelry'').

Across the various scenarios, a total of twenty-five emotional episodes occurred. Each episode was analyzed for the presence of five categories of negative emotional actions. *Facial actions* included furrowing brow (eyebrows pushed downward), frowning (chin jutting out with furrowed brow), grimacing, showing teeth, narrowing or closing of the eyes, and pursing lips (upper and lower lip pressed together). *Vocalizations* included crying/wailing (with or without tears); pouting (mild repeated vocalization with or without frown); growling/negative exclamations (sustained guttural vocalization), screaming (high-pitched voice), grunting (single exhalation of breath accompanied by single, short vocalization), sniffling (quick inhaling through nostrils), whimpering, sighing (pronounced inhalation or exhalation of breath), fretting (combination of mild crying or whining with negative tone and/or rubbing eyes), and displaying negative/angry vocal tone. *Gazing patterns* included gazing at persons (e.g., mother, peer, sibling), at object or task, and off task. *Bodily actions* included clenching fist, shaking arms (arms extended outward and moving), rubbing eyes, banging fist/hands/elbows, raising arms in air (above the torso), holding head (placing hands on head), placing hands on hips, kicking feet, and stomping feet. In addition, bodily actions included lying down on one's side/back/stomach, slumping body or shoulders, sulking, shrugging shoulders, crouching, arching body back, lurching forward, jumping up and down, and falling down. *Instrumental actions* included pushing other, hitting other, grabbing other, grabbing object, throwing object, pointing, and rocking.

A hierarchical cluster analysis was conducted to determine the degree to which one can identify patterns of negative emotional acts that tend to co-occur in this child. The resulting tree diagram is displayed in Figure 5.3. The cluster analysis produced evidence of four clusters of emotional behaviors. The first cluster, which we will refer to as *sadness/task withdrawal*, seems to group behaviors related to task withdrawal or sadness (i.e., lying down, falling down, whining, hiding eyes) with several anger-related behaviors (i.e., sulking, holding head, negative angry tone, furrowing brow, and growling). The second cluster, which we will refer to as *frustration*, is composed mainly of behaviors that reflect frustrated discharge or emotional activation following frustration (i.e., gasping, grunting, putting hands on hips, pouting, pointing, jumping up and down, fretting, throwing object, rocking, hitting object, banging fists, kicking legs, and sniffling) with some more typically anger-related behaviors (i.e., showing teeth, narrowing eyes). The third cluster, which seems to reflect what might be called *interpersonal anger*, consists of behaviors directed at others (i.e., pushing other, grabbing other) and other negative emotional reactions (e.g., moaning, screaming). The fourth cluster, which seems less interpretable, contains pulling objects, rubbing eyes, and crying.

We then examined the extent to which several categories of negative emotion components varied in mean frequency as a function of type of context. A MANOVA revealed a significant difference in the number and type of anger-related behaviors during independent, mother-child, and child-child activity, $F(10, 36) = 2.08$, $p < .05$. Hand, arm, and leg movements, $F(2, 22) = 3.02$, $p < .07$, and postural movements, $F(2, 22) = 6.40$, $p < .01$, varied as a function of the three contexts. As indicated in Table 5.1, indicators of bodily collapse (i.e., sulking, slumping shoulders, lying down, falling) were significantly more frequent in independent than in mother-child ($p < .01$) or child-child activity ($p < .01$). There was a trend toward more frequent hand, arm, and leg movements (i.e., clenched fist, shaking arms, banging fists/hands/elbows) during mother-child interaction than during child-child interaction ($p = .06$), but not during independent activity.

These analyses suggest that Nina's emotional reactions to goal-frustrations self-organized into at least three categories: frustrated anger, interpersonal anger, and sadness/withdrawal. Each of these different emo-

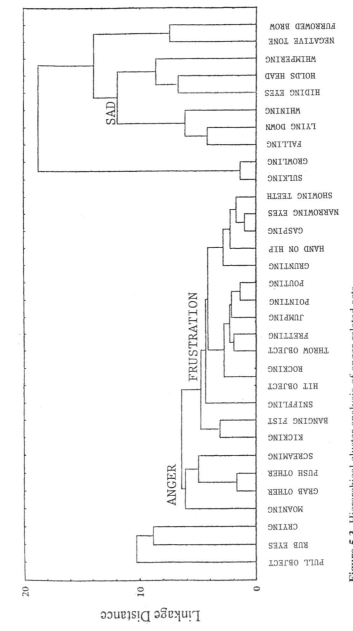

Figure 5.3. Hierarchical cluster analysis of anger-related acts.

140

Table 5.1. *Mean number of anger-relevant behaviors produced during independent, mother-child, and child-child activity*

Context	Facial activity	Vocalization	Hand, arm, and leg movements	Bodily collapse
Independent (*n* = 4)	.75 (.96)	5.00 (4.08)	2.25 (2.87)	3.75 (3.30)
Mother-child (*n* = 14)	.64 (1.34)	5.79 (7.20)	5.07 (5.58)	.86 (.94)
Child-child (*n* = 7)	1.00 (1.83)	3.29 (3.50)	.14 (.38)	.57 (1.33)

tional syndromes can occur in a variety of different social contexts. To illustrate the self-organization of these emotional experiences, consider the following emotional episodes. The first describes instances of frustration:

> Nina was just learning to ride her tricycle, and so Nina's mother brought her outside, saying "What I want you to do is ride your bike." Nina climbed on her bike and applied pressure to the pedals, which did not move. Nina applied still more pressure, looked up, narrowed her eyes, strained, grunted, and showed her teeth. The pedals yielded and the tricycle moved forward. Nina looked up, smiled, and oriented to the videocamera. Nina then looked down as the tricycle then stopped moving. Growling, she looked down at her tricycle pedals. She then climbed off the tricycle and looking down with her shoulders shrugged, stomped her feet while walking in a circle. She then crouched down on the ground next to her tricycle, and looked down with her hands on her face. After her mother said "Don't you want to ride your bike?" Nina held her head and with a furrowed brow said "I can't. It's making me crazy. It's going that way (motions) and I want it to go that way (motions)." She looked at her mother, who said "Well, try it." Nina responded again "I want it to go that way," looked down and stomped toward her tricycle with her shoulders slumped.

This scenario illustrates several aspects of the self-organization of frustration. First, after unsuccessfully attempting to move the pedals, Nina exhibited a frustrated reaction and exerted additional effort. One might suggest that her frustration reaction functioned to increase her will or resolve to move against the tricycle pedals. In this instance, her *energized frustration* facilitated task success, which brought about positive affect. After the second goal-failure, however, Nina exhibited what we call *frustrated discharge* (stomping feet, etc.) upon task withdrawal. When queried by her mother, Nina is explicit about the want violation that mediated her frustration: "It's [the tricycle] going that way [gestures in one direction] and I want it to go that way [gestures in other direction]."

Compare this frustration experience, produced in individual play, with an experience of interpersonal anger produced in child-child play. The richly textured self-organization of this anger episode is represented in Figure 5.4. Figure 5.4 displays not only how each child's actions are organized *sequentially over time*, it also depicts how each child's actions unfold *simultaneously in relation to each other*. As such, Figure 5.4 illustrates how anger displays are put together by processes that occur both between as well as within children.

In Figure 5.4, Nina and Karrie are fighting over who will get to play with a Minnie Mouse doll. The scenario begins with both girls holding onto Minnie and attempting to pull the doll from each other. In the second series of frames, the pulling intensifies, and Karrie, who is dominating the interaction, begins to pry Nina's hands from the doll. Sensing this change, Nina exhibits a series of angry behaviors (in bold) and demands the doll. When the prying does not yield the doll, Karrie returns to pulling. At this point, the girls begin an exchange in which they offer reasons why each should get the doll. These reasons (e.g., "it's my favorite," "you got it already," "you can't borrow it," "it's mine") not only represent strategies to obtain the wanted doll, but also illustrate the ways in which the girls' anger involves the appropriation of an incipient sociomoral framework. In so doing, each girl makes rudimentary appraisals that the other has not only violated a *want* but has also violated an *ought*; each child's rationale represents an attempt to use rudimentary sociomoral standards to justify who is entitled to (i.e., should) play with the doll. In addition, throughout the episode, the girls visually reference Nina's mother, as if to make an appeal to her moral authority about who should play with the doll. After this exchange, Karrie again attempts to pry the doll from Nina's hands. This time, she succeeds, producing an intense angry reaction from Nina directed at Karrie. Karrie runs away, and Nina falls to the floor in withdrawal.

This experience of interpersonal anger bears some similarity to the frustration experiences described earlier. The two share common elements (e.g., furrowed brows, growls, etc.), arising out of local goal obstructions, and involve attempts to move against goal violations. However, although

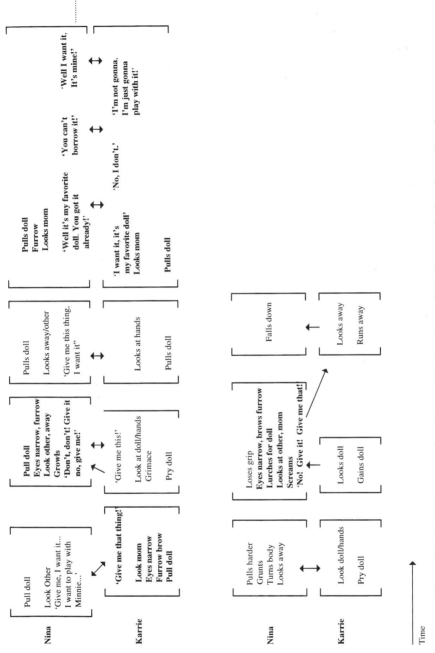

Figure 5.4. The joint construction of anger. Bracketed material indicates episodes of coordinated actions. Boldface indicates anger-related acts. Single arrows indicate direct influence from one set of actions to another. Double arrows indicate coregulation between individuals.

143

similar, the two episodes self-organize in different ways. Nina's frustration, which is structured around attempts to move her tricycle, is characterized by bursts of energized activity and frustrated discharge against a passive and difficult-to-control object. By contrast, her interpersonal anger is directed at another person (Karrie). Thus, Nina's angry actions take different forms (e.g., evolving fluctuations in vocal and facial activity; shifting focus on object, other, or an authority figure; appeals to moral rules; pulling/resisting the object) as they adjust themselves to Karrie's ongoing actions. In addition, her interpersonal anger involves a strong moral component that is jointly negotiated over time; her frustration lacks a significant moral dimension. These descriptions suggest ways in which anger experiences self-organize into different attractors that display both core stability and dynamic variability.

Developmental Sources of Variation in Anger Experiences

Another source of the variation in emotional states involves transformations engendered by developmental processes. Like Sroufe (1996), we suggest that anger episodes undergo qualitative transformation in ontogenesis even as core aspects of such states are preserved. Transformations in the capacity to make motive-relevant appraisals within specific sociocultural contexts are an important source of emotional development. In what follows, we examine developmental changes in anger-related appraisals and their implications for changes in the experience of anger.

Even a casual examination of the theoretical and empirical literature on anger indicates some striking differences in the conditions that elicit signs of anger in infants and adults. Among infants, theorists have suggested that anger reactions are precipitated by goal blockage or frustration (Barrett and Campos, 1987; M. Lewis, 1993). Consistent with this claim, Stenberg and Campos (1990) reported that a range of procedures involving different types of goal frustration (e.g., arm restraint, taking objects from a child's mouth or hands, wiping the face with a cloth) could precipitate anger displays in infants. We refer to such eliciting conditions as *want violations*. By contrast, theory and research with respect to adults consistently make reference to a moral dimension in the experience of anger. In anger, individuals attribute responsibility or *blame* to agents who can otherwise control their actions for violations of conditions that one believes *ought* to exist (de Rivera, 1981; Lazarus, 1991; Mascolo and Griffin, 1998; Mascolo and Mancuso, 1990; Roseman, 1984; Roseman, Spindel, and Jose, 1990;

Shaver et al., 1987; Smith and Ellsworth, 1985; Weiner, 1985). Such violations consist of *ought violations*.

Using dynamic skill theory (Fischer, 1980; Mascolo and Fischer, 1998) as a tool for predicting developmental transformations in action and representation, Mascolo and Griffin (1998) proposed a developmental model describing changes in anger appraisals from simple want violations toward increasingly sophisticated want and ought violations. Selected steps of this model are depicted in Table 5.2. The first anger displays (step A1) occur early in ontogenesis with disruptions in an infant's capacity to coordinate simple action-outcome contingencies. M. Lewis, Allessandri, and Sullivan (1990) trained two-, four-, six-, and eight-month-old infants to arm pull to produce an interesting audiovisual display. Termination of the arm pull–outcome contingency resulted in increased arm pulling and angry facial behavior. This first step is made possible by the onset of what Fischer and associates (1990) call *reflex mappings*, or the capacity to actively coordinate simple action elements. Specifically, in M. Lewis and associates' (1990) study, infants were able to coordinate a simple relation between *swiping* an arm and *seeing* the resulting outcome. The cessation of this contingency produced frustrated reactions. It is important to note the importance of social context in organizing this reaction. The operant procedures used to evoke anger provide immediate feedback, *which actually helps to put together* the rudimentary action-outcome appraisal that mediated the emotional reaction. Thus, the early emergence of frustration reactions is under the *joint control* of child and context. As indicated in steps A2 and A3, anger-related want violations continue to evolve over the course of infancy.

At the end of infancy, with the onset of the capacity to form single (symbolic) representations, children gain the capacity to compare events to representations of the ways in which the world *should* be. As such, the onset of representational intelligence prompts a transformation from the capacity to experience anger in terms of want violations to a capacity to exhibit anger in the context of ought violations. For example, around this time, children can begin to construct categories for what is considered *me* or *mine* (Mascolo and Fischer, 1998; Mascolo and Griffin, 1998). Thus, children can become angry when a sibling takes a toy considered ''mine,'' or when the mother attends to another child rather than to the self. Although such violations clearly implicate a child's *wants*, they also involve primitive sociomoral standards specifying concrete values of possession and ownership. As indicated in Table 5.2, with increased development at

Table 5.2. *Steps in the development of anger appraisals*

Step	Form of appraisal	Age of onset	Example of step
Reflex Tier			
Reflex mappings	Distress over failure to control simple contingency or effect	7–8 weeks	Swiping of the arm that formerly led to pleasurable outcome is disrupted.
Sensorimotor Tier			
Single sensorimotor acts	Frustration over failure of caregiver to respond to child when wanted	4 months	Seen caregiver who previously responded to child's cries fails to respond.
Sensorimotor mappings	Frustration over failure to obtain covered wanted object	7–8 months	Child is frustrated when barrier is placed between child and wanted ball.
Representations Tier			
Single representations	Anger over intrusion on objects considered ''mine''	18–24 months	Other takes toy seen as ''mine''; child becomes angry and says ''mine,'' etc.
Representational mappings	Anger mediated by concrete comparison	3.5–4.5 years	Parent gives a larger piece of cake to sibling; event not necessarily called ''unfair.''
Representational systems	Anger over transgressions of rule-related events seen as unfair, violation of reciprocity, etc.	5–7 years	Sibling takes toy, child says ''No fair. I didn't take your ball when you were playing so don't take mine!''
Abstract Tier			
Single abstractions and beyond	Anger over violation of abstract standards defining personal boundaries, relationships or rules	10–11 years and beyond	Anger at intrusion on self's privacy or restriction of freedom, etc. Anger at oppression, social injustice

Note: Levels are based on changes in action and representation as specified by Fischer's (1980; Fischer et al., 1990) dynamic skill theory. Ages represent general age of emergence among North American individuals in contexts that support the generation of the appraisals in question. Age range and content-specific violations will vary as a function of a myriad of variables, including culture, social context, family history, temperament, gender, and other considerations.

the levels of representational mappings and systems, children construct increasingly powerful albeit concrete ought violations. Still further, with the onset of the abstract tier of development, adolescents become capable of constructing appraisals that embody increasingly sophisticated relations between events and increasingly abstract, intangible motive-relevant standards, identities, relationships, or moral rules.

How do changes in appraisals coact with other component systems to prompt transformations in the experience of anger? Fine-grained observation of the changing organization of appraisal-affect-action complexes in development is currently lacking. Nonetheless, one might suggest several ways in which appraisal systems coact with other component and embedded systems in the self-organization of novel experiences of anger. First, an individual's appraisal systems coact with social context in the construction of higher-order anger experiences. For example, as indicated earlier, the operant procedures used to precipitate anger reactions in young infants provide the type of contextual support that actually helps to put together simple sensorimotor event appraisals. With development, children gain the capacity to coordinate for themselves event appraisals that have their origins in jointly regulated activity. The individual's reconstruction of jointly constructed appraisals occurs throughout ontogenesis at each new level of development.

Second, changes in appraisal systems prompt reorganizations of experiential and action components of anger experiences. For example, an important aspect of anger involves a strengthening of an individual's will or resolve to move against the source of a violation (de Rivera, 1981). The strengthening of will both energizes and channels an individual's attention and action. As such, it embodies both experiential and motive-action elements. One might suggest that in infancy, anger involves a strengthening of will to move against the source of a want violation. The capacity to construct ought violations elevates the experience of anger to a higher plane. Ought violations are accompanied by a strengthening of an individual's will to remove a challenge to what *ought* to exist (de Rivera, 1981). This is no trivial change. In the context of ought violations, we no longer simply want to remove a local goal obstruction; instead, we want our oughts (moral standards) to be acknowledged and respected. For example, if a colleague were to borrow a needed journal without permission, the simple return of the volume would be unlikely to assuage the unwilling lender's anger. Although the book's return would resolve the local goal violation, it would not remove the ought violation. One's will to remove the ought violation would likely remain strong until the offender apologized, thus addressing the moral violation.

The capacity for symbolic functioning also prompts transformations in overt action tendencies. With the development of symbolic capacities, physical action tendencies (e.g., physical opposition or aggression) can be replaced by symbolic communications. These can include verbal attacks, indirect communications (e.g., slamming doors, remaining silent), and gestures. Development of representational skills supports the construction of higher-order motive-action tendencies, such as the desire to retaliate, to gain revenge, or to restore balance to the scales of justice. Theoretical and empirical analysis of the codevelopment of appraisal, affect, and action systems has been virtually nonexistent.

Self-Organization as an Integrative Explanatory Principle

As felt experiences, emotions arise from the self-organization of multiple component processes and systems. Key to a component systems view of emotion is the idea that although the systems that compose any given emotional experience are *distinct*, they nonetheless play *inseparable* roles in the formation of those experiences. As such, order and variability in emotion processes emerge from relations among distinct systems, rather than from the operation of any single system itself. From a component systems view, traditional dualisms employed for understanding emotion begin to lose their force. It is not profitable to view emotional forms as either innate or acquired, basic or derived, individual or social. Instead, as products of coacting systems, emotional experiences are emergent within biogenetic constraints, variable within broad stabilities, and individual within social relations. A full articulation of a systems approach to emotions may well require a reconsideration of dichotomies that constrain traditional thinking about psychological development.

Note

1. I am indebted to Carroll Izard for calling attention to the simple yet important difference between characterizing systems as *distinct* and characterizing them as *independent*. To say that systems are distinct is to imply that they are not the same. However, one system can be distinct from another without being independent of it (e.g., the cardiovascular and respiratory systems are distinct yet interdependent). Most approaches to emotion do concur with some version of this thesis. Even theorists who postulate that undifferentiated autonomic arousal underlies all reports of emotion (e.g., Mandler, 1984) nonetheless assert that ANS arousal is distinct

from – not the same as – the cognitive processes that are presumed to generate and evaluate that arousal.

References

Ackerman, B. P., Abe, J. A., and Izard, C. E. (1998). Differential emotions theory and emotional development: Mindful of modularity. In M. F. Mascolo and S. Griffin (Eds.), *What develops in emotional development?* (pp. 85–106). New York: Plenum.

Barrett, K. C. (1998). A functionalist perspective on the development of emotions. In M. F. Mascolo and S. Griffin (Eds.), *What develops in emotional development?* (pp. 109–133). New York: Plenum.

Barrett, K. C., and Campos, J. J. (1987). Perspectives on emotional development II: A functional approach to emotions. In J. D. Osofsky (Ed.), *Handbook of infant development* (2nd ed., pp. 555–578). New York: Wiley.

Barton, S. (1994). Chaos, self-organization and psychology. *American Psychologist, 49*, 5–14.

Brown, T. (1994). Affective dimensions of meaning. In W. F. Overton and D. S. Palermo (Eds.), *The nature and ontogenesis of meaning* (pp. 167–190). Hillsdale, NJ: Erlbaum.

Brown, T., and Kozak, A. (1998). Emotion and the possibility of psychologists entering into heaven. In M. F. Mascolo and S. Griffin (Eds.), *What develops in emotional development?* (pp. 135–155). New York: Plenum.

Campos, J. J. (1994). The new functionalism in emotion. *SRCD Newsletter* (Spring). Chicago: Society for Research in Child Development.

Camras, L. A. (1992). Expressive development and basic emotions. *Cognition and Emotion, 6*, 269–283.

de Rivera, J. (1981). The structure of anger. In J. H. de Rivera (Ed.), *Conceptual encounter* (pp. 35–82). Washington, DC: University Press of America.

Dickson, K. L., Fogel, A., and Messinger, D. (1998). The development of emotion from a social process view. In M. F. Mascolo and S. Griffin (Eds.), *What develops in emotional development?* (pp. 253–271). New York: Plenum.

Ekman, P. (1984). Expression and the nature of emotion. In. K. R. Scherer and P. Ekman (Eds.), *Approaches to emotion* (pp. 319–343). Hillsdale, NJ: Erlbaum.

Ekman, P., and Friesen, W. V. (1971). Constants across cultures in the face and emotion. *Journal of Personality and Social Psychology, 17*, 124–129.

Ekman, P., Levenson, R. W., and Friesen, W. V. (1983). Autonomic nervous system activity distinguishes between emotions. *Science, 221*, 1208–1210.

Fischer, K. W. (1980). A theory of cognitive development: The control and construction of hierarchies of skills. *Psychological Review, 87*, 447–531.

Fischer, K. W., and Bidell, T. R. (1998). Dynamic development of psychological structures in action and thought. In W. Damon (series ed.) and R. Lerner (vol. ed.), *Handbook of child psychology: Vol. 1. Theoretical models of human development* (5th ed., pp. 467–561). New York: Wiley.

Fischer, K. W., Shaver, P. R, and Carnochan, P. (1990). How emotions develop and how they organize development. *Cognition and Emotion, 4*, 81–128.

Fogel, A. (1993). *Development through relationships: Origins of communication, self and culture*. Chicago: University of Chicago Press.

Fogel, A., Lyra, M. D., and Valsiner, J. (Eds.). (1997). *Dynamics and indeterminism in developmental and social processes*. Mahwah, NJ: Erlbaum.

Fogel, A., Nwokah, E., Dedo, J. Y., Messinger, D., Dickson, K. L., Matusov, E., and Holt, S. A. (1992). Social process theory of emotion: A dynamic systems perspective. *Social Development, 1*, 122–142.

Fogel, A., and Thelen, E. (1987). Development of early expressive end communicative action: Reinterpreting the evidence from a dynamic systems perspective. *Developmental Psychology, 23*, 747–761.

Frijda, N. (1986). *The emotions*. New York: Cambridge University Press.

Frijda, N. H., and Mesquita, B. (1998). The analysis of emotions: Dimensions of variation. In M. F. Mascolo and S. Griffin (Eds.), *What develops in emotional development?* (pp. 273–295). New York: Plenum.

Gergen, K. J. (1985). Social pragmatics and the origins of psychological discourse. In K. J. Gergen and K. E. Davis (Eds.), *The social construction of the person* (pp. 111–127). New York: Springer-Verlag.

Gottleib, G. (1992). *Individual development and evolution: The genesis of novel behavior*. New York: Oxford University Press.

Harré, R., and Finlay-Jones, R. (1986). Emotion talk across the times. In R. Harré (Ed.), *The social construction of emotions* (pp. 220–233). Oxford: Basil Blackwell.

Harré, R., and Gillett, G. (1994). *The discursive mind*. Thousand Oaks, CA: Sage.

Izard, C. (1977). *Human emotions*. New York: Plenum.

Izard, C. (1991). *The psychology of emotions*. New York: Plenum.

Izard, C. E., and Malatesta, C. Z. (1987). Perspectives on emotional development I: Differential emotions theory of early emotional development. In J. Osofsky (Ed.), *Handbook of infant development* (2nd ed., pp. 495–554). New York: Wiley.

Kagan, J. (1978). On emotion and its development: A working paper. In M. Lewis and L. A. Rosenblum (Eds.), *The development of affect* (pp. 11–42). New York: Plenum.

Laird, J. D. (1984). The real role of facial response in experience of emotion: A reply to Tourangeau and Ellsworth, and others. *Journal of Personality and Social Psychology, 47*, 909–917.

Lazarus, R. S. (1991). *Emotion and adaptation*. New York: Oxford University Press.

LeDoux, J. E. (1994). Emotion-specific physiological activity: Don't forget about CNS physiology. In P. Ekman and R. J. Davidson (Eds.), *The nature of emotion* (pp. 248–251). New York: Oxford University Press

Levenson, R. W. (1994). The search for autonomic specificity. In P. Ekman and R. J. Davidson (Eds.), *The nature of emotion* (pp. 252–257). New York: Oxford University Press.

Lewis, M. (1993). The development of anger and rage. In R. A. Glick and S. P. Roose (Eds.), *Rage, power and aggression* (pp. 148–172). New Haven, CT: Yale University Press.

Lewis, M. (1998). The development and structure of emotions. In M. F. Mascolo and S. Griffin (Eds.), *What develops in emotional development?* (pp. 29–50). New York: Plenum.

Lewis, M., Alessandri, S., and Sullivan, M. W. (1990). Expectancy, loss of control and anger in young infants. *Developmental Psychology, 26*, 745–751.

Lewis, M. D. (1995). Cognition-emotion feedback and the self-organization of developmental paths. *Human Development, 38*, 71–102.

Lewis, M. D. (1996). Self-organising cognitive appraisals. *Cognition and Emotion, 10*, 1–25.

Lewis, M. D., and Douglas, L. (1998). A dynamic systems approach to cognition-emotion interactions in development. In M. F. Mascolo and S. Griffin (Eds.), *What develops in emotional development?* (pp. 159–188). New York: Plenum.

Lutz, C. (1988). *Unnatural emotions.* Chicago: University of Chicago Press.

Mandler, G. (1984). *Mind and body.* New York: Norton.

Mascolo, M. F., and Fischer, K. W. (1998). The development of self as the coordination of component systems. In M. Ferrari and R. Sternberg (Eds.), *Self-awareness: Its nature and development* (pp. 332–384). New York: Guilford.

Mascolo, M. F., and Griffin, S. (1998). Alternative trajectories in the development of anger. In M. F. Mascolo and S. Griffin (Eds.), *What develops in emotional development?* (pp. 219–249). New York: Plenum.

Mascolo, M. F., and Harkins, D. (1998). Toward a component systems model of emotional development. In M. F. Mascolo and S. Griffin (Eds.), *What develops in emotional development?* (pp. 189–217). New York: Plenum.

Mascolo, M. F., and Mancuso, J. C. (1990). The functioning of epigenetically evolved emotion systems: A constructive analysis. *International Journal of Personal Construct Theory, 3*, 205–222.

Mascolo, M. F., Pollack, R., and Fischer, K. W. (1997). Keeping the constructor in development: An epigenetic systems approach. *Journal of Constructivist Psychology, 10*, 25–49.

Panksepp, J., Knutson, B., and Pruitt, D. L. (1998). Toward a neuroscience of emotion: The epigenetic foundations of emotional development. In M. F. Mascolo and S. Griffin (Eds.), *What develops in emotional development?* (pp. 53–84). New York: Plenum.

Roseman, I. J. (1984). Cognitive determinants of emotions: A structural theory. In P. Shaver (Ed.), *Review of personality and social psychology* (vol. 5, pp. 11–36). Beverly Hills, CA: Sage.

Roseman, I. J., Antoniou, A. A., and Jose, P. E. (1996). Appraisal determinants of emotions: Constructing a more accurate and comprehensive theory. *Cognition and Emotion, 10*, 241–277.

Roseman, I. J., Spindel, M. S., and Jose, P. E. (1990). Appraisals of emotion-eliciting events: Testing a theory of discrete emotions. *Journal of Personality and Social Psychology, 59*, 899–915.

Russell, J. A. (1991). In defense of a prototype approach to emotion concepts. *Journal of Personality and Social Psychology, 60*, 37–47.

Russell, J. A., and Fehr, B. (1994). Fuzzy concepts in a fuzzy hierarchy: Varieties of anger. *Journal of Personality and Social Psychology, 67*, 186–205.

Scherer, K. (1994). Toward a concept of ''modal emotions.'' In P. Ekman and R. J. Davidson (Eds.), *The nature of emotion* (pp. 25–31). New York: Oxford University Press.

Shaver, P., Schwartz, J., Kirson, D., and O'Connor, C. (1987). Emotion knowledge: Further exploration of a prototype approach. *Journal of Personality and Social Psychology, 52*, 1061–1086.

Shweder, R. (1994). "You're not sick, you're just in love": Emotion as an interpretive system. In P. Ekman and R. J. Davidson (Eds.), *The nature of emotion* (pp. 32–44). Oxford: Oxford University Press.

Smith, C. A., and Ellsworth, P. C. (1985). Patterns of cognitive appraisal in emotion. *Journal of Personality and Social Psychology, 48*, 813–838.

Solomon, R. (1976). *The passions*. New York: Anchor/Doubleday.

Sroufe, L. A. (1996). *Emotional development: The organization of emotional life in the early years*. New York: Cambridge University Press.

Stenberg, C. R., and Campos, J. J. (1990). The development of anger expressions in infancy. In N. L. Stein, B. Leventhal, and T. Trabasso (Eds.), *Psychological and biological approaches to emotions* (pp. 247–282). Hillsdale, NJ: Erlbaum.

Thelen, E. (1990). Dynamic systems and the generation of individual differences. In J. Colombo and J. Fagen (Eds.), *Individual differences in infancy: Reliability, stability, prediction* (pp. 19–43). Hillsdale, NJ: Erlbaum.

Thelen, E., and Smith, L. B. (1994). *A dynamic systems approach to the development of cognition and action*. Cambridge, MA: MIT Press.

Tomkins, S. S. (1962). *Affect, imagery and consciousness: Vol. 1. The positive affects*. New York: Springer.

Trevarthen, C. (1984). Emotions in infancy: Regulators of contact and relationships with persons. In K. R. Scherer and P. Ekman (Eds.), *Approaches to emotion* (pp. 129–157). Hillsdale, NJ: Erlbuam.

van Geert, P. (1994). *Dynamic systems of development: Change between complexity and chaos*. London: Harvester Wheatsheaf.

Weiner, B. (1985). An attributional theory of achievement motivation and emotion. *Psychological Review, 92*, 548–573.

PART II

Neurobiological Perspectives

6 The Self-Organization of the Right Brain and the Neurobiology of Emotional Development

Allan N. Schore

Dynamical systems theory is now being extensively utilized in physics, chemistry, and biology to explore the emergence of pattern and order in inanimate and animate complex systems. A central principle of this perspective is that a dynamical complex system is assembled as a product of the interactions of the elements of the system in a particular context. The early organization of the human brain is a prototypical example of a hierarchically structured complex system that is dynamically assembled and expresses a capacity to evolve toward a state of higher organization. In this chapter I offer evidence to show that the context in which the infant's brain develops, especially the early-developing right hemisphere, is within the emotion-transacting relationship with the primary caregiver. Referring to my work on the neurobiology of emotional development, I will suggest that three dynamical systems concepts – state changes, self-organization, and the central role of energy flows – must not be used only as metaphors but rather directly incorporated in their literal form into the core of models of human development.

A fundamental focus of nonlinear dynamical systems theory is the modeling of complex patterns of *state changes* in all physical and biological systems. This clearly implies that the basic unit of analysis of the process of human development is not changes in behavior, cognition, or even affect, but rather the ontogenetic appearance of more and more complex psychobiological states that underlie these state-dependent emergent functions (Schore, 1994). Lydic (1987, p. 14) points out that "studies that ignore organismic state are analogous to the experiments of physics that ignore time" and that the ubiquity of state-dependent organismic changes "reminds us that biological systems are highly dynamic and notoriously nonlinear." He then concludes that continued progress in our understanding of state phenomena will require a deeper explication of the role played

155

by the brain systems that biochemically regulate all brain and bodily state phenomena – various discrete groups of bioaminergic neurons of the subcortical reticular formation that innervate wide areas of the brain through diffuse projections. The unique anatomical capacities of these systems to affect large areas simultaneously allow for their central involvement in global, state-associated (Flicker, McCarley, and Hobson, 1981; Foote, 1987) brain functions.

The concept of psychobiological state lies at the common boundary of the psychological and biological sciences, and as such it can go far to overcome the myopia of "Descartes' error," "the separation of the most refined operations of mind from the structure and operation of a biological organism" (Damasio, 1994, p. 250). At all points of human development, but especially in infancy, the continually developing mind cannot be understood without reference to the continually maturing body, and their ongoing interactions become an important interface for the organizing self. This perspective necessitates an infusion of recent data from developmental psychobiology into the disciplines of developmental psychology and developmental psychopathology. Indeed, in a recent text of this field, Michel and Moore (1995) declare that dynamical system theories are "good models on which to construct the developmental psychobiological approach" (p. 31).

A second core assumption of systems theory is that *self-organization* is characterized by the emergence and stabilization of novel forms from the interaction of lower-order components and involves "the specification and crystallization of structure" (Lewis, 1995). I will argue that this mechanism also describes how hierarchical structural systems in the developing brain self-organize. The developmental neurosciences are now identifying the "lower" autonomic and "higher" central brain systems that organize in infancy and become capable of generating and regulating psychobiological states. These homeostatic structures that maintain stability are primarily lateralized in the early developing right brain (Chiron et al., 1997), which is, more than the left, well connected to the limbic system and the mechanisms of autonomic and behavioral arousal; and their maturation is experience-dependent. In light of the ontogenetic principle that the most important information for the successful development of the human brain is conveyed by the social rather than the physical environment, I have proposed that "the self-organization of the developing brain occurs in the context of another self, another brain" (Schore, 1996, p. 60). This organization, like all aspects of human brain maturation, is nonlinear and shows discontinuous developmental patterns.

And lastly, another cardinal feature of nonlinear theory is that it assigns the sources of new adaptive forms to the self-organizing properties of systems that use *energy* in order to facilitate the cooperativity of simpler subsystem components into a hierarchically structured complex system (Thelen, 1989). This model therefore emphasizes the central roles of thermodynamics – the science of energy flow – and bioenergetics – the study of how energy is used for the work of establishing biological order – toward the understanding of the creation of new complex structural forms. The functional activity of the brain is an energy-requiring process. One of the most striking aspects of development is found in the growing brain's rapidly increasing capacity to generate and sustain higher and higher levels of energy metabolism over the first two years of life.

The biosynthetic processes that underlie the proliferation of synaptic connections in the postnatally developing brain demand, in addition to sufficient quantities of essential nutrients, massive amounts of energy, so much so that the metabolic rate of the young child's brain is significantly greater than that of adults (Kennedy and Sokoloff, 1957). Sequential increments in metabolic rates take place in various regions of the brain during postnatal development, and this accounts for the finding that the brain matures in discontinuous discrete stages. Due to the relationship between energy metabolism and physiological function, this metabolic progression is central to the emergence of ''higher'' brain systems and the appearance of more complex behaviors. A central principle of systems theory asserts that self-organization increases the rate of energy transfer, and the more ordered the complexity, the faster the energy flows (Goerner, 1995).

The energy metabolism of the brain is regulated and coordinated by biogenic amines that are delivered to widely distributed regions by ascending, unmyelinated projections from the brain stem. Ontogenetic changes in these monoaminergic systems result in progressive increases in organismic energy metabolism. These neuromodulators, in concert with different subtypes of their receptors that determine whether they augment local excitatory or inhibitory activity, alter and synchronize the input-output characteristics of brain cell populations in accord with changes in arousal. In human infancy these same bioagents that regulate central arousal and bodily states play an essential ontogenetic role – they also act as morphogenetic agents that induce the growth and organization of the developing brain (see Schore, 1994). Most intriguingly, it is now evident that these bioamines are regulated by the interaction between caregiver and infant. Neurobiological studies can thus offer us valuable information about how social factors modulate the effects of state organization on development, that is, about how early interpersonal experiences induce the bioenergetic changes that support the growth of brain interconnections, and therefore more complex structures and emergent functions.

This latter problem is, of course, a central focus of models of self-organization. In order to further explore this question, in this chapter I will propose models of the nonlinear phenomena of attachment dynamics, of the role of bioamines in self-organizational processes of synaptic connectivity, and of the energy-dependent imprinting of neural circuitry in the infant brain. In this application of self-organizational concepts to developmental models of both resistance against and vulnerability to mental disorders, I will particularly focus on the experience-dependent maturation of a frontolimbic system that regulates psychobiological states and organismic energy balance in a nonlinear fashion. This prefrontal system is expanded in the right hemisphere and plays a superior role in enabling the organism to cope actively and passively with stress.

Functional Properties of Self-Organizing Developmental Systems

A fundamental property of any developing living system is that it is open to and interactive with its particular environment. This applies to the human infant, which actively seeks environmental input, adjusts to the variations of this input, transforms it with its organizing properties, and incorporates it into its developing form. In such reciprocal interchanges, the dynamic activity of the developing system, in turn, produces changes in the proximal environment. As a result of these continuous self-environment interactions, the system establishes dynamic equilibria both within itself, and between itself and its environment (Michel and Moore, 1995). It is important to note that in the physical sciences dynamical systems theories imply that ''the environment'' is singularly the physical environment. But in the case of a living system, one that proceeds through development to ultimately attain a mature form that can pass on its genomes, these primordial interactions are with the social environment – others of its species, and in particular, the primary caregiver.

A central tenet of dynamical systems theory prescribes that in these early transactions the developing biological system is openly exchanging both energy and matter with the environment. Indeed, ongoing development requires an ''open'' system, one that inputs free energy from the environment, uses it for matter-energy transformations, and exports it in degraded form. As a result of incorporating the dissipation of energy and matter of its environment into itself, the developing system moves away from equilibrium and remains for periods of time in a state of disequilibrium, one that exhibits negative entropy. In this manner the flow of energy through the system creates conditions for strong deviations from thermodynamic equilibrium, and this results in the phenomenon of self-organization. When a system is "far-from-equilibrium" (Prigogine and Stengers, 1984) energy is continually dissipated in the very process that binds the elements of the system together, allowing the elements to "behave in a synchronous fashion, to couple with each other through ongoing feedback, and to act together in macroscopic entities rather than independent entities" (Lewis, 1995, p. 79).

As the patterns of relations among the components of a self-organizing system become increasingly interconnected and well-ordered, it is more capable of maintaining a coherence of organization in relation to variations in the environment. Given a particular organization and a particular environmental context, the system prefers a certain range of states. A system passes through a succession of a finite number of states, but it must eventually reenter a state that it has previously encountered. These cycles of contiguous states represent the dynamic attractors of the system, and the path taken by the system from one state to another defines a "trajectory" that describes the evolution of the system. If the system is driven away from its stationary state, it will tend to return to that state; the time it takes to return to a stationary state is a function of the stability of the system. The stability of a system is dependent upon its capacity to transition between and thereby exist within a range of possible states, and this property is a consequence of its dynamic processes.

Self-organization, the process whereby order and complexity create more order and complexity, proceeds hierarchically, as each level of self-organization builds on the level that precedes it. Different levels of organization are represented in hierarchical models of development, and maturation in infancy is best characterized by an alternation of rapid development and slower rates, even plateaus, which delimit "stages" (McGuiness, Pribram, and Pirnazar, 1990). Developmental change results from a series of states of stability and instability and phase transitions in the attractor landscape that irreversibly alter the trajectory of the system and allow for the organization of new states of matter-dissipative structures. These "points of bifurcation," when new states can potentially evolve from preceding ones, occur in the context of a "mutually determining organism-environment interaction" (Schwalbe, 1991). During these intervals, the open system, due to increasingly complex interconnections within its components and the creation of feedback mechanisms, can act not only on the output of an environmental system with which it is interacting, but also iteratively to amplify its own output, and so is sensitive to fluctuations of both external and internal processes. Complex systems thus show sensitive dependence on initial conditions – the state of the system when fluctuations first initiate change – and small differences can be amplified into large effects over many cycles of iteration. These fluctuations drive the system to explore new states.

Most importantly, environmental perturbations that occur during points of bifurcation create nonlinear breaks in organization and discontinuous changes in system states. According to Schwalbe (1991, p. 276),

> Chaos . . . arises at the point of phase transitions, when systems are "choosing" between different process structures. What occurs at these points is that random fluctuations in energy can be amplified throughout the entire system so that a new process structure is formed. Chaos in dynamical systems is thus a product of the same forces that create process structures and give rise to self-organization.

Nonlinearity, the source of rapid change and novel structure, is thus also the source of potential order and stability. It is now well established that nonlinearity can produce either positive (amplifying) or negative (dampening) feedback, stability or instability, convergence (coupling or entrainment) or divergence (Goerner, 1995). Shinbrot and colleagues (1993) report that chaotic systems are extremely sensitive to small perturbations, and that these tiny feedback perturbations control their trajectories. These researchers experimentally demonstrate that small perturbations can be used both to stabilize regular dynamic behaviors and to direct chaotic trajectories rapidly to a "desired state." They also show that, using only tiny perturbations, one can switch among a rich variety of dynamical behaviors as circumstances change. Referring to "the advantage of chaos," they conclude that "[i]ncorporating chaos deliberately into practical systems therefore offers the possibility of achieving greater flexibility in their performance" (p. 411). These findings fit nicely with Thelen's (1995) assertion that times of instability are essential to give a developing system flexibility to select adaptive capacities.

Developing organisms "internalize" environmental forces by becoming appropriately structured in relation to them; and by incorporating an internal model of these exogenous signals they develop adaptive homeostatic regulatory mechanisms that allow for stability in the face of external variation. The regulation of the organism, which maintains internal stability and output regulation and enables an effective response to external stimuli, therefore depends on the formation of a dynamic model of the external environment. Self-organizing systems are thus systems that are capable of generating new internal representations in response to changing environmental conditions.

These abstract self-organizational principles apply in a general way to all living systems. The next question is, how do these overarching principles specifically apply to the ontogeny of the human infant, itself described as "very nonlinear" (Thelen, 1989)? Schwalbe (1991) portrays the human as "a nonlinear dynamic system," an inherently dynamic energy-transformation regime that co-evolves with its environment, one that self-organizes when exposed to an energy flux. In a scenario that resembles attachment dynamics, he postulates that the infant becomes "attuned to" an external object in its environment that consistently responds in a stimulating manner to the infant's spontaneous impulsive energy dissipating behaviors.

The concept of energy, central to dynamical systems theory, is rarely used in developmental psychology. In a recent article on the self-organization of developmental paths, Lewis (1995) asks, "What is the best analogy for energy in psychological systems?" He points out that the energy flowthrough for self-organization has been conceived of as "information," an idea that fits well with Harold's (1986) formulation that information is a special kind of energy required for the work of establishing biological order. He then goes on to argue that information can be defined subjectively as that which is relevant to an individual's goals or needs, an idea that echoes recent concepts of emotions as adaptive functions that guide attention to the most relevant aspects of the environment, and of emotional appraisals as monitoring and interpreting events in order to determine their significance to the self. Lewis concludes that there is no better marker of such information than the emotion that accompanies it, that emotions amplify fluctuations to act in self-organization, and that the processing of relevant information in the presence of emotion may be analogous to the flowthrough of energy in a state of disequilibrium. Stability is a property of interpersonal attractors that maintain their organization by perpetuating equilibrium as well as by resolving emotional disequilibrium.

In applying nonlinear systems concepts to development, Lewis emphasizes the salience of "dyadic self-organization," which is epitomized by the creation of specific forms of communication between the mother and infant. When emotion is present in this dyadic interaction, each partner's behavior is monitored by the other, and this results in a coupling between the output of one partner's loop and the input of the other's to form a larger feedback configuration. These transactions represent a flow of inter-personal information accompanying emotion, and critical fluctuations, am-plified by positive feedback, lead to disequilibrium and self-organization. Attachment patterns are posited to arise through consolidating interpreta-tions (working models) of caregiving contingencies, and such representa-tions take into account both emotional responses to caregiving fluctuations and maternal behavioral characteristics. Core attachment organizations sta-bilize with age and branch into attachment categories, and in this manner emotional experiences with caregivers set the course of the individual's behavioral style and emotional disposition (Lewis, 1995).

Nonlinear State Changes and the Organization of Attachment Dynamics

In previous work I have proposed that emotional transactions involving synchronized ordered patterns of energy transmissions (directed flows of energy) represent the fundamental core of the attachment dynamic (Schore, 1994). This conception, congruent with nonlinear dynamical models, fo-cuses on reciprocal affective exchanges in which the caregiver psychobio-logically regulates changes in the infant's state. These interactions occur in sensitive periods of infancy, phases when energy is high in the infant and the parent for receptivity to each other's cues and for adapting to each other. The creation of this dynamical system of "contingent responsivity" occurs in the context of face-to-face interactions, and it relies heavily upon the processing of visual and auditory (prosodic) information emanating from the most potent source of stimulation in the infant's environment – the mother's face. The human face is a unique stimulus whose features display biologically significant information, and it functions as a continu-ous real-time readout of internal processes.

Indeed, over the first year of life visual experiences play a paramount role in human development (Schore, 1994, 1996). A recent functional magnetic resonance imaging (fMRI) study reveals that beginning at eight weeks, a dramatic rise in metabolic rate occurs in the cerebral cortex, heralding a significant advance in brain maturation (Yamada et al., 1997). Visual stimulation specifically induces a rapid change in energy meta-bolism in the occipital cortex, and the authors conclude that this reflects the onset of a critical period during which synaptic connections in the primary visual cortex are modified by visual experience. It is at this very time that face-to-face interactions, occurring within the primordial experiences of human play, first appear (Cohn and Tronick, 1987). Although these interpersonal experiences of mutual visual regard and "affect synchrony" are of brief duration, because they expose the infant to essential elements of social and cognitive information within a context of high levels of positive arousal (Feldman, Greenbaum, and Yirmiya, 1999), and because they occur during a critical period of brain maturation (Schore, 1994), they have long-enduring effects (Johnson and Vecera, 1993).

These face-to-face dialogues of mother-infant affect synchrony thus create a match between the expression of arousal-accelerating, positively valenced internal states. Dynamically fluctuating moment-to-moment state sharing represents an organized dialogue occurring within milliseconds, and it acts as an interactive matrix in which both partners match states and then simultaneously adjust their social attention, stimulation, and accelerating arousal in response to the partner's signals. In order for this to happen, the mother must monitor the infant's state as well as her own, and then resonate not with the child's overt behavior but with certain qualities of its internal state, such as contour, intensity, and temporal features. In physics, a property of resonance is sympathetic vibration, which is the tendency of one resonance system to enlarge and augment its activity through matching the resonance frequency pattern of another resonance system. In this mutually synchronized attunement of emotionally driven facial expression, prosodic vocalization, and kinesic behaviors, the dyad co-constructs a mutual regulatory system of arousal that contains a "positively amplifying circuit mutually affirming both partners" (Wright, 1991).

In such facial mirroring transactions (see Figure 6.1) the caregiver facilitates a state transition, manifested in a change in patterns of "energetic arousal," and a shift from quiet alertness (point A) into an intensely positive affective state (point F). Stern (1990) describes exchanges of smiles in escalating overlapping waves that propel the other into "higher orbit." At resonance, energy transfer from the external agent to the resonant system is maximal (Katsuri, Amtey, and Beall, 1984). In accord with complex systems theory, an environmental perturbation triggers a rapid and discontinuous change in state, a far-from-equilibrium organization that leads to the potential for achieving novel states of temporal stability. Schwalbe (1991) posits that the nonlinear self acts iteratively, so that minor changes, occurring at the right moment, can be amplified in the system, thus launching it into a qualitatively different state. Patterns of information emanating from the caregiver's face, especially of low visual and auditory frequencies (Ornstein, 1997), thus trigger metabolic energy shifts in the infant. The caregiver is thus modulating changes in the child's energetic

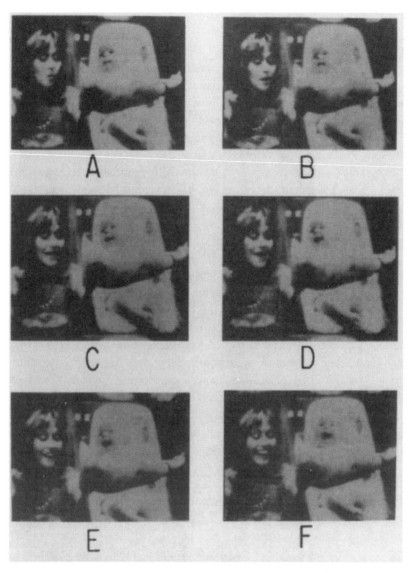

Figure 6.1. Photographs of a "mirroring" sequence. Mother and infant are seated face to face, looking at each other. At point A, mother shows a "kiss-face," and infant's lips are partially drawn in, resulting in a tight, sober-faced expression. At point B, mother's mouth has widened into a slightly positive expression, and infant's face has relaxed with a hint of widening in the mouth, also a slighly positive expression. At point C, both mother and infant show a slight smile, further widened at point D. At point E, the infant breaks into a "full gape smile." At point F, the infant has shifted the orientation of his head further to his left, and upward, which heightens the evocativeness of the gape-smile. Total elapsed time is under three seconds (from Beebe and Lachmann, 1988).

state, since arousal levels are known to be associated with changes in metabolic energy. Indeed, energy shifts are the most basic and fundamental features of emotion; discontinuous states are experienced as affect responses, and nonlinear psychic bifurcations are manifest as rapid affective shifts.

In light of the fact that in these interchanges the infant's and mother's homeostatic systems are "open" and linked together (Hofer, 1990) and are "semipermeable to regulation from the other" (Pipp, 1993), the transition embedded in the psychobiological attunement of the dyad involves an alteration in the infant's bodily state. These dyadic entrainments of physiological rhythms increase over the first year, since the baby's ability to adjust the amount of interaction with mother in accordance with internal states increases with physiological and psychological maturity. An essential attachment function is to promote the synchrony or regulation of biological and behavioral systems on an organismic level. Damasio concludes that emotions are the highest-order direct expression of bioregulation in complex organisms (1998), and that primordial representations of bodily states are the building blocks and scaffolding of development (1994). The infant's core sense of self is bodily based, and since bodily processes abide by the laws of nonlinear dynamics (Goldberger, Rigney, and West, 1990), the emerging self is grounded in biologically mediated properties (Pipp, 1993).

Even more specifically, synchronized gaze transactions induce changes in the infant's bodily states by maternal regulation of the energy-expending sympathetic and energy-conserving parasympathetic branches of the child's developing autonomic nervous system (ANS). This interactive mechanism represents a mutual entrainment of the mother's and infant's brains, including a coupling of the activation of the subcortical bioaminergic nuclei that mediate somatic states, emotional arousal, and trophic influences on the developing cortex. I suggest that the regulated affective interchanges of early play sequences serve as an enriched environment in which "mothers invest extra energy in their young to promote larger brains" (Gibbons, 1998, p. 1347). In support of this model, Trevarthen (1993) argues that the epigenetic program of brain growth requires brain-brain interaction and occurs in the context of a traffic of visual and prosodic auditory signals that induce instant positive emotional states in both infant and mother (see Figure 6.2). The resonance of the dyad ultimately permits the intercoordination of positive affective brain states. Trevarthen concludes that "the affective regulations of brain growth" are embedded in the context of an intimate relationship, and that they promote the development of cerebral circuits.

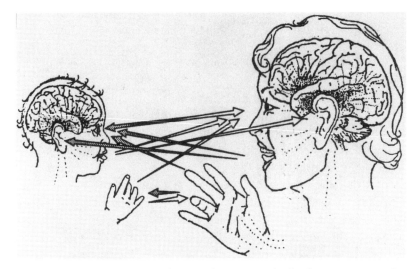

Figure 6.2. Channels of face-to-face communication in proto-conversation. Proto-conversation is mediated by eye-to-eye orientations, vocalizations, hand gestures, and movements of the arms and head, all acting in coordination to express interpersonal awareness and emotions (adapted from Trevarthen, 1993).

Regulation of the Energy Metabolism in Critical Periods of Neural Development

In her recent writings Thelen (1995) asserts that dynamical systems theory needs to be more closely tied into a theory of brain development that addresses the fundamental question, how is the brain molded through experience? Although nonlinear systems theory has been used to model brain functions, the problem of what causes the infant brain to change, and of how this organization is influenced by the interaction of genetic programming and environmental history, has not received much attention. Yet, Cicchetti and Tucker (1994) now emphasize that the identification of the brain's self-organizing mechanisms is a primary challenge of science, and that indeed it may reveal the best description of development. These authors also point out that certain interactions between an "open homeostatic system" and the environment are critical to the differentiation of brain tissue, and that particular environmental experiences during sensitive periods are necessary for the induction of certain developmental changes that result from the maturation of the infant brain.

This leads to the fundamental questions, what specific kinds of experiences induce brain maturation, and how do such early experiences influence brain organization? I have proposed that attachment experiences essentially represent affective transactions in which the caregiver modulates changes in the infant's arousal levels, and thereby in its energetic state. More specifically, this is accomplished by her psychobiological regulation of dopamine and noradrenaline in the infant's developing brain (Hofer, 1990). These catecholamines are centrally involved in the regulation of brain metabolic energy levels, morphogenesis, and the maturation of cortical areas during different developmental stages. Since the bioaminergic "reticular" systems that are responsible for various states of arousal are in an intense state of active growth in infancy, the regulatory transactions embedded in the emotional relationship are occurring at a time when the infant's arousal circuitries are expanding (Harkness and Tucker, this volume). Central catecholaminergic neurons undergo an accelerated development in mammalian infancy, and these periods are also a time when regional catecholaminergic receptors are amplified (see Schore, 1994, 1997b for detailed references).

Thus, during early critical periods, biogenic amines, the same agents that regulate emotion and motivation throughout the lifespan, play an important role in the responsiveness of the cortex to environmental stimulation and in the regulation of the temporal framework of developmental processes. These neuromodulators influence the ontogeny of cortical circuitry and have long-lasting effects on synaptic plasticity and on biochemical processes that mediate developmental influences. Their activation of both glycogenolysis, a cascade of biochemical reactions that trigger the release of glucose in conditions of intense activity, and of the hexose monophosphate shunt, a pathway that mediates biosynthetic processes, underscores their preeminent role in the regulation of energy substrate availability in the developing brain. Bioaminergic axons, which are highly collateralized, modulate cerebral circulatory systems and the blood-brain barrier that delivers and exports metabolic substrate to the brain, thereby regulating the responsivity of large areas of the brain to inputs in a coordinated manner (see Schore, 1994 for a detailed discussion).

A central tenet of dynamical systems theory holds that at particular critical moments, a flow of energy allows the components of a self-organizing system to become increasingly interconnected, and in this manner organismic form is constructed in developmental processes. These moments occur in instances of imprinting, the very rapid form of learning that irreversibly stamps early experience upon the developing nervous system and mediates attachment bond formation. It is now thought that a stimulus that elicits a high level of catecholamine-generated arousal facilitates the imprinting process and exerts an enduring influence on neural development (a perfect description of the emotionally expressive face of the attachment object), and that certain types of early learning experiences associated with new levels of arousal lead to rapid increases in the volume of hemispheric blood flow. Both imprinting and arousal are associated with increased metabolic activity, and both are regulated by catecholamines, agents that have pronounced effects on cerebral energy metabolism (see Schore, 1994) and cerebral blood flow (Krimer et al., 1998).

During very early development, the neonatal cerebral metabolic rate that sustains early cortical function is very low. But as infancy proceeds, blood flow, known to correlate with changes in arousal and to be an indicator of regional oxidative metabolism, rises. Indeed, the dramatic transformations of energy production that occur in particular portions of the maturing nervous system during specific postnatal temporal intervals represent the physiological basis of developmental-stage and critical-period phenomena, and these events allow for the onset of increasing complexity of structure and efficiency and integration of function, just as described by dynamical systems theory. In earlier work (Schore, 1994) I have proposed that the onset of a critical period of growth in a differentiating brain region is defined by a sudden switch from anaerobic to aerobic energy metabolism. This allows for larger and larger flows of energy within more and more interconnected elements that can be used for self-organizational processes. Since these bioenergetic transformations are coordinated over long distances, they underlie the critical-period construction of a neural circuit – a self-contained neuronal network that sustains a nerve impulse by channeling it repeatedly through the same network.

The organization of these circuits occurs during a period of synaptogenesis and dendritic growth, processes that are regulated by bioamines. In critical periods catecholamines induce dynamic changes in the shape and branching patterns of dendrites and in the growth of dendritic spines. These spines have the greatest energy requirements in the brain, and they act as potential sites of synaptic contact that modulate rapid changes in the nervous system throughout the course of its development (Perkel and Perkel, 1985). In light of the fact that in a critical period of a developing brain region energy metabolism peaks when dendrites are growing and neurons are attaining a new state of organization, and that dendritic spines have the greatest energy requirements in the brain, I would characterize their local cellular environment at this specific time as a ''far-from-equilibrium system.'' It is now held that energy-regulating bioamines modulate ion channels in dendrites, and that excitatory events occurring in dendrites within a "narrow time window" produce a "much bigger response" than events occurring outside this window, thereby allowing for interactions among synapses to be "highly nonlinear" (Johnston et al., 1996).

Expanding upon these ideas, I suggest that although dendritic spines represent a unique site for receiving communications from other cells, these points of interface with the local environment, especially in critical periods, also potentially expose the neuron to a state of "oxidative stress," thereby making the cell vulnerable to "apoptosis" or "programmed cell death" (Margolis, Chuang, and Post, 1994). Apoptosis plays a crucial role in the early development and growth regulation of living systems. This same mechanism may underlie the developmental process of circuit pruning, the selective loss of connections and redistribution of inputs that allows for the appearance of an emergent function. Regressive events such as cell death and the elimination of long axon collaterals and dendritic processes are essential mechanisms of brain maturation. The critical period expansion and retraction of limbic dendritic fields is thus directly influenced by the social environment.

A large body of evidence supports the principle that cortical networks are generated by a genetically programmed initial overabundant production of synaptic connections, which is then followed by a process of competitive interaction to select those connections that are most effectively entrained to environmental information. "Parcellation," the activity-dependent fine tuning of connections and winnowing of surplus circuitry, is responsible for the loss of early transient ontogenetic adaptations, but this same mechanism of functional segregation also allows the developing brain to become increasingly complex, a property of a self-organizing system. Development, the process of self-assembly, thus involves both progressive and regressive phenomena, and is best characterized as a sequence of processes of organization, disorganization, and reorganization.

The Organization of a Regulatory System in the Orbitofrontal Cortex that Manifests Chaotic Dynamics

According to biological approaches to self-organization, attractors maintain the system's organization by acting as adaptive homeostatic regulatory mechanisms that allow for stability in the face of environmental change. Of particular importance to the regulation of nonlinear emotional states are cortical-subcortical circuits, especially those that directly link cortical areas that process current information about changes in the external social environment with subcortical information about concurrent alterations in internal bodily states. These systems are hierarchically arranged, and they onset in a fixed progression over the first year. Although the amygdala, a limbic structure that appraises only crude information about external stimuli, is on line at birth, a critical period for the development of corticolimbic association areas onsets in the second and third quarters of the first year, involving maturation of the anterior cingulate cortex, an area involved in play and separation behaviors, laughing and crying vocalizations, face representations, and modulation of autonomic activity (MacLean, 1993; Paus et al., 1993).

By the end of this year the orbitoinsular region of the inferior prefrontal cortex (see Figure 6.3), an area that receives information from the ventral object-processing visual stream (Rolls, 1996) and contains neurons that fire in response to faces (Scalaidhe, Wilson, and Goldman-Rakic, 1997), becomes preeminently involved in the processing of interpersonal signals

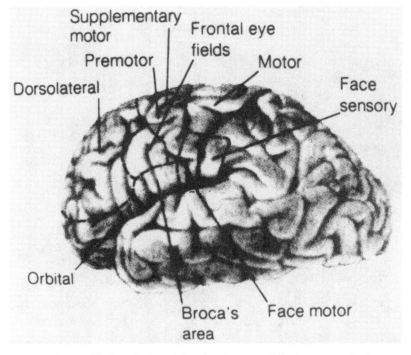

Figure 6.3. Boundaries of functional zones of the human cerebral cortex, showing the orbital and dorsolateral prefrontal areas (from Kolb and Whishaw, 1990).

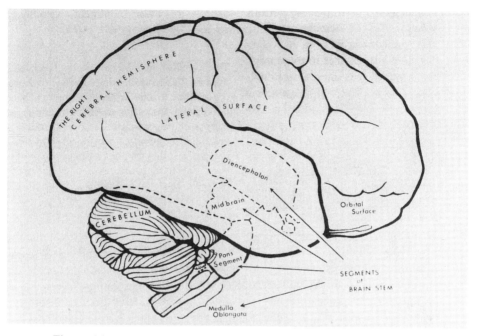

Figure 6.4. Relationships of brain stem structures to the orbital surface of the right hemisphere (from Smith, 1981).

necessary for the initiation of social interactions and in the regulation of arousal and body states, properties that account for its central involvement in attachment neurobiology. The orbitofrontal system matures in the last half of the second year, a watershed time for the appearance of a number of adaptive capacities. These advances reflect the role of the frontal lobe in the development of infant self-regulatory behavior, and are relevant to Cicchetti and Tucker's (1994) assertion that the homeostatic, self-regulating structures of the mind are the major stabilities in the chaotic dynamics of psychological and neural development. Due to the fact that orbital activity is essentially implicated in homeostatic regulation (Schore, 1994), *the operational nature of this prefrontal cortex is best described as a nonlinear dynamical system.*

The functional properties of this structural system can only be understood in reference to its unique neuroanatomical characteristics. The frontolimbic areas of the cortex are "hidden" in the ventral and medial surfaces of the prefrontal lobe (Price, Carmichael, and Drevets, 1996). Due to its location at the interface of cortex and subcortex (see Figure 6.4), this ventromedial prefrontal cortex acts as a "convergence zone" and is one of the few brain regions that is "privy to signals about virtually any activity taking place in our beings' mind or body at any given time" (Damasio, 1994, p. 181). In addition to receiving input from all sensory association areas of the posterior cortex and outputs to motor areas in the anterior cortex and ventral striatum, it uniquely projects extensive pathways to limbic areas in the temporal pole, central nucleus of the amygdala, and olfactory areas, to dopamine neurons in the ventral tegmental area of the anterior reticular formation, and to subcortical drive centers in the ventro-medial and paraventricular hypothalamus that are associated with the sym-pathetic branch of the autonomic nervous system. This excitatory limbic circuit, the ventral tegmental limbic forebrain-midbrain circuit, is involved with the generation of positively valenced states associated with motiva-tional reward, approach behavior, and active coping strategies.

Orbitofrontal regions also send axons onto subcortical targets in para-sympathetic autonomic areas of the lateral hypothalamus, and to noradren-ergic neurons in the medullary solitary nucleus and the vagal complex in the brain stem caudal reticular formation, thereby completing the organi-zation of another limbic circuit, the lateral tegmental limbic forebrain-midbrain circuit that activates the onset of an inhibitory, negatively val-enced state associated with avoidance and passive coping. The functioning of the two limbic circuits underlies the observation that emotions organize behavior along a basic appetitive-aversive dimension associated with either a behavioral set involving approach and attachment, or a set disposing avoidance, escape, and defense (see Schore, 1994, 1996, 1997b).

The orbital corticolimbic system, along with the insular cortex, anterior cingulate, and amygdala, is a component of the "rostral limbic system" (Devinsky, Morrell, and Vogt, 1995). Situated at the hierarchical apex of the emotion-generating limbic system, it functions as a "senior executive" of limbic arousal (Joseph, 1996). But in addition, it acts as a major center of CNS hierarchical control over the energy-expending sympathetic and energy-conserving parasympathetic branches of the ANS, thereby regulat-ing, respectively, ergotropic high arousal and trophotropic low arousal bodily states (Gellhorn, 1970). Due to its direct connections with both the ANS (Neafsey, 1990) and the spinal cord (Burstein and Potrebic, 1993), it plays an important cortical role in the feedback from bodily systems, what Damasio (1994) calls "somatic markers," and in the nonlinear mechanism of visceral regulation (Skinner et al., 1992). These reciprocal connections allow for an essential orbitofrontal role in *the highest level of control of behavior, especially in relation to emotion* (Price et al., 1996), *the moti-*

vational control of goal-directed behavior (Tremblay and Schultz, 1999), *the representation of highly integrated information on the organismic state* (Tucker, 1992), and *the modulation of energy balance* (McGregor and Atrens, 1991).

By being directly connected into heteromodal areas of the cortex as well as into both limbic circuits, the sensory perception of an environmental perturbation can be associated with the adaptive switching of bodily states in response to changes (or expected changes) in the external environment that are appraised to be personally meaningful (Schore, 1998). These rapidly acting orbitofrontal appraisals of the social environment are accomplished at levels beneath awareness by a visual and auditory scanning of information emanating from an emotionally expressive face, and they act as nonconscious biases that guide behavior before conscious knowledge does (Bechara et al., 1997). This cortex, via implicit processing (Rolls, 1996), performs a "valence tagging" function, in which perceptions receive a positive or negative affective charge. The orbitofrontal system, the "administrator of the basolimbic forebrain circuitry" (Nelson, 1994), is a central component of the mechanism by which "forebrain circuits concerned with the recognition and interpretation of life experiences are capable of influencing virtually all, if not all, regulatory mechanisms in the body" (Wolf, 1995, p. 90).

In such organism-environment interactions there is a sensitive dependence on initial conditions, and these heightened affective moments represent "points of bifurcation" of the potential activation of the two fronto-limbic circuits. Mender (1994) points out that in a competitive system, steep gain increases in response to stimulus input, combined with arousal, can create explosive bursts of neural activity and hence discontinuous jumps between discrete aggregate states of neuronal networks. As a result, distributed aggregates of neurons can shift abruptly and simultaneously from one complex activity pattern to another in response to the smallest of inputs. In this manner the appraisal of an external or internal stimulus as self-relevant will trigger synchronized state changes in organismic systems, and this is expressed in highly emotionally charged "affect bursts" (Scherer, 1994). It is interesting to note that dopamine neurons involved in emotional states show a "nonlinear" relationship between impulse flow and dopamine release, and shift from single-spike to "burst firing" (Gonon, 1988) in response to an environmental stimulus that is "ethologically salient" (a good description of sensory stimulation emanating from the mother), and that this effect is induced by medial prefrontal activity (Overton and Clark, 1997).

Bertalanffy (1974) asserts that a small change in an anterior "higher" controlling center "may by way of amplification mechanisms cause large changes in the total system. In this way a hierarchical order of parts or processes may be established" (p. 1104). I suggest that the orbitofrontal cortex represents this controlling center, and that it is intimately involved in the mechanism by which affect acts as an "analog amplifier" that extends the duration of whatever activates it. In accord with chaos theory, "[t]iny differences in input could quickly become overwhelming differences in output" (Gleick, 1987, p. 8). Chaotic periods of activity within the excitatory and inhibitory limbic circuits reflect sudden psychobiological state transitions. Orbitofrontal activity is associated with affective shifts, the alteration of behavior in response to fluctuations in the emotional significance of stimuli (Dias, Robbins, and Roberts, 1996). In optimal frontolimbic operations, these shifts from one emotional state to another are experienced as rhythms in feeling states and are fluid and smooth, a flexible capacity of a coherent dynamical system.

The activity of this prefrontal system is responsible for *the regulation of motivational states* and *the adjustment or correction of emotional responses*. It is specialized for generating and storing cognitive interactive representations (internal working models) that contain information about state transitions, and for physiologically coding the fact that state changes associated with homeostatic disruptions will be set right. Regulated emotional states represent desired attractors that maintain emotional equilibrium and resolve emotional disequilibrium. Chaotic variability in brain self-regulatory activity may be necessary for flexibility and adaptability in a changing environment (Freeman, this volume). According to Ciompi (1991), under certain conditions feedback processes in "affective cognitive systems" are capable of "provoking sudden non-linear jumps, far away from equilibrium, leading to chaotic conditions or to the formation of new 'dissipative structures' " (p. 98). Recent work indicates that the orbitofrontal system is specialized for "cognitive-emotional interactions" (Barbas, 1995) and the processing of feedback information (Elliot, Frith, and Dolan, 1997), and that neurons in the right prefrontal cortex with balanced excitatory and inhibitory inputs show chaotic behavior (van Vreeswijk and Sompolinsky, 1996).

The Right Brain as a Nonlinear System

The fact that the orbital prefrontal area is expanded in the right hemisphere has been suggested to account for the dominance of this hemisphere in the processing of emotional information (Falk et al., 1990). The right cerebral cortex plays an important role in the processing of individual faces early in life (de Schonen et al., 1993), in the infant's recognition of arousal-inducing maternal facial affective expressions (Nelson, 1987), in the infant's response to the prosody of motherese (Fernald, 1989), and in early language development (Locke, 1993; Schumann, 1997). In describing the greater involvement of the right hemisphere in infancy, Semrud-Clikeman and Hynd (1990, p. 198) state:

> The emotional experience of the infant develops through the sounds, images, and pictures that constitute much of an infant's early learning experience, and are disproportionately stored or processed in the right hemisphere during the formative stages of brain ontogeny.

Based on EEG and neuroimaging data, Ryan, Kuhl, and Deci (1997, p. 719) now propose that "[t]he positive emotional exchange resulting from autonomy-supportive parenting involves participation of right hemispheric cortical and subcortical systems that participate in global, tonic emotional modulation."

Indeed, the right hemisphere is centrally involved in human attachment and in the development of reciprocal interactions within the mother-infant regulatory system (Henry, 1997; Schore, 1994, 1997a; Siegel, 1999; Wang, 1997). In earlier work I presented a substantial body of multidisciplinary evidence that indicates that the high intensity affective communications that culminate in the development of the attachment system are essentially right hemisphere–to–right hemisphere arousal regulating energy transmissions between the primary caregiver and infant. Attachment dynamics continue in ongoing development, and the ventromedial region of the right cortex that neurobiologically mediates these dynamics plays a crucial role in the processing of information emanating from the human face throughout the lifespan.

Descending projections from the prefrontal cortex to subcortical structures are known to mature during infancy, and the "primitive" right hemisphere, more than the left, has dense reciprocal interconnections with limbic and subcortical structures and contains an increased emphasis on paralimbic networks (Tucker, 1992). These reciprocal right frontal–subcortical connections, especially with bioaminergic and hypothalamic neuroendocrine nuclei, account for the unique contribution of the right hemisphere in regulating homeostasis and modulating physiological state in response to internal and external feedback. The representation of visceral and somatic states is under primary control of the right hemisphere, and the somatic marker mechanism, tuned by critical learning interactions in development, is more connected into the right ventromedial area. Wittling and Pfluger (1990) conclude that the right hemisphere is dominant for "the metacontrol of fundamental physiological and endocrinological functions whose primary control centers are located in subcortical regions of the brain" (p. 260). This cortical asymmetry is an extension of an autonomic asymmetry – at all levels of the nervous system, the right side of the brain provides the primary central regulation of homeostasis and physiological reactivity (Porges, Doussard-Roosevelt, and Maiti, 1994).

Expanding upon these neurophysiological and neuroanatomical relationships, Porges proposes that the right vagus is involved in the regulation of emotion and communication. Porges' right brain circuit of emotion regulation is thus identical to the inhibitory lateral tegmental noradrenergic limbic circuit that is hierarchically dominated by the right orbitofrontal cortex. As opposed to sympathetically driven "fight-flight" active coping strategies, parasympathetically mediated passive coping mechanisms expressed in immobility and withdrawal allow for conservation–withdrawal, the capacity that improves survival efficiency through inactive disengagement and unresponsiveness to environmental input in order "to conserve resources." With regard to the other ventral tegmental dopaminergic limbic circuit, psychopharmacological research shows that emotionally stressful experiences result in greater dopaminergic activation of the right over the left prefrontal cortex (Fitzgerald et al., 1989). In a study of the mesocortical dopaminergic system, the authors conclude that the right cortex is at the top of a hierarchy for the processing of prolonged emotionally stressful inputs, and that endogenous dopaminergic modulation facilitates adaptive responses (Sullivan and Szechtman, 1995). They posit that under intense inputs, a left to right shift occurs in intrinsic neural activity.

These ideas correspond with the assertion that this "nondominant" (!) hemisphere plays a central role in the control of vital functions supporting survival and enabling the organism to cope with stressors (Wittling and Schweiger, 1993). I suggest that upon its maturation in the middle of the second year, the orbitofrontal area of the right hemisphere acts as an "executive control system" for the entire right brain. Its essential role in adaptive capacities is seen in the activation of the right orbitofrontal regulatory system during classical conditioning of an emotional response, which Hugdahl and colleagues (1995) define as the implicit learning of the relationship between events that allows the organism to represent its environment. Ryan and colleagues (1997) conclude that the operation of the right prefrontal cortex is integral to autonomous regulation, and that the activation of this system facilitates increases in positive affect in response to optimally challenging or personally meaningful situations, and decreases in negative affect in response to stressful events. The essential aspect of this function is highlighted by Westin (1997, p. 542), who asserts that "[t]he attempt to regulate affect – to minimize unpleasant feelings and to maximize pleasant ones – is the driving force in human motivation."

These findings bear upon an ongoing debate concerning hemispheric asymmetry and the regulation of emotions (Canli, 1999). There is now general agreement that right cortical posterior association regions are centrally involved in the perception of all emotional information. However, with regard to the production and experience and thereby the regulation of emotion, there is a controversy, with some suggesting that the right hemisphere regulates all emotions (the right hemisphere hypothesis – e.g., Borod et al., 1996; Heilman & Bowers, 1990), while others suggest a model in which the right is specialized for negative and the left for positive emotions (the valence hypothesis – e.g., Davidson et al., 1990). In general, studies examining hemispheric lateralization for emotional *nonverbal* stimuli (e.g., faces) have provided support for the right hemispheric model of emotional lateralization (Ali and Cimino, 1997), a finding that fits with the conception that the right hemisphere contains a "nonverbal affect lexicon," a vocabulary for nonverbal affective signals such as facial expressions, gestures, and prosody (Bowers, Bauer, and Heilman, 1993). Conditioned autonomic responses after subliminal presentations of facial expressions occur only when faces are presented to the right hemisphere (Johnsen and Hugdahl, 1991), clearly implying that future studies should use tachistoscopic facial stimuli. Furthermore, the majority of these studies have been done with adults, but recent infant studies (e.g., Nass and Koch, 1991) report that the right hemisphere plays a crucial role in mediating emotional expression from a very early point in development (note that in Figure 6.1, at point F, in the high arousal elated state, the infant turns his head to the left, indicating right hemispheric activation), and that infants with right posterior brain damage show a persistent deficit in the expression of *positive* affect (Reilly et al., 1995).

It is important to note that emotions have, in addition to a valence (hedonic) dimension, an intensity or arousal (energetic) dimension. Many of the "primary" emotions are ergotropic-dominant, energy-expending high arousal, or trophotropic-dominant, energy-conserving low arousal affects, and these "primitive" affects appear early in development, arise automatically, are expressed in facial movements, and are correlated with differentiable ANS activity. Due to the lateralization of catecholaminergic systems in the right hemisphere, it is dominant in the regulation of arousal and is more closely associated with regulation of heart rate than the left. This hemisphere is specialized for processing the autonomic (Wittling et al., 1998; Yoon et al., 1997), neuroendocrine (Kalogeras et al., 1996; Wittling and Pfluger, 1990), and cognitive (Spence, Shapiro, and Zaidel, 1996) correlates of emotional states. The structural and functional qualities of the right cortex, which has a higher metabolic rate than the left, thus account for its essential role in emotional processes that involve significant alterations of arousal.

The developmental approach presented here is compatible with a model in which the early-maturing right hemisphere modulates all nonverbal "primary" emotions, regardless of valence, while the later-maturing left (which does not begin its growth spurt until the last half of the second year) modulates verbal "social" emotions and enhances positive and inhibits negative emotional behavior (Ross, Homan, and Buck, 1994). It also supports the views that the right hemisphere mediates pleasure and pain and the more intrinsically primitive emotions, and that although the left cortex acts to inhibit emotional expression generated in the limbic areas of the right half of the brain, the right brain contains a circuit of emotion regulation that is involved in the modulation of "primary" emotions and "intense emotional-homeostatic processes" (Porges, 1995). Thus, the experience and regulation of affects mediated by extremes of arousal – both high, like terror, excitement, and elation, and low, like shame – would involve more right hemispheric activity, in contrast to their left hemispheric–driven counterparts – anxiety, interest, enjoyment, and guilt.

The right cortex is also specialized for globally directed attention, holistic analysis, and the processing of novel information. As opposed to the left hemisphere's "linear" consecutive analysis of information (Schore, 1999; Tucker, 1981), the processing style of the right hemisphere has been described as *nonlinear*, "based on multiple converging determinants rather than on a single causal chain" (Galin, 1974). According to Ramachandran and colleagues (1996), the cognitive style of the right hemisphere shows a highly sensitive dependence on initial conditions and perturbations, a property of chaotic systems. I conclude that the orbitofrontal cortex, especially in the right brain, is particularly suited to amplifying appraisals of short-acting, small fluctuations into larger effects, and that it is primarily activated in "far-from-equilibrium" states of heightened ergotropic and/or trophotropic emotional arousal that create a potential for achieving novel states and a new stability.

The nonlinear right hemisphere, the substrate of early attachment processes, ends its initial growth phase in the second year, when the linear left hemisphere begins one, but it cycles back into growth phases at later periods of the life cycle (Thatcher, 1994). This allows for the continuity of attachment mechanisms in subsequent functioning, and yet also for the potential continuing reorganization of the emotion-processing right brain throughout life. The orbitofrontal regions, centrally involved in the regulation of psychobiological state and energy balance and in the experience of emotion (Baker, Frith, and Dolan, 1997), the emotional modulation of experience (Mesulam, 1998), and "emotion-related learning" (Rolls et al., 1994), are unique in that they retain the neuroanatomic and biochemical features of early development, and for this reason they are the most plastic areas of the cortex (Barbas, 1995).

If, however, an infant, especially one born with a genetically encoded altered neurophysiologic reactivity, does not have adequate experiences of being part of an open dynamical system with an emotionally responsive adult human, its corticolimbic organization will be poorly capable of coping with the stressful chaotic dynamics that are inherent in all human relationships. Such a system tends to become static and closed, and invested in defensive structures to guard against anticipated interactive assaults that potentially trigger disorganizing and emotionally painful psychobiological states. Due to its avoidance of novel situations and diminished capacity to cope with challenging situations, it does not expose itself to new socioemotional learning experiences that are required for the continuing experience-dependent growth of the right brain. This structural limitation, in turn, negatively impacts the future trajectory of self-organization.

References

Ali, N., and Cimino, C. R. (1997). Hemispheric lateralization of perception and memory for emotional verbal stimuli in normal individuals. *Neuropsychology, 11*, 114–125.

Baker, S. C., Frith, C. D., and Dolan, R. J. (1997). The interaction between mood and cognitive function studied with PET. *Psychological Medicine, 27*, 565–578.

Barbas, H. (1995). Anatomic basis of cognitive-emotional interactions in the primate prefrontal cortex. *Neuroscience and Biobehavioral Reviews, 19*, 499–510.

Bechara, A., Damasio, H., Tranel, D., and Damasio, A. R. (1997). Deciding advantageously before knowing the advantageous strategy. *Science, 275*, 1293–1295.

Beebe, B., and Lachmann, F. M. (1988). Mother-infant mutual influence and precursors of psychic structure. In A. Goldberg (Ed.), *Progress in self psychology, Vol. 3* (pp. 3–25). Hillsdale, NJ: Analytic Press.

Bertalanffy, L. von (1974). General systems theory and psychiatry. In S. Arieti (Ed.), *American handbook of psychiatry* (vol. 1, pp. 1095–1117). New York: Basic Books.

Borod, J. C., Rorie, K. D., Haywood, C. S., Andelman, F., Obler, L. K., Welkowitz,

J., Bloom, R. L., and Tweedy, J. R. (1996). Hemispheric specialization for discourse reports of emotional experiences: Relationships to demographic, neurological, and perceptual variables. *Neuropsychologia, 34,* 351–359.

Bowers, D., Bauer, R. M., and Heilman, K. M. (1993). The nonverbal affect lexicon: Theoretical perspectives from neuropsychological studies of affect perception. *Neuropsychology, 7,* 433–444.

Burstein, R., and Potrebic, S. (1993). Retrograde labeling of neurons in the spinal cord that project directly to the amygdala or the orbital cortex in the rat. *Journal of Comparative Neurology, 335,* 469–483.

Canli, T. (1999), Hemispheric asymmetry in the experience of emotion: A perspective from functional imaging. *The Neuroscientist, 5,* 201–207.

Chiron, C., Jambaque, I., Nabbout, R., Lounes, R., Syrota, A., and Dulac, O. (1997). The right brain is dominant in human infants. *Brain, 120,* 1057–1065.

Cicchetti, D., and Tucker, D. (1994). Development and self-regulatory structures of the mind. *Development and Psychopathology, 6,* 533–549.

Ciompi, L. (1991). Affects as central organising and integrating factors. A new psychosocial/biological model of the psyche. *British Journal of Psychiatry, 159,* 97–105.

Cohn, J. F., and Tronick, E. Z. (1987). Mother-infant face-to-face interaction: The sequence of dyadic states at 3, 6, and 9 months. *Developmental Psychology, 23,* 68–87.

Damasio, A. R. (1994). *Descartes' error: Emotion, reason, and the human brain.* New York: Grosset/Putnam.

Damasio, A. R. (1998). Emotion in the perspective of an integrated nervous system. *Brain Research Reviews, 26,* 83–86.

Davidson, R., Ekman, P., Saron, C., Senulis, J., and Friesen, W.V. (1990). Approach-withdrawal and cerebral asymmetry: Emotion expression and brain physiology I. *Journal of Personality and Social Psychology, 58,* 330–341.

de Schonen, S., Deruelle, C., Mancini, J., and Pascalis, O. (1993). Hemispheric differences in face processing and brain maturation. In B. de Boysson-Bardies, S. de Schonen, P. Jusczyk, P. McNeilage, and J. Morton (Eds.), *Developmental neurocognition: Speech and face processing in the first year of life* (pp. 149–163). Dordrecht: Kluwer.

Devinsky, O., Morrell, M. J., and Vogt, B. A. (1995). Contributions of anterior cingulate cortex to behaviour. *Brain, 118,* 279–306.

Dias, R., Robbins, T. W., and Roberts, A. C. (1996). Dissociation in prefrontal cortex of affective and attentional shifts. *Nature, 380,* 69–72.

Elliot, R., Frith, C. D., and Dolan, R. J. (1997). Differential neural response to positive and negative feedback in planning and guessing tasks. *Neuropsychologia, 35,* 1395–1404.

Falk, D., Hildebolt, C., Cheverud, J., Vannier, M., Helmkamp, R. C., and Konigsberg, L. (1990). Cortical asymmetries in frontal lobes of Rhesus monkeys (Macaca mulatta). *Brain Research, 512,* 40–45.

Feldman, R., Greenbaum, C. W., and Yirmiya, N. (1999). Mothert-infant affect synchrony as an antecedent of the emergence of self-control. *Developmental Psychology, 35,* 223–231.

Fernald, A. (1989). Intonation and communicative interest in mother's speech to infants: Is the melody the message? *Child Development, 60,* 1497–1510.

Fitzgerald, L. W., Keller, R. W., Glick. S. D., and Carlson, J. N. (1989). The effects of stressor controllability on regional changes in mesocorticolimbic dopamine activity. *Society of Neuroscience Abstracts, 15*, 1316.

Flicker, C., McCarley, R. W., and Hobson, J. A. (1981). Aminergic neurons: State control and plasticity in three model systems. *Cellular and Molecular Neurobiology, 1*, 123–166.

Foote, S. L. (1987). Extrathalamic modulation of cortical function. *Annual Review of Neuroscience, 10*, 67–95.

Galin, D. (1974). Lateral specialization and psychiatric issues: Speculations on development and the evolution of consciousness. *Annals of the New York Academy of Sciences, 299*, 397–411.

Gellhorn, E. (1970). The emotions and the ergotropic and trophotropic systems. *Psychologische Forschung, 34*, 48–94.

Gibbons, A. (1998). Solving the brain's energy crisis. *Science, 280*, 1345–1347.

Gleick, J. (1987). *Chaos: Making a new science*. New York: Viking Penguin.

Goerner, S. (1995). Chaos, evolution, and deep ecology. In R. Robertson and A. Combs (Eds.), *Chaos theory in psychology and the life sciences* (pp. 17–38). Mahwah, NJ: Erlbaum.

Goldberger, A. L., Rigney, D. R., and West, B. J. (1990). Chaos and fractals in human physiology. *Scientific American, 262* (February), 43–49.

Gonon, F. G. (1988). Nonlinear relationship between impulse flow and dopamine release by midbrain dopaminergic neurons as studied by *in vivo* electrochemistry. *Neuroscience, 24*, 19–28.

Harold, F. M. (1986). *The vital force: A study of bioenergetics*. New York: W. H. Freeman.

Heilman, K., and Bowers, D. (1990). Neuropsychological studies of emotional changes induced by right and left hemispheric studies. In N. Stein, B. Leventhal, and T. Trabasso (Eds.), *Psychological and biological approaches to emotion* (pp. 97–113). Mahwah, NJ: Erlbaum.

Henry, J. P. (1997). Psychological and physiological response to stress: The right hemisphere and the hypothalamo-pituitary-adrenal axis, an inquiry into problems of human bonding. *Acta Physiologica Scandinavica*, Suppl. 640, 10–25.

Hofer, M. A (1990). Early symbiotic processes: Hard evidence from a soft place. In R. A. Glick and S. Bone (Eds.), *Pleasure beyond the pleasure principle* (pp. 55–78). New Haven, CT: Yale University Press.

Hugdahl, K., Berardi, A., Thompson, W. L., Kosslyn, S. M., Macy, R., Baker, D. P., Alpert, N. M., and LeDoux, J. E. (1995). Brain mechanisms in human classical conditioning: A PET blood flow study. *NeuroReport, 6*, 1723–1728.

Johnsen, B. H., and Hugdahl, K. (1991). Hemispheric asymmetry in conditioning to facial emotional expressions. *Psychophysiology, 28*, 154–162.

Johnson, M. H., and Vecera, S. P. (1993). Cortical parcellation and the development of face processing. In B. de Boysson-Bardies, S. de Schonen, P. Jusczyk, P. McNeilage, and J. Morton (Eds.), *Developmental neurocognition: Speech and face processing in the first year of life* (pp. 135–148). Dordrecht: Kluwer.

Johnston, D., Magee, J. C., Colbert, C. M., and Christie, B. R. (1996). Active properties of neuronal dendrites. *Annual Review of Neuroscience, 19*, 165–186.

Joseph, R. (1996). *Neuropsychiatry, neuropsychology, and clinical neuroscience* (2nd ed.). Baltimore: Williams and Wilkins.

Kalogeras, K. T., Nieman, L. K., Friedman, T. C., Doppman, J. L., Cutler, G. B., Jr., Chrousos, G. P., Wilder, R. L., Gold, P. W., and Yanovski, J. A. (1996). Inferior petrosal sinus sampling in healthy human subjects reveals a unilateral corticotropin-releasing hormone-induced arginine vasopressin release associated with ipsilateral adrenocorticotropin secretion. *Journal of Clinical Investigation, 97*, 2045–2050.

Katsuri, S., Amtey, S., and Beall, P. (1984). *NMR data handbook for biomedical applications*. New York: Pergamon.

Kennedy, C., and Sokoloff, L. (1957). An adaptation of the nitrous oxide method to the study of the cerebral circulation in children: Normal values for cerebral blood flow and cerebral metabolic rate in childhood. *Journal of Clinical Investigation, 36*, 1130–1137.

Kolb, B., & Whishaw, I. Q. (1990). *Fundamentals of human neuropsychology* (3rd ed.) New York: Freeman.

Krimer, L. S., Muly, E. C., III, Williams, G. V., and Goldman-Rakic, P. S. (1998). Dopaminergic regulation of cerebral cortical microcirculation. *Nature Neuroscience, 1*, 286–289.

Lewis, M. D. (1995). Cognition-emotion feedback and the self-organization of developmental paths. *Human Development, 38*, 71–102.

Locke, J. L. (1993). *The child's path to spoken language*. Cambridge, MA: Harvard University Press.

Lydic, R. (1987). State-dependent aspects of regulatory physiology. *The Federation of American Societies for Experimental Biology Journal, 1*, 6–15.

MacLean, P. D. (1993). Perspectives on cingulate cortex in the limbic system. In B. A. Vogt and M. Gabriel (Eds.), *Neurobiology of cingulate cortex and limbic thalamus: A comprehensive handbook* (pp. 1–15). Boston: Birkhauser.

Margolis, R. L., Chuang, D. M., and Post, R. M. (1994). Programmed cell death: Implications for neuropsychiatric disorders. *Biological Psychiatry, 35*, 946–956.

McGregor, I. S., and Atrens, D. M. (1991). Prefrontal cortex self-stimulation and energy balance. *Behavorial Neuroscience, 105*, 870–883.

McGuiness, D., Pribram, K. H., and Pirnazar, M. (1990). Upstaging the stage model. In C. N. Alexander and E. Langer (Eds.), *Higher stages of human development* (pp. 97–113). New York: Oxford University Press.

Mender, D. M. (1994). *The myth of neuropsychiatry: A look at paradoxes, physics, and the human brain*. New York: Plenum.

Mesulam, M.-M. (1998). From sensation to cognition. *Brain, 121*, 1013–1052.

Michel, G. F., and Moore, C. L. (1995). *Developmental psychobiology*. Cambridge, MA: MIT Press.

Nass, R., and Koch, D. (1991). Innate specialization for emotion: Temperament differences in children with left versus right damage. In N. Amir, I. Rapin, and D. Branski (Eds.), *Pediatric neurology: Behavior and cognition of the child with brain dysfunction* (vol. 1, pp. 1–17). Basel: Karger.

Neafsey, E. J. (1990). Prefrontal cortical control of the autonomic nervous system: Anatomical and physiological observations. *Progress in Brain Research, 85*, 147–166.

Nelson, C. A. (1987). The recognition of facial expressions in the first two years of life: Mechanisms of development. *Child Development, 58*, 889–909.

Nelson, C. A. (1994). Neural bases of infant temperament. In J. E. Bates and T. D.

Wachs (Eds.), *Temperament: Individual differences at the interface of biology and behavior* (pp. 47–82). Washington, DC: American Psychological Association.

Ornstein, R. (1997). *The right mind: Making sense of the hemispheres.* New York: Harcourt Brace.

Overton, P. G., and Clark, D. (1997). Burst firing in midbrain dopaminergic neurons. *Brain Research Reviews, 25,* 312–334.

Paus, T., Petrides, M., Evans, A. C., and Meyer, E. (1993). Role of the human anterior cingulate cortex in the control of oculomotor, manual, and speech responses: A positron emission tomography study. *Journal of Neurophysiology, 70,* 453–469.

Perkel, D. H., and Perkel, D. J. (1985). Dendritic spines: Role of active membranes in modulating synaptic efficacy. *Brain Research, 325,* 331–335.

Pipp, S. (1993). Infant's knowledge of self, other, and relationship. In U. Neisser (Ed.), *The perceived self* (pp. 185–204). New York: Cambridge University Press.

Porges, S. W. (1995). Orienting in a defensive world: Mammalian modifications of our evolutionary heritage: A polyvagal theory. *Psychophysiology, 32,* 301–318.

Porges, S. W., Doussard-Roosevelt, J. A., and Maiti, A. K. (1994). Vagal tone and the physiological regulation of emotion. In N. A Fox (Ed.), *The development of emotion regulation: Biological and behavioral considerations. Monographs of the Society for Research in Child Development, 59* (2-3, serial no. 240), pp. 167–186.

Price, J. L., Carmichael, S. T., and Drevets, W. C. (1996). Networks related to the orbital and medial prefrontal cortex: A substrate for emotional behavior? *Progress in Brain Research, 107,* 523–536.

Prigogine, I., and Stengers, I. (1984). *Order out of chaos.* New York: Bantam.

Ramachandran, V. S., Levi, L., Stone, L., Rogers-Ramachandran, D., McKinney, R., Stalcup, M., Arcilla, G., Zweifler, R., Shatz, A., and Flippin, A. (1996). Illusions of body image: What they reveal about human nature. In R. Llinas and P. S. Churchland (Eds.), *The mind-brain continuum: Sensory processes* (pp. 29–60). Cambridge, MA: MIT Press.

Reilly, J. S., Stiles, J., Larsen, J., and Trauner, D. (1995). Affective expression in infants with focal brain damage. *Neuropsychologia, 33,* 83–99.

Rolls, E. T. (1996). The orbitofrontal cortex. *Philosophical Transactions of the Royal Society of London, Series B, 351,* 1433–1444.

Rolls, E. D., Hornak, J., Wade, D., and McGrath, J. (1994). Emotion-related learning in patients with social and emotional changes associated with frontal lobe damage. *Journal of Neurology, Neurosurgery, and Psychiatry, 57,* 1518–1524.

Ross, E. D., Homan, R. W., and Buck, R. (1994). Differential hemispheric lateralization of primary and social emotions: Implications for developing a comprehensive neurology for emotions, repression, and the subconscious. *Neuropsychiatry, Neuropsychology, and Behavioral Neurology, 7,* 1–19.

Ryan, R. M., Kuhl, J., and Deci, E. L. (1997). Nature and autonomy: An organizational view of social and neurobiological aspects of self-regulation in behavior and development. *Development and Psychopathology, 9,* 701–728.

Scalaidhe, S. P., Wilson, A. W., and Goldman-Rakic, P. S. (1997). Areal segregation of face-processing neurons in prefrontal cortex. *Science, 278,* 1135–1138.

Scherer, K. R. (1994). Affect bursts. In S. H. van Goozen, N. E. van de Poll, and J. A.

Sergeant (Eds.), *Emotions: Essays on emotion theory* (pp. 161–193). Mahwah, NJ: Erlbaum.

Schore, A. N. (1994). *Affect regulation and the origin of the self: The neurobiology of emotional development.* Mahwah, NJ: Erlbaum.

Schore, A. N. (1996). The experience-dependent maturation of a regulatory system in the orbital prefrontal cortex and the origin of developmental psychopathology. *Development and Psychopathology, 8,* 59–87.

Schore, A. N. (1997a). Interdisciplinary developmental research as a source of clinical models. In M. Moskowitz, C. Monk, C. Kaye, and S. Ellman (Eds.), *The neurobiological and developmental basis for psychotherapeutic intervention* (pp. 1–71). Northvale, NJ: Aronson.

Schore, A. N. (1997b). Early organization of the nonlinear right brain and development of a predisposition to psychiatric disorders. *Development and Psychopathology, 9,* 595–631.

Schore, A. N. (1998). The experience-dependent maturation of an evaluative system in the cortex. In K. H. Pribram (Ed.), *Brain and values: Is a biological science of values possible?* (pp. 337–358). Mahwah, NJ: Erlbaum.

Schore, A. N. (1999). Commentary on Freud's affect theory in the light of contemporary neuroscience. *Neuro-Psychoanalysis, 1,* 49–55.

Schumann, J. H. (1997). *The neurobiology of affect in language.* Malden, MA: Blackwell.

Schwalbe, M. L. (1991). The autogenesis of the self. *Journal of the Theory of Social Behavior, 21,* 269–295.

Semrud-Clikeman, M., and Hynd, G. W. (1990). Right hemisphere dysfunction in nonverbal learning disabilities: Social, academic, and adaptive functioning in adults and children. *Psychological Bulletin, 107,* 196–209.

Shinbrot, T., Grebogi, C., Ott, E., and Yorke, J. A. (1993). Using small perturbations to control chaos. *Nature, 363,* 411–417.

Siegel, D. J. (1999). *The developing mind: Toward a neurobiology of interpersonal experience.* New York: Guilford.

Skinner, J. E., Molnar, M., Vybiral, T., and Mitra, M. (1992). Application of chaos theory to biology and medicine. *Integrative Physiology and Behavioral Science, 27,* 43–57.

Smith, C. G. (1981). *Serial dissection of the human brain.* Baltimore: Urban and Scwarzenberg.

Spence, S., Shapiro, D., and Zaidel, E. (1996). The role of the right hemisphere in the physiological and cognitive components of emotional processing. *Psychophysiology, 33,* 112–122.

Stern, D. N. (1990). Joy and satisfaction in infancy. In R. A. Glick and S. Bone (Eds.), *Pleasure beyond the pleasure principle* (pp. 13–25). New Haven, CT: Yale University Press.

Sullivan, R. M., and Szechtman, H. (1995). Asymmetrical influence of mesocortical dopamine depletion on stress ulcer development and subcortical dopamine systems in rats: Implications for psychopathology. *Neuroscience, 65,* 757–766.

Thatcher, R. W. (1994). Cyclical cortical reorganization: Origins of human cognitive development. In G. Dawson and K. W. Fischer (Eds.), *Human behavior and the developing brain* (pp. 232–266). New York: Guilford.

Thelen, E. (1989). Self-organization in developmental processes: Can systems approaches work? In M. R. Gunnar and E. Thelen (Eds.), *Minnesota Symposium on Child Psychology: Vol. 22. Systems and development* (pp. 77–118). Hillsdale, NJ: Erlbaum.

Thelen, E. (1995). Motor development: A new synthesis. *American Psychologist, 50*, 79–95.

Tremblay, L., and Schultz, W. (1999). Relative reward preference in primate orbito-frontal cortex. *Nature, 398*, 704–708.

Trevarthen, C. (1993). The self born in intersubjectivity: The psychology of an infant communicating. In U. Neisser (Ed.), *The perceived self: Ecological and interpersonal sources of self-knowledge* (pp. 121–173). New York: Cambridge University Press.

Tucker, D. M. (1981). Lateral brain function, emotion, and conceptualization. *Psychological Bulletin, 89*, 19–46.

Tucker, D. M. (1992). Developing emotions and cortical networks. In M. R. Gunnar and C. A. Nelson (Eds.), *Minnesota Symposium on Child Psychology: Vol. 24. Developmental behavioral neuroscience* (pp. 75–128). Hillsdale, NJ: Erlbaum.

van Vreeswijk, C., and Sompolinsky, H. (1996). Chaos in neuronal networks with balanced excitatory and inhibitory activity. *Science, 274*, 1724–1726.

Wang, S. (1997). Traumatic stress and attachment. *Acta Physiologica Scandinavica*, Suppl. 640, 164–169.

Westin, D. (1997). Towards a clinically and empirically sound theory of motivation. *International Journal of Psychoanalysis, 78*, 521–548.

Wittling, W., Block, A., Schweiger, E., and Genzel, S. (1998). Hemisphere asymmetry in sympathetic control of the human myocardium. *Brain and Cognition, 38*, 17–35.

Wittling, W., and Pfluger, M. (1990). Neuroendocrine hemisphere asymmetries: Salivary cortisol secretion during lateralized viewing of emotion-related and neutral films. *Brain and Cognition, 14*, 243–265.

Wittling, W., and Schweiger, E. (1993). Neuroendocrine brain asymmetry and physical complaints. *Neuropsychologia, 31*, 591–608.

Wolf, S. (1995). Psychosocial forces and neural mechanisms in disease: Defining the question and collecting the evidence. *Integrative Physiological and Behavioral Science, 30*, 85–94.

Wright, K. (1991). *Vision and separation: Between mother and baby*. Northvale, NJ: Aronson.

Yamada, H., Sadato, N., Konishi, Y., Kimura, K., Tanaka, M., Yonekura, Y., and Ishii, Y. (1997). A rapid metabolic change in infants detected by fMRI. *Neuro-Report, 8*, 3775–3778.

Yoon, B-U., Morillo, C. A., Cechetto, D. F., and Hachinski, V. (1997). Cerebral hemispheric lateralization in cardiac autonomic control. *Archives of Neurology, 54*, 741–744.

7 Motivation of Neural Plasticity: Neural Mechanisms in the Self-Organization of Depression

Kate L. Harkness and Don M. Tucker

In this chapter we outline a theoretical framework for self-organization in the development of a neurological and cognitive-emotional vulnerability to major depression. We begin by outlining the basis for plasticity in embryonic and early infant neural systems. Early plasticity, we argue, forms the basis for learning and, by extension, may determine the organization of the cognitive and emotional schemas that drive behavior. Disruptions in the mechanisms of plasticity may lead to disruptions in emotional, motivational, and cognitive self-organization, rendering the person vulnerable to affective psychopathology throughout life.

Disruptions at two levels of neurological control of plasticity and self-organization may lead to vulnerability to depression. First, arousal states, under the control of brain stem and thalamic centers, are necessary to support the neural plasticity underlying learning. We propose that deficits in arousal due to early neglect and/or loss experiences may impair normal developmental plasticity. Second, we propose that particularly traumatic events, such as childhood sexual abuse, may form enduring memory traces in cortical and limbic areas. These memories, and the emotional dysregulation they engender, may then sensitize (or "kindle") individuals to such experiences in the future. In support of these two hypotheses, we review the mechanisms of arousal control and memory consolidation, and their likely roles in neural plasticity. We then theorize on how these may be related to the neurological and cognitive sequelae of early neglect and trauma both in animal models and in studies with humans.

A general and overarching hypothesis that encompasses the two specific learning models just outlined follows from an analysis of neural plasticity within a self-organizing neural network such as the child's brain. We argue that self-organization, in general, is a cumulative and dynamic process, with each new learning experience building upon the existing neuropsychological representation interactively. Using learning in distributed neural networks as a metaphor for human learning, we describe how cognitive schemas tend toward stability over time, and we argue that these schemas are invariably constrained by their developmental histories. We argue that the cumulative nature of self-organization may be a pernicious problem for individuals who experience early adversity. First, adverse early experiences, because they are emotionally charged, may constrain plasticity, leading to the early formation of a relatively stable depressogenic schema. Second, in the process of self-organization, learning on the basis of future experiences may be interpreted in the context of the existing neuropsychological representation. The existing network of associations sensitizes the person to similar future events, increasing the likelihood of reacting to these events with episodes of major depression.

Arousal, Motivation, and the Activity-Dependent Specification of Cortical Anatomy

Early behavioral and anatomical observations have suggested that, rather than being a fixed, mechanical process of translating shape instructions from a genetic blueprint, embryonic neural morphogenesis is self-organizing (Hamburger, 1977; Herrick, 1965). Early in embryonic neural development there is a massive, indiscriminate synaptogenesis and axonal and dendritic sprouting, creating a highly interconnected, undifferentiated nerve network (Huttenlocher, 1990). This network is then pared down and sculpted based upon functional usage. Self-organization is intrinsic to morphogenesis, and the embryo spontaneously emits rhythmic motor patterns that provide input to somatosensory, kinesthetic, and other sensory systems (Hamburger, 1977). As a result, functional sensorimotor circuits become strengthened, while unused circuits are lost. This process has been described as Darwinian, in the sense that activity operates to strengthen connections while disuse causes the unused connections to atrophy (Changeux and Dehaene, 1989).

One of the more remarkable insights of modern neuroscience has been that these basic mechanisms of embryonic neural morphogenesis continue to operate into the extended mammalian juvenile period. Based upon the information exchange between perceptual and motor systems and the environment, useful connections are strengthened, and unused connections are pruned (Innocenti, 1983; Neville et al., 1998). Current theoretical models hold that this mechanism of synaptic pruning and strengthening may form the basis for learning (Singer, 1987; von der Malsburg and Singer, 1988).

In most mammals, this neural plasticity declines substantially within a few years after birth, particularly at the point of sexual maturity. Human development, however, represents an exaggerated neoteny, with extensive plasticity maintained throughout the two decades of childhood and adolescence. This sensitive period of childhood and adolescence is when brain systems are both critically dependent on and maximally sensitive to environmental influence. The result of such a long period of plasticity in humans may be a degree of individual variability in neuroanatomy, and thus personality, that is unique in the animal kingdom. The capacity for neural plasticity continues to decline as the brain matures, with different critical periods for different cognitive skills (Neville, 1995), and this decline is precisely marked by indicators of maturation such as myelination. However, despite the progressive decrease in plasticity, research in the last few years has shown that even adult mammals may retain the capacity to reorganize cortical maps, at least on the basis of significant new sensory experience (Recanzone et al., 1992).

If the specification of cortical networks is activity-dependent, then not only local synaptic traffic but also global controls on neural activation may need to be intact for normal behavioral and neuroanatomical development. In recent experimental models of developmental neural plasticity, perceptual networks often show plasticity only when they are engaged together with a functional response (von der Malsburg and Singer, 1988), as if the activation of the circuit must be supported by global arousal and motivational controls. For example, in the kitten model of ocular dominance plasticity, paralyzing the kitten is sufficient to block plasticity, but plasticity returns within thirty to sixty minutes if the visual stimulation is accompanied by global neural arousal produced by nonspecific thalamic or brain stem reticular stimulation (Singer, 1987). The neurotransmitter projection systems (specifically, norepinephrine and acetylcholine) that mediate the brain stem reticular controls on arousal must be intact to allow plastic reorganization in response to altered visual input (Singer, 1987). Recently, the forebrain arousal and motivational controls from the cholinergic nucleus basalis have been shown to modulate the reorganization of auditory cortex in response to new learning experiences (Kilgard and Merzenich, 1998). Kilgard and Merzenich point out that behavioral learning has been known to be under motivational control since the first experimental studies of behavior a century ago. We should not be surprised, therefore, to recognize that the neural plasticity underlying this learning is also under motivational control.

Given this evidence from animal studies, it becomes important to question whether brain development in humans may be disrupted by impaired arousal. Arousal in children is closely linked to social interaction (Derryberry and Rothbart, 1988; Rothbart, Posner, and Boylan, 1990). It follows that impoverished social interactions might result in low levels of arousal and thus an inadequate neurological substrate for activity-dependent specification. Children of depressed mothers are an important group to study within this framework. Due to the mother's own arousal deficits, it has been hypothesized that these children may not be receiving a sufficiently stimulating environment, thus leading to deficits in the emergence of their own emotional and cognitive structures. Depressed mothers play with their children less than do nondepressed mothers, and they display more negative affect toward their children in play (Lang et al., 1996). Children growing up with a depressed mother may therefore be at risk for neurological as well as behavioral dysfunction.

Infants of depressed mothers tend to display less activity, more frequent negative facial expressions, and greater sleep difficulties than infants of nondepressed mothers (Jones et al., 1997). In addition, the infants of depressed mothers show poor orienting skills, specifically in localizing sounds and tracking moving stimuli. Even as early as one month, infants of depressed mothers display reduced left frontal EEG activation relative to infants of nondepressed mothers (Dawson et al., 1997; Jones et al., 1997). It has been hypothesized that infants of depressed mothers may have higher sensory thresholds and require more arousing stimuli in order to respond appropriately to cues in the environment (Abrams et al., 1995). Whatever the mechanisms, by preschool age children of depressed mothers exhibit greater levels of psychopathology (both internalizing and externalizing disorders) than children of nondepressed mothers (Field et al., 1996).

Due to the correlational nature of the above studies, it is not clear whether differences between children of depressed and nondepressed mothers are due to differences in the postnatal interactional environment, deficits in the intrauterine environment, or simply the transmission of vulnerable temperamental traits. However, given the animal studies of arousal and neural plasticity, a compelling hypothesis is that the depressed mother's poor emotional organization is conveyed to the child, resulting in a chronic pattern of low neural arousal and, as a result, deficits in plastic learning and emotional self-organization. The arousal deficits of childhood depression also have direct implications for motivation and emotional outlook throughout development. Although arousal has traditionally been treated in psychological theory as a dimension independent of emotional valence, more recent investigation into the neuromodulator controls on brain arousal have suggested that high and low neurological arousal states are inherently charged with hedonic and anhedonic mood states, respectively. This is seen in the variation in motivation and cognitive bias between depression and mania (Tucker and Williamson, 1984). Therefore, if low neural arousal frames the process of early neurological development, then psychological development may be characterized by the formation of self-schemas centered around themes of loss, hopelessness, and low self-worth, as well as a vulnerability to experience depressed mood.

Memory Consolidation and Corticolimbic Kindling

In addition to brain stem and thalamic arousal controls, there are also important control processes emanating from cortical and limbic networks (Tucker, 1992). We argue that these processes control the consolidation of emotionally charged experiences. Specifically, information of a traumatic nature (e.g., abuse) may become overconsolidated due to its hyperexcitation of limbic networks. This process provides a further constraint on plasticity through formation of a schema biasing cognition toward themes of danger, helplessness, and guilt.

For humans as well as for other animals, the consolidation of memory requires intact commerce between paralimbic and neocortical networks (Squire, 1992). The anatomical studies of the last two decades have clarified that neocortical networks evolve from paralimbic networks, and that the two levels remain integrated in a structured, coherent architecture (Pandya and Yeterian, 1985, 1990). The neuropsychological model of cognition that emerges from these studies suggests that brain function unfolds like an onion, with layered neocortical networks emanating from a core of highly reactive limbic cortices (Derryberry and Tucker, 1991; Tucker, 1992). Because the limbic networks are more densely interconnected than are neocortical networks, the limbic cortices provide holistic representations of motivational significance that may energize the process of memory consolidation for self-relevant information. This limbic excitability may then regulate the process of memory consolidation according to the personal significance of the information (Tucker and Luu, 1998). We can thus theorize that if limbic activity is poorly controlled, due to either neural or emotional pathology, the result may be an overconsolidation of emotionally charged experiences. Particularly significant for the cumulative nature of schema development, the human behavioral evidence suggests that memory consolidation may not be limited to minutes or hours, but may extend over days or even years (Gustafsson and Wigstrom, 1988; Squire, 1987; Teyler, 1986).

The neurophysiology of a hyperexcited limbic network is seen in the process of electrophysiological kindling in animals. Kindling involves the sensitization to seizure-inducing electrical current applied to, primarily, limbic areas (Doane and Livingston, 1986; Goddard, McIntyre, and Leech, 1969). When electrical stimulation is initially applied to a limbic site, substantial current is required to generate seizures. However, when stimulation is repeated at intermittent intervals, progressively lower current thresholds are required to generate the same intensity of seizure, and eventually seizures occur spontaneously (Goddard et al., 1969). Kindling has been demonstrated in numerous species and in a variety of brain areas. Subcortical limbic areas, particularly the hippocampus and amygdala, appear to be most sensitive to kindling effects (Goddard et al., 1986). The limbic hyperexcitability produced by kindling results in cognitive and emotional dysregulation. For example, kindling of the amygdala in cats often produces a long-term heightening of the fear or anxiety response to threat (Adamec and McKay, 1993).

The most direct human parallel to electrophysiological kindling is temporal lobe epilepsy (TLE), which involves internal electrophysiologically induced limbic seizures. In TLE, the ongoing seizure disorder appears to produce an exaggerated degree of limbic constraint on cognition (Bear, 1979). The psychological changes in these patients illustrate how memory consolidation may become overly constrained by limbic activity. When the epileptic focus is in the temporal lobe of the nondominant right hemisphere, the patient shows exaggerated emotionality and poor emotional control, consistent with an exaggeration of the right hemisphere's contributions to emotional experience and expression (Bear and Fedio, 1977). More interesting are the symptoms when the limbic focus occurs in the dominant left hemisphere. The left temporal epileptic may show obsessive intellectual concerns, often writing extensive philosophical or religious treatises (Bear and Fedio, 1977). For either hemisphere, the normal cognitive processes of that side of the brain are exaggerated, as if limbic activity had become disinhibited from normal cortical constraint.

Interestingly, electrical kindling has been found to cross-sensitize to environmental stress sensitization (Adamec and McKay, 1993). In animals, electrical kindling and environmental stress sensitization appear to share mechanisms, resulting in similar neurochemical and behavioral changes (e.g., hypercortisolism and heightened fear response; Adamec and McKay, 1993; Adamec, Sayin, and Brown, 1991; Corcoran and Weiss, 1989). Perhaps most important for an integrated neurobehavioral theory of memory is the observation that kindling and seizure activity can be classically conditioned (Janowsky, Laxer, and Rushmer, 1980).

Based upon the similarities between kindling and stress sensitization, Post and his colleagues have suggested that kindling may be analogous to the neuropathological process involved in traumatic stress sensitization and depression recurrence in humans (e.g., Post, 1992; Post, Weiss, and Leverich, 1994). That is, traumatic life events, especially those experienced during a period of intense synaptogenesis and plasticity, may create a vulnerability in limbic areas that increases emotional reactivity to similar events in the future. Clinical evidence for stress sensitization in depression comes from several studies demonstrating that, while severe negative life events are required to precipitate early episodes of the disorder, increasingly less severe events are observed to trigger onset as the disorder progresses across multiple recurrences. In addition, recurrent episodes of depression tend to cycle more quickly as the disorder progresses (e.g., Ezquiaga, Gutierrez, and Lopez, 1987; Ghaziuddin, Ghaziuddin, and Stein, 1990). We agree with Post's hypothesis. However, we suggest that kindling is more than an analogy. Given the evidence for the cross-sensitization of kindling and emotional stress, and the observation of classical conditioning of the kindling response, we hypothesize that early traumatic experiences, such as childhood abuse, may literally kindle limbic areas. As reviewed here, environmental trauma is associated with neurological damage in the limbic areas that are most responsive to electrophysiological kindling.

Early adversity may thus create a vulnerability to depression in two ways. First, poor and/or neglectful mother-child interactions may impair plasticity by impairing the self-regulation of neural arousal that forms the physiological substrate for activity-dependent specification of synaptic connections. Second, early traumatic abuse may constrain plasticity by sensitizing limbic excitability, leading to an overconsolidation of the traumatic information. Memory thus becomes fixated by the traumatic concern to the detriment of future, perhaps more adaptive, learning.

The Role of Early Experience in Adult Depression

An assumption of our theoretical model is that there is a causal link between early life events and depression onset. The role of early negative life experience has for decades played a central role in theorizing about etiological factors in the development of adult depression. However, only recently has its role been subjected to rigorous scientific scrutiny, with the development of sophisticated interview methods for capturing these early events and the psychosocial context in which they occur (e.g., the Childhood Experience of Care and Abuse Scale [CECA]; Bifulco, Brown, and Harris, 1994). Studies using such methods have consistently found a strong relationship between early loss and abuse events and the onset of major depression.

In two community studies of working-class women living in London, Harris, Brown, and Bifulco (1986) found that those who had lost a mother by death or separation prior to age seventeen had a 22 percent chance of developing an episode of depression in the three-year study period, versus a 4 percent chance in those without any loss experiences in childhood. A similar pattern of results was found regarding the relationship between early abuse and depression. Specifically, in a longitudinal study of 286 women, 64 percent of the 25 women in the sample who had experienced childhood sexual abuse developed depression at some point in the three-year study period, versus 26 percent of the non–sexually abused women (Bifulco, Brown, and Adler, 1991).

Central to a theory of self-organization of personality is that no single life experience is capable of completely determining personality and schema formation. That is, one single trauma does not "brand" itself into the limbic system and determine all subsequent personality adjustment; instead, self-organization is the result of the dynamic interaction between cognitive appraisals, emotional responses, and environmental contexts over time (Lewis, 1996, 1997). This theoretical proposal is supported by the clinical evidence relating early adversity to depression. For example, in the literature relating early loss of mother to depression, several researchers have found that the experience of loss on its own does not translate into increased depression risk. Instead, an environment characterized by lack of adequate parental care subsequent to early parental loss is required to model the relationship between early loss and adulthood depression (Bifulco et al., 1987; Breier et al., 1988; Harris et al., 1986). This experience of loss and subsequent neglect may be similar in its theme, and engender similar neurological effects, to the chronically impoverished context experienced by children of depressed mothers discussed earlier (e.g., Dawson et al., 1997).

Similarly, in the literature relating early abuse to depression, Bifulco and colleagues (1991) found that the rates of depression varied with the severity and frequency of abuse: 100 percent of women who had experienced repeated forced sexual intercourse developed depression, versus 78 percent of those who had experienced repeated abuse with no intercourse, versus only 30 percent for those who had experienced single incidents of abuse with no intercourse. This rate of 30 percent in the single-incident group was not significantly different from the rate of 26 percent observed in the non–sexually abused group (Bifulco et al., 1991). Thus, single traumatic incidents do not appear to determine adult depression; instead, an environmental context of ongoing adversity is necessary. This chronically stressful environment facilitates assimilation of the early abuse or loss, and may prevent the development of adaptive and protective cognitive and emotional mechanisms.

These studies illustrate that two very different types of early negative contexts – loss/neglect and repeated abuse – are able to precipitate major depression. As discussed earlier, within a neuropsychological model of activity-dependent cortical organization, this chronic environmental adversity can be expected to produce in these children enduring alterations of neural organization. For the neglected child, the global arousal mechanisms that should be engaged in the service of play, exploration, and challenge may be shut down, resulting in inadequate plastic learning. As a result, a relatively stable schema may be formed early in life involving themes of loss, hopelessness, and low self-worth, thus creating a vulnerability to depression. For the abused and traumatized child, the consolidation processes mediating between limbic and cortical networks may become hyperexcitable. The result may be an overconsolidation of the traumatic abuse experiences, and the formation of an enduring traumatic memory template. Although the basic mechanisms of arousal control and corticolimbic consolidation are integral to normal memory, traumatic experience may cause them to become pathological, not only in a psychological but also in a neurological sense.

Neurological Sequelae of Early Trauma – Animal Models

Animal studies have shown that stress may alter the early plasticity of brain regions required for normal behavioral development. For example, neonatal stress in rats (i.e., restraint, tail shock, swimming, and shaking) has been found to lead to a downregulation of hippocampal glucocorticoid receptors and cell death of hippocampal neurons (MagariInos and McEwen, 1995; McEwen, 1994; Sapolsky and Pulsinelli, 1985). These neurological changes were accompanied by behavioral performance deficits, perhaps due to an impairment of long-term potentiation (LTP) and enhancement of long-term depression (LTD) in the CA1 area of the hippocampus (Kim, Foy, and Thompson, 1996). The stressors to which animals were exposed in these studies (e.g., tail shock and restraint) posed threats to the animals that may model early abuse experiences in humans.

Stressors evoking themes of loss have also been associated with neurological abnormalities in animals. Maternal deprivation results in long-lasting hypercortisolism in both rats and monkeys (e.g., Plotsky and Meaney, 1993; Rosenfeld, Wetmore, and Levine, 1992), and this effect has been found to last into adulthood (Plotsky and Meaney, 1993). MacLean (1986) has implicated the cingulate subdivision of the limbic system in the audio-vocal communication necessary for maintaining maternal-offspring contact (i.e., the isolation call). Opiate receptors are found in high concentration in the cingulate cortex, and opiates are released during maternal-infant contact (Kehoe, 1989). In addition, the administration of morphine leads to a cessation of the isolation call in separated animals (Kehoe, 1989). MacLean (1986) suggests that the thalamocingulate division may be implicated in generation of ''separation feelings'' conducive to drug addiction and depression.

Rats that have undergone maternal separation are more likely to engage in a pattern of cocaine and alcohol self-administration than their nonseparated litter mates (Plotsky, 1997). Interestingly, Plotsky (1997) found that the endocrine abnormalities and increased cocaine and alcohol sensitivity associated with separation were partially reversed by selective serotonin reuptake inhibitor (SSRI) antidepressants. Once the SSRIs were withdrawn, however, these abnormalities reverted to pretreatment levels. The sensitivity of these deprived animals to drugs of reward suggests that, parallel to neglected children, these animals may experience chronic deficits in hedonic arousal. They may seek to correct this deficiency through self-medication.

Neurological Sequelae of Trauma in Humans

Recent studies have begun to investigate the neurological sequelae of early trauma in humans. To date, only early abuse experiences have been examined. Since early loss also appears to be a strong precipitant to depression, future studies investigating the effects of early loss on neurological development in humans are needed to provide a full account of neurological vulnerability to depression. In addition, the psychopathological conditions studied are not limited to depression, but include a wide range of disorders. Nevertheless, these studies are providing support for the core role of the limbic system in traumatic processing.

Shearer and colleagues (1990) found that women with borderline personality disorder (BPD) who reported a history of sexual abuse were significantly more likely to have a concomitant diagnosis of partial seizure disorder than were BPD patients with no abuse history. These researchers suggest that the repetitive abuse experiences may "kindle" limbic substrates, "eventually manifested in adulthood as some combination of complex partial seizure disorder and chronic PTSD [post-traumatic stress disorder]" (Shearer et al., 1990, p. 216). A similar study by Teicher and colleagues (1993) utilized a checklist designed to assess limbic system dysfunction in order to compare adult psychiatric patients (with PTSD, major depression, and panic disorder) who had experienced early abuse (sexual and/or physical) to a control group of patients with no such early abuse. The checklist assessed for the presence of symptom categories often encountered as ictal TLE phenomena, including brief hallucinations and automatisms, as well as visual, somatic, and dissociative disturbances. Compared to controls, patients who had suffered early sexual, physical, or both forms of abuse exhibited 49 percent, 39 percent, and 113 percent greater scores, respectively.

In addition, Ito and colleagues demonstrated that children with psychiatric diagnoses who had suffered early physical and/or sexual abuse had an increased prevalence of resting EEG abnormalities localized to left fronto-temporal regions (Ito et al., 1993). Consistent with the laterality of these abnormalities, the abused children demonstrated better visual-spatial ability than verbal ability. These results are similar to the reduced left frontal activation observed in infants of depressed mothers described earlier (Jones et al., 1997). In addition, in an auditory EEG study, Schiffer, Teicher, and Papanicolaou (1995) found that adult participants with a history of childhood trauma had significantly reduced left hemisphere versus right hemisphere activity when evoking an unpleasant memory, compared to a non-traumatized group. This asymmetry during traumatic recall was also found in a positron emission tomography (PET) study of eight combat veterans with PTSD (Rauch et al., 1996). Specifically, in this study, increased cerebral blood flow was observed in right limbic and paralimbic regions during traumatic remembering versus recollection of neutral memories (Rauch et al., 1996). These results together suggest that the role of the left hemisphere may be decreased, while the role of the right hemisphere may be increased, in the processing of negative information in traumatized individuals.

Further evidence for the effects of traumatic life events on brain areas, even when the life events are encountered in adulthood, comes from recent brain imaging studies conducted in patients with PTSD. A study by Bremner and colleagues using structural magnetic resonance imaging (MRI) found that the average hippocampal volume of twenty-six combat veterans with PTSD was 8 percent lower than that of twenty-two combat veterans without PTSD. This difference was statistically significant, and no differences in the volumes of other brain regions were found. Furthermore, deficits on the Wechsler Memory Scale were associated with smaller hippocampal volume in the PTSD patients only (Bremner et al., 1995). Recent MRI findings suggest that a decrease in hippocampal volume is also associated with abuse-related PTSD (Bremner et al., 1997). Seventeen survivors of childhood physical and/or sexual abuse had a 12 percent smaller left hippocampal volume relative to nonabused controls. A trend for reduced hippocampal left/right ratio in six PTSD veterans versus seven normal controls has also been observed in one PET study (Semple et al., 1993). These studies are only correlational. Nevertheless, the finding that only the combat veterans with PTSD had smaller hippocampal volumes suggests that emotional dysregulation following trauma may be required for the trauma to result in enduring neurostructural changes.

Therefore, in both animal and human studies, traumatic events appear to produce structural abnormalities in limbic areas, particularly the hippocampus, that have cognitive correlates. Although traumatic neuropsychological effects may also be seen in adulthood, they may be particularly pronounced for traumas of childhood, when the extensive plasticity of the cortex makes the brain vulnerable to disorganizing emotional influences.

Cumulative Self-Organization and the Stability-Plasticity Dilemma

When the young mind is understood as emerging from a self-organizing neural network, the self must be recognized as a cumulative process, with each new learning experience building upon the existing neural and cognitive representation in a dynamic and interactional fashion. The representational capacity of the human cortex is not the result of any single experience, but the cumulative result of its entire developmental history. The human learning process is perhaps analogous to the way in which learning occurs in distributed neural networks (Rumelhart and McClelland, 1986).

As in neural networks, the brain areas responsible for motivational and emotional learning, specifically limbic areas, are highly interconnected (Innocenti, 1983). This high degree of interconnectivity may result in a highly integrated mode of learning for the primary functions of motivation and emotion. Specifically, as each new perceptual experience is integrated within the network, through an extended consolidation process, it is constrained by the representational inertia of the entire network.

Because new input must be distributed across the same connectional weights that carry historical experience, parallel processing networks face a fundamental challenge that has been characterized as the stability-plasticity dilemma (Grossberg, 1980, 1984). If new input is fully integrated, as the result of strong plasticity, then the representation of past experience must be degraded, producing catastrophic instability. Conversely, the network's developmental context (its stable connectional inertia) frames the recognition of each new input pattern, and the opportunity for plasticity that remains. Therefore, to the extent that the continuity of the self is maintained, new experiences can only be understood as they are organized and framed by the templates of past experience.

Because increasing stability occurs with maturity, early experiences and the motivational and emotional biases they engender may apply enduring and unavoidable constraints on information processing. For example, as a result of early neglectful or traumatic events that bias stabilizing representational networks, some individuals may develop integrated conceptual networks that are organized around depressive themes. These cognitive schemas continue to self-organize throughout life, through dynamic interactions with the environment. However, because of their increasing stability, the schemas may impose and maintain the depressive bias in the absence of recurring trauma.

The Cognitive-Emotional Sequelae of Early Trauma: The Development of a Depressogenic Schema

So far, we have provided evidence relating early adversity to depression onset. We have also reviewed several studies suggesting that part of the pathological link between early adversity and depression may be the environment's detrimental effect on developing brain networks. Neural organization may thus become entrained by adverse life circumstances, increasing the sensitivity of the networks to similar future experiences. What remains to be examined are the cognitive and emotional correlates of these neurological effects.

Lewis (1996, 1997) proposes that the self-organization of normal personality is a dynamic process of coupling cognitive appraisals with emotional states over repeated experiences. As coupled cognitive and emotional elements reinforce each other, a coherent appraisal becomes increasingly likely, first in similar situations, and eventually in less similar situations. Lewis describes this emerging predictability in the system as "a reduction in degrees of freedom in the system's response to any given situation, or . . . in the system as a whole" (Lewis, 1996, p. 14). The parallel to kindling in corticolimbic networks is interesting. Over time, Lewis describes the personality system as tending toward stability, forming a coherent and well-articulated "cognitive gestalt" that drives future situational appraisals and emotional reactions (Lewis, 1996, 1997).

In depression, the cognitive gestalt that emerges from development has been called a "depressogenic schema" (Beck, 1987). Depression research has framed the schema concept within the present-centered models of cognitive science (i.e., spreading activation), but it has also acknowledged the importance of developmental stress. Repeated experiences of loss, neglect, or abuse continually activate cognitive themes of abandonment and worthlessness, coupled with feelings of hopelessness and guilt. The experience of many such situations leads to the spreading of activation to an increasingly articulated and broad set of appraisals and emotions. As a result, these depressive elements become strengthened, to the detriment of more positive and adaptive cognitive and emotional elements. Consistent with the theory of spreading activation, activating one part of the network will serve to activate other parts, making negative memories more salient and increasing the probability of forming a negative appraisal of current events. This initial activation serves to magnify depressed mood, which in turn further activates the cognitive network. The end result of this process is a "downward spiral" of mood and cognition (Lewinsohn et al., 1988) in which minor dysphoria evolves into persistent and more severe depression (e.g., Segal et al., 1996). The strong depressive schema that emerges is then increasingly accessible across varied situations. The principles of self-organization and schema development provide a theoretical framework for understanding the results reported in the literature on early trauma and neurological dysfunction. Thus, single traumatic events are not sufficient for predicting depression onset. Instead, depression results from an enduring pattern of poor parent-child interaction and repeated abuse or loss. This progression of insults appears necessary to constrain the ongoing process of self-organization.

Understanding the cumulative, nonlinear nature of self-organization may help explain why, despite a similar exposure to discrete early traumatic life events, some individuals develop a depressive cognitive bias and some do not. For example, imagine two unrelated children, Sarah and Andrew, who lose their mothers. For both children, this loss engenders neurological dysregulation (e.g., noradrenergic depletion and hypercortisolism), cognitive appraisals of abandonment and isolation, and feelings of helplessness. The neural architecture is then sensitized, priming the depressogenic appraisal-emotion couplings, and reducing the threshold for activation by future loss situations. However, subsequent experience may act on the dynamic systems in very different ways, leading to differing operations of self-organization and therefore different depression vulnerabilities. Because self-organization is cumulative, even very small differences in experience may have drastically different end effects, as demonstrated by extending the above hypothetical example further into the future.

Soon after the death of her mother, Sarah experiences a school failure that may even have been generated by the very symptoms of depression experienced subsequent to her loss. This additional stressor serves to reactivate Sarah's depressogenic cognitive structure, strengthening and broadening it to include additional themes (e.g., relating to low self-worth). Therefore, when faced with the next stressor (e.g., the loss of a friend), Sarah is primed to again react with a recurrence of depression. By the time Sarah reaches adulthood, she may have developed a fully articulated and wide-ranging network of depressogenic appraisal-emotion couplings. These associations are easily evoked in a wide array of situations, such as a romantic disappointment, that are only incidentally related to the original loss.

By contrast, let us say that Andrew does not experience a school-related failure but continues to perform acceptably. Because of this, the school domain continues to be a source of ego strength. As a result, Andrew may begin to form a cognitive gestalt that includes elements related to success and high self-worth. Therefore, when faced with the next stressor (e.g., the loss of a friend), Andrew is not as vulnerable to depression recurrence. By adulthood, Andrew may have developed an engaging, hopeful approach to the environment that lessens his vulnerability to depression. Because of cumulative self-organization, small differences in initial conditions may produce large changes in outcome.

The Maintenance of Depression: Self-Organization Through Adulthood

When a depressive style becomes entrenched, there are a number of consequences for adult functioning. First, at the neurological level, the corticolimbic networks subserving emotional regulation, arousal, and traumatic memory may become sensitized, increasing the likelihood that an individual will respond to a stressor with dysregulated emotion. Second, at the cognitive level, there is an ever-expanding and coherent network of appraisal-emotion associations that recruit and replay the memory of the negative environmental context. As a result, feelings of hopelessness, guilt, and depression and thoughts of low self-worth, abandonment, and worthlessness remain always at the surface of consciousness, ready to be primed by future environmental stimuli. An increasingly broad array of events is then able to activate these depressogenic themes, leading to an intensification of the depressed mood and the ultimate development of a major depressive episode. The ready accessibility of depressogenic cognitive gestalts over more adaptive schemas has been repeatedly demonstrated in the experimental literature relating to depression in adulthood. For example, depressed individuals have been found to recall more negative memories than positive or neutral memories, and to selectively recall material previously learned in a depressed mood (Singer and Salovey, 1988; Teasdale, 1983). In addition, when in a depressive episode, individuals will magnify the significance of even minor negative events, while minimizing the importance of positive events (Beck, 1987).

Evidence that self-organization in depression is an ongoing and dynamic process comes from studies suggesting that the depressogenic cognitive-emotion gestalts continue to evolve in adulthood. For example, Post (1992) has suggested that, despite the increasing stability of brain areas in adulthood, corticolimbic networks continue to be sensitized by negative environmental events and the repeated experience of emotional dysregulation:

> Stressors related to loss, separation, and self-esteem that are associated with the onset of depressive episodes may not only play an important pathophysiological role in the triggering of an affective episode, but also, because of the neurobiological encoding of memory-like functions related to these stressors, provide a long-term vulnerability to subsequent recurrences and perhaps a mechanism for triggering episodes with lesser degrees of psychosocial stress. (p. 1004)

According to Post (1992), the continued experience of stress and depression sensitizes neural networks to such a degree that even a symbol of past loss may be enough to trigger a depressive episode. As reviewed earlier, several studies have demonstrated that, while severe events are required to precipitate early episodes of depression, increasingly less severe events are required to generate successive episode recurrences (e.g., Ezquiaga et al., 1987; Ghaziuddin et al., 1994). These results and supporting theory suggest that the depressogenic cognitive-emotional gestalt continues to strengthen over time. In addition, the supporting neural architecture continues to kindle, increasing the probability that an increasingly diverse array of environmental events will trigger a depressive episode.

Conclusion: The Price of Plasticity

We have argued that neural plasticity may be at risk if emotional and motivational arousal are poorly regulated – either at the global level of reticular and thalamic arousal control or at the more local level of cortico-limbic memory consolidation. Particularly when integrated within processes of memory and self-representation, early insults of emotional deprivation and trauma may lead to the formation of stable depressogenic schemas. The cognitive and emotional appraisals making up these schemas continue to interact dynamically with the environment throughout development, framing information processing within a depressive lens. The child and later adult become increasingly susceptible to recurrences of depression, as a growing array of environmental triggers activate the negative schemas and again recruit the depressive affect.

By this reasoning, it is fairly straightforward to see how a depressive bias could arise. However, what often seems to distinguish clinical depression from normal depressed emotion is not that it occurs, but that it persists in the face of new opportunities. Why are maladaptive patterns maintained when healthier, more rewarding ways of coping with life seem easily available? A possible answer is suggested by the cumulative nature of representations within a massively interconnected network, such as is found in the human brain. The stability-plasticity dilemma may be more than an abstract, computational principle. It may reflect the reality of development within a highly parallel network. Because plasticity and change occur only at the expense of stability, the adult depressive may continue to suffer emotionally in order to maintain the continuity of the self.

The stability-plasticity dilemma states that fully incorporating new information invariably produces interference with the previous historical memory. If this is the case, treatments for depression that work at the overt symptom level, while providing temporary symptom relief and short-term depressive episode remission, may not result in enduring changes and prolonged recovery. The limitation of symptomatic treatment is being recognized by cognitive therapy researchers who have begun proposing schema change as a necessary process in therapy for preventing relapse and recurrence (Padesky, 1994; Young, 1994). The primary technique used for achieving change involves weakening maladaptive schemas (e.g., "I'm worthless") and developing and strengthening more adaptive schemas (e.g., "I'm OK").

As an additional aid to achieving cognitive change and preventing the relapse and recurrence of depression, Teasdale and colleagues have recently proposed using techniques of mindfulness meditation (MM; Kabat-Zinn, 1990) as an adjunct to cognitive therapy in a technique they call attentional control training (Teasdale, Segal, and Williams, 1995). They propose that MM helps patients to become fully aware of their thoughts and feelings in the moment and, thus, may help to bring to full consciousness schematic material that may previously have been more automatically influencing mood and behavior: "Mindfulness training appears to be associated with a reduction in the tendency to 'float away' into ruminative, elaborative thought streams . . . that . . . play such an important role in relapse" (Teasdale et al., 1995, p. 34). Schema change therapy and attentional control training are still being developed, and controlled trials have not been conducted. Nevertheless, we propose that the stability/plasticity dilemma may provide a theoretical basis for recognizing the potential benefits of these innovations.

To the extent that the new information to be incorporated is both novel and emotionally significant enough to capture the memory consolidation process, the disruption of prior memory is potentially substantial. Taken as a whole (as it must be taken in a parallel network), prior memory incorporates personally significant values, needs, and modes of being in the world. This cumulative store of past experience comprises the self. Because of the stability-plasticity dilemma, the full incorporation of the novelty of a significant new experience invariably disrupts the historical self. The process of memory consolidation can therefore be seen as a kind of negotiation of self-maintenance, an arbitration between a stable identity and the capacity for new learning (Tucker and Desmond, 1997). For those with a stable but flexible identity and approach to the environment, each new challenge of understanding is a chance to incorporate knowledge of reality within a larger, evolving self. For those for whom early experience has prematurely determined a depressogenic construction of the self, the price of new learning may be out of reach.

Acknowledgment

We thank Mark A. Sabbagh for his very helpful comments on earlier drafts of this manuscript.

References

Abrams, S. M., Field, T., Scafidi, F., and Prodromidis, M. (1995). Newborns of depressed mothers. *Infant Mental Health Journal, 16*, 233–239.

Adamec, R. E., and McKay, D. (1993). Amygdala kindling, anxiety, and corticotrophin releasing factor (CRF). *Physiology and Behavior, 54*, 423–431.

Adamec, R. E., Sayin, U., and Brown, A. (1991). The effects of corticotrophin releasing factor (CRF) and handling stress on behavior in the elevated plus-maze test of anxiety. *Journal of Psychopharmacology, 5*, 175–186.

Bear, D. M. (1979). Temporal lobe epilepsy – A syndrome of temporal-limbic hyperconnection. *Cortex, 15*, 357–384.

Bear, D. M., and Fedio, P. (1977). Quantitative analysis of interictal behavior in temporal lobe epilepsy. *Archives of Neurology, 34*, 454–467.

Beck, A. T. (1987). Cognitive models of depression. *Journal of Cognitive Psychotherapy, 1*, 5–37.

Bifulco, A., Brown, G. W., and Adler, Z. (1991). Early sexual abuse and clinical depression in adult life. *British Journal of Psychiatry, 159*, 115–122.

Bifulco, A. T., Brown, G. W., and Harris, T. O. (1987). Childhood loss of parent, lack of adequate parental care and adult depression: A replication. *Journal of Affective Disorders, 12*, 115–128.

Bifulco, A. T., Brown, G. W., and Harris, T. O. (1994). Childhood Experience of Care and Abuse (CECA): A retrospective interview measure. *Journal of Child Psychology and Psychiatry, 35*, 1419–1435.

Breier, A., Kelsoe, J. R., Kirwin, P. D., Beller, S. A., Wolkowitz, O. M., and Pickar, D. (1988). Early parental loss and development of adult psychopathology. *Archives of General Psychiatry, 45*, 987–993.

Bremner, J. D., Randall, P., Scott, T. M., Bronen, R. A., Seibyl, J. P., Southwick, S. M., Delaney, R. C., McCarthy, G., Charney, D. S., and Innis, R. B. (1995). MRI-based measurement of hippocampal volume in patients with combat-related posttraumatic stress disorder. *American Journal of Psychiatry, 152*, 973–981.

Bremner, J. D, Randall, P., Vermetten, E., Staib, L., Bronen, R. A., Mazure, C., Capelli, S., McCarthy, G., Innis, R. B., and Charney, D. S. (1997). Magnetic resonance imaging-based measurement of hippocampal volume in posttraumatic stress disorder related to childhood physical and sexual abuse: A preliminary report. *Biological Psychiatry, 41*, 23–32.

Changeux, J., and Dehaene, S. (1989). Neuronal models of cognitive functions. *Cognition, 33*, 63–109.

Corcoran, M. E., and Weiss, G. K. (1989). Noradrenaline and kindling revisited. In J. A. Wada (Ed.), *Kindling 4: Mechanisms of behavioral biology* (pp. 141–156). New York: Plenum.

Dawson, G., Frey, K., Panagiotides, H., Osterling, J., and Hessl, D. (1997). Infants of depressed mothers exhibit atypical frontal brain activity: A replication and extension of previous findings. *Journal of Child Psychology and Psychiatry, 38*, 179–186.

Derryberry, D., and Rothbart, M. K. (1988). Arousal, affect, and attention as components of temperament. *Journal of Personality and Social Psychology, 55*, 958–966.

Derryberry, D., and Tucker, D. M. (1991). The adaptive base of the neural hierarchy: Elementary motivational controls on network function. In R. Dienstbier (Ed.), *Nebraska Symposium on Motivation: Vol. 38. Perspectives on motivation* (pp. 289–342). Lincoln: University of Nebraska Press.

Doane, B. K., and Livingston, K. E. (1986). *The limbic system: Functional organization and clinical disorders*. New York: Raven Press.

Ezquiaga, E., Gutierrez, J. L., and Lopez, A. G. (1987). Psychosocial factors and episode number in depression. *Journal of Affective Disorders, 12*, 135–138.

Field, T., Lang, C., Martinez, A., and Yando, R. (1996). Preschool follow-up of infants of dysphoric mothers. *Journal of Clinical Child Psychology, 25*, 272–279.

Ghaziuddin, M., Ghaziuddin, N., and Stein, G. S. (1990). Life events and the recurrence of depression. *Canadian Journal of Psychiatry, 35*, 239–242.

Goddard, G. V., Dragunow, M., Maru, E., and MacLeod, E. K. (1986). Kindling and the forces that oppose it. In B. K. Doane and K. E. Livingston (Eds.), *The limbic system: Functional organization and clinical disorders* (pp. 95–108). New York: Raven Press.

Goddard, G. V., McIntyre, D. C., and Leech, C. K. (1969). A permanent change in brain function resulting from daily electrical stimulation. *Experimental Neurology, 25*, 295–330.

Grossberg, S. (1980). How does a brain build a cognitive code? *Psychological Review, 87*, 1–51.

Grossberg, S. (1984). Some psychophysiological and pharmacological correlates of a developmental, cognitive and motivational theory. *Annals of the New York Academy of Sciences, 425*, 58–151.

Gustafsson, B., and Wigstrom, H. (1988). Physiological mechanisms underlying long-term potentiation. *Trends in Neuroscience, 11*, 156–162.

Hamburger, V. (1977). The developmental history of the motor neuron. *Neuroscience Research Progress Bulletin, 15*, 1–37.

Harris, T., Brown, G. W., and Bifulco, A. (1986). Loss of parent in childhood and adult psychiatric disorder: The role of lack of adequate parental care. *Psychological Medicine, 16*, 641–659.

Herrick, C. J. (1965). *The brain of the tiger salamander, Ambystoma tigrinum*. Chicago: University of Chicago Press.

Huttenlocher, P. R. (1990). Morphometric study of human cerebral cortex development. *Neuropsychologia, 28*, 517–527.

Innocenti, G. M. (1983). Exuberant callosal projections between the developing hemispheres. In R. Villani, I. Papo, M. Giovanelli, S. M. Gaini, and G. Tomei (Eds.), *Advances in neurotraumatology* (pp. 5–10). Amsterdam: Excerpta Medica.

Ito, Y., Teicher, M. H., Glod, C. A., Harper, D., Magnus, E., and Gelbard, H. A. (1993). Increased prevalence of electrophysiological abnormalities in children with psychological, physical, and sexual abuse. *Journal of Neuropsychiatry, 5,* 401–408.

Janowsky, J. S., Laxer, K. D., and Rushmer, D. S. (1980). Classical conditioning of kindled seizures. *Epilepsia, 21,* 393–398.

Jones, N. A., Field, T., Fox, N. A., Lundy, B., and Davalos, M. (1997). EEG activation in 1-month-old infants of depressed mothers. *Development and Psychopathology, 9,* 491–505.

Kabat-Zinn, J. (1990). *Full catastrophe living: The program of the Stress Reduction Clinic at the University of Massachusetts Medical Center.* New York: Dell.

Kehoe, P. (1989). The neuropharmacology of neonatal rat's separation vocalizations. In S. Breznitz and O. Zinder (Eds.), *Molecular biology of stress: Proceedings of a Director's Sponsors-UCLA Symposium* (pp. 307–317). New York: Liss.

Kilgard, M. P., and Merzenich, M. M. (1998). Cortical map reorganization enabled by nucleus basalis activity. *Science, 279,* 1714–1718.

Kim, J. J., Foy, M. R., and Thompson, R. F. (1996). Behavioral stress modifies hippocampal plasticity through N-methyl-D-asparate receptor activation. *Proceedings of the National Academy of Sciences, 93,* 4750–4753.

Lang, C., Field, T., Pickens, J., Martinez, A. Bendell D., Yando R., and Routh, D. (1996). Preschoolers of dysphoric mothers. *Journal of Child Psychology and Psychiatry and Allied Disciplines, 37,* 221–224.

Lewinsohn, P. M., Hoberman, H., Teri, L., and Hautzinger, M. (1988). An integrative theory of depression. In S. Reiss and R. Bootzin (Eds.), *Theoretical issues in behavior therapy* (pp. 331-359). New York: Academic Press.

Lewis, M. D. (1996). Self-organising cognitive appraisals. *Cognition and Emotion, 10,* 1–25.

Lewis, M. D. (1997). Personality self-organization: Cascading constraints on cognition-emotion interaction. In A. Fogel, M. C. Lyra, and J. Valsiner (Eds.), *Dynamics and indeterminism in developmental and social processes* (pp. 193–216). Mahwah, NJ: Erlbaum.

MacLean, P. D. (1986). Culminating developments in the evolution of the limbic system: The thalamocingulate division. In B. K. Doane and K. E. Livingston (Eds.), *The limbic system: Functional organization and clinical disorders* (pp. 1–28). New York: Raven Press.

MagariInos, A. M., and McEwen, B. S. (1995). Stress-induced atrophy of apical dendrites of hippocampal CA3c neurons: Comparison of stressors. *Neuroscience, 69,* 83–88.

McEwen, B. S. (1994). Corticosteroids and hippocampal plasticity. *Annals of the New York Academy of Sciences, 746,* 134–142.

Neville, H. J. (1995). Developmental specificity in neurocognitive development in humans. In M. M. Gazzaniga (Ed.), *The cognitive neurosciences* (pp. 219–231). Cambridge, MA: MIT Press.

Neville, H. J., Bavelier, D., Corina, D., Rauschecker, J., Karni, A., Lalwani, A., Braun, A., Clark, V., Jezzard, P., and Turner, R. (1998). Cerebral organization for language in deaf and hearing subjects: Biological constraints and effects of experience. *Proceedings of the National Academy of Sciences 95,* 922-929.

Padesky, C. A. (1994). Schema change processes in cognitive therapy. *Clinical Psychology and Psychotherapy, 1*, 267–278.

Pandya, D. N., and Yeterian, E. H. (1985). Architecture and connections of cortical association areas. In A. Peters and E. G. Jones (Eds.), *Cerebral cortex: Vol. 4. Association and auditory cortices* (pp. 3–61). New York: Plenum.

Pandya, D. N., and Yeterian, E. H. (1990). Prefrontal cortex in relation to other cortical areas in rhesus monkey: Architecture and connections. In H. B. M. Uylings, C. G. Van Eden, J. P. De Bruin, M. A. Corner, and M. G. Feenstra (Eds.), *The prefrontal cortex: Its structure, function and pathology* (pp. 63–94). New York: Elsevier.

Plotsky, P. M. (1997). Long-term consequences of adverse early experience: A rodent model [abstract]. *Biological Psychiatry, 41*, 77S.

Plotsky, P. M., and Meaney, M. J. (1993). Early, postnatal experience alters hypothalamic corticotropin-releasing factor (CRF) mRNA, median eminence CRF content and stress-induced release in adult rats. *Brain Research Molecular Brain Research, 18*, 195–200.

Post, R. M. (1992). Transduction of psychosocial stress into the neurobiology of recurrent affective disorder. *American Journal of Psychiatry, 149*, 999–1010.

Post, R. M., Weiss, S. R., and Leverich, G. S. (1994). Recurrent affective disorder: Roots in developmental neurobiology and illness progression based on changes in gene expression. *Development and Psychopathology, 6*, 781–813.

Rauch, S. L., van der Kolk, B. A., Fisler, R. E., Alpert, N. M., Orr, S. P., Savage, C. R., Fischman, A. J., Jenike, M. A., and Pitman, R. K. (1996). A symptom provocation study of posttraumatic stress disorder using positron emission tomography and script-driven imagery. *Archives of General Psychiatry, 53*, 380–387.

Recanzone, G. H., Merzenich, M. M., Jenkins, W. M., Grajski, K., and Dinse, H. R. (1992). Topographic reorganization of the hand representation in cortical area 3b of owl monkeys trained in a frequency-discrimination task. *Journal of Neurophysiology, 67*, 1031–1056.

Rosenfeld, P., Wetmore, J. B., and Levine, S. (1992). Effects of repeated maternal separations on the adrenocortical response to stress of preweanling rats. *Physiology and Behavior, 52*, 787–791.

Rothbart, M. K., Posner, M. I., and Boylan, A. (1990). Regulatory mechanisms in infant development. In J. T. Enns (Ed.), *The development of attention: Research and theory* (pp. 47–66). New York: Elsevier.

Rumelhart, D. E., McClelland, J. L., and the PDP Research Group. (1986). *Parallel distributed processing: Explorations in the microstructure of cognition. Volume I: Foundations.* Cambridge, MA: MIT Press.

Sapolsky, R. M., and Pulsinelli, W. A. (1985). Glucocorticoids potentiate ischemic injury to neurons: Therapeutic implications. *Science, 229*, 1397–1400.

Schiffer, F., Teicher, M. H., and Papanicolaou, A. C. (1995). Evoked potential evidence for right brain activity during the recall of traumatic memories. *Journal of Neuropsychiatry and Clinical Neurosciences, 7*, 169–175.

Segal, Z. V., Williams, J. M., Teasdale, J. D., and Gemar, M. (1996). A cognitive science perspective on kindling and episode sensitization in recurrent affective disorder. *Psychological Medicine, 26*, 371–380.

Semple, W. E., Goyer, P., McCormick, R., Morris, E., Compton, B., Muswick, G.,

Nelson, D., Donovan, B., Leisure, G., Berridge, M., Miraldi, F., and Schulz, S. C. (1993). Preliminary report: Brain blood flow using PET in patients with posttraumatic stress disorder and substance-abuse histories. *Biological Psychiatry, 34*, 115–118.

Shearer, S. L., Peters, C. P., Quaytman, M. S., and Ogden, R. L. (1990). Frequency and correlates of childhood sexual and physical abuse histories in adult female borderline inpatients. *American Journal of Psychiatry, 147*, 214–216.

Singer, J. A., and Salovey, P. (1988). Mood and memory: Evaluating the network theory of affect. *Clinical Psychology Review, 8*, 211–251.

Singer, W. (1987). Activity-dependent self-organization of synaptic connections as a substrate of learning. In J. P. Changeux and M. Konishi (Eds.), *The neural and molecular basis of learning* (pp. 301–336). New York: Wiley.

Squire, L. R. (1987). *Memory and brain.* New York: Oxford University Press.

Squire, L. R. (1992). Memory and the hippocampus: A synthesis from findings with rats, monkeys, and humans. *Psychological Review, 99*, 195–231.

Teasdale, J. D. (1983). Negative thinking in depression: Cause, effect, or reciprocal relationship? *Advances in Behaviour Research and Therapy, 5*, 3–25.

Teasdale, J. D., Segal, Z., and Williams, M. G. (1995). How does cognitive therapy prevent depressive relapse and why should attentional control (mindfulness) training help? *Behaviour Research and Therapy, 33*, 25–39.

Teicher, M. H., Glod, C. A., Surrey, J., and Swett, C. (1993). Early childhood abuse and limbic system ratings in adult psychiatric outpatients. *Journal of Neuropsychiatry, 5*, 301–306.

Teyler, T. J. (1986). Memory: Electrophysiological analogs. In J. L. Martinez, Jr., and R. P. Kesner (Eds.), *Learning and memory: A biological view* (pp. 237-265). Orlando, FL: Academic Press.

Tucker, D. M. (1992). Developing emotions and cortical networks. In M. R. Gunnar and C. Nelson (Eds.), *Minnesota Symposium on Child Psychology: Vol 24. Developmental behavioral neuroscience* (pp. 75–128). Hillsdale, NJ: Erlbaum.

Tucker, D. M., and Desmond, R. (1997). Aging and the plasticity of the self. In K. W. Schaie and M. P. Lawton (Eds.), *Annual review of gerontology and geriatrics* (pp. 266–281). New York: Springer.

Tucker, D. M., and Luu, P. (1998). Cathexis revisited: Corticolimbic resonance and the adaptive control of memory. *Annals of the New York Academy of Sciences, 843*, 134-152.

Tucker, D. M., and Williamson, P. A. (1984). Asymmetric neural control systems in human self-regulation. *Psychological Review, 91*, 185-215.

von der Malsburg, C., and Singer, W. (1988). Principles of cortical network organization. In P. Rakic and W. Singer (Eds.), *Neurobiology of neocortex* (pp. 69–99). New York: Wiley.

Young, J. E. (1994). *Cognitive therapy for personality disorders: A schema-focused approach.* Sarasota, FL: Professional Resource Press.

8 Emotion Is Essential to All Intentional Behaviors

Walter J. Freeman

Introduction

The problem of understanding emotion has emerged as one of the major challenges for the social, psychological, and psychiatric disciplines. The root of the problem goes very far back in the history of Western science and philosophy, whence came the primary assumptions that people of European origin use to explain the nature of mind, and how the mind relates to the body and to the world through learning. A singular clue to the form of one of these assumptions is provided by the distinction often made between emotion and reason. This is a "commonsense" notion used to explain the motives of observed behaviors. Motives are reasons that explain the actions we witness with respect to the state of mind of the perpetrators. In this philosophical interpretation, actions stem either from reasoned judgments of available options in the light of self-interest or the greater good, or they are based in an internal force that is out of conscious control and beyond rational choice – blind emotion.

An alternative view, one that I will elaborate here, holds that because this dichotomy treats emotion as bad and reason as good, it fails to recognize them as properties of a larger whole. All actions are emotional, and at the same time they have their reasons and explanations. This is the nature of intentional behavior. I will begin with a historical review of the philosophical grounds from which this dichotomy arose and will follow that review with a description of brain function in the genesis of intention through the nonlinear dynamics of neural populations. I will conclude with some remarks on the interrelation of consciousness and emotion, in an attempt to recast the distinction between rational and emotional people in the light of neurodynamics.

209

Plato, Aristotle, and Aquinas

A major cleavage that fuels debates on the nature of mind derives from the ancient Greeks: Is perception active or passive? According to Plato, it was passive. He drew a distinction between intellect and sense, both being immaterial and belonging to the soul. The intellect was born with ideal forms of objects in the world, and the senses presented imperfect copies of those forms. For each object the intellect sought the corresponding subjective ideal form through the exercise of reason. Thus the experiences from the world of objects and events were passively impressed onto the senses. According to Aristotle it was active. There were no ideal forms in the mind. The organism moved in accordance with its biological destiny, which was initiated by the Prime Mover (God). The actions of the intellect were to define and seek objects with its sensorimotor power, and with its cogitative power to construct forms of them by abstraction and induction from the examples that were presented by the senses. The forms of mental contents constructed from stimuli were inscribed by the intellect with its mnemonic power onto an initially blank slate, the "tabula rasa." Emotion was treated in both systems as an aspect of the animality of man, the rational animal – a residue of corporeality that was to be subjugated by reason.

In the early Middle Ages the Platonic view was dominant mainly through the work of St. Augustine. In the thirteenth century St. Thomas Aquinas transformed the Aristotelian view of biological destiny to intention ("stretching forth") by distinguishing the Christian will from largely unconscious striving, and by conceiving the imagination ("phantasia") as the source of the endogenous forms of perception. He had this to say in his *Summa Theologica* (Aquinas, 1272/1952) about the nature of intentionality, as he defined it to include other animals as well as man:

> *A1: Whether intention is an act of the intellect or of the will?* Intention, as the very word denotes, means to tend to something. Now both the action of the mover and the movement of the thing moved tend to something. But that the movement of the thing moved tends to anything is due to the action of the mover. Consequently intention belongs first and principally to that which moves to the end; hence we say that an architect or anyone who is in authority, by his command moves others to that which he intends. Now the will moves all the other powers of the soul to the end. Therefore it is evident that intention, properly speaking, is an act of the will . . . in regard to the end. Now the will stands in a threefold relation to the end. First,

absolutely. And in this way we have volition, whereby we will absolutely to have health and so forth. Secondly, it considers the end, as its place of rest. And in this way enjoyment regards the end. Thirdly, it considers the end as the term towards which something is ordered; and thus intention regards the end. For when we speak of intending to have health, we mean not only that we will to have it, but that we will to have it by means of something else. . . .

A4: Whether intention of the end is the same act as the volition of the means? Accordingly, in so far as the movement of the will is to the means, as ordered to the end, it is called choice; but the movement of the will to the end as acquired by the means, is called intention. A sign of this is that we can have intention of the end without having determined the means which are the object of choice.

This distinction between will or volition based on choice (for which we might now read ''consciousness'') and intent (which may or may not be conscious) was rapidly and wholeheartedly adopted by the western European community, and it had far-reaching consequences for the growth of middle-class morality and the belief in the capability of individuals to accept responsibility and take action to change things in the world that needed changing. In my opinion the growth of science and technology through the later Middle Ages in large part stemmed from that liberation and its philosophical justification of individual freedom. However, emotions were not given the status assigned to will nor clearly distinguished from intent. Consciousness is a modern concept for which no real equivalent exists in ancient or medieval world views, and emotions appear to be best translated as the ''passions'' of the soul, in reference to suffering caused by external forces foreign to one's true nature.

During the Renaissance, Western thought returned to Plato largely through the work of Descartes, who conceived the revolutionary approach of describing the world and the mind in terms of linear algebra and geometry, without place for the faculty of imagination. In his view the animal machine in man was guided by the soul as its ''pilot,'' which sought knowledge through reasoning about the passive imprints of sensations, in order to arrive at absolute mathematical truth. Fantasy, intention, and emotion were dismissed along with imagination as being nonmathematical and therefore unscientific. The origin of ''passions'' coming from outside one's ''true nature'' was left unexplained.

In the postmodern era, Descartes' pilot has been fired. The reasons usually given are that the soul does not exist, or that the concept doesn't explain anything, or that the soul is a matter of personal belief, not a scientific principle. In philosophy, intentionality was reinstated in modified form by Franz Brentano (1889/1969) to signify the relations between representations in the mind and objects in the world, and thereby to distinguish humans from machines. In the medical and biological sciences, explanations of the mind are sought in terms of the functions of the body through studies of behavior, and by analysis of the brain through chemistry and imaging. Emotions have become matters of central concern, particularly in the context of the affective disorders, where the tendency has been to see them as determined by the machinery of the brain, and most recently by a family of neurohormones in the brain stem, but not in relation to volition or intention.

There is another and less easily grasped reason for the decline of confidence in the Cartesian pilot. For the past three centuries, the functions of mind and brain have been described in terms of the linear dynamics of Newton and Leibnitz, which was enabled by the Cartesian revolution in mathematics. The passive model of perception is entirely appropriate for linear causality, in terms of conditioned and unconditioned reflexes, neural networks, and the chemistry of neuromodulators, because brain structures and operations are seen as determined by genes, developmental processes, and the environment. Perception is thought to work through the imprint of objects and events from the environment, which is called information processing. Mental contents are seen as formed by neural connections that are determined by genes, and modified by learning from stimuli, particularly during critical periods of growth. Representations of objects and events are stored in memory banks as ideal forms, each having attached to it a label as to its value for the organism, and they are used to classify new inputs by retrieval, cross-correlation, template matching, error reduction, modification of wiring in neural networks by Hebbian synapses, and assignment of value by passage through the emotional generators of the brain in the basal ganglia and brain stem. Questions of how the brain can a priori create its own goals and then find the appropriate search images in its memory banks are not well handled. The loss of the Cartesian pilot has left a large gap in the theory, because no one wants a homunculus, but cognitivists have no replacement.

In the first half of the twentieth century some pragmatists, existentialists, and gestaltists broke from the Platonic tradition by incorporating concepts of the source of value in action (Dewey, 1914), the importance of preexisting goals and expectations (Merleau-Ponty, 1945/1962), and the role of affordances in governing perceptions (Gibson, 1979). Merleau-Ponty drew heavily on the clinical neurology of his epoch to reintroduce intentionality in its Thomist sense, as the outward "tending" of brain activity with sensory consequences that completed what he called the "intentional arc." Despite the strong neural basis of these concepts, most neuroscientists have failed to respond to or accommodate them, in part because of their complexity, but in larger part because of the lack of a coherent theory of the deep origin of goal structures in the brains of animals and humans.

However, in the second half of the twentieth century a sharp break in the mathematical, physical, and chemical sciences has occurred with the development of nonlinear dynamics, which was made possible by the emergence of computer technology. Recognition of "dissipative structures" by Prigogine (1980), of "macroscopic order parameters" by Haken (1983), and of "positive negentropic information flows" by various authors writing on self-organization in chaotic systems has opened new avenues to pursue the age-old question: How do goals and their derivative values and expectancies arise in brains? Proposed new answers are expressed in terms of "circular causality" in philosophy (Cartwright, 1989), psychology (Rosch, 1994) and physics (Haken, 1983), which is a convenient term to address the intrinsic indeterminacy of feedback, by which the components of a system can in large part determine their own behavior. The theory of chaos and nonlinear dynamics, when applied to the functions of brains, can answer the fundamental mystery posed by the concept of intent, by showing how goals, their attendant values, and the creative actions by which they are pursued can arise in brains. Every intentional act is preceded by the formation of its character prior to its execution. And if perception is active, then things that are perceived in the body and the world must in an important sense preexist in the sensory cortices as the predicted consequences of acts of searching.

Emotion as the Anticipation of Intentional Action

Intentional action begins with the emergent construction within the brain of goals comprising its possible future states, which will require that actions be directed by the brain in order that those futures be realized. The departure from a state of calm rest without anticipation is aptly named: e(x)motion ("ex" = "outward"). An emotional state need not be revealed in immediate overt actions, but it certainly implies the high probability of actions that will soon be directed outward from an individual into the world. Such states are easily recognized and explained as intentional in many situations, but in others they seem to boil up spontaneously and illogically within an individual in defiance of intent. The behaviors may be in apparent contradiction to sensory triggers that seem trivial, contrary, or insufficient to account for the intensity of actions. Yet they may have an internal logic that comes to light only after probing into and reflecting on the history of the individual. Philosophers refer to such actions as "incontinent" (Davidson, 1980, pp. 21–42).

A way of making sense of emotion is to identify it with the intention to act in the near future, and then to note increasing levels of the complexity of contextualization. Most basically, emotion is outward movement. It is the "stretching forth" of intentionality, which is seen in primitive animals preparing to attack in order to gain food, territory, or resources to reproduce, to find shelter, or to escape impending harm (Panksepp, 1998). The key characteristic is that the action wells up from within the organism. It is not a reflex. It is directed toward some future state, which is being determined by the organism in conjunction with its perceptions of its evolving condition and its history. This primitive form of emotion is called "motivation" or "drive" by behaviorists. These are bad choices of terms, because they confuse intention, which is action that is to be taken, with biological imperatives such as the need for food and water, which are the reasons and explanations for the actions. Behaviorists (passivists) treat behaviors as fixed action patterns released by stimuli from the environment, and they cannot explain phenomena such as curiosity, self-improvement, and self-sacrifice. Their terms are also commonly conflated with arousal, which is a nonspecific increase in the sensitivity of the nervous system that need not be locked into any incipient action. In other words, the concepts of motivation and drive lack the two key properties of emotion, which are endogenous origin and intentionality; and I propose to avoid using them.

At a more physiological level, emotion includes the behavioral expression of internal states of the brain. The behaviors that are directed through interactions with the world toward the future state of an organism predictably require adaptations of the body to support the intentional motor activity. These preparations consist of taking an appropriate postural stance with the musculoskeletal system, and mobilizing the metabolic support systems. The latter include the cardiovascular, respiratory, and endocrine systems, which will be called upon to supply oxygen and nutrients to the muscles, to remove the waste products of energy expenditure, and to facilitate oxidative catabolism. It is the directedness of these preparations in the positioning of the body, the heightening of respiration, the twitching of the tail, and so on, that reveal to observers the emergence of the likelihood of approach, attack, or escape.

Among social animals that live in packs and tribes, these preparatory changes in the body of an organism have become, through evolutionary adaptation, external representations of internal states of meaning and expected action. The display of panting, pawing, stomping the ground, erecting the hair or sexual organs, or moving the face or limbs can serve as signals from each organism to others in its surround (Darwin, 1872). For that to occur a basis must have been formed by previous shared experience, which requires prior intentional learning of and for coordinated behaviors among the members of that society. This aspect of emotion is called social communication.

At a more complex level, emotions are experiences. They are the feelings that accompany the emergent actions that address the anticipated futures of gain or loss in one's attachments to others, one's livelihood and safety, and the perceived possibility or impossibility of changing the world to one's liking or advantage: joy, grief, fear, rage, hope, despair. Though we associate them with objects in the world, these feelings, which philosophers call *qualia* – such as the sweetness of fruit, the repugnance of carrion, the inviting softness of velvet – are internally derived and do not belong to those objects.

The mechanisms of these feelings remain in dispute. The physiologist Walter Cannon, in the passivist-materialist tradition, identified them with the activity of neurons in the head ganglion of the autonomic nervous system, which is in the hypothalamus. The psychologist William James (1890), in the activist-pragmatist tradition, proposed that the feelings were sensed after the fact, so to speak, through the changes in the body induced by the activity of the autonomic nervous system, such as the sinking of the stomach, which is known to occur in states of fear, the bristling of hairs in the skin, the pounding of the pulse, the flushing of the face, and so on. Physiologists view these feelings as epiphenomena. Pragmatists see them as integral parts of the ongoing interaction between one's self and one's social environment. Through these bodily processes one becomes aware of one's emotional state, and, through those signals, one's friends and enemies can typically become aware of that state at the same time as one's self. The perception of one's own action and state, and of the states and actions of one's interactors, shapes the basis for one's own next action. It is neither necessary nor feasible to separate the expression of autonomic states and one's perceptions of them, whether conscious or not, in the intentional loop. They evolve as an organic whole.

The perception of feelings may or may not be accompanied by the process of awareness. Behavior without awareness is called automatic, instinctive, unthinking, and implicitly cognitive. Acting in accustomed roles, engaging in a highly practiced sports routine, and driving a car are examples. Are they emotional? Competitive sports and dramatic performances are obviously so. Evidence that driving a car is intensely emotional is found in the frenzy of concern that a fuel shortage causes, and in the lavish care that many owners bestow upon their machines, even giving them priority over their families. A behavioral action cannot be distinguished as rational or emotional by judging whether the actor is or is not aware of his or her behavioral state and action.

The most complex level of emotion involves social evaluation and assignment of responsibility for actions taken. In the classical Platonic view, in which reason is apposed to emotion, actions that conform to social standards of considerate, productive behavior are said to be rational. Actions that appear to lack the prior logical analysis called premeditation, and that bring unwanted damage to one's self and to others in one's community, are said to be emotional. Yet both kinds of actions are emotional and intentional, in that both emerge from within the individual and are directed to short- or long-term goals. They clearly differ from one another. The biological basis for that difference lies in the self-organizing properties of brains, through which actions are constrained or deferred by a global self-organizing process. We experience that neurodynamic process through being aware or conscious. But consciousness does not generate emotion. It has much more to do with the control of emotion, and in that respect is closely akin to its predecessor, conscience (''knowing together'').

Understanding emotion at all of these levels depends on an answer to this prior question: How do intentional behaviors, all of which are emotive, whether or not they are conscious, emerge through the self-organization of neural activity in even the most primitive brains?

The Architecture of Stimulus-Response Determinism

Most people know the appearance of the human brain, because it has so often been displayed in popular publications, owing to widespread interest in brain imaging during normal human behavior. This knowledge can serve to highlight the differences in emphasis between the passivist-materialist-cognitivist view of the brain as an input-dependent processor of information and representations (Figure 8.1), and the activist-existentialist-pragmatist view of the brain as a semiautonomous generator of goal-directed behavior (Figure 8.2).

In the materialist and cognitive conceptions, the starting point for analysis is assigned to the sensory receptors, either in the skin (as shown by

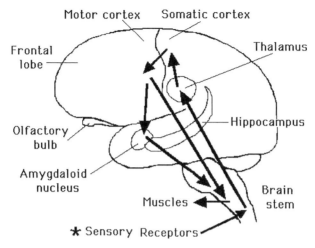

Figure 8.1. The passivist-cognitivist view. Perception begins with sensory stimulation (*) that provides the information to be processed. Three serial neurons (upward arrows) carry it through the thalamus to the primary sensory cortex, from which it is transmitted to the frontal lobes. Similar stages hold for visual and auditory information. The processed information is sent directly to the brain stem and indirectly through the amygdaloid nucleus, where emotion is attached, before final delivery to the muscles. This serial pathway constitutes a linear causal chain (from Freeman, 1999).

the * in Figure 8.1), eyes, ears, or other portal at which information from the world is transduced from energy to action potentials. Bundles of axons serve as channels to carry the information to the brain stem, where it is processed through nuclear relays and converged into the thalamus (upward arrows), which is a central sensory clearinghouse at the top of the brain stem. The information is already subdivided by the receptors in respect to its features – color, motion, tonal modulation, and so on. The thalamus sorts the information for transmission to small areas within each of the primary sensory cortices, which are specialized to deal with their designated kinds of information. Most of the channels have some degree of topographic order, so that the information is said to be mapped from the sensory arrays into each of the small cortical areas.

Within the thalamus, each relay nucleus inhibits the other nuclei. This is called "competitive inhibition." The nucleus that is most strongly excited is said to suppress the others around it. These others, being inhibited, fail to inhibit the excited nucleus, so it is most likely to fire. This process is also called "winner-take-all." It is thought to select information for

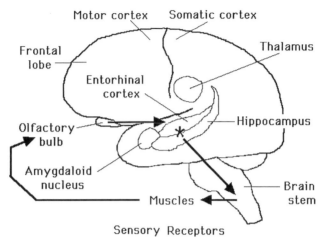

Figure 8.2. The activist-pragmatist view. Perception begins with emergence of a goal through self-organizing dynamics in the limbic system, specifically in the interaction between the hippocampus and the entorhinal cortex (*). Commands sent to the brain stem cause changes in sensory inflow. At the same time, corollary discharges are sent to the primary sensory cortices to prepare them for the anticipated sensory barrage. For simplicity, only the olfactory feedback is shown. All other senses participate by transmitting to and receiving from the entorhinal cortex, which interacts with the hippocampus. The loop starting and ending in (*) illustrates circular causality (from Freeman, 1999).

transmission to the cortex in the process of selective attention. The hinge that squeaks the loudest gets the oil.

The sensory input is believed to excite receptor neurons, whose pulses represent the primitive elements of sensation that are called features. These representations of features are combined into representations of objects when they are transmitted from the primary sensory cortices to adjacent association areas. For example, the integration of lines and colors might image a face, a set of phonemes might form a sentence, and a sequence of joint angles and tissue pressures might represent a gesture. The representations of objects are thought to be transmitted from the association cortices to the frontal lobes, where objects are assembled into concepts, and meaning and value are attached to them.

The architecture of the motor systems is similar to that of the sensory systems in respect to topographic mapping, both in the cerebral cortex and in the cerebellar cortex. Working backward from the muscles along the downward arrows in Figure 8.1, the final central relay in the outgoing channels is provided by pools of motor neurons in the spinal cord and brain stem. These are driven by networks of neurons in the basal ganglia, which include a part of the thalamus. At the crest of the chain is the motor cortex in the frontal lobe, which maintains a topographic map of the musculoskeletal system. The motor cortex in turn is controlled by the premotor and supplementary motor areas that lie in progressively more anterior positions. In this view, the frontal lobes are the site of selection and organization of motor activity in accordance with the objective perception of sensory input. It is there that the rational information processing selects the appropriate motor commands that are to be issued through the motor cortex. Emotion is added to color the output commands by side channels that include the amygdaloid nucleus, which is well known for its involvement in emotional behavior. Studies initiated sixty years ago by Klüver and Bucy (1939) showed that bilateral amygdaloidectomy produced hyperorality and hypersexuality and reduced tendencies to violent behavior in monkeys. The findings led some neurosurgeons to apply the operation in humans to curb violent behavior in adults (Kling, 1972; Mark and Ervin, 1970) and to diminish hyperactivity in children (Narabayashi, 1972). Extensive experience was then accumulated on the effects of stimulation in humans (Eleftherion, 1972; Mark, Ervin, and Sweet, 1972). This structure has recently been given emphasis by imaging studies of the emotion of fear (LeDoux, 1996). In fact, the amygdala is involved in the expression and experience of all emotions, but it is much more difficult to elicit and control love, anger, jealousy, contempt, pity, and so forth in subjects who are immobilized in the machinery that is required for functional brain imaging. Sex is problematic because of the requirement that subjects not move, and because of puritanical attitudes about masturbation in public.

The pathways indicated by the arrows in Figure 8.1 for the transmission of sensory information about objects and the motor commands sound complicated, but the interpretations are based on straightforward engineering concepts. They are, in fact, models that are very well supported by experimental measurements of the pulse trains of neurons in response to well-designed stimulus configurations. However, these models lead to a number of unsolved problems. First, the thalamic winner-take-all mechanism fails to account for expectancy, in which attention is directed toward a stimulus that is not yet present. Second, the corticocortical pathways that link the primary sensory cortices to the frontal lobes are well documented, but no one knows how the features in the small specialized maps are combined to represent objects, or even how an object is defined. How are the elements, sometimes called ''primitives'' by cognitivists, combined to obtain a table and a chair rather than a chairtable? This is known as the binding problem (Hardcastle, 1994). It is unsolved. Third, the role of the limbic system is underemphasized and misrepresented. It is known to be involved with, even required for, spatial navigation, the formation of explicit memories, and the emotional coloring of motor responses. The neural mechanisms by which the limbic system performs these functions are bundled into "higher functions" that are to be analyzed after the problems of cognition have been solved. Fourth, olfaction does not fit within these architectures and is widely ignored.

The Architecture of Intentional Action

In the activist-pragmatist view (Figure 8.2) the topographic organization of the primary sensory and motor systems, which include the receptors, the muscles, and the dedicated areas of cortex, is accepted as outlined in the preceding section, but the starting point for analysis is assigned to the limbic system (*), not the sensory receptors. This is because perception is defined as a form of intentional action, not as a late stage of sensation. The consequences of this change in perspective include reassigning the pivotal roles of the thalamus and the frontal lobes to the limbic system.

In primitive vertebrates the limbic system comprises the entire forebrain, including naturally both cortical and subcortical structures, as in all definitions of "limbic." The various goal-directed activities that these free-ranging animals sustain clearly support the assertion that these animals have limited forms of intentional action. In the human brain the vast enlargement of the neocortical lobes makes it difficult to see that the primitive components not only have persisted, but have become enlarged. For example, topologically the hippocampus still occupies part of the surface of each cerebral hemisphere, but the folding and twisting of the hemisphere during its embryological growth relocates it, so that it now seems buried deep within the brain. Although it is only one part of a distributed system of modules comprising the limbic system, its central location and characteristic cellular architecture make it a useful focus for understanding limbic dynamics. In metaphorical terms, it is more like the hub of a wheel than the memory bank or central processor of a computer.

Whereas in the salamander and other primitive vertebrates (Herrick, 1948) the hippocampus receives input directly from the primary sensory areas, in humans and other mammals there is a collection of intervening cortical areas that feed into the entorhinal cortex and parahippocampal gyrus. These stages include the inferotemporal cortex receiving visual input, the posterior cingulate gyrus receiving somatic and other parietal input, the superior temporal gyrus receiving auditory input, the insula receiving visceral input, and the orbital frontal region transmitting via the uncinate fasciculus. The entorhinal cortex is the main gateway to the hippocampus. It is also the main target for hippocampal output by way of the subiculum and parahippocampal gyrus, so the two modules constantly communicate between each other. They occupy the medial temporal lobe of each hemisphere, along with the amygdaloid nucleus, the orbital striatum, and the tail of the caudate nucleus.

The most remarkable feature of the entorhinal cortex is that it not only receives and combines input from all of the primary sensory areas in the cerebral hemisphere; it also sends its output back again to all of them, after its previous activity has been integrated over time in the hippocampus. This reciprocal interaction in mammalian brains is carried out through multiple synaptic relays to and from all sensory and motor areas of neocortex. Other pathways support direct interactions between pairs of these areas, but the most significant aspect of limbic architecture is the multisensory convergence and integration that underlies the assembly of multisensory gestalts, mediates spatial orientation, and provides the basis for laying down explicit memories (Clark and Squire, 1998).

The organization of brain dynamics is schematized in Figure 8.3 as a set of nested loops. The loops have been simplified deliberately by lumping together many subsidiary components and lesser loops, in order to show the forest, not the trees. At the core is the spacetime loop, which represents the interaction of the hippocampus with the adjacent neocortex, mainly the entorhinal cortex. There are two outstanding properties of this spacetime loop. First, the hippocampus has been shown experimentally to be deeply involved in the orientation of behavior in space and in time. Cognitivists attribute these functions to ''place cells'' (Wilson and McNaughton, 1993). These are neurons that fire pulses whenever an animal orients itself in a particular place or direction in its field of action, so they are conceived to provide spatial information for navigation.

Cognitivists believe that the hippocampus maintains a cognitive map (Tolman, 1948) and a short-term memory bank, which serve to represent the environment as a part of the world picture within each animal. Pragmatists hold that there is no representational ''map'' in the brain, but that the hippocampus maintains an experience-dependent field of synapses among its neurons. This field continually shapes and revises the action patterns that form under the interactions of the limbic system with other modules in the brain, as the animal moves through its environment. Every

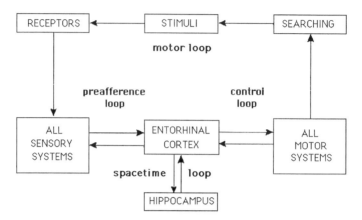

DYNAMIC ARCHITECTURE OF THE LIMBIC SYSTEM

Figure 8.3. The organization of brain dynamics as a set of loops of interaction in which the limbic system is embedded. The global interaction between the self and the world is shown as the pathway through the environment from motor output to sensory receptors. The proprioceptive and interoceptive loops are closed outside the brain but inside the body. The preafferent loops are within the brain, updating the sensory cortices to expect the consequences of incipient actions. They differ from the motor control loops that include the neurohumoral regulation of the brain by itself. The spacetime loop indicates the interaction between the components of the limbic system by which experience is organized for intentional action through time and space (from Freeman, 1999).

intentional act takes place in space through time. The space is the personal realm in which the organism has moved in previous explorations and now continues to move toward its immediate goals. The time is the personal lapse that every movement in space requires, and that orders each sequence of past, present, and expected states (Hendriks-Jansen, 1996; Tani, 1996). Fully integrated intentional action requires this learned framework, but it is a dynamic operator, not a repository of facts or geometric forms. As in the case of other forms of memory, it is not localized to the limbic system but is broadly distributed.

We experience this kind of navigation in our first exposure to a new city, when we can get from a hotel to a bus station by rote but not by an optimal plan. Similarly there is no global abstraction by which a machine might know where it is and where it wants to go. Humans have the high-level capability for expanding and elaborating the field of action by virtue of the frontal lobes, and we experience that as having foresight, but we cannot infer that road atlases or decision trees reside there or in the hippocampus, except in a metaphorical sense. The important point here is that perception is action that is directed through space and time, and the limbic system provides for the formation of distributed memory that organizes action with respect to the world.

The second salient property of this spacetime loop is that the neural populations within its modules have the same and similar kinds of interconnections and interactive dynamics as those in the primary sensory cortices. The EEGs generated by these structures have similar waveforms in time and space, and they show similar kinds of change with behavioral and brain states as do the sensory cortices. In the language of dynamics, the populations comprising the spacetime loop construct and maintain an array of *attractors*. What this means is that the limbic system has some preferred patterns of activity. Each pattern is governed by an attractor with a *basin of attraction*. The basin is defined by the full range of conditions of the brain in which the pattern emerges. A collection of patterns is governed by an *attractor landscape*, such that the limbic system can only be in one attractor at a time, but it can jump from one to another. Each jump is the occasion of an instability. That is, the brain is continually changing its state, because it is volatile and unstable. Again, there are some preferred pathways among the basins, which leads to the idea of a pathway or *trajectory* that supports a habitual pattern of thought and behavior. That emerges as a sequence of briefly stable patterns, each giving way to the next after its brief moment of life, occasionally coming to awareness as a chain of movements or a familiar train of thought.

Each attractor provides for a certain brain state, and the jump from one state to another is called a *state transition*. These states recur at a rate of three to seven per second in the manner of a motion picture film. That is a characteristic frequency of hippocampal EEG called ''theta activity,'' which is provided by neuron populations in the septal nuclei and regulated by the brain stem. The spatiotemporal patterns result from the self-organizing dynamics within the spacetime loop (Freeman, 1992). They are shaped and modulated by the feedback from the larger loops in which the spacetime loop is embedded, but the locus for the critical instabilities that shape the trajectory is found in this core of the limbic system. It is the organized and fruitful evolution of limbic patterns through chaotic instabilities that governs the flow of intentional action (Freeman, 1995).

The Dynamics of the Motor Control Loops

The bulk of entorhinal output goes either to the hippocampus or back to the sensory cortices, but some of it enters into the motor systems. Similarly, the bulk of hippocampal output goes back to the entorhinal cortex, but some of it also goes directly downstream. These arrangements reflect a general principle of brain organization: the larger fraction of the output of each module goes back directly or indirectly to the module from which it gets its input, and only a smaller fraction goes onward.

There are two main motor systems that receive and respond to limbic activity, and that feed back reports about their contributions. In the lateral side of each hemisphere in the forebrain a main target is the amygdaloid nucleus already mentioned. The downward component of its outflow is directed toward the motor nuclei in the brain stem and spinal cord (Figure 8.1) that control the musculoskeletal system through what is called the "lateral forebrain bundle." In the medial side of each hemisphere the main targets are the septum, accumbens nucleus, and hypothalamus, with relays into the ventral tegmental area, all of which control the autonomic and neuroendocrine chemical and metabolic supports for the musculoskeletal system through what is called the "medial forebrain bundle." These autonomic and hormonal supports are involved in all emotional expressions, not only in the periphery, where their effects are visible to everyone, but also inside the brain itself. The internal ascending pathways from the brain stem that diverge broadly through the cerebrum are well documented. A more recent development is a better understanding of how brain tissues use neurohormones to regulate their own blood supply. The consequences of the changes that these systems bring about in the function of the body cannot fail to alter the sensory input from the proprioceptor neurons in the muscles and the interoceptor neurons in the viscera, which operate concomitantly with the exteroceptor neurons in the eye, ear, and skin, and continually influence the somatosensory areas of the forebrain, including the thalamus and cortex. Considering the rapidity with which an emotional state can emerge – such as a flash of anger, a knifelike fear, a surge of pity or jealousy – whether the trigger is the sight of a rival, the recollection of a missed appointment, an odor of smoke, or the embarrassing rumble of one's bowel at tea, the occasion is best understood as a global first-order state transition involving all parts of the brain and body acting in concert. Of course, onsets can also be gradual. However, this description of the dynamics does not yet serve to distinguish, for example, the quale experienced in aerobic exercise from the quale of hot pursuit. There is more to emotion than the limbic system.

What role does the motor cortex in the frontal lobe have in this schema? The limbic output goes from the amygdaloid nucleus into other parts of the basal ganglia, and from the hypothalamus into the thalamus. By these routes limbic control is broadly established in the frontal lobe, which is motor in two senses. In the narrow sense, the primary motor cortex (Figure 8.1) controls the position of the limbs, and also of the head and eyes, to optimize the sensory inflow in accordance with the goal-directed actions that are initiated in the limbic system. It does not initiate the actions or formulate their intents.

In the broad sense, the frontal lobe refines and elaborates the predictions of future states and possible outcomes toward which intentional action is directed. In primitive animals there is little or no frontal cortex, and their intentional action is correspondingly impoverished. Even in cats and dogs, and in large-brained animals such as elephants and whales, the frontal lobe comprises only a small fraction of each hemisphere. These animals are short-sighted and have brief attention spans. The great apes presage the emergence of the dominance of the frontal lobes in humans. Two aspects are noteworthy. The dorsal and lateral areas of the frontal lobe are concerned with cognitive functions such as logic and reasoning in prediction. The medial and ventral areas are concerned with social skills and the capacity for deep interpersonal relationships. These contributions can be summarized as foresight and insight. The frontal lobe guides and enriches intentional action but does not initiate it. In respect to emotion, it provides the operations that distinguish between pity and compassion, pride and arrogance, humility and obsequiousness, and so on, in an incredible range of nuances of feeling and value. The tale has often been told, most recently by Damasio (1994), of the emotional impoverishment of Phineas Gage by damage to his frontal lobes.

A remarkable feature of the human brain is the fact that it embodies the principle noted earlier of the dominance of feedback (recursion, re-entry, self-activation) in brain architecture. This is immediately apparent on inspection of the organization of neurons in all parts of the brain. Each neuron is embedded in a dense fabric of axons and dendrites, which is called "neuropil," in which its thousands of connections form. Most of the connections for each neuron are from others in its neighborhood, but about 10 percent come from distant structures. For example, the frontal lobes provide about 80 percent of the descending axons from the forebrain into the basal ganglia and brain stem, but only a small fraction reaches the motor nuclei. Virtually all of the output of the basal ganglia goes back to the cortex, either directly or through the thalamus. Virtually all of the output of the brain stem goes back to the cortex, through the thalamus or the cerebellum. These massive internal feedback pathways are crucial for learning, practice, rehearsal, and play in forming the detailed structure of experience, which is the history of the organism that provides the wholeness and richness of intentionality that is unique to each individual. This texture provides the unique qualia of emotion in each of us, which are our inner experiences of impending actions. If the classes of such actions are reduced to the dichotomy of approach versus avoidance, then the experiences of feeling can be reduced to the bivalence of pleasure versus pain, but that simplification leaves out the options of deferring action, of declining to act, of weaseling around in search of angles, or perhaps of just seeking more information. Curiosity can inspire growing dread of what will be found. Who can stop before it is too late?

Undoubtedly these large, strongly interconnected populations have the capacity for self-organizing nonlinear dynamics, comparable to those of the primary sensory (Barrie, Freeman, and Lenhart, 1996) and limbic modules. They are active participants in shaping the complex behaviors in which humans excel, far beyond the capacities of even our closest relatives among the great apes. What is important in this context is the dynamics that we share with both our closest and our more distant relatives (Darwin, 1872). The essential insights we need in order to explain the dynamics are most likely to come from measurements of the limbic activities during normal behavior.

The Neurohumoral Dynamics of Emotions

An essential part of the motor system is found in the brain stem of all vertebrates, from the simplest to the most advanced. This is a collection of nuclei with neurons that are specialized to secrete types of chemicals that are called neuromodulators. Whereas neurotransmitters are chemicals released at synapses that immediately excite or inhibit the postsynaptic neurons, the neuromodulators enhance or diminish the effectiveness of the synapses, typically without having immediate excitatory or inhibitory actions of their own, and typically effecting long-lasting changes in the strengths and durations of synaptic actions. The nuclei are arranged in pairs on both sides of the brain stem, extending from the hindbrain into the base of the forebrain, everywhere embedded in the core of the brain stem, the centrencephalic gray matter, and the reticular formation (Magoun, 1962).

These nuclei receive their input from many parts of the sensory and motor systems of the brain. Most important is the limbic input to these nuclei that modulates the emotion of intentional action. There are several dozen neuromodulators, which are grouped in two main classes based on their chemical structures: the neuroamines and the neuropeptides (Panksepp, 1998; Pert, 1997). The axons of these modulatory neurons typically branch widely and infiltrate among neurons in the neuropil without making terminal synapses. They secrete their chemicals that permeate throughout both cerebral hemispheres. Their actions are global, not local. This functional architecture is a major determinant of the unity of intentionality, because the entire forebrain is simultaneously affected by the action of each pair of nuclei. To some extent the differing nuclei interact by competitive inhibition, which may enhance winner-take-all capture of the forebrain by the nuclei.

The types of modulation include generalized arousal by histamine; sedation and the induction of sleep by serotonin; modulation of circadian rhythms by melatonin; the introduction of value by the reward hormone cholecystokinin (CCK); the relief of pain by the endorphins; the release of aggressive behavior by vasopressin; the enabling of the appearance of maternal behavior by oxytocin; the facilitation of changes in synaptic gains with imprinting and learning by acetylcholine and norepinephrine (Gray, Freeman, and Skinner, 1986), which is crucial for updating intention in light of the consequences of previous actions; and the control by dopamine of energy level and of movement, as in exploratory behavior and the initiation of new projects (Panksepp, 1998).

The changes in synaptic strengths with learning, as mediated by neurohormones, are not restricted to a particular sensory modality or motor system, where a particular conditioned stimulus (CS) evokes a particular conditioned response (CR). In conformance with the unity of intentionality, the changes occur everywhere in the forebrain that the simultaneous activity of pre- and postsynaptic neurons meets the conditions for Hebbian learning, in which the strength of synapses is modified by the activities of the neurons simultaneously on both sides of the synapse. The changes are also cumulative, which meets the requirement for continuing additions to the personal history constituting the evolving wholeness of intentionality. When a new fact, skill, or insight is learned, the widespread synaptic changes knit the modification into the entire intentional structure of meaning that is embedded in the neuropil.

Neuromodulators combine their actions in the states of people and animals that we describe in terms of mood, affect, mania, depression, and so on. It is not clear how these complex interactions take place, or how the modulators are related to specific emotions of individuals, as they are experienced through awareness, but it is certain that all of them are involved in expressing emotions and learning from experience.

The Dynamics of the Preafference Loop

When internally organized action patterns radiate from the limbic system, they are not packets of information or representational commands, as cognitivists would describe them. They are solicitations to other parts of the brain to enter into cooperative activity, by which the spatiotemporal patterns of both the initiator and the coparticipants engage in a kind of communal dance. The linking together in a global pattern is not a directive by which the limbic system imposes a predictive schema onto the motor systems. It is a process of evolution by consensus to which each of the sensory and motor modules makes its unique contribution. Each sensory module provides a porthole through which to view the world, which is specified by its receptor neurons. The motor modules provide the linkage through the motor neurons to the movers of the body and the metabolic support systems. For the limbic system the contributions are the spacetime field, the feedback regulation of the neuromodulator nuclei in the reticular core, and the simultaneous integration of the input from all of the sensory areas that establishes the unity of perception. That integration provides the basis for the synthesis of intent.

All of the solicitations for cooperation radiating to the motor systems are simultaneously radiated to all of the primary sensory cortices through the bidirectional connections schematized in Figure 8.3. The existence of these influences upon other parts of the brain has been postulated for over a century. The transmissions have been called "efference copies" and "corollary discharges." They are highly significant in perception, because they provide the basis on which the consequences of impending motor actions are predicted for the coming inflows to each of the sensory ports in the process of preafference (Kay and Freeman, 1998). When we move our heads and eyes to look, it is this process that tells us the motion we see is in our bodies and not in the world. When we speak, this process tells us that the voice we hear is our own and not another's. Preafference takes place entirely within the brain. It is not to be confused with the proprioceptive loop, which feeds through the body back to the sensory receptors and the somatosensory cortex.

Corollary discharges are carried by action potentials, as are virtually all corticocortical transmissions, with a subtle but significant difference from forward motor transmissions. The spacetime loop has two directions of both inflow and outflow. In my view, the forward flow in from the sensory modules and out to the motor modules is carried by spatiotemporal activity patterns (Barrie et al., 1996) comprised of pulses whose effects are at the microscopic level, to direct their targets into appropriate attractors. The feedback flow from the motor modules to the limbic system and on to the sensory modules as corollary discharges is also carried by activity patterns of pulses, but their effects are at the macroscopic level, to serve as order parameters, shape the attractor landscapes, and facilitate the selective learning that characterizes intentionality (Freeman, 1995).

Preafference in the forebrain has even more important contributions to make. When a goal-directed state emerges by a nonlinear state transition with its focus in the limbic system, it contains within it the expectancy of a sequence of sensory inputs. Those anticipated inputs are highly specific to a planned sequence of actions along the way to achieving a specific goal, as well as to a future state of reward, whether it is food, safety, or the feeling of power and comprehension that accompanies activation of the dopamine receptors. These expected inputs are the sights, sounds, smells, and feels of searching and observing. The organism has some idea, whether correct or mistaken, of what it is looking for. The scent of prey combined with the touch of wind on the skin instantly involves the ears to listen and the eyes to look for waving grass. These are the gestalt processes of expectation and attention, which are sustained by the motor control and preafference loops. Without preconfiguration, there is no perception. Without sensory feedback, there is no intentional action.

Everyone agrees that central processing takes time, whether for information, representations, or intentional states. Minimal estimates are provided (Libet, 1994) by measurements of reaction times between conditioned stimuli and responses (about 0.25 to 0.75 second), which are longer than the reaction times between unconditioned stimuli and responses (less than 0.1 second). Only a small fraction of this interval is taken by the conduction delays between receptors and the brain, between the brain modules, and from the brain to the muscles. Most of the interval is required for binding features into higher-order brain states, or for retrieving and matching stored representations for cross-correlation with present input, or for seeking appropriate basins of attraction and constructing spatiotemporal patterns in an itinerant trajectory, depending on one's point of view.

Neocortex as an Organ of Mammalian Intentionality

Recent findings obtained by recording EEGs from the scalps of human volunteers (Lehmann, Ozaki, and Pal, 1987) indicate that cooperation between the modules in each hemisphere is not by sequential transmission of information packets or representations bouncing from one area to another, with local processing by computational or logical algorithms. That hypothesis might be compared to the response of billiard balls to the impact of the cue stick upon one of them, with the outcome being determined by Newtonian dynamics. The global spatiotemporal pattern formation revealed by EEG recording shows that the sensory and limbic areas of each hemisphere can rapidly enter into a cooperative state, which persists on the order of a tenth of a second before dissolving to make way for the next state. The cooperation does not develop by entrainment of coupled oscillators into synchronous oscillation. Instead, the cooperation depends on the entry of the entire hemisphere into a global chaotic attractor.

An explanation in terms of brain dynamics is through generalization of the process by which local spatiotemporal patterns form. The microscopic activity of the neurons in each sensory cortex couples them together by synaptic transmission, and when the coupling is strong enough, the population becomes unstable and undergoes a state transition. Thereby a new macroscopic state emerges, which constrains and enslaves the neurons that create and sustain it, in a process of circular causality (Cartwright, 1989; Haken, 1983). The neurons express their membership in the coordination of their firing patterns, even though they do not synchronize to fire simultaneously. It appears that the macroscopic patterns radiate through various axonal pathways in each hemisphere. The interactions on the global scale engender state transitions of the entire hemisphere by triggering instabilities, such that new global macroscopic states are continually being created. Each global macroscopic state constrains and enslaves the modules that have created it throughout the hemisphere.

Consciousness as a Dynamic Operator

Neurodynamics offers a new and enlarged conceptual framework, in which interrelationships among parts creating wholes can be described without need for causal agents to effect changes. An elementary example is the self-organization of a neural population by its component neurons. The neuropil in each area of cortex contains millions of neurons interacting by synaptic transmission. The density of action is low, diffuse, and widespread. Under the impact of sensory stimulation, or by the release of a modulatory chemical from another part of the brain, or by the inevitable process of growth and maturation, all the neurons together form a macroscopic pattern of activity. That pattern simultaneously constrains the activities of the neurons that support it. The microscopic activity flows in one direction, upward in the hierarchy, and simultaneously the macroscopic activity flows in the other direction, downward. With the arrival of a new stimulus or under the impact of a new condition, this entire cortex can be destabilized, so that it jumps into a new state, and then into another, and another, in a sequence forming a trajectory. It is not meaningful to ask how individual neurons can cause global state transitions, any more than it is meaningful to ask how some molecules of air and water can cause a hurricane. This macroscopic way of thinking about matter has become so familiar to physical scientists since its introduction a century ago by Boltzmann, that it is difficult to see why it is not better understood by neurobiologists working with neurons.

The primary sensory cortices are also components in a larger system, together with the various parts of the limbic system. Each of these components is liable to destabilization at any time, in part because of the feedback connections that support the interaction between populations. Perception can and does follow the impact of sensory bombardment, but that which is perceived has already been prepared for in two ways. One way is by the residue from past experience, the synaptic modifications, which shape the connections in the neuropil of each sensory cortex to form nerve cell assemblies. Each assembly opens the door to a preferred spatial pattern, which is constructed by the learned attractors in the basin formed in the past. The set of basins forms an attractor landscape. The second way is by reciprocal relations with all other sensory cortices through the entorhinal cortex. Input by preafferent pathways can bias the attractor landscapes of the cortices, and that can enhance the basins of attraction that conform to the goals emerging through the limbic system.

The sensory cortices are continually bombarded by receptors, irrespective of intention, and each module of the brain is subject to destabilization at any time, owing to its intrinsic dynamics. Some form of global coordination must exist to explain the unity of intentional action, and the perseverance of goal-directed states in the face of distractions and unexpected obstacles. My hypothesis is that the interactions of the neural populations create a brainwide level of shared activity. The populations are not locked together in synchronous discharge, because they preserve a degree of autonomy. Synchrony seldom occurs among the individual neurons in the local populations, either. The entire community of brain modules must be considered as creating a global dynamic framework. The micro-macro relation that binds single neurons into populations, then, is a precursor for the binding of the limbic and sensory systems into a brain state.

This description can explain the formation of global spatiotemporal patterns but not their function and significance. It still leaves unexplained their relation to awareness. What is it? I want to propose a hypothesis as to just what is going on, in which consciousness is interpreted in neurobiological terms as a sequence of states of awareness. The limbic and sensory systems transmit to each other by action potentials as microscopic elements in a hierarchically upward direction. They create a global state, which acts downwardly to constrain the parts. The constraints are exercised by action potentials on divergent pathways that enhance the global content. The constraint of each module acting on others diminishes the freedom of all of them. The likelihood that any one of them will destabilize, take control, and impose its activity onto other modules is reduced. In particular, it is less likely that any one or a subset of modules can capture the motor systems and shape behaviors with minimal contributions from the other parts.

My hypothesis is that a global spatiotemporal pattern in each hemisphere is the principal brain correlate of awareness. The interactive populations of the brain are continually creating new local patterns of chaotic activity that are transmitted widely and that influence the trajectory of the global state. That is how the content of meaning emerges and grows in richness, range, and complexity. Only a small fraction of the total variance of the activity in each of the modules is incorporated into the global pattern. Yet that small part is crucial. Just as the individual neuron is subject to continual bombardment at its synapses, yet can only report out a pulse intermittently on its sole axon, and just as the population is built from the seemingly random activity of millions of neurons, yet can only form one attractor pattern at a time, so the whole hemisphere, in achieving unity from its myriad shifting parts, can sustain only one global spatiotemporal pattern at a time, but that unified pattern jumps continually, producing the chaotic but purposeful stream of consciousness.

The crucial role that awareness plays, according to this hypothesis, is to prevent precipitous action, not by inhibition, but by quenching local chaotic fluctuations in the manner described by Prigogine, through sustained interactions acting as a global constraint. Thus awareness is a higher-order state, one that harnesses the component subsystems and minimizes the likelihood of renegade state transitions in them. Consciousness as a sequence of global states is not an agent that initiates action. Nor is it an epiphenomenon. It is a state variable that constrains erratic activity by quenching local fluctuations. It is an order parameter and operator that comes into play in the action-perception cycle after an action has been taken, and during the learning phase of perception. This is the part of intentionality in which the consequences of the just-completed action are being organized and integrated, and a new action is in planning but not yet in execution. Consciousness holds back on premature action, and by giving time for maturation, it improves the likelihood of the expression of the long-term promise of an intentional being in considered behavior. David Chalmers (1996) has characterized as "the hard problem" the question of why we have experience at all. The answer is simple. Humans who can't stop to think don't survive long in competition with those who can. William James (1879) described consciousness as "an organ added for the sake of steering a nervous system grown too complex to regulate itself." But it is not an organ in the sense of some new part of the brain. Instead, it is a higher and more inclusive form of self-organization.

The view of consciousness as a dynamic state variable clarifies the issue of emotion versus reason. Emotion can be measured by the magnitudes of the tendencies to chaotic fluctuations in brain modules, and reason can be seen as an expression of a high level of assimilation to the world, meaning knowledge that endows a rational mind with control of remarkable power. Consciousness does not construct the trajectory of reason. It provides the global linkage for smoothing chaotic fluctuations through global interaction and for building a life history. By these criteria, an action can be intensely emotional and yet strictly controlled. Actions that are considered to be thoughtless, ill-conceived, rash, incontinent, inattentive, or even unconscious, and that are commonly and incorrectly labeled as "emotional," can be described in dynamic terms as an escape of chaotic fluctuations from a global order parameter, prematurely in respect to unity of mind and long-term growth toward the wholeness of intentionality. Without emotion there is no action, but without conscious control, there is the potential for self-abasement, self-destruction, and the heartless infliction of violence on others.

When we speak of people as "highly emotional," in this view we refer to their having high levels of chaotic activity in the various components of their brains, which cannot be achieved without a corresponding high level of the global cooperativity that manifests itself in consciousness. The levels of energy build inexorably through the dynamic tensions of controlled internal conflicts. In other words, emotionality is not a weakness but a sign of strength, because its depth, range, and complexity beyond the instinctual attitudes of other animals cannot develop without structuring by reason and language. The highest and most complex levels of emotion are seen in poets and other natural leaders who have the greatest range of personal insight, cultural vision, and predictive power. Emotion is chaotic, but, after all, by one definition chaos is controlled noise.

Acknowledgments

This work was supported by a grant from the National Institute of Mental Health entitled Correlation of EEG and Behavior. Much of the material here has been adapted from a chapter in a monograph entitled *How Brains Make Up Their Minds* published by Weidenfeld and Nicolson in London, UK, July 1999.

References

Aquinas, St. Thomas. (1952). *Summa theologica*. Translated by Fathers of the English Dominican Province. Revised by Daniel J. Sullivan. Published by William Benton as Volume 19 in the Great Books Series. Chicago: Encyclopedia Britannica. (Original work published 1272.)

Barrie, J. M., Freeman, W. J., and Lenhart, M. (1996). Modulation by discriminative training of spatial patterns of gamma EEG amplitude and phase in neocortex of rabbits. *Journal of Neurophysiology, 76*, 520–539.

Brentano, F. C. (1969). *The origin of our knowledge of right and wrong*. (R. M. Chisolm and E. H. Schneewind, trans.) New York: Humanities Press. (Original work published 1889.)

Cartwright, N. (1989). *Nature's capacities and their measurement*. Oxford: Clarendon Press.

Chalmers, D. J. (1996). *The conscious mind: In search of a fundamental theory*. New York: Oxford University Press.

Clark, R. E., and Squire, L. R. (1998). Classical conditioning and brain systems: The role of awareness. *Science, 280*, 77–81.

Damasio, A. R. (1994). *Descartes' error: Emotion, reason, and the human brain*. New York: Putnam.

Darwin, C. (1872). *The expression of emotion in man and animals*. London: Murray.

Davidson, D. (1980). Essay 2. In *Essays on actions and events* (pp. 21–42). Oxford: Clarendon

Dewey, J. (1914). Psychological doctrine in philosophical teaching. *Journal of Philosophy 11*, 505–512.

Eleftherion, B. E. (Ed.) (1972). *The neurobiology of the amygdala*. New York: Plenum.

Freeman, W. J. (1992). Tutorial in neurobiology: From single neurons to brain chaos. *International Journal of Bifurcation and Chaos, 2*, 451–482.

Freeman, W. J. (1995). *Societies of brains: A study in the neuroscience of love and hate*. Mahwah, NJ: Erlbaum.

Freeman, W. J. (1999). *How brains make up their minds*. London: Weidenfeld and Nicolson.

Gibson, J. J. (1979). *The ecological approach to visual perception*. Boston: Houghton Mifflin.

Gray, C. M., Freeman W. J., and Skinner, J. E. (1986). Chemical dependencies of learning in the rabbit olfactory bulb: Acquisition of the transient spatial-pattern change depends on norepinephrine. *Behavioral Neuroscience, 100*, 585–596.

Haken, H. (1983). *Synergetics: An introduction*. Berlin: Springer.

Hardcastle, V. G. (1994). Psychology's binding problem and possible neurobiological solutions. *Journal of Consciousness Studies, 1,* 66–90.

Hendriks-Jansen, H. (1996). *Catching ourselves in the act: Situated activity, interactive emergence, evolution, and human thought.* Cambridge, MA: MIT Press.

Herrick, C. J. (1948). *The brain of the tiger salamander, Ambystoma tigrinum.* Chicago: University of Chicago Press.

James, W. (1879). Are we automata? *Mind, 4,* 1–21.

James, W. (1890). *The principles of psychology.* New York: Holt.

Kay, L. M., and Freeman, W. J. (1998). Bidirectional processing in the olfactory-limbic axis during olfactory behavior. *Behavioral Neuroscience, 112,* 541–553.

Kling, A. (1972). Effects of amygdalectomy on social-affective behavior in nonhuman primates. In B. E. Eleftherion (Ed.), *The neurobiology of the amygdala* (pp. 511–536). New York: Plenum.

Klüver, H., and Bucy, P. (1939). Preliminary analysis of functions of the temporal lobe in monkeys. *Archives of Neurology and Psychiatry, 42,* 979–1000.

LeDoux, J. E. (1996). *The emotional brain: The mysterious underpinnings of emotional life.* New York: Simon and Schuster.

Lehmann, D., Ozaki, H., and Pal, I. (1987). EEG alpha map series: Brain micro-states by space-oriented adaptive segmentation. *Electroencephalography and Clinical Neurophysiology, 67,* 271–288.

Libet, B. (1994). *Neurophysiology of consciousness: Selected papers and new essays.* Boston: Birkhauser.

Magoun, H. W. (1962). *The waking brain* (2nd ed.). Springfield, IL: Thomas.

Mark, V. H., and Ervin, F. R. (1970). *Violence and the brain.* New York: Harper and Row.

Mark, V. H., Ervin, F. R., and Sweet, W. H. (1972). Deep temporal lobe stimulation in man. In B. E. Eleftherion (Ed.), *The neurobiology of the amygdala* (pp. 485–507). New York: Plenum.

Merleau-Ponty, M. (1962). *Phenomenology of perception.* (C. Smith, trans.) New York: Humanities Press. (Original work published 1945.)

Narabayashi, H. (1972). Stereotaxic amygdaloidotomy. In B. E. Eleftherion (Ed.), *The neurobiology of the amygdala* (pp. 459–483). New York: Plenum.

Panksepp, J. (1998). *Affective neuroscience: The foundations of human and animal emotions.* Oxford: Oxford University Press.

Pert, C. B. (1997). *Molecules of emotion: Why you feel the way you feel.* New York: Scribner.

Prigogine, I. (1980). *From being to becoming: Time and complexity in the physical sciences.* San Francisco: Freeman.

Rosch, E. (1994). Is causality circular? Event structure in folk psychology, cognitive science and Buddhist logic. *Journal of Consciousness Studies, 1,* 50–65.

Tani, J. (1996). Model-based learning for mobile robot navigation from the dynamical systems perspective. *IEEE Transactions on Systems, Man and Cybernetics, 26B,* 421–436.

Tolman, E. C. (1948). Cognitive maps in rats and men. *Psychological Review, 55,* 189–208.

Wilson, M. A., and McNaughton, B. L. (1993). Dynamics of the hippocampal ensemble code for space. *Science, 261,* 1055–1058.

9   The Neurodynamics of Emotions: An Evolutionary-Neurodevelopmental View

Jaak Panksepp

My goals will be threefold: (1) to provide a brief synopsis of emotional systems in the mammalian brain as detailed in Panksepp (1998a); (2) to introduce problems we face in trying to measure emotions directly from the signals of the brain as monitored through electroencephalographic (EEG) recordings, along with some discussion of the potential benefits of nonlinear approaches to analyzing such signals; and (3) to discuss the self-organizational aspects of emotional systems in ontogenetic development, and how we might go about measuring such processes behaviorally (largely in animal models). Finally, I will try to stitch these diverse themes together into a conceptual view of emotional development as it may epigenetically emerge within the living human brain/mind. The available data on all three of these issues is regrettably meager, leaving too much room for speculation.

My overall aim is to conceptualize how the neurodynamic changes within the brain create emotions, and how such changes modulate emotional development. By "neurodynamic" I mean those brain electrical and/or chemical activities that reflect the coherent activities of functional ensembles of neurons. Here I will focus on the electrical activities of groups of neurons as measured using EEG approaches, since this is the only routine measure that can monitor human neuronal activities in real time.

I. An Overview of Brain Emotional Systems

Although we currently know little about the neurodynamics of emotional processes, we do know a great deal about the behavioral, neuroanatomical, and neurochemical aspects of many emotional systems of the mammalian brain. The anatomical localization of certain basic emotion circuits has been achieved most convincingly using classical electrical stimulation of the brain (ESB) procedures and by observing the behavioral and psycholog-

236

ical consequences of various forms of experimental and clinical damage to
animal and human brains (see Panksepp, 1982, 1996, 1998a). To highlight
the fact that I will be discussing distinct emotional circuits of the brain, I
will employ capitalized labels for certain emotional systems. The use of
vernacular terms for these neural systems provides a heuristic to remind us
that the subcortically situated core systems for emotionality are organized
homologously in the brains of all mammals and may generate remarkably
similar internal feelings (affective states) in all of us. These systems are
envisioned to arouse global psychological states in the brain by activating
widespread brain activities, from the energization of action readiness to the
mood-congruent dynamics of cognitive activities. The basic emotions reflect evolutionary memories that provide an intrinsic way for animals to
project potentially adaptive behaviors into the future. Emotional systems
may be the primal governors of various self-organizing functions of the
brain, such as the self, consciousness, and intentionality.

   Emotional command pathways for FEAR, RAGE, PANIC (i.e., separation distress), SEEKING, PLAY, LUST and maternal CARE course between centromedial areas of the midbrain, such as the periaqueductal gray
(PAG), through specific zones of the diencephalon. PANIC and PLAY are
more concentrated in medial thalamic and anterior cingulate zones, while
all the other circuits course more through the hypothalamus and project to
such higher areas as the amygdala and other basal ganglia as well as frontal
cortical areas. However, all systems are widely ramifying, two-way avenues of communication that connect lower brain areas controlling reflexive,
autonomic, and hormonal response systems with those higher cerebral
systems that integrate information about objects in space and time, yielding
complex modes of learning, planning, and the generation of varied behavior
sequences. At the lower reaches of the brain such as the PAG, emotional
systems may help guide attentional processes mediated by ascending reticular systems, and provide a solid substrate of biological values for the
construction of primary-process or core consciousness (Panksepp, 1998a,
b). Thus, the various emotional command systems interact strongly with
each other, with dynamics we can presently only imagine, as well as with
the higher areas of the brain that more directly create our thoughts, perceptions, and cultural fabrics. A reasonable hypothesis is that the intrinsic
neurodynamics of the various emotional systems generate internally experienced affect by serving as global attractors for a great deal of emotion
state–specific or mood-congruent brain activities. Here I will envision the
epigenetic spread and colonization of the rest of the brain by these attractors as being a major force in emotional development.

Diffuse higher spheres of influence within the brain emerge epigenetically from distinct emotional processes interacting with higher brain areas. SEEKING systems strongly modulate frontal areas, FEAR and RAGE find loci of control in temporal lobe areas, and the prosocial emotions (including the pain of loss) are concentrated in medial paleocortical areas such as the anterior cingulate and insula. Through learning, these circuits come to be modulated by a large variety of inputs, from simple cues to complex cognitive appraisals. The natural caudal to rostral maturation of such processes in the brain may tell us a great deal about emotional development in human children. If one simply visualizes the brain effects of any emotional episode (using immunocytochemistry or in situ hybridization for oncogenes such as cFos (see Panksepp, 1998a), one sees dramatic arousal effects throughout the cortex and cerebellum, and many other brain areas that are not at all essential for arousing and synchronizing emotional processes (e.g., Kollack-Walker, Watson, and Akil, 1997). What this tells us is that the ramification of emotional effects through the brain is much more widespread than the locations of the integrative "command systems" that lie at the essential subcortical core of emotional processing in the brain. The precise manner in which cognitive activities become intermeshed with affective values remains largely unknown, but is an issue of first importance. Since the basic emotional systems have a "mind of their own," it may be that self-organizing aspects of each emotional system can reinforce certain developmental trajectories.

Some of the major neurochemical substrates for these command systems have been revealed by immunocytochemical studies and the administration of neurochemicals directly into relevant brain areas, where one can specifically increase and decrease behavioral measures of anticipatory eagerness, anger, fearfulness, separation distress, sexuality, nurturance, and playfulness (Panksepp, 1986, 1991, 1998a). It is within such "command" neurochemistries that we can see especially deep and useful evolutionary homologies, supporting the conclusion that there are ancestral cladistic (line-of-descent) relationships among these primitive emotional systems in all mammals. For instance, the hormones that help mothers deliver and feed children (oxytocin and prolactin) figure heavily in the modulation of maternal behaviors, separation distress, and the construction of social bonds. We know a great deal about the details of such systems in animal brains (for a comprehensive summary, see Panksepp, 1998a).

The imaging of the electrical and chemical neurodynamics will be more difficult to achieve than the cataloging of neural trajectories. In animals, chemical neurodynamics can be measured to some extent by evaluating synaptic release of transmitters using a variety of approaches ranging from push-pull sampling of brain fluids to *in vivo* voltametric measures of certain brain chemicals (for review, see Panksepp, 1998a, Chapter 6). Because of serious "plumbing" and ethical problems, these approaches are not applicable to human research. Since on-line measurements of brain electrical activities are relatively easily achieved from the cranial surface, EEG approaches will receive focused attention in the present chapter.

The measurement of electrical neurodynamics may benefit substantially from the intensive application of nonlinear techniques. Since the ripples of activity induced by all emotional systems are bound to spread widely throughout the brain, it is possible to at least imagine how topographic EEG techniques might be able to image the flickers of emotional dynamics in real time. Perhaps the greatest barrier to success is the fact that emotional dynamics can become idiosyncratic in higher brain regions through individual learning, along with the distance of those areas from the core generators of emotionality. However, there are systematic ways to proceed, as I will try to clarify.

II. Problems in Measuring the Emotions of the Brain

A. *Emotions Will Eventually Need to be Measured Directly from the Brain*

How might we eventually measure the various types of emotional arousal directly – from the ongoing neurodynamics that create primary-process feelings within the brain? This feat has not yet been accomplished, but with modern computational brain recordings and the techniques of nonlinear dynamics, there are some new and credible strategies to pursue. However, the optimal approaches may not emerge from the spectacular types of brain analysis that can be achieved with positron emission tomography (PET) and functional magnetic resonance imaging (fMRI). Although those techniques prevail in the clarification of neuroanatomical and neurochemical aspects of the higher *human* brain function (George et al., 1996; Lane et al., 1997), they cannot resolve the real-time neurodynamics of brain states that we experience as moods and emotional feelings. The classical approach of electroencephalography (EEG) and its princely cousin, magnetoencephalography (MEG), possess the essential characteristic that the newer technologies do not – they can follow the activities of ensembles of neurons in real time. MEG can also be used to compute source localizations for signals within the higher regions of the brain

(Williamson et al., 1997), although it remains too expensive for routine experimental use, especially in animals.

Unfortunately, both have one great shortcoming. Surface recording cannot resolve subcortical activities. Without surgical interventions, we cannot harvest signals from the deeper regions of the brain that are essential for generating emotions (Panksepp, 1998a). Although the electrical signals that can be harvested from the surface of the brain are strongly influenced by subcortical processes, including ascending neurotransmitter pathways such as acetylcholine, dopamine, norepinephrine, and serotonin, those generalized modulatory systems do not create specific emotions in the brain (Panksepp, 1986). Specific emotions appear to be largely created by excitatory amino acid circuits that are selectively modulated by a large number of neuropeptide circuits, most of which are subcortically situated (Panksepp, 1993).

It is possible that specific emotions will never be recorded clearly from the surface of the human brain; only the nonspecific dimensions such as great general arousal and positive and negative valence (Davidson, 1993) may be accessible at such a distance from the source generators. However, some of the shortcomings of surface recordings can be circumvented in routine animal research through the use of depth recordings. Well-placed electrodes within the trajectories of emotional systems may be able to monitor neural dynamics that distinguish the various emotions. Obviously, such recordings are bound to be hampered by various spatial problems, such as the massive interdigitation of many distinct systems within deep reticular areas of the brain, but the hope is that with properly situated electrodes at many relevant points in the brain, many emotions may generate distinct neurodynamic signatures in the spatiotemporal electrical fields within the brain.

B. A Role for EEG Recordings in Monitoring Brain Emotional Processes

With only a few notable exceptions (e.g., Freeman, 1992, and Vanderwolf, 1992, as well as much of sleep research), the EEG approach fell into disuse in animal research several decades ago when the more precise and seemingly more informative measures of single neuron activity became routinely available. However, since single-unit techniques cannot be readily deployed in human research on emotions, there is little chance of deriving useful empirical generalizations regarding human and animal brain functions using those approaches. Our inability to use such techniques for routine human research may be just as well from a psychological point of view: Global brain functions such as emotions emerge from the coordination of widely distributed ensembles of neurons that cannot be adequately sampled with single-unit techniques.

On the other hand, the EEG can monitor the integrated dendritic activities of large populations of neurons that may reflect emotion-specific signals. With the addition of nonlinear dynamic methodologies to the existing linear approaches such as peak frequency, power spectrum, and coherence analyses, we are experiencing a renaissance in the utilization of EEG to probe brain functions (Basar, 1990; Nunez, 1995). How well such sophisticated EEG measures, applied to subcortical recording sites, can monitor specific emotional processes remains uncertain, but our understanding of the neuroanatomy of emotional systems can now help us guide the placement of recording electrodes in optimal orientations within several emotional systems (Panksepp, 1998a). With the current availability of computational power, EEG signals can be processed and analyzed in ever more sophisticated ways, and there are good reasons to believe that a renewed implementation of such approaches in animal brain research can begin to yield powerful integrative concepts (Freeman, 1995). Furthermore, the fact that EEG techniques can be used identically in animals and humans can promote interdisciplinary bridge building that will be essential to yield meaningful answers to essential questions concerning the nature of mind, both emotional and cognitive.

Global psychological processes may be linked more clearly to such integrated brain potentials (i.e., EEG signals) than to flickering trains of action potentials from individual neurons. Although both types of measures exhibit chaotic features (Basar, 1990; Mpitsos et al., 1988), the nonlinear analysis of dendritic potentials may be especially useful in decoding behavioral states (Freeman, 1995; Kelso, 1995). Considering that ''the mind'' is fundamentally a neuroelectrical phenomenon, EEG recordings may give us access to the fluctuating ''texture'' and ''clothing'' of the mind, while action potentials, to continue this metaphor, may only help highlight the stitches that keep the psychic garments together. One of the great challenges for developmental psychology will be to describe, in some detail, how this clothing changes as a function of endogenous and epigenetic development (Adamec, 1993; Panksepp, Knutson, and Pruitt, 1998; Thatcher, 1994). A great deal of this work will have to be done in animal models.

Few have succeeded in such pursuits (and few have tried), but the tools now exist for revolutionary types of research. With sufficiently dense, multisite recording arrays and computational sophistication, we may be able first to visualize how subcortical circuits in animals become aroused during emotions, and then to develop ways to detect the faint glimmers of emotion-specific signals from EEG recordings off the surface of the human cranium. Although the resulting measures of neurodynamics may not require nonlinear approaches, those approaches are especially enticing. Many believe the analysis of nonlinear dynamics in neural tissue will allow us eventually to understand how the brain generates mind (Kelso, 1995; MacCormac and Stamenov, 1996). The empirical underpinnings for such brain analyses are now well developed (e.g., Basar, 1990; Freeman, 1992; Nunez, 1995), and a summary of how the new science of complexity is fertilizing theoretical and empirical worldviews in psychology is summarized in an appendix to this chapter. Such approaches remain to be utilized for analyzing the brain representations of emotion, but a great deal of work has been done using traditional EEG measures.

C. On Measuring the Activity of Emotional Systems of the Brain

So, how close have we come to measuring emotions from the human brain? There is some pertinent albeit indirect data from PET and MRI studies (see George et al., 1996, for a review), but for reasons already discussed, I will focus here on the available EEG work. The topographic patterns of alpha activity from surface recordings differ between negative and positive emotional states (Ahern and Schwartz, 1985; Meyers and Smith, 1986), and these differences increase with emotional intensity (Harman and Ray, 1977). Some of these effects can be distinguished from attentional responses, since the patterns are measurably different during cognitive and affective appraisal of the same stimuli (Smith et al., 1987).

One compelling line of research indicates that positive and negative affective processes can be monitored from frontal recordings. Positive emotionality (approach) is characterized by predominant left frontal arousal, while negative affect (withdrawal) is characterized by right frontal arousal (Davidson, 1993). Similar types of brain changes have been observed in neonates (Davidson and Fox, 1989; Dawson et al., 1997), and corresponding long-term mood dispositions can also be distinguished in adults (Henriques and Davidson, 1991; Schaffer, Davidson, and Saron, 1983).

To determine whether EEG technology has the potential to distinguish among basic affect programs, I developed expertise in modifying my own emotional states using the Sentic Cycle procedure of Clynes (1977). When changes in EEG alpha blocking within the 8-13 Hz range were monitored from my cranial surface as I was experiencing different emotions, clear and robust differential patterns were evident for various emotions. A second-by-second analysis yielded some global regional differences in the broad 8-13 Hz alpha band (Figure 9.1). Even more remarkable images were evident with finer 0.25 sec analyses of the same data in single frequency bins, but the flickering EEG changes in the various frequency bins were so complex as to defy straightforward description (data not shown). Unfortunately, this Sentic Cycle technique was not easily implemented among our undergraduate students, and we shifted our EEG work to analyze responses to more explicit exteroceptive affective stimuli (i.e., music).

Since affectively distinct information is easily encoded in music, and the EEG is quite sensitive to musical variables (Petsche et al., 1988), we decided to use standardized pieces of happy and sad music as our stimuli (Terwogt and van Grinsven, 1991). The computational methodology we employed (the same as in Fig. 9.1) was the sensitive event related desynchronization (ERD)/event related synchronization (ERS) algorithm, which evaluates cerebral arousal by the relative degrees of alpha power reduction (ERDs) or alpha power increases (ERSs) in the EEG (Pfurtscheller, 1992). For optimal application of this technique, repeated trials need to be run and averaged. Accordingly, we used repeated presentations of well-standardized 12- to 13-second segments of happy and sad music with 10-second intertrial intervals. We computed ERD and ERS changes (within the 8-12 Hz alpha range) from 19 topographically arranged electrodes according to the international 10/20 system. Control conditions consisted of counterbalanced periods during which subjects were exposed to a human voice or pink noise.

The results for ten females and six males (summarized in Panksepp and Bekkedal, 1997) indicated that there were large changes in EEG to all of the stimuli but, at best, only modest discrimination among them. Across stimuli, females generally exhibited more ERSs than males during the first third of the stimulus period, while males exhibited more ERDs. In general, females exhibited slightly more ERDs to the happy music and slightly more ERSs to the sad music, while males exhibited the opposite pattern (for topographic maps, see Panksepp and Bekkedal, 1997). Although the subjects easily discriminated the affect the music was intended to convey, few reported that this type of listening session evoked any clear affective states in them. Most found the repeated presentation of the same segment of music unmoving in this laboratory setting. However, when well-motivated male subjects listened to their own self-selected happy and sad

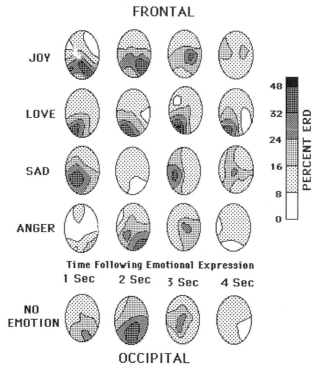

Figure 9.1. Global regional differences in EEG alpha-blocking activity during various emotional states. Percent event-related desynchronization (ERD) evaluates relative degrees of alpha power reduction.

selections (presented in the same segmented manner, but presented from beginning to end, without repetitions), robust cerebral arousal or ERDs were observed in response to the sad pieces, while more ERSs were evident to the happy music (Figure 9.2). These results affirmed that distinct changes in patterns of cerebral arousal are evident in response to happy and sad pieces of music.

To further analyze the potential utility of such measures, we proceeded to analyze the ERS/ERD responsivity of the cerebral surface to very simple affective stimuli – namely, four brief and powerful emotion-specific human sounds (~1 sec in duration). Expressive sounds were selected so as to reflect the orthogonal affective dimensions of positive-negative valence crossed with the dimensions of arousal (as in Lang, 1995). The positive and negative stimuli of high arousal were the sounds of joy and anger respectively, while those for positive and negative low arousal were plea-

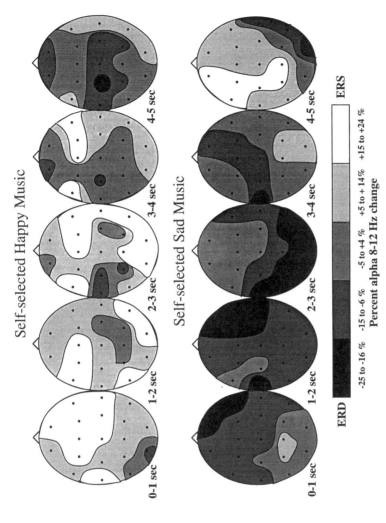

Self-selected Happy Music

0-1 sec   1-2 sec   2-3 sec   3-4 sec   4-5 sec

Self-selected Sad Music

0-1 sec   1-2 sec   2-3 sec   3-4 sec   4-5 sec

ERD

-25 to -16 %   -15 to -6 %   -5 to +4 %   +5 to + 14%   +15 to +24 %

Percent alpha 8-12 Hz change

ERS

Figure 9.2. Global regional differences in alpha power reduction (ERD) and alpha power increases (ERS) in response to self-selected happy and sad pieces of music.

245

sure and sadness. Pure tones were used as control stimuli. As in the previous experiment, there were many EEG changes to these stimuli, but not of sufficient clarity to permit us to distinguish the various emotional stimuli (for results, see Bekkedal, 1997). The clearest difference was in the gender domain once again, with females exhibiting more ERSs in the theta range to anger stimuli than males, while males responded with more ERDs than females to the pleasure stimuli. These data suggest that the patterns may be different in males and females, which may highlight their different emotional concerns.

We conducted similar experiments contrasting emotional sounds in autistic and control populations. Even though various EEG differences emerged (especially a reduced coherence of EEG in frontal areas of autistic individuals), again the primitive emotional sounds could not be distinguished from each other via such surface recordings (Floriana, 1997). Finally, we decided to see if somatically generated affect would yield a clearer picture: We analyzed the cerebral consequences of thermal stimuli applied to the forearms just above and below pain thresholds in normal individuals. We were not able to discriminate these hot and warm stimuli using EEG criteria, and this appeared to be at least partially due to individual reactivity to pain. Individuals who found the mild pain distressing exhibited ERSs, while those who were not bothered by this type of mild pain exhibited more ERDs (Whitestone, 1996).

In short, our aim – to seek emotion-specific signatures from topographic EEG recordings – has not yielded the coherent patterns we had hoped to find. Even though frontal asymmetries do reflect positive and negative arousal (Davidson, 1993), no one has yet distinguished the specific types of basic emotion from one another using EEG criteria. In retrospect, this is not surprising. If the primal generators for emotionality are subcortically situated, scalp recordings are probably too distant from the primary generators to provide unambiguous information. Let us recall that the fierce subcortical neuronal "storms" that occur in dreaming, as reflected in PGO (pons, geniculate, occipital cortex) spikes, are not detectable with surface EEG recordings of the sleeping human brain. Of course, it is possible that processing such degraded signals through neural-net computer algorithms that are designed to detect hidden features may help solve such problems. Indeed, dimensional nonlinear analytic approaches may help illuminate systematic patterns in EEG signals (which, after all, are squiggly lines that convey no intrinsic psychological meaning) that are not evident using the more traditional approaches, but at present, the literature only holds out modest hope that such approaches might work (see appendix).

With the present state of the art, I believe we must backtrack and focus on several critical dimensions of the problem: (1) What type of model system might be able to discriminate the neurodynamics of discrete emotions? (2) What might it mean, in neural terms, to have emotional feelings in the brain? There is only space to reflect on these issues briefly, but I will conclude that there is still reason to believe that we may eventually derive direct neurodynamic measures of emotionality from the mammalian brain.

(1) Model system considerations. Since we know a great deal about the emotion systems in other species, such as cats, rats, and primates, it is presently most reasonable to attempt to obtain clear signals of the neurodynamics of emotional states in these creatures. Indeed, powerful emotion- and motivation-related changes in EEG signals have been detected from primitive cortical areas that cannot be accessed with surface EEG recordings in humans, such as the olfactory projection areas of the prepyriform cortex (Freeman, 1960). Those types of experiments now need to be conducted with depth recordings where recording electrodes are nestled right in the trajectory of basic emotional systems. Since we now know a great deal about the emotional circuits of animal brains, we are in a position to position electrodes with some finesse. An optimal way to seek emotion-specific signatures in EEG recordings would be (i) to artificially evoke emotional responses by either electrical or chemical stimulation of the appropriate subcortical circuits (Panksepp, 1982, 1991, 1998a), (ii) to record from diverse locations along the circuitry, and (iii) to see how the signals are transformed or degraded as they pass into more distant areas of the brain. To reduce background noise, much of this work could be done in anesthetized animals, since one can readily activate various forms of emotional arousal in such animals (Ikemoto and Panksepp, 1994; Panksepp et al., 1991). Only during subsequent stages of analysis should one introduce naturalistic models of the various emotional responses (e.g., Freeman, 1960).

At present, the wisest strategy may be to orient multiple electrodes within brain zones where we find concentrations of executive neurons that elaborate primitive emotional states. The periaqueductal gray (PAG) of the midbrain is an optimal location, for it is now clear that all emotional systems converge there, often as columnar units (Bandler and Keay, 1996). There is reason to believe that this part of the brain provides a primal neural scaffolding for the emergence of affective consciousness (Panksepp, 1998a).

(2) On the neural nature of emotional feelings. Many affective feelings may be critically linked to PAG functions. Although a high level of aware-

ness is certainly not a local property of the PAG itself, such functions may emerge from the higher brain areas that are recursively linked to the PAG, especially in temporal and frontal lobes (Damasio, 1994; Mantyh, 1982; Panksepp et al., 1991; Sesack et al., 1989). Obviously, affective consciousness, like all other forms of consciousness, is hierarchically organized in the brain, with the higher functions being decisively dependent on the integrity of the lower functions, but not vice versa (Panksepp, 1998a). However, the potential reiterations and expansions of the basic affective themes, perhaps first elaborated within the PAG, to higher brain areas, may eventually allow the neurodynamics of discrete emotions to be detected on the cortical surface.

The postulation of a primal affective processor (a "simple, ego-type life form" or SELF), as a key actor, as opposed to an observer, within the Cartesian Theater, may help us cultivate a more satisfactory understanding of emotional feelings than presently exists (for an elaboration of this theoretical view, see Panksepp, 1998a, Chapter 16). Essentially, the SELF is conceived to consist of reverberatory neuronal patterns – perhaps with an epicenter in the PAG – that incorporate key aspects of somatic and visceral bodily components into a coherent neurodynamic form (Panksepp, 1998b). Emotional feelings may constitute changing resonances in this system that can be broadcast widely in the brain, even though they may be quite difficult to monitor. If this is the case, then it might be easier initially to focus on the integrated behavioral outputs of such systems than on EEG signals to determine whether the time-series analysis of repetitive emotional behaviors will reflect nonlinear or even chaotic processes.

III. On the Measurement of Nonlinear Processes in Emotional Behaviors, and Implications for Self-Organizing Aspects of Emotional Development

A. Optimal Behavioral Choices for a Future Dynamic Analysis of Emotional Processes

In order to generate theoretically important phase portraits for the fundamental emotions of the brain, a reasonable starting point is to apply nonlinear techniques to spontaneous affective behavior patterns that animals normally exhibit in nature. This assertion is based on the assumption that emotions are most clearly reflected in the instinctual as opposed to the learned tendencies of animals. As soon as a learned behavior pattern is selected for analysis (e.g., Hoyert, 1992), habit structures will emerge, and the results will not be as clearly interpretable with regard to the nature of the unconditioned brain systems that normally govern emotional tendencies. To my knowledge, there is presently no published study that has performed a nonlinear, time-series analysis of an emotionally interesting natural *behavioral* pattern in any mammalian species. Indeed, only a handful of published reports exist where natural behavior patterns of animals have been subjected to nonlinear analysis (e.g., the vigilant behavior of birds: Ferriere et al., 1996).

To determine if an emotional process exhibits chaotic determinism, one will need to harvest sustained sequences of clearly operationalized emotional behaviors or physiological changes. For certain emotions, such as fear, this would be hard to achieve, since one common response is behavioral immobility (freezing) and another is a precipitous flight response. Somewhat better success might be had with angry behaviors, since one could quantify the temporal patterns of successive attacks and bites during systematic provocations. Of course, the free flow of agonistic interaction between two animals could yield a variety of problems that would compromise clean and sustained measures of these behavioral patterns. Perhaps the joint behaviors of a fairly evenly matched dueling pair of animals (like two boxers or wrestlers), with repeated shifts in who was prevailing, could be a productive model for analysis. However, such research is bound to be messy, especially for EEG work, where one would have to worry about tangled leads. I would suggest that two other types of basic emotional measures, namely rough-and-tumble play and separation distress vocalizations, have excellent behavioral characteristics for a nonlinear analysis. The separation distress calls of young animals isolated from their normal social environment (Panksepp et al., 1980) and the flow of behavior that occurs during rough-housing play (Panksepp, Siviy, and Normansell, 1984; Vanderschuren, Niesink, and Van Ree, 1997) are powerful, well-operationalized behaviors that lend themselves nicely to extended time-series analyses. Both are easily operationalized and sustained for sufficiently long periods of time to permit harvesting of high-quality time-series data sets that are essential for dynamic systems analysis. Also, there is reason to suppose that such emotional systems are especially important for emotional development in human children, as reflected in secure and insecure attachments and various impulse control disorders.

Separation distress calls in various species including primates, dogs, guinea pigs, and domestic birds (Panksepp, Newman, and Insel, 1992) consist of long periods of discrete vocalizations, and the intervocalization intervals could be easily quantified. Thus, large sets of behaviors indicative of a sustained emotional response could be easily gathered in many animals. Also, since there is now a large literature on the neurochemical systems that control such vocalizations (Panksepp et al., 1988), there are many interesting independent variables that could be studied to determine how the potential attractors for these emotional responses are modulated. Also, this emotional system has now been strongly linked to human psychopathologies like depression (Kramer et al., 1998).

Bouts of rough-and-tumble play can also yield promising data sets. Ludic behavior patterns are characterized by the repeated emission of many discrete, easily operationalized behaviors that would be ideal endpoints for the generation of emotion-relevant phase diagrams. The two ideal play behaviors to quantify are the time series of dorsal contacts (one animal soliciting play by pouncing on another animal's back) and pins (those discrete moments of time when one animal has its back to the ground with the other animal above). One could do separate analyses for each animal, as well as an analysis for the conjoint output of each dyad. Parenthetically, to minimize the nightmare of tangled leads in such EEG studies of play, one animal could be made unplayful with drugs, and thereby one could simply monitor the play solicitations of a single animal. Also, since the active phases of play generate considerable force on the floor of the play chamber, one could conduct concurrent analyses on automated activity counts generated at various thresholds of force. The implications of play research for understanding spontaneously emerging childhood problems like attention deficit/hyperactivity disorders (ADHD) are many (Panksepp, 1998d).

In addition, during play young rats emit repeated 50 KHz vocalizations (Knutson, Burgdorf, and Panksepp, 1998). We have provisionally concluded that these vocalizations may be homologous to playful laughter in children (Panksepp, 1998a), which makes them an especially apt subject for nonlinear analysis. It will be most interesting to see how the dynamics of such behavior patterns change as animals progress through various developmental stages. Indeed, such dependent measures could serve as test cases for the ability of nonlinear dynamics to yield new insights into the natural behavior patterns of mammals. If we can distinguish joyous from distressed attractors, across several dependent measures, it would lend confidence to the utility of such approaches. I am personally not yet convinced that a major new doorway to understanding these emotional processes will necessarily emerge from nonlinear analyses (for a critique, see the appendix at the end of this chapter), but the approach needs to be fully evaluated.

B. Some Practical Developmental Prospects: From ADHD to Autism

The mathematical tools of nonlinear dynamics do raise the possibility that we will be able to empirically characterize processes, especially coherent internal functions of the brain, that were beyond our scientific imagination just a few years ago. We can now image how we might begin to systematically measure basic emotional issues that we could previously only conceptualize as verbal metaphors or as outputs of relatively static neural circuits. With some luck, nonlinear tools may help us decode processes in animal and human brains/minds that have never been visualized with objective tools. Already, we have powerful and complex images of motor development in infancy (Thelen and Smith, 1995), cognitive dynamics (Port and van Gelder, 1995; van Geert, 1991), and the cyclic waves of reorganization that occur during human brain development (Thatcher, 1994).

The new behavioral measures of emotion in animals, in conjunction with EEG measures and dynamic theoretical views, may yield totally new views of affective development. I have advocated the view that at the heart of these affective developments is a neurosymbolically embodied core SELF that receives strong inputs from a variety of basic bodily and emotional systems (Panksepp, 1998a,b). This type of brain organization may be reflected especially clearly in the precipitous emotional responses that prevail in the behavioral repertoire of infants, where emotional feelings and bodily actions always go together. The dictates of these systems interacting with the world may be essential for the emergence and maturation of higher levels of consciousness. In mature adults, these feelings may come to be largely hidden under a shroud of behavioral inhibition that permits one to enact behavioral possibilities in the absence of behavioral actions. Presumably, in adult brains, value tagging – whereby affective evaluative responses are linked to various world events – is transpiring continuously, outside the realm of behavioral observation. When the interactions of emotions and cognitions or the ability to elaborate a sufficient level of behavioral inhibition is compromised, we would have a variety of distinct childhood ''disorders.''

In ADHD, the more primitive impulses and urges may remain ascendant because of the failure of frontal lobe maturation (Barkley, 1997; Castellanos et al., 1996). Without adequate frontal lobe functions, children will not be able to buffer their instinctual energies with the expectations of society. They will not be able to conceptualize the views and expectations of others – to formulate a sufficiently deep and complex theory of other minds. I suspect that such problems could be alleviated substantially by providing greater access to and cathartic release of the intrinsic affective regulators that normally promote the maturation of the higher brain areas – perhaps processes such as those that generate rough-and-tumble play within the brain (Panksepp, 1998c). We should seriously consider the possibility that the self-organizing aspects of various emotional systems may be thwarted by certain societal practices, such as expecting young children to sit attentively for hours when their internal play urges are insistent (Panksepp, 1998d).

Many things can go wrong in the natural developmental progression, from early periods of life when behavior is controlled largely by primitive instinctual energies to later periods when higher cognitive and social regulatory controls emerge. For instance, there seems to be a disconnection between the primary processes of social emotions and emergent cognitive and behavioral controls in childhood disorders such as autism (Bauman and Kemper, 1995). Had we standardized phase diagrams of early motor development and emotional responsivity for infants, might autism be diagnosed at earlier ages through the analysis of motor patterns (see Teitelbaum et al., 1996)? The earlier the diagnosis, the more opportunities there will be to shift development toward more desirable trajectories. In pursuing such enterprises, we should entertain all options, not just the cognitive/ environmental ones traditionally favored by psychologists.

Could the behavior of such developmentally delayed children be improved by promoting the arousal of certain attractor patterns in their brains? Perhaps such feats could be achieved by the application of certain patterns of rapid transcranial magnetic stimulation (rTMS), a procedure that has shown considerable promise as a somatic treatment of depression (George et al., 1996). Alternatively, might certain neurofeedback or other neurotraining procedures (Lubar et al., 1995) be used to promote desirable neural strength and deterministic chaotic patterns within the brain? Could the ability of music to mold the emotional dynamics of the brain be helpful (Panksepp and Bekkedal, 1997)? Whether nonlinear analyses of the underlying brain systems will eventually allow us to develop earlier and better interventions for such children remains to be seen. But whenever there are such strikingly new paths of empiricism to be pursued, there are reasons for cautious optimism.

C. A Neurotheoretical View of Emotional Self-Organization in the Brain

Aside from the characterization of the fundamental neural systems for affective processes, perhaps the most pressing issue for understanding emotional development is the specification of how emotional values inter-penetrate with cognitive activities. As a child gains experience with the world, various events, people, and objects come to be associated with different emotional meanings. We know practically nothing about how this really happens. There are many possibilities, ranging from some type of simple value tagging (via processes like classical conditioning) to some type of primal neuroelectric wave fronts from primitive regions of the brain that impose an ordered affective coherence on the inflow of perceptual impressions and/or cognitive processing. For didactic purposes, let us focus just on these two possibilities.

First, with classically conditioned value tagging, we have two general suboptions: (1) that cognitive activities become imbued or interpenetrated with affective values, or more simply (2) that value-neutral cognitive processes develop access routes (by some type of reinforcement process) to the primary-process emotional systems discussed at the outset of this chapter. I would not be surprised if both types of processes occur, although the second is much easier to model mechanistically. The second type of general process, albeit not independent of classical conditioning conceptions, views brains quite differently – as dynamic interacting neuroelectric fields as opposed to node-based information transfer devices.

In general, I tend to favor such dynamic views of brain organization as put forward by Walter Freeman (see his chapter in this volume). My take on this view is that certain types of neural reverberations establish primal state spaces within the brain that can expand and contract dynamically, both in short- and long-term time frames, depending on the balanced interactions of key systems. In my estimation, the major possible state spaces are dictated by the arousals of the primal emotional systems, and those systems have certain intrinsic dynamics that help establish coherent, emotion-specific forms of action and cognitive readiness. In other words, these primal state spaces, generated early in development by the arousal of emotional value systems, interact dynamically in increasingly complex and recursive ways with all of the higher cognitive mechanisms. These inter-actions are self-organizing. They are initially strongly influenced by the integrative forces of the basic emotional value systems, and they prioritize the events that will subsequently have the most influence on thought and behavior. In this way, increasingly complex symbolic valence structures emerge that have an ever-increasing ability to guide future thoughts and behaviors. If the intrinsic valence structures of emotional systems do help create various higher affective state spaces within certain cortical regions, there are bound to be enormous differences in the patterning of these spaces from individual to individual. Because of many such idiosyncrasies, electrical recordings from higher regions of the brain may ultimately be of marginal value in characterizing the intrinsic dynamics of emotional systems.

In somewhat simpler terms, let me envision how all this may transpire during the emotional maturation of a child. At birth, a child's brain organization is largely affective, with basic emotional systems orchestrating responses to the world that assails it. These emotional systems, in conjunction with the maturation of SELF structures and sensory-motor capacities, rain down values into the higher regions of the brain. Although we do not understand the nature of this penetrating ''rain,'' presumably the resultant values consist of certain types of neural resonances that still reflect the intrinsic, ancient rhythms of the basic emotional systems. The types of affective resonances that tend to prevail within the cognitive reaches of the brain (partially due to genetic strengths and weaknesses and partially due to life experiences) establish the cognitive personality structures and styles of each child.

In these ways, world events become imbued with a special affective meaning that can guide actions. Certain people, groups, and cultures become lovable, others become despicable, others threatening, and yet others fear- or awe-inspiring. If the confluence of forces are primarily those of love, trust, and security (presumably because of abundant maternal nurturance, well-regulated separation response experiences, and abundant joyful play experiences), the child will carry a secure base into all future social activities. If, on the other hand, these forces work in the opposite direction for the child, insecure attachments and many life worries and problems will emerge. In other words, as one's emotional balances or imbalances become established as social facts, the cognitive apparatus will be permanently imbued with an affective tone that will put a characteristic stamp on an individual's life activities.

In sharing this epigenetic view of the confluence of basic emotional and cognitive activities, I would not like to argue that perceptual processes are intrinsically affect-free. Although few have developed ideas along these lines, I do believe that a different category of affects may be an intrinsic part of our perceptual apparatus. It would seem negligent of evolution to have left the major exteroperceptive systems – vision and hearing – without any intrinsic values. I suspect that such value structures are typically and especially clearly manifested in our concepts of beauty and ugliness. To some major yet unmeasured extent, I think the higher aesthetic responses emerge from perceptual inputs that have special symmetries, special harmonies, and special coherences with subtle genetically provided ''Kantian'' templates within our neuroperceptual apparatus. Such ideas need more development.

D. Conclusions and Prospects for a Dynamic Understanding of Emotions and Emotional Development

Everything the brain does is organized by massive cascades of interacting components. Some of these components mature spontaneously during development, while others are molded by experience (Panksepp, Knutson, and Pruitt, 1998). Mind apparently emerges from the resulting neuroelectric dynamics. Considering the massive complexities of dendritic potentials and the ballistic barrages of action potentials within this neurodynamic weave, mere mathematical procedures may not be able to provide satisfactory clarification of the underlying neurodynamics and the resulting psychodynamics (Van Eeenwyck, 1996).

Although the precise manner in which neuronal field activities create minds by interacting with environments remains unfathomed, we are at least beginning to understand where we can look for some lasting answers to some of these fundamental questions. The emerging dynamic views of brain functions are at the leading edge of such developments. Although no one has yet demonstrated that deterministic chaos is essential for any brain function or that chaotic bifurcations create divergent thoughts and feelings, such ideas are exciting, provocative, and at times empirically testable (see the following appendix).

Appendix: The Science of Complexity: A Holistic View of Brain Functions from the Outside

Dynamic systems theory has enlivened several areas of psychology that were languishing scientifically (albeit not professionally) because they were confronted by complexities that could not be decisively clarified or sufficiently quantified using statistical and linear tools. A suitable nonlinear methodology borrowed from theoretical physics (Li and Yorke, 1975) has now kindled the imagination of many psychologists. Developmental and social psychologists (Fogel, Lyra, and Valsiner, 1997; Smith and Thelen, 1993; Vallacher and Nowak, 1997), indeed psychologists of all persuasions (Barton, 1994), are becoming entranced by the conceptual frameworks afforded by the metaphors and mathematics of complexity. Behavioral neuroscientists as a group have shown less enthusiasm for such endeavors, partially because they already have very powerful tools to analyze the causes of behaviors. In any case, nonlinear analytic techniques now allow us to seek predictable patterns in seemingly random events; they allow us to estimate the number of dynamically interacting variables that are needed to model (if not explain) many psychobehavioral processes that previously seemed random, or at least capricious. We can finally image predictable fractal patterns of strange attractors embedded in the massive variability and turbulence of physical (Abraham and Shaw, 1992; Crutchfield et al., 1986; Gleick, 1987) and social worlds (see Vallacher and Nowak, 1997, with commentaries).

We can now characterize the self-organizing and bifurcating complexities of creatures behaving and interacting in their natural environments with greater precision (Thelen and Smith, 1995). The new procedures have the potential to describe mental abilities (Kelso, 1995; MacCormac and Stamenov, 1996), the flow of emotions during psychoanalytic crises (Reidbord and Redington, 1992), the intricacies of social and family dynamics (Gottman, this volume), and the predictably unpredictable ways of some of our other influential cultural institutions (Vaga, 1994). Mathematical modeling of nonlinear complexities is finally allowing us to extract meaningful sets of underlying variables from the confluence of real-world events. By gathering a sufficient amount of time-series data on processes of interest, we can now aspire to characterize the abstract, outward shadows of the underlying dynamics from a single continuous data line. By converting a continuous time axis into a recurrent frequency axis, we can depict coherent images of behavioral phenotypes by drawing their fractal geometries – the phase portraits of the underlying, and previously invisible, attractors. The flow of behavioral events that once seemed random often contains hidden patterns that may inform us of coherences that may reflect the abstract shapes of mental states.

The bifurcations in chaotic phase diagrams, because of their sensitivity to small changes in initial conditions, offer unique ways to image, and potentially understand, how seemingly modest events, like the scorn or glint in lovers' eyes, can escalate into major emotional eruptions with powerful behavioral consequences. As has long been recognized, complex and robust emotional states of mind can be precipitated by energetically modest conditioned stimuli and seemingly minor fluctuations in cognitive appraisals, but now we can aspire to quantify and model such pervasive interactions in the neuropsychological world. By so doing we can better conceptualize the multilayered, two-way interactions between thoughts and feelings that occur within the brain (see Lewis, 1996, for an overview of how we might systematize such an interactive systems view). Causal influences moving in multiple and recursive directions is a better image of the realities typically found in nature than is the useful but simplistic "billiard-ball" causality of engineering, which has so decisively helped build our modern world. The pursuit of one-way causality will, of course, continue to provide us with important mechanistic answers, with strategies that work.

On the cautionary side, the newly minted dynamic metaphors for twenty-first-century science (Goerner, 1994) have many hidden dangers – many siren-song seductions for the unwary. The shortcomings are beginning to be enumerated and appreciated (Horgan, 1995; Rapp, 1993). These nonlinear tools are largely descriptive and not necessarily the scalpels we need to probe the ultracomplex *causal* underbelly of nature. As with all scientific pursuits, the quality of nonlinear analyses is highly constrained by the quality of data, and sufficiently large and interesting data sets are more difficult to obtain than the ones we have come to trust when we simply aspire to contrast statistical differences among various experimental groups. Although we can now treat what appeared to be statistical noise or error variance as part of the essence of the phenomena we are seeking to describe, there is presently no assurance that such approaches will provide more valid and useful conclusions than those derived from traditional approaches.

In sum, while the tools of nonlinear dynamics can help us describe behavior patterns more accurately than ever before, they provide no fast and fail-safe way to fathom the underlying principles that control our thoughts, feelings, and actions. Sufficiently long segments of interesting behavioral and physiological patterns during stable psychological states remain notoriously difficult to harvest. The techniques have been most successfully applied to systematic descriptions of repetitive motor behaviors that can readily be documented in the time domain (Kelso, 1995), ranging from pigeons pecking on fixed interval schedules (Hoyert, 1992) to humans clapping over nothing special (Fitzpatrick, Schmidt, and Carello, 1996).

Several investigators have pursued more challenging undertakings, yielding some noteworthy findings. The changing patterns of chaotic attractors evident in the EEG have been monitored within the deepening stages of human sleep (Roschke and Aldenhoff, 1991). The transient visual effects produced by stroboscopic stimulation have yielded some interesting patterns (Stwertka, 1993). Some of the most compelling contributions have come from the analysis of real-time physiological signals, such as heart rate and EEG (Basar, 1990; Elbert et al., 1994). But truly memorable findings, with useful consequences, have been few and far between.

For decades now, physicists have been searching for practical applications for nonlinear techniques, but a disappointingly small number have emerged (Herbert, 1996). Perhaps breakthrough applications will come in the area of diagnostics. One provocative finding is that diminished chaotic dimensionality in heart rate may help predict the probability of cardiac infarction (Skinner, 1993), raising the possibility that comparable brain measures may eventually be used to predict strokes and perhaps even psychiatric problems (Elbert et al., 1992; Globus and Arpaia, 1994).

Although the neural hieroglyphics of affective processes remain to be clarified using nonlinear techniques, the nature of psychiatric ailments have been clarified by analyzing complex rhythms in patients' EEGs (Elbert et al., 1994). Low-dimensional chaotic cycling has been detected in manic-depressive episodes as monitored using serial mood ratings (Gottschalk, Bauer, and Whybrow, 1995), even though no unusual patterns were detected with measures of linear rhythmicity (i.e., power spectral analysis). Others are seeking to identify emotionally important transitions in therapist-client relationships by visualizing the complexity of cardiac dynamics (Reidbord and Redington, 1995). Whether these approaches will yield major insights in basic emotion research and child development remains to be seen.

By providing a conceptual structure that begins to capture holistically the subtle interactions of many variables that impinge on organisms in the real world, the tools of nonlinear dynamics offer hope that we will be able to objectively monitor qualitative psychological and neural processes that have never been measured before (Lutzenberger, Flor, and Birbaumer, 1997; Milton et al., 1989). Walter Freeman's classic work on olfactory perceptual processes in animals (Freeman, 1992, 1995; Skarda and Freeman, 1990) epitomizes such a possibility. Such approaches may eventually provide diagnostic measures of developmental problems that can lead to psychiatric disturbances.

References

Abraham, R. H., and Shaw, C. D. (1992). *Dynamics: The geometry of behavior.* Redwood City, CA: Addison-Wesley.
Adamec, R. E. (1993). Lasting effect of FG-7142 on anxiety, aggression and limbic physiology in the rat. *Journal of Neurophysiology, 3,* 232–248.

Ahern, G. L., and Schwartz, G. E. (1985). Differential lateralization for positive and negative emotion in the human brain: EEG spectral analysis. *Neuropsychologia, 23*, 745–755.

Bandler, R., and Keay, K. A. (1996). Columnar organization in the midbrain periaqueductal gray and the integration of emotional expression. In G. Holstege, R. Bandler and C. B. Saper (Eds.), *The emotional motor system: Progress in brain research* (vol. 107, pp. 287–300). Amsterdam: Elsevier.

Barkley, R. A. (1997). *ADHD and the nature of self-control.* New York: Guilford.

Barton, S. (1994). Chaos, self-organization, and psychology. *American Psychologist, 49*, 5–14.

Basar, E. (Ed.). (1990). *Chaos in brain.* New York: Springer-Verlag.

Bauman, M. L., and Kemper, T. L. (1995). Neuroanatomical observations of the brain in autism. In J. Panksepp (Ed.), *Advances in biological psychiatry* (vol. 1, pp. 1–26). Greenwich, CT: JAI Press.

Bekkedal, M. Y. V. (1997). *Emotion in the brain: EEG changes in response to emotional vocalizations.* Unpublished doctoral dissertation, Bowling Green State University, Bowling Green, OH.

Castellanos, F. X., Giedd, J. N., March, W. L., Hamburger, S. D., Vaituzis, A. C., Dickerstein, D. P., Sarfatti, S. E., Vauss, Y. C., Snell, J. W., Rajapakse, J. C., and Rapoport, J. L. (1996). Quantitative brain magnetic resonance imaging in attention-deficit hyperactivity disorder. *Archives of General Psychiatry, 53*, 607–616.

Clynes, M. (1977). *Sentics: The touch of emotions.* New York: Doubleday/Anchor.

Crutchfield, J. P., Farmer, J. D., Packard, H. and Shaw, R. S. (1986). Chaos. *Scientific American, 255* (Dec.), 46–57.

Damasio, A. R. (1994). *Descartes' error: Emotion, reason, and the human brain.* New York: G. P. Putnam's Sons.

Davidson, R. J. (1993). The neuropsychology of emotions and affective style. In M. Lewis and J. M. Haviland (Eds.), *Handbook of emotions* (pp. 143–154), New York: Guilford.

Davidson, R. J., and Fox, N. A. (1989). Frontal brain asymmetry predicts infants' response to maternal separation. *Journal of Abnormal Psychology, 98*, 127–131.

Dawson, G., Panagiotides, H., Klinger, L. G., and Spieker, S. (1997). Infants of depressed and nondepressed mothers exhibit differences in frontal brain electrical activity during the expression of negative emotions. *Developmental Psychology, 33*, 650–656.

Elbert, T., Lutzenberger, W., Rockstroh, B., Berg, P., and Cohen, R. (1992). Physical aspects of the EEG in schizophrenics. *Biological Psychiatry, 32*, 181–193.

Elbert, T., Ray, W. J., Kowalik, Z. J., Skinner, J. E., Graf, K. E., and Birbaumer, N. (1994). Chaos and physiology: Deterministic chaos in excitable cell assemblies. *Physiological Reviews, 74*, 1–47.

Ferriere, R., Cazelles, B., Cezilly, F., and Desportes, J.-P. (1996). Predictability and chaos in bird vigilant behaviour. *Animal Behaviour, 52*, 457–472.

Fitzpatrick, P., Schmidt, R. C., and Carello, C. (1996). Dynamical patterns in clapping behavior. *Journal of Experimental Psychology: Human Perception and Performance, 22*, 707–724.

Floriana, J. (1997). *An examination of cerebral processing of auditory non-verbal affective stimuli in autism through event-related desynchronization*. Unpublished doctoral dissertation, Bowling Green State University, Bowling Green, OH.

Fogel, A., Lyra, M. C., and Valsiner, J. (Eds.). (1997). *Dynamics and indeterminism in developmental and social processes*. Mahwah, NJ: Erlbaum.

Freeman, W. J. (1960). Correlation of electrical activity of prepyriform cortex and behavior in cat. *Journal of Neurophysiology, 23*, 111–131.

Freeman, W. J. (1992). Tutorial on neurobiology: From single neurons to brain chaos. *International Journal of Bifurcation and Chaos, 2*, 451–482.

Freeman, W. J. (1995). *Societies of brain: A study in the neuroscience of love and hate*. Hillsdale, NJ: Erlbaum.

George, M. S., Kettner, T. A., Kimbrell, T. A., Steedman, J. M., and Post, R. M. (1996). What functional imaging has revealed about the brain basis of mood and emotion. In J. Panksepp (Ed.), *Advances in biological psychiatry* (vol. 2, pp. 63–114). Greenwich, CT: JAI Press.

Gleick, J. (1987). *Chaos*. New York: Viking.

Globus, G. G., and Arpaia, J. P. (1994). Psychiatry and the new dynamics. *Biological Psychiatry, 35*, 352–364.

Goerner, S. J. (1994). *Chaos and the evolving ecological universe*. Langhorne, PA: Gordon and Breach.

Gottschalk, A., Bauer, M. S., and Whybrow, P. C. (1995). Evidence of chaotic mood variation in bipolar disorder. *Archives of General Psychiatry, 52*, 947–959.

Harman, D. W., and Ray, W. J. (1977). Hemispheric activity during affective verbal stimuli: An EEG study. *Neuropsychologia, 15*, 457–460.

Henriques, J. B., and Davidson, R. J. (1991). Left frontal hypo-activation in depression. *Journal of Abnormal Psychology, 100*, 535–545.

Herbert, D. E. (Ed.). (1996). *Chaos and the changing nature of science and medicine: An introduction*. Woodbury, NY: American Institute of Physics.

Horgan, J. (1995). From complexity to perplexity. *Scientific American, 272* (June), 104–109.

Hoyert, M. S. (1992). Order and chaos in fixed-interval schedules of reinforcment. *Journal of Experimental Analysis of Behavior, 57*, 339–363.

Ikemoto, S., and Panksepp, J. (1994). The relationship between self-stimulation and sniffing in rats: Does a common brain system mediate these behaviors? *Behavioral Brain Research, 61*, 143–162.

Kelso, J. A. (1995). *Dynamic patterns: The self-organization of brain and behavior*. Cambridge, MA: MIT Press.

Knutson, B., Burgdorf, J., and Panksepp, J. (1998). Anticipation of play elicits high-frequency ultrasonic vocalizations in young rats. *Journal of Comparative Psychology, 112*, 1–9.

Kollack-Walker, S., Watson, S. J. and Akil, H. (1997). Social stress in hamsters: Defeat activates specific neurocircuits within the brain. *Journal of Neuroscience, 15*, 8842–8855.

Kramer, M. S., Cutler, N., Feighner, J., Shrivastava, R., Carman, J., Sramek, J. J., Reines, S. A., Liu, G., Snavely, D., Wyatt-Knowles, E., Hale, J. J., Mills, S. G., MacCoss, M., Swain, C. J., Harrison, T., Till, R. G., Hefti, F., Scolnick, E. M., Cascieri, M. A., Chicchi, G. G., Sadowski, S., Williams, A. R., Hewson, L., Smith,

D., and Rupniak, N. M. (1998). Distinct mechanisms for antidepressant activity by blockade of central substance P receptors. *Science, 281,* 1640–1645.

Lane, R. D., Reiman, E. M., Bradley, M. M., Lang, P. J., Ahern, G. L., Davidson, R. J., and Schwartz, G. E. (1997). Neuroanatomical correlates of pleasant and unpleasant emotion. *Neuropsychologia, 35,* 1437–1444.

Lewis, M. D. (1996). Self-organising cognitive appraisals. *Cognition and Emotion, 10,* 1–25.

Lang, P. J. (1995). The emotion probe. *American Psychologist, 50,* 372–385.

Li, T., and Yorke, J. A. (1975). Period three implies chaos. *American Mathematical Monthly, 82,* 985–992.

Lubar, J. F., Swartwood, M. O., Swartwood, J. N. and O'Donnell, P. H. (1995). Evaluation of the effectiveness of EEG neurofeedback training for ADHD in a clinical setting as measured by changes in T.O.V.A. scores, behavioral ratings, and WISC-R performance. *Biofeedback and Self Regulation, 20,* 83–99.

Lutzenberger, W., Flor, H., and Birbaumer, N. (1997). Enhanced dimensional complexity of the EEG during memory for personal pain in chronic pain patients. *Neuroscience Letters, 22,* 167–170.

MacCormac, E., and Stamenov, M. I. (Eds.) (1996). *Fractals of brain, fractals of mind.* Amsterdam: John Benjamins.

Mantyh, P. W. (1982). Forebrain projections to the periaqueductal gray in the monkey, with observations in the cat and rat. *The Journal of Comparative Neurology, 206,* 146–158.

Meyers, M. B., and Smith, B. D. (1986). Hemispheric asymmetry and emotion: Effects of nonverbal affective stimuli. *Biological Psychology, 22,* 11–22.

Milton, J. G., Longtin, A., Beuter, A., Mackey, M. C., and Glass, L. (1989). Complex dynamics and bifurcations in neurology. *Journal of Theoretical Biology, 138,* 129–147.

Mpitsos, G. J., Burton, R. M., Creech, H. C., and Sonila, S. O. (1988). Evidence for chaos in spike trains of neurons that generate rhythmic motor patterns. *Brain Research Bulletin, 21,* 529–538.

Nunez, P. L. (Ed.) (1995). *Neocortical dynamics and human EEG rhythms.* New York: Oxford University Press.

Panksepp, J. (1982). Toward a general psychobiological theory of emotions. *The Behavioral and Brain Sciences, 5,* 407–467.

Panksepp, J. (1986). The neurochemistry of behavior. *Annual Review of Psychology, 37,* 77–107.

Panksepp, J. (1991). Affective neuroscience: A conceptual framework for the neurobiological study of emotions. In K. Strongman (Ed.), *International reviews of emotion research* (pp. 59–99). Chichester: Wiley.

Panksepp, J. (1993). Neurochemical control of moods and emotions: Amino acids to neuropeptides. In M. Lewis and J. Haviland (Eds.), *The handbook of emotions* (pp. 87–107). New York: Guilford.

Panksepp, J. (1996). Affective neuroscience: A paradigm to study the animate circuits for human emotions. In R. Kavanaugh, B. Zimmerberg, and S. Fine (Eds.), *Emotions: An interdisciplinary approach* (pp. 29–60). Hillsdale, NJ: Erlbaum.

Panksepp, J. (1998a). *Affective neuroscience: The foundations of human and animal emotions.* New York: Oxford University Press.

Panksepp, J. (1998b). The periconscious substrates of consciousness: Affective states and the evolutionary origins of the SELF. *Journal of Consciousness Studies, 5,* 566–582.

Panksepp, J. (1998c). The quest for long-term health and happiness: To play or not to play, that is the question. *Psychological Inquiry, 9,* 56–66.

Panksepp, J. (1998d). A critical analysis of ADHD, psychostimulants, and intolerance of childhood playfulness: A tragedy in the making? *Current Directions in Psychological Science, 7,* 91–98.

Panksepp, J., and Bekkedal, M. Y. V. (1997). The affective cerebral consequence of music: Happy versus sad effects on the EEG and clinical implications. *International Journal of Arts Medicine, 5,* 18–27.

Panksepp, J., Herman, B. H., Villberg, T., Bishop, P., and DeEskinazi, F. G. (1980). Endogenous opioids and social behavior. *Neuroscience and Biobehavioral Reviews, 4,* 473–487.

Panksepp, J., Knutson, B., and Pruitt, D. (1998). Toward a neuroscience of emotion: The epigenetic foundations of emotional development. In M. F. Mascolo and S. Griffin (Eds.), *What develops in emotional development?* (pp. 53–84). New York: Plenum.

Panksepp, J., Newman, J. D., and Insel, T. R. (1992). Critical conceptual issues in the analysis of separation distress systems of the brain. In K. T. Strongman (Ed.), *International review of studies on emotion* (vol. 2, pp. 51–72). Chichester: Wiley.

Panksepp, J., Normansell, L., Herman, B., Bishop, P., and Crepeau, L. (1988). Neural and neurochemical control of the separation distress call. In J. D. Newman (Ed.), *The physiological control of mammalian vocalizations* (pp. 263–300), New York: Plenum.

Panksepp, J., Sacks, D. S., Crepeau, L., and Abbott, B. B. (1991). The psycho- and neuro-biology of fear systems in the brain. In M. R. Denny (Ed.), *Aversive events and behavior* (pp. 7–59). New York: Erlbaum.

Panksepp, J., Siviy, S., and Normansell, L. (1984). The psychobiology of play: Theoretical and methodological perspectives. *Neuroscience and Biobehavioral Reviews, 8,* 465–492.

Petsche, H., Lindener, K., Rappelsberger, P., and Gruber, G. (1988). The EEG: An adequate method to concretize brain processes elicited by music. *Music Perception, 6,* 133–160.

Pfurtscheller, G. (1992). Event-related synchronization (ERS): An electrophysiological correlate of cortical areas at rest. *Electroencephalography and Clinical Neurophysiology, 42,* 817–826.

Port, R. F., and van Gelder, T. (1995). *Mind as motion: Exploration in the dynamics of cognition.* Cambridge, MA: MIT Press.

Rapp, P. E. (1993). Chaos in the neurosciences: Cautionary tales from the frontier. *Biologist, 40,* 89–94.

Reidbord, S. P., and Redington, D. J. (1992). Chaotic dynamics in autonomic nervous system activity of a patient during a psychotherapy session. *Biological Psychiatry, 31,* 993–1007.

Reidbord, S. P., and Redington, D. J. (1995). The dynamics of mind and body during clinical interviews: Research trends, potential, and future directions. In R. F. Port and T. van Gelder (Eds.), *Mind as motion: Exploration in the dynamics of cognition* (pp. 527–547). Cambridge, MA: MIT Press.

Roschke, J., and Aldenhoff, J. (1991). A nonlinear approach to brain function: Deterministic chaos and sleep EEG. *Sleep, 15*, 95–101.

Schaffer, C. E., Davidson, R. J., and Saron, C. (1983). Frontal and parietal EEG asymmetries in depressed and non-depressed subjects. *Biological Psychiatry, 18*, 753–762.

Sesack, S. R., Deutsch, A. Y., Roth, R. H., and Bunney, B. (1989). Topographic organization of the efferent projections of the medial prefrontal cortex in the rat: An anterograde tract-tracing study with *Phaeolus vulgaris* leucoagglutinin. *The Journal of Comparative Neurology, 190*, 213–242.

Skarda, C. A., and Freeman, W. J. (1990). Chaos and the new sciences of the brain. *Concepts in Neuroscience, 1*, 275–285.

Skinner, J. E. (1993). Neurocardiology: Brain mechanisms underlying fatal cardiac arrhythmias. *Neurologic Clinics, 11*, 325–351.

Smith, B. D., Meyers, M., Kline, R., and Bozman, A. (1987). Hemispheric asymmetry and emotion: Lateralized parietal processing of affect and cognition. *Biological Psychology, 25*, 247–260.

Smith, L. B., and Thelen, E. (Eds.). (1993). *A dynamic systems approach to development*. Cambridge, MA: MIT Press.

Stwertka, S. A. (1993). The stroboscopic patterns as dissipative structures. *Neuroscience and Biobehavioral Reviews, 17*, 69–78.

Teitelbaum, P., Maurer, R. G., Fyman, J., Teitelbaum, O. B., Vilensky, J., and Creedon, M. P. (1996). Dimensions of disintegration in the stereotyped locomotion characteristic of Parkinsonism and autism. In R. L. Sprague and K. M. Newell (Eds.), *Stereotyped movements: Brain and behavior relationships* (pp. 167–193). Washington, DC: American Psychological Association.

Terwogt, M. M., and van Grinsven, F. (1991). Musical expression of moodstates. *Psychology of Music, 19*, 99–109.

Thatcher, R. W. (1994). Cyclic cortical reorganization: Origins of human cognitive development. In G. Dawson and K. W. Fischer (Eds.), *Human behavior and the developing brain* (pp. 232–266). New York: Guilford.

Thelen, E., and Smith, L. B. (1995). *A dynamic systems approach to the development of cognition and action*. Cambridge, MA: MIT Press.

Vaga, T. (1994). *Profiting from chaos: Using chaos theory for market timing, stock selection, and option valuation*. New York: McGraw-Hill.

Vallacher, R. R., and Nowak, A. (1997). The emergence of dynamical social psychology. *Psychological Inquiry, 8*, 73–99.

Vanderschuren, L. J., Niesink, R. J., and Van Ree, J. M. (1997). The neurobiology of social play behavior in rats. *Neuroscience and Biobehavioral Reviews, 21*, 309–326.

Vanderwolf, C. H. (1992). The electrocorticogram in relation to physiology and behavior – A new analysis. *Electroencephalography and Clinical Neurophysiology, 82*, 165–175.

Van Eeenwyck, J. R. (1996). Chaotic dynamics and the development of consciousness. In E. MacCormac and M. I. Stamenov (Eds.), *Fractals of brain, fractals of mind* (pp. 323–346). Amsterdam: John Benjamins.

van Geert, P. (1991). A dynamic systems model of cognitive and language growth. *Psychological Review, 98*, 3–53.

Whitestone, D. (1996). *Cortical reflections of pain: An investigation utilizing event related desynchronization (ERD) mapping.* Unpublished doctoral dissertation, Bowling Green State University, Bowling Green, OH.

Williamson, S. J., Kaufman, L., Lu, Z.-L., Wang, J.-Z., and Karron, D. (1997). Study of human occipital alpha rhythm: The alphon hypothesis of alpha suppression. *International Journal of Psychophysiology, 26*, 63–76.

PART III

Interpersonal Processes

10   The Self-Organization of Parent-Child Relations: Beyond Bidirectional Models

Isabela Granic

The study of parent-child relations has been one of the most active areas of research and theory building in developmental psychology. In general, socialization theories have evolved from unidirectional, main effect models to more complex bidirectional and transactional models (Maccoby, 1992; Maccoby and Martin, 1983). There now exists considerable evidence that children influence their parents' behavior as much, and in some cases more, than parents influence their children (e.g., Anderson, Lytton, and Romney, 1986; Bell and Chapman, 1986; Bronstein, 1984; Dix, Rubel, and Zambarano, 1989; Grusec and Kuczynski, 1980; Kandel and Wu, 1995; Patterson, Reid, and Dishion, 1992). Thus, socialization is not just something that is done to the child, but rather an outcome of what each partner brings to the process (e.g., Chamberlain and Patterson, 1995). Nevertheless, the reciprocal nature of parent-child relations seems to have implications that far exceed contemporary theorizing.

This chapter represents a preliminary attempt to develop a model of socialization that goes beyond viewing parent-child relationships as simply clusters of bidirectional influences. I will argue that current socialization theories have come to an impasse, one that can be overcome by applying the principles of self-organization. Through this new lens, bidirectionality is seen as a crucial, but preliminary, step toward a more comprehensive explanatory model of parent-child relations.

In the first part of this chapter, research on the bidirectionality of socialization processes will be reviewed, and some limitations will be highlighted. I will go on to suggest how these limitations may be addressed by reconceptualizing socialization as a self-organizing, emergent process. Throughout this discussion, conceptual links with past models of parent-child processes will be provided, and the potential extensions made by a self-organization view will be explored. Once this general self-organization

267

framework for socialization has been sketched, the next section of the chapter will examine how it may be applied specifically to understanding aggressive parent-child interactions. Aggressive behavior is the most frequently studied "outcome" in socialization studies (Rothbaum and Weisz, 1994), presumably because noncompliant, aggressive children represent a breakdown in the socialization process. By exploring the utility of self-organization principles in this specific context, it is hoped that the strengths of this new framework will be further explicated. I will conclude by outlining some promising research directions that incorporate principles of self-organization and discuss their implications for extending our present socialization models.

From Unidirectional to Bidirectional Influences

In early socialization models, parental behaviors were usually understood as the "antecedents," and children's behaviors were "outcomes" (Maccoby, 1992; Maccoby and Martin, 1983). This unidirectional perspective emerged largely from two main camps: behaviorism and psychoanalytic theory (for reviews, see Cairns, 1983). For behaviorists, parents could be viewed as teachers who socialized children through the mechanisms of classical and instrumental conditioning. Children were considered open vessels into which knowledge and expertise could be poured. While psychoanalytic theory espoused vastly different propositions, it too conceptualized the child as a product of parenting practices, although psychoanalysts viewed the parents as mainly teaching children to curb their free expression of desires and wishes.

Contemporary socialization theorists have largely abandoned this unidirectional perspective for bidirectional and interactive models (for reviews, see Lytton, 1990; Maccoby, 1992; Maccoby and Martin, 1983). This new view emerged from at least two sources: (1) In the 1970s, influential writers (Bell, 1968; Bell and Harper, 1977; Parke, 1977) began insisting that the direction of causality inferred from past correlational research had been misinterpreted and that child effects on parents needed to be more rigorously examined (Maccoby, 1992). (2) During this same period, sophisticated microanalytic techniques were developed for studying the moment-to-moment interactions of parents and children. Videotaping and computer technologies allowed investigators to study, on a fine-grained level, the extent to which each member of the dyad influenced the other (Maccoby and Martin, 1983). These developments informed and complemented one another and have led to the view of children as active agents participating with their parents in "linked streams of behavior that provide the experiential context for socialization" (Snyder et al., 1994, p. 306).

Bell (1968; Bell and Chapman, 1986; Bell and Harper, 1977) is credited as one of the first developmentalists to conceptualize the parent-child relationship as one of bidirectional (or reciprocal) influences. As a first step toward the development of a theory of reciprocal socialization, he proposed a control system model in which parents and children regulate each other's behavior in order to maintain a state of equilibrium. According to Bell, both parent and child develop upper and lower limits of tolerance for the intensity, frequency, and acceptability of specific behaviors by the other based on their interactional history. When the upper limit of one member of the dyad is approached by the other, the former attempts to dampen or redirect the other's intolerable behavior. Alternatively, when the lower limit is reached, attempts to stimulate the other are initiated.

Since Bell's model was initially presented, an extensive body of research has emerged confirming the extent to which children influence their parents' behavior (reviewed in Bell and Chapman, 1986). Among the more compelling examples are the temperament studies that have shown that mothers of children with difficult temperaments respond to their children with more controlling (e.g., Bates, 1980) and fewer teaching behaviors (e.g., Maccoby and Martin, 1983). Young children's difficult temperaments have also been causally linked to parental permissiveness toward aggression and a reduction of socialization pressures (Olweus, 1980; Patterson, 1982). Studies have also suggested that mothers of normally compliant children become significantly more negative when they interact with problem children (Anderson, Lytton, and Romney, 1986).

Bell's model was successful in stimulating a wave of research focusing on child effects that had been neglected previously; however, his ultimate goal of an "eventual synthesis into a theory of reciprocal interaction" (Bell and Chapman, 1986, p. 602) has not yet been realized. Part of the problem may be that the research designs he suggested to isolate child effects were based on the same set of assumptions that had guided past research efforts – assumptions based on linearity and independence. Thus, bidirectionality for Bell and his colleagues seemed to refer simply to the fact that, in some interactions, parents influence children's behavior, and in others, the reverse is true. But reciprocity, especially in developing systems, implies much more than two separate causal arrows.

Through innovations in videotaping and computer technologies, the study of real-time interactions of infants and toddlers with their mothers has provided the empirical basis for redefining socialization as not only reciprocal in Bell's more restricted sense, but also circular (Maccoby, 1984; Maccoby, 1992; Maccoby and Martin, 1983). Reconceptualizing parent-child relations as circular requires that the two causal arrows become linked into one continuous process: the child's behavior influences the parent's behavior, which in turn influences the child, and so on. These processes can be observed both on real and developmental time scales. Considerable evidence of circular processes in real-time parent-infant interactions has accrued, but due to space limitations, only a few highlights will be provided (see Maccoby and Martin, 1983, for a review; Schore, this volume). Mother-infant gazing patterns have been described as coordinated, communicative acts (e.g., Fogel, 1993; Stern, 1974; Trevarthen, 1993). The infant's gaze elicits the mother's gaze, which in turn perpetuates the infant's gaze (Brazelton, Koslowski, and Main, 1974; Stern, 1974; Stern et al., 1977). Schore (1997) describes the effect of these synchronized gaze transactions as inducing bodily changes in the infant; this may be the means by which the mother regulates the infant's autonomic nervous system. In turn, the infant impacts on the mother's nervous system. Schore describes this coordination as "mutual entrainment of the mother's and infant's brains" (1997, p. 602). Fogel similarly refers to dyadic interactions as "simultaneous co-action" (Fogel, 1993). Thus, real-time parent-child interactions can be understood as circular processes in which it is impossible to pinpoint the discrete influence of one partner on the other at any given moment in time.

Circular parent-child processes can be seen on a developmental time scale as well. The research on temperament reviewed earlier provides important examples. A child's difficult temperament may lead the frustrated mother to reduce socialization efforts and, over time, become more permissive of aggressive behavior. This permissiveness may, in turn, exacerbate the child's aggression problems (Bates and Bayles, 1988; Olweus, 1980; Tronick, Ricks, and Cohn, 1982). Over development, the child's escalating aggression will likely cause the mother to reject the child increasingly, and so on (Patterson, Reid, and Dishion, 1992).

These real-time and developmental-time processes point to the transactional nature of parent-child relations. The transactional model of development (Sameroff, 1975, 1983; Sameroff and Chandler, 1975; Sameroff and Emde, 1989) suggests that developing individuals are embedded in a rich variety of interacting contextual forces that continuously alter their organizational structures, while their actions simultaneously change these very contextual forces. Thus, in real-time dyadic interactions, circularity can be seen as continuously unfolding influences in which the child's behavior prompts the mother to respond, and this response in turn alters the child's behavior, and so on. Similarly, in developmental time, each partner's style, as well as reciprocal dyadic patterns, can be viewed as a product of past interactions that go on to constrain parent-child behavioral repertoires in the future (e.g., Dumas and LaFreniere, 1993, 1995; Fogel, 1993; La-Freniere and Dumas, 1992; Sameroff and Chandler, 1975; Sameroff and Emde, 1989; Sroufe, 1996; Trevarthen, 1993).

Toward a Self-Organization Model

Up to this point, I have stressed some of the important contributions made by researchers concerned with parent-child processes. I have argued that socialization is a circular, interactive process, one in which it is difficult to isolate either causal arrow on a moment-to-moment or a developmental time scale. Instead, socialization can best be conceptualized as a recursive process, leading some theorists to regard the parent-child dyad as one *integrated system* (e.g., Maccoby and Martin, 1983) with emergent properties attributable to neither participant alone (e.g., Maccoby, 1992). These emergent dyadic properties can be seen as dynamic products of the parent-child *transactional history* that go on to constrain future interactions (e.g., Dumas and LaFreniere, 1995; LaFreniere and Dumas, 1992). In general, then, the study of socialization processes seems to have progressed from being concerned with simple linear contingencies, to reciprocal (bidirectional) effects, to an increased interest in circular interactional patterns and the *relationships* to which they give rise (Dumas and LaFreniere, 1995; Hart, Ladd, and Burleson, 1990; Kochanska, 1992; Maccoby, 1992).

Despite these advances, we still lack a theoretical framework that can integrate these new insights into one coherent model. Researchers have identified circular processes on real and developmental time scales, but the connection between the two scales remains unclear. Also, our current models of socialization seem to rely mostly on principles of homeostasis and reciprocity. These are helpful for understanding stability in parent-child relations, but they lack the explanatory power to address changes in these relationships. If parent-child relationships are to be examined as developing systems, an appropriate theoretical framework must address the underpinnings of both stability and change. Finally, the connection between circular interactions and emergent dyadic states is not well understood. New theoretical tools are needed to examine how they are related. I propose that a self-organization framework helps to explicate processes including circularity, emergent relational patterns, and historical constraints. Further, this new framework may provide principles for understanding both change and stability in the development of the parent-child system.

Principles of Self-Organization

Principles of self-organization have proven essential in understanding change and stability in diverse fields including physics (e.g., Haken, 1977), chemistry (e.g., Prigogine and Stengers, 1984), biology (e.g., Kauffman, 1993; Kelso, 1995), and evolution (e.g., Goerner, 1995). Recently, these principles have been imported into the social sciences. A number of developmentalists have begun to understand ontogenesis from a self-organization perspective (e.g., Fogel, 1993; Lewis, 1995; Thelen and Smith, 1994). Social psychologists (Vallacher and Nowak, 1994; Vallacher and Nowak, 1997) and developmental psychopathologists (Cicchetti and Rogosch, 1997; Deater-Deckard and Dodge, 1997; Lewis & Granic, 1999) have also begun to explore the utility of these principles. For these theorists, self-organization has become a powerful concept through which the development of complex psychological systems can be better understood.

Self-organization refers to the auto-organization or emergent order in complex adaptive systems. Dynamic (or dynamical) systems (DS) theory is a mathematical framework that can be used for studying the emergence and stabilization of novel forms in the process of self-organization (Prigogine and Stengers, 1984). For the purposes of this chapter, I will be using DS terms metaphorically; that is, I am not suggesting that there are precise mathematical equations that can describe the development of parent-child relationships. Instead, following other developmentalists (e.g., Fogel, 1993; Fogel and Thelen, 1987; Keating, 1990; Lewis, 1995, 1997; Thelen and Smith, 1994; Thelen and Ulrich, 1991), I have found that the mathematical concepts have important heuristic value for conceptualizing development as self-organization. Below are six main principles of self-organizing systems that seem particularly useful for reconceptualizing parent-child relations.

Nonequilibrium

Self-organizing systems in nature are open systems *far from thermodynamic equilibrium* that are maintained through the constant importing and dissipating of energy. Nonequilibrium is the necessary condition for the spontaneous emergence and stabilization of novel forms. It is also this condition that makes self-organizing systems inherently adaptive to changes in their environment (Prigogine and Stengers, 1984).

What does it mean to interpret the parent-child relationship as a system that is far from equilibrium? Interestingly, the notion extends Bell and Chapman's (1986) contention that "the most significant socialization occurs at times of destabilization" (p. 596). According to their model, the parent-child system is generally in a state of equilibrium, with each member meeting the other's expectations. But when one member breaches the other's upper or lower limit of tolerance, the control system becomes activated and some sort of action is taken to restore the system to a state of balance. For Bell and Chapman, socialization episodes represent the dyadic system's movement from relative nonequilibrium to equilibrium. For models of self-organization, nonequilibrium is a ubiquitous state of the system, but this does not preclude stability.

Stabilization

Patterns of interaction or stable states are called *attractors* in DS terminology. They emerge through *coupling*, or cooperativity among lower-order (more basic) system elements. Attractors may best be understood as absorbing states that "attract" the system. Behavior self-organizes to these attractors in real time. Over developmental time, attractors represent the recurrent patterns that have stabilized in the system. Attractors can be depicted topographically as valleys on a dynamic landscape. The deeper the attractor, the more absorbing it is and, thus, the more resistant to small changes in the environment. As the system develops, a unique *state space*, defined as a model of all possible states a system can attain, is configured by several attractors.

Recurrent patterns of parent-child interactions can be conceptualized as dyadic attractors. One classic example may be found in the alternating pattern of speech acts (Bruner, 1975). Infants and their mothers begin communicating by matching their gazes and vocalizations. Later, this matching develops and stabilizes into the familiar turn-taking attractor that characterizes most normal conversations. Another example can be found in Patterson's (1982) description of "coercive cycles" in which the parent and aggressive child engage in a pattern of mutually aversive interchanges. These coercive cycles can be understood as attractors that have stabilized from repeated real-time disciplinary interactions. The advantages of viewing social interaction patterns as dyadic attractors that emerge over development have been convincingly articulated by Alan Fogel and his colleagues (e.g., Fogel, 1993; Fogel and Thelen, 1987; Fogel et al., 1992).

Energy flowthrough is the means by which elements of a system far from equilibrium couple, forming attractors (Prigogine and Stengers, 1984). Some theorists (e.g., Bateson, 1972; Brent, 1978; Fogel and Branco, 1997; Jantsch, 1980; Sameroff, 1983) have suggested that "information" may be the psychological equivalent of "energy." Lewis (1995) has defined information in psychological systems as simply *that which is relevant to an individual's goals and needs.* This account has been explicated mainly on an intraindividual level, but it also has some important implications for thinking about dyadic relationships (Fogel and Branco, 1997). In particular, parent-child interactions may be largely constituted by each partner's ongoing perceptions of whether the other is facilitating or blocking the former's goals; this information flow may be the necessary condition for self-organizing socialization attractors. To examine the mechanisms underlying the emergence of these dyadic attractors, a third self-organization principle is introduced.

Feedback Processes

Systems far from equilibrium self-organize through the interplay of two basic mechanisms: positive and negative feedback. Feedback processes have powerful implications for understanding stability and change in developing systems. *Positive feedback* is the means by which interactions among system elements amplify particular variations, leading to the emergence of novelty. Thus, new dynamic organizations emerge when small fluctuations become the conduit for energy flowthrough by way of positive feedback cycles. *Negative feedback* is the means by which elements continue to be linked and stability is realized. Self-organizing systems become increasingly complex through the interaction of both feedback processes; positive feedback catalyzes hierarchical reorganization in response to environmental changes, and these new organizations are maintained through the self-stabilizing properties of negative feedback. These mechanisms of stability and change have been sufficient to explain phenomena ranging from self-maintaining cyclical chemical reactions (e.g., Prigogine and Stengers, 1984) to brain functioning (e.g., Freeman, this volume) to evolution (e.g., Goerner, 1995); they may be equally crucial for understanding socialization processes.

Feedback may be the mechanism by which characteristic dyadic states develop and crystallize. Certainly recent reconceptualizations of bidirectionality as a circular, recursive process resonate well with this notion (e.g., Maccoby, 1992). Several investigators in the field have recognized the importance of feedback to describe dyadic processes (e.g., Cairns, 1979; Maccoby and Martin, 1983; Patterson, 1982, 1995; Sameroff, 1995; Schore, 1997, this volume; Wilson and Gottman, 1995). For instance, Cairns (in Maccoby & Martin, 1983) has suggested that the "continuing reverberations" of mutual influences between dyad members can be understood as feedback in real time. Likewise, Patterson specifies the role of feedback in coercive family processes: "the child is an active participant whose behavior is a reaction to the behavior of the other family members and also constitutes a stimulus for their behaviors. A behavioral event is an effect and a cause . . ." (Patterson, 1982, p. 196). Although feedback processes have been discussed by several theorists, most have focused exclusively on the self-maintaining mechanism of negative feedback (e.g., Bell's control model; Patterson's coercion model); this may be one reason that we still have a limited understanding of the processes underlying change in dyadic patterns.

Nonlinear Change

Through the amplification properties of positive feedback, nonlinear changes in the organizational structure of a dynamic system can be observed. These abrupt changes are referred to as *phase shifts*, and they occur at *points of bifurcation*, or junctures, in the system's development. At these thresholds, small fluctuations have the potential to disproportionately affect the status of other elements, leading to the emergence of new forms. Novelty does not have to originate from outside the system; it can emerge spontaneously through feedback within the system. At bifurcation points, these systems are extremely sensitive, adapting rapidly to both internal and environmental perturbations. Between these points, however, self-organizing systems tend toward coherence and stability.

The parent-child system may cross several bifurcation points along its developmental trajectory. At these thresholds of instability, the system may undergo rapid reorganizations that have the potential to radically alter the dyadic pathway. An example of this type of nonlinear change at the developmental time scale can be seen in Mahler, Pine, and Bergman's (1975) "rapprochement crisis" that is said to occur when the infant is between eighteen and twenty-four months old. The "crisis" is characterized by the infant's fluctuating need to cling to mother on the one hand and to begin to explore independently on the other. According to cognitive-developmental theories (e.g., Case, 1985), this is also a period of dramatic cognitive reorganization. At the end of this highly unstable rapprochement crisis, Mahler and colleagues observed what may be considered the emergence and stabilization of interaction patterns that did not exist in the dyads' repertoires before the phase shift. According to DS principles, these rapid changes in dyadic patterns may have been catalyzed by small changes in the cognitive system that were augmented through positive feedback cycles between dyad members.

Interdependent Time Scales

The final DS premise important for the current discussion is the interplay between different time scales of self-organization. Self-organization at the moment-to-moment (real-time) scale constrains self-organization at the developmental scale, which in turn constrains real-time behavior (van Gelder and Port, 1995). The notion of interdependent time scales suggests that developmental parent-child patterns arise from real-time interactions that recur. As these patterns are continuously reexperienced over occasions, they can be represented as deeper and deeper attractors on a dyadic state space. This increasingly specified dyadic state space can be said to encompass the history of the system (cf. Thelen and Smith, 1994), and, as such, it constrains the types of real-time interactions in which the dyad will engage. In other words, based on prior experience, the likelihood of a parent and child interacting in a particular manner is increasingly predetermined.

Tronick and colleagues' (e.g., Tronick et al., 1982) findings on mother-infant coordinated social interchanges provide good examples of the interdependence of time scales. Their research has shown that, from the emotions experienced during real-time mother-infant interactions, an affective bias or mood stabilizes in the child. This crystallized affective state is considered a developmental amalgam of the repeated positive or negative emotions generated during dyadic interactions. In turn, a particular mood that has crystallized over development is thought to bias the infant's perceptions and behavioral tendencies in real time. For instance, a child who has developed an anxious affective style is likely to evaluate new situations as threatening and to withdraw from them quickly.

Having briefly reviewed several DS concepts, I now go on to examine how they can address previously identified gaps in socialization models. As mentioned, the parent-child dyad has begun to be viewed as one system qualitatively different from and, therefore, irreducible to its separate parts (Maccoby, 1992). A self-organization framework helps to transform this largely metaphorical insight into an idea that can be modeled. The next section represents a preliminary step toward this goal. I will attempt to delineate the hierarchy of subsystems and the elements that comprise them, paying particular attention to feedback processes and the interplay of parent-child patterns at different time scales. By doing so, I hope to achieve a more specific reintegration of the subsystems into their relational "whole."

A note on the scope of this discussion is necessary. The structures that I label systems or subsystems depend on an arbitrary reference point. For instance, a child may be considered a subsystem of a dyad, but the brain may be one of his or her many organic subsystems, which in turn may be constituted by several more emotional and cognitive subsystems. In each of these cases, any subsystem can also be considered a system, depending on the level of analysis. Although each level of the hierarchy is significant, my objective is to address some of the psychological systems and their components that seem most important for understanding parent-child relations. I will not be touching on levels of the hierarchy that may be above the parent-child dyad (i.e., family, society) nor on those that fall below psychological structures within individuals (i.e., neuroanatomical structures, hormonal patterns).

Self-Organizing Individual Attractors

The parent-child system seems to be made up of two obvious subsystems: the parent and the child. Before we can understand how these subsystems reciprocally interact as one dyadic system, each may need to be broken down into its own respective subsystems and components. Thus, it may be useful to refer to models of personality development and to examine the interacting components that have been proposed to account for stable personality patterns.

Emotional developmentalists have suggested that emotions and cognitive appraisals are the basic psychological elements that interact to form global personality structures (e.g., Izard, 1977; Lewis, 1995; Magai and McFadden, 1995; Malatesta and Wilson, 1988; Tomkins, 1987, 1991). Emotions are elicited from cognitive evaluations of events relative to an individual's personal goals (Frijda, 1986; Lazarus, 1982, 1984; Oatley and Johnson-Laird, 1987). They focus an individual's attention on certain aspects of a situation, prompting changes in action readiness (Frijda, 1986).

Emotions also serve to organize the cognitive system by imposing a specific mode of operation that may include attentional demands and memory biases (Oatley and Johnson-Laird, 1987). Thus, through the interaction of emotion and cognition, recurrent organizational states – variously labeled "affective-cognitive" structures (Izard, 1977), "emotional interpretations" (Lewis, 1997), and "emotion traits" (Malatesta and Wilson, 1988) – sensitize the individual to particular ways of processing information and engaging with the world.

Several theorists have begun to understand the relation between cognitive processes and emotion as a feedback loop (e.g., Lewis, 1995, 1997; Teasdale, 1983; Teasdale and Barnard, 1993). Particularly relevant for this discussion is Lewis's model (1995, 1997), which posits that positive feedback between emotion and cognition is the basis for self-organizing personality development. Neither emotion nor cognition is accorded causal priority. Cognitive appraisals are conceptualized as emerging in coordination with emotions, each amplifying the other in real time. According to this view, from moment to moment, emotion focuses an individual's attention on particular goal-relevant elements in a situation. An appraisal forms, further generating emotion, which is in turn fed back into the system over repeated iterations. Stability results from a recurrence of feedback between specific appraisals and emotions that, over time, becomes self-sustaining (i.e., negative feedback). Over developmental time, repeated cycles of feedback increase the tendency for particular elements to cohere (Thelen and Smith, 1994). These cognition-emotion structures have been conceptualized as attractors that have stabilized over personality development (Lewis, 1995).

Consider the *hostile attributional bias* as an example of an attractor on a personality state space. Dodge and his colleagues (e.g., Dodge, 1980; Dodge and Somberg, 1987; Dodge et al., 1986) have demonstrated that aggressive boys are predisposed to attribute hostile intent to others, even when the situation is ambiguous. From a DS perspective, the aggressive youth has developed a cognition-emotion attractor through many past experiences that were characterized by anger and appraisals of others as hostile and threatening (Granic and Butler, 1998; Granic and Lewis, 1997). When next he finds himself in an ambiguous social context, very few situational cues are needed to catalyze the emergence of hostile cognitive components that spontaneously couple with feelings of anger, further generating hostile appraisals. Recurrent feedback between anger and these negative cognitive components stabilizes over developmental time into what may be called a hostile attribution attractor.

Calling a hostile attributional bias an attractor does not simply provide a different label for the same concept. Instead, an attractor reconceptualizes stability. According to the principles of self-organization, the hostile attributional bias is not a static mental representation that is stored and then retrieved to be used as a template for assessing a situation. Instead, it is a temporal form in the sense that it coalesces in real time through feedback among its components. Thus, *stability* in self-organizing systems does not imply stillness; rather, behavior evolves predictably toward an attractor in real time, producing a reliable pattern of change.

Self-Organizing Dyadic Attractors

Personality attractors do not develop in a vacuum – quite the contrary, a number of theorists suggest that development is a fundamentally relational process (e.g., Bowlby, 1969; Fogel, 1993; Fogel and Thelen, 1987; Laible and Thompson, this volume; Schore, this volume). Although Lewis (1995) has considered some implications of extending his model to dyadic interactions, he does so briefly and with little attention to what is probably the most important dyadic system: the parent-child relationship. Given what we understand about self-organizing processes in general and their role in personality development in particular, what are the implications for modeling parent-child relations?

One way to extend the individual personality model is to posit that the separate affective-cognitive structures of the parent and the child may be the interacting subsystems that coalesce in dyadic interactions. Through repeated feedback cycles, particular parent and child affective-cognitive couplings may reciprocally select one another and become further coupled into a more complex, dyadic configuration. Given that few parent-child relationships can be exclusively characterized by a single stable state, a variety of dyadic attractors on one integrative state space may be a useful way to represent the emergent dyadic ''whole.'' A unique dyadic landscape can represent the range of possible interaction patterns toward which dyadic self-organization can evolve in real time. It can also inform us of the developmental history of that parent-child system.

Research on cognitive-emotional processes in parenting may help to ground the notion of intercoupled parent and child attractors and frame dyadic self-organization in terms of information flow. Socialization often involves the clash of incompatible goals (Grusec, Rudy, and Martini, 1997), and invariably these processes are emotional (Dix, 1991) – parents want children to get enough sleep or to clean up their rooms, which may be incompatible with children's wishes to stay up late or watch television. The specific positive or negative emotions involved in socialization episodes may depend, in part, on the parent's appraisals of why the child is compliant or noncompliant and the degree to which she controls these outcomes (e.g., Abramson, Seligman, and Teasdale, 1978; Dix, 1991; Weiner, 1979). The direction of influence may be extended to the child as well. The extent to which a child is angry at her mother for not letting her stay up late "just to finish this one game" may depend on appraisals of why the parent is being so rigid and the degree to which the child feels she has control over the situation. For each partner, the information flow in real time regarding the other's goal-facilitating or goal-blocking behaviors may promote coupling among both partners' attractors.

There is some evidence that emotion and appraisals of goal-relevant information reciprocally select one another during socialization episodes. Lay and colleagues (1989) have shown that a child is more likely to comply with a parent's command if a positive mood is induced in him or her. From a self-organization perspective, the child is in a "cooperative" or positive attractor in which excitement or joy is fundamentally linked to goal-facilitating appraisals in an iterative feedback process. Also, Parpal and Maccoby (1985) have shown that children comply more with parental commands if the parent has previously complied with the child's directives. Here we see some suggestion of reciprocal coupling of cognitive-affective structures. It may be that children who perceive their mothers as furthering their goals feel positive emotions that feed back with appraisals of the mother as a cooperative and supportive partner. This happy-supportive attractor may be expressed behaviorally by complying with the mother's next directive. The child's behavior, in turn, seems to trigger goal-facilitating appraisals and positive emotions in the mother. Their respective affective-cognitive structures seem to be linked in a feedback cycle, self-organizing moment to moment toward a joyful-cooperative dyadic attractor. This parent-child pattern may stabilize over development, providing the context in which mutual socialization goals may be realized.

Alternatively, after years of failed disciplinary attempts, a mother may have developed an affective-cognitive structure characterized by anger and appraisals of her child as oppositional and inherently "bad." As a result of these disciplinary interactions, her child may have developed his own angry attractor, but his appraisals center around his mother, whom he perceives as perpetually frustrating his goals. Through repeated interactions, their two attractors may become linked in a feedback loop such that the mother's attractor and the behavior with which it is expressed "pulls for" her son's angry attractor and the behaviors to which it is linked. Each member's behavior amplifies the other's anger and accompanying appraisals, coalescing into a hostile dyadic attractor. Recurring feedback processes stabilize this interaction pattern, making it difficult to perturb.

Developmental Constraints

Dyadic attractors specify real-time interactions, and they also serve as developmental constraints. Over years, both partners develop characteristic ways of interacting with the other – individual personality configurations become more and more entrenched over occasions and, in parallel, dyadic attractors increasingly deepen and become stronger. The developmental result is a highly articulated dyadic state space that has been configured from past dyadic self-organization and that constrains future interactions. The notion of self-organizing developmental constraints is consistent with Rothbaum and Weisz's (1994) interpretation of their meta-analysis findings. They argued that, over time, parents develop ''generalized expectations'' about their children that influence subsequent interactions; the same may be said for children's expectations about their parents. For the angry parent-child dyad discussed above, the hostile attractor may grow so strong that most of their interactions are doomed to end in anger and frustration; interacting positively and empathically may become an increasingly remote possibility.

Furthermore, consistent with the DS idea of nonlinear relations among components of a system, less and less activation is necessary to trigger the convergence of developmental forms. Returning to the angry parent-child dyad, it may be that early in their relationship the parent and child mutually annoyed each other for hours, and only a large insult resulted in a highly aversive and angry interaction. But after the hostile dyadic attractor has become deeply entrenched over time, the most subtle aversive behavior by one partner (e.g., child rolling his eyes, mother exaggerating her sigh) may initiate the spontaneous emergence of the full-blown hostile dyadic attractor. Consistent with this conceptualization, Patterson has suggested that ''well practiced conflict exchanges among family members are . . . examples of automatic or schematic processes that form small islands of increased predictability in ongoing family interaction'' (Patterson, 1995, p. 87).

Past research on parental attributions provides additional support for the notion that, as development proceeds, less activation is necessary to catalyze the emergence of dyadic patterns. For instance, studies have shown that once a mother's negative attributions of her child have repeatedly elicited anger, the mother tends to become angry even when the child's behavior is not particularly aversive (Brunk and Henggeler, 1984; Dix, 1991; Mash and Johnston, 1982). Even when anger is elicited from a situation that does not involve the child's actions, parents tend to anticipate that future interactions with the child will be aversive (Dix, 1991). With respect to the child's attributions of the parent, much less has been empirically established. In one study, though, both aggressive children and parents tended to misattribute hostile intent to the other, and this was related to the aggressiveness of their interactions (MacKinnon-Lewis et al., 1992). Thus, there is some empirical support for the idea that, once interaction patterns have crystallized over development, there are fewer degrees of freedom in the system. The recruitment of only one or a few elements of the system – emotional or cognitive – may trigger the real-time emergence of a developmentally established dyadic configuration.

Like any complex self-organizing system, the developing parent-child relationship can be conceptualized as moving from a diffused, undifferentiated organization toward one that is increasingly predictable. In part, this may be due to what Lewis (1997) calls *cascading constraints* – over development, attractors emerge that are both the origin and the product of increasing specificity throughout the system. Particular dyadic configurations that have emerged in real time and stabilized over development may be considered cascading constraints. They are the product of past interactions, and they go on to constrain degrees of freedom along the subsequent dyadic trajectory. Scripts or relational themes may be useful ways of understanding cascading dyadic constraints; after they have emerged, they increasingly guide the developmental process by influencing new elements that become incorporated into the system. The developmental unfolding of these constraints can be exemplified by the process of generalization or increasing uniformity in the relationship.

Increasing stability and uniformity in the parent-child relationship may rely on two additional types of constraints. The first are *prespecified constraints*, that is, constraints that are part of the original structure of the system (Lewis, 1997). For the parent-child system, the infant's temperament and the mother's already articulated personality state space may be construed as two such prespecified constraints. They are complementary parts of the system that do not emerge over development. Instead, they constitute the structure of the system at its inception and provide the initial conditions to which self-organizing systems are highly sensitive. Early in their relationship, a child with an easy, flexible temperament will likely elicit warm, supportive behavior from a responsive mother. The reciprocally positive affective interactions that arise from these initial conditions may form the basis of a secure attachment relationship that may subsequently constrain the dyadic developmental trajectory. Also, the parent initially influences the system's development through the much more articulated state space that she ''brings'' to the relationship. For instance, a depressed mother's ''angry-resentful'' and ''sad-helpless'' personality attractors may be considered prespecified constraints for the dyadic system. The negative personality structures with which she begins her relationship with the infant may manifest in withdrawn and irritable behavior (e.g., Demos, 1986), which in turn may become coupled with the infant's distress and withdrawal. Thus, positive feedback processes in the more malleable early stage of the parent-child system catalyze the emergence of specific dyadic attractors that influence the subsequent unfolding of particular relational pathways.

Another source of increasing specificity and stability is the principle of mutual constraints among hierarchical levels. I have mentioned that personality attractors seem to interact to form particular dyadic attractors; but, likewise, these dyadic patterns may constrain the very individual structures of which they are constituted. This means that, as the child develops, her unique personality state space is partially configured by the dyadic attractors in which she participates. These dyadic attractors, in turn, constrain the features of intraindividual personality structures. Consider again the parent-child relationship characterized by a very deep, angry dyadic attractor. The child in this dyad will be less likely to develop an empathic (Zahn-Waxler and Radke-Yarrow, 1990; Zahn-Waxler, Radke-Yarrow, and King, 1979) or friendly personality configuration, given the constraints laid down by the parent-child system. Similarly, the mother may develop a new depressive-helpless configuration as a result of many failed socialization efforts with her child.

There may be a final, more macro-level constraint under which the others are nested and which may determine dyadic development more globally. Despite the potential for extreme variations in intraindividual attractors, it may be that their interactions are limited in such a way that distinct types of dyadic forms are more viable than others. The possibility of self-organizing ''typical forms'' has been elaborated in the biological and evolutionary sciences by Brian Goodwin (1987, 1994). Arguing for a structuralist approach to morphogenesis, Goodwin suggests that there are transformational principles that constrain the ways in which system components can coassemble. There seem to be organizational ''laws'' that manifest as regularities in all biological systems. For example, underlying the incredible diversity of shapes, sizes, and colors of higher plants is a startling degree of order – there are only three ways in which their leaves can be patterned on a stem! Perhaps similar regularities may be found in the patterns of intercoupled elements in dyadic attractors (Fogel, 1993). For example, it seems unlikely that a warm, supportive personality structure can easily couple with an angry, resentful configuration. The goal-relevant information flow that fuels intercoupling may not be able to support these incompatible appraisals and emotions. Specifically, if one partner is perceiving the other as goal-blocking and feels angry, the action tendency is to remove the obstacle (i.e., to refuse to comply, or to command the other to comply). This makes it highly unlikely that the other dyad member will perceive the situation as goal-facilitating and feel appropriately content. Thus, there may be certain dyadic configurations that are more probable than others, based on the complementary properties of emotional appraisals.

What sorts of appraisal structures exhibit more complementarity than others? Research by Dumas and his colleagues suggests some viable parent-child combinations (Dumas and LaFreniere, 1993, 1995; LaFreniere and Dumas, 1992). For example, an overcontrolling, critical parental style tends to be linked to anxious personality structures in children. Alternatively, distant, inconsistent patterns of interacting are connected to aggressive patterns in children. There may be an intrinsic complementarity between a critical attractor and an anxious, withdrawn one. Similarly, two angry configurations may more easily be reciprocally selective than other combinations. These intercoupled personality attractors seem to fit together better than others. Thus, intercoupled attractors may be constrained by "relational laws" that configure parent-child relationships in only a limited number of ways.

Homeorhesis and Generic Developmental Paths

If there are certain intercoupled forms that are more likely than others to develop, the principles of prespecified and cascading constraints suggest that these forms may probabilistically determine a limited number of generic developmental pathways. *Homeorhetic processes* (Sameroff, 1995) may account for the unfolding of these "typical" paths. In homeorhesis, the interplay between positive and negative feedback processes stabilizes the system around a *trajectory*. Physical growth and normal cognitive development are two examples of such self-maintaining trajectories. They can be contrasted with homeostatic processes that stabilize through negative feedback around a fixed or set point (e.g., the setting of a thermostat).

Bell's model emphasizes homeostatic processes in dyadic relationships – the system stabilizes according to a set tolerance level. Although homeostasis may be an accurate description of the intercoupled dyadic configurations that emerge in real time, homeorhesis may be a better description of stability in dyadic systems in developmental time (cf. Sameroff, 1995). It may be that the dyadic attractors that stabilize through homeostatic feedback processes contribute, in turn, to the homeorhetic unfolding of parent-child relationships. These homeorhetic processes are trajectory attractors that "pull" the dyadic system forward through a series of developmental changes and reorganizations. One specific example of self-sustaining dyadic trajectories is Gottman and his colleagues' (Ryan et al., this volume; Gottman, 1993) three types of stable and two types of unstable marriages. Each type of couple was found to follow a characteristic developmental trajectory toward continued success in marriage (i.e., they remained together) or toward divorce. Another example of a self-sustaining dyadic trajectory may be found in Patterson's description of the development and maintenance of coercive family processes (e.g., Patterson, 1982; Patterson, Reid, and Dishion, 1992). A more detailed account of the homeorhetic influences underlying coercive dyads is presented in the final section of this chapter.

There may be an additional factor that contributes to the development of particular dyadic trajectories. They may depend on normative environmental perturbations that act upon the system over the course of development. For example, the beginning of formal education is a bifurcation point through which most parents and children pass (in Western cultures, at least). During this transitional period, the child is exposed to unfamiliar caregivers and peers and the mother is separated from her child for an extended period for perhaps the first time. According to the principles of self-organization, when dyads reach this bifurcation point, the potential for new dyadic attractors to arise increases dramatically. The specific types of novel parent-child patterns that self-organize at this bifurcation point will depend partially on previously established structures. But the relational system is also highly sensitive to small fluctuations at this threshold of instability. The increase in degrees of freedom may mean that minor incidents (e.g., a peer refuses to share with the child, the parent is five minutes late to pick up the child) result in a cascade toward a major change in the parent-child system. Some dyads may develop a new configuration characterized by parental anxiety/child fearfulness, others may develop a parental supportive/child autonomy-seeking attractor. Moreover, normative perturbations to the parent-child system need not originate from the external environment; changes may occur in response to internal fluctuations as well. Puberty is a good example of an internal perturbation that can lead to significant reorganization in the parent-child relationship (e.g., Brooks-Gunn and Reiter, 1990; Steinberg, 1990). Although certainly there is behavioral variability with respect to how dyads cope with these events, there may be only a limited number of ways that the dyadic system can stably reorganize in response to normative perturbations.

Summary

Up to this point, I have attempted to outline some promising ways in which we can conceptualize the development of the parent-child system. I have suggested that repeated real-time interactions give rise to a limited number of intercoupled cognitive-affective configurations that can be represented as attractors on a dyadic state space. Real-time feedback between dyad members was suggested as the underlying mechanism that catalyzes the emergence of dyadic configurations. Over developmental time, dyadic attractors serve as cascading constraints; they are the product of past self-organization, and they increasingly narrow the possibilities for further development. Prespecified constraints were discussed as an additional source of stability, providing the initial conditions from which the parent-child system develops.

Finally, I suggested that dyadic systems may be probabilistically determined by homeorhetic tendencies. These tendencies may be one of several higher-order "relational laws," similar to transformational principles in biology, that stipulate a limited number of viable developmental trajectories. In the final section of this chapter, I attempt to apply this model of self-organizing parent-child relations to one particular "type" of dyadic trajectory – the development of aggressive parent-child relationships. By doing so, I hope to demonstrate the potential explanatory power inherent in a self-organization framework.

Aggressive Parent-Child Relations

One of the most active branches of socialization research has been the area of aggressive parent-child relations, probably because of the serious developmental consequences of early aggressive behavior. Early onset of aggression leads to severe psychosocial maladjustment across several domains (Loeber, 1990), including poor peer relations (Behar and Stewart, 1982), impaired academic functioning (Tremblay et al., 1992), depression, alcoholism, and substance abuse (Tremblay et al., 1994). From a self-organization perspective, how do aggressive parent-child relationships develop?

The process seems to begin with hundreds of similar, mildly aversive interactions (Patterson, 1982). These early interactions may be influenced by prespecified constraints on the dyadic system. One of these constraints may be the child's difficult temperament at birth (e.g., Bates and Bayles, 1988; Patterson and Bank, 1989). Another is likely to be the mother's proneness to negative affect, specifically depression, which may influence her perception of the child early in the relationship, perhaps even before birth (e.g., Brody and Forehand, 1986; Elder, Caspi, and Van Nguyen, 1986; Forehand, Brody, and Smith, 1986; MacKinnon-Lewis et al., 1992). Given these initial conditions, recurrent difficult interactions between mother and child are probable. In fact, Patterson and colleagues (1992) have found that, in clinically referred dyads, an aggressive child is likely to experience an aversive intrusion from a family member at least once every minute. Typically, these intrusions are minor ones (e.g., mother scolds child for playing video games for too long) characterized by a vague command in an irritated tone of voice (Patterson, 1982, 1995). In response, the aggressive child tends to be noncompliant and to counterattack by arguing, yelling, and whining. Through many iterations of similarly frustrating episodes, the mother may develop a personality configuration characterized by irritability and anger and appraisals of her child as difficult and intentionally ''bad.'' Simultaneously, the child may develop his own compatible cognitive-emotional configuration characterized by anger and attributions of his mother as hostile and unfair (MacKinnon-Lewis et al., 1992). During these conflictual interactions, both partners are angry and perceive the other as intentionally frustrating some goal (e.g., mother wants child to do homework, but child wants to continue playing video games). Repeated feedback between these two individual personality configurations may enhance their complementarity, resulting in the self-organization of one intercoupled *coercive attractor.*

The principle of interdependent time scales stipulates that recurrent coercive patterns that self-organize in real time emerge as attractors over development; these developmental patterns, in turn, constrain dyadic behavior in real time. Through development, the coercive intercoupled configuration may be strengthened simply by its reemergence in many similar situations – there is less and less room for conscious intentionality on the part of either participant. Patterson makes a fascinating observation along these lines: "Many of the parents referred to [our clinic] are gentle, non-aggressive people. They perceive both themselves and their child as being under the influence of forces beyond their control. Some parents express extreme guilt because of the beatings they have given their children" (Patterson, 1982, p. 156). According to self-organization principles, coupling among complementary elements (i.e., mutual anger and hostile attributions) and the consequent convergence to the coercive attractor may be what constitutes those "forces beyond their control."

Nonlinear relations among constituents of the coercive configuration may be an additional reason why parents and children do not feel they have control over their aggressive interactions. Once interaction patterns have crystallized, a self-organization approach suggests that fewer and fewer contextual cues will be necessary to catalyze the real-time emergence of the full-blown coercive attractor. This idea is supported by studies that have shown that, over months and years, coercive interactions tend to *begin* at a higher level of intensity (e.g., physical fighting rather than whining) and to intensify more rapidly within an episode (Patterson, 1982; Patterson et al., 1992; Snyder et al., 1994). Patterson (1982) has suggested that in any given coercive episode that ends in hitting, one or the other partner "may move so quickly through a sequence that the victim is hardly aware that the confrontation has begun . . ." (p. 157) Perhaps the dyad is actually not moving through a sequence – a nonlinear, real-time phase shift may be a more accurate description.

It is important to note that the coercive dyadic configuration may be represented as one among several attractors on a dyadic state space. Self-organizing dyadic systems have the potential to be drawn toward several attractors, depending on contextual constraints. This is a significant point to highlight, because most models of aggressive parent-child relations neglect to consider that not all of the interactions of aggressive dyads are hostile and coercive. Most research has focused exclusively on identifying either negative or positive patterns, but even severely aggressive dyads sometimes engage in positive interactions, and even the most healthy dyads can engage in hostile arguments. It seems important for a comprehensive model of aggressive socialization processes to address the variety of dyadic states that comprise the system – to adopt a "state space wide" perspective. How easily can a dyad change from a hostile to a supportive interaction pattern? Under what conditions does a dyadic system exhibit this sort of flexibility? Are there contexts in which the system is unable to get "unstuck" from a hostile attractor? Developmental issues may also be uniquely addressed. In what ways do dyadic state spaces become reconfigured at bifurcation points? What new attractors – perhaps avoidant, conciliatory, or provocative – emerge during, for instance, early adolescence? Which ones disappear? These are just a few examples of the new questions that can be posed through a "state space wide" approach to studying aggressive families (Granic, 1998).

Homeorhesis in dyadic development may be another avenue through which to examine aggressive parent-child relationships. Recall that homeorhesis can be viewed as an attractor for a developmental trajectory. There may be several aggressive parent-child trajectories, but two conditions are needed to define any one of them as homeorhetic. The first is evidence that dyads stabilize according to a characteristic developmental path. Over three decades of research with aggressive families has led Patterson's group to specify at least one such potentially characteristic trajectory (Patterson, 1982; Patterson et al., 1992). The path begins with the parent repeatedly requesting compliance from her toddler, who in turn responds oppositionally (e.g., whining, tantrums). During these early years, permissive (e.g., Baumrind, 1971; Baumrind, 1991; Patterson, 1982) and indiscriminant parenting (e.g., reprimanding the child's constructive behavior, laughing at a child's aggressive attempts; Dumas and LaFreniere, 1995) and noncompliant, angry, and aggressive behavior on the part of the child characterize the dyad. As the dyad proceeds on this trajectory, coercive parent-child exchanges grow longer in duration and escalate in amplitude so that physical assault becomes more probable (Snyder et al., 1994). Next, the preadolescent begins coercing his parent into allowing him to go out unsupervised, thus increasing his chances of interacting with like-minded deviant peers (e.g., Dishion et al., 1995; Dishion et al., 1996; Elliot, Huizinga, and Ageton, 1985). The parent and child interact less and less (Patterson and Bank, 1989), they no longer have even brief episodes of pleasant interchange, and discipline and monitoring disappear from the dyadic repertoire (Patterson, 1982; Patterson et al., 1992). In these later periods, the aggressive dyad becomes almost exclusively characterized by mutual hostility and rejection. Patterson maintains that this coercive trajectory characterizes two-thirds of the hundreds of families he and his colleagues have seen at their clinic (Patterson et al., 1992). Thus, there seems to be some indication of homeorhesis in aggressive dyads – the majority of aggressive dyads seem to be "pulled" along a characteristic developmental trajectory.

The second condition for homeorhesis is that the developmental trajectory shows evidence of an attractor. There should be some indication of the "stickiness" of the trajectory; that is, once perturbed, the dyadic system should rapidly return to its path. This criterion for homeorhesis points to the self-maintaining properties of the system (Sameroff, 1995). Studies aimed at evaluating the effectiveness of treatment with aggressive parent-child dyads assume that coercive dyads are changeable. Treatment is aimed at perturbing the system in hopes of triggering a reorganization that will permit the dyad to escape from the aggressive trajectory that Patterson discusses. If there are strong homeorhetic tendencies underlying the aggressive parent-child system, then this should prove extremely difficult. Indeed, this is the case. Although some treatment programs have been effective in producing positive changes in dyadic behavior (e.g., Patterson, Chamberlain, and Reid, 1982), even among the most advanced, empirically validated programs the overwhelming majority fail to push most aggressive dyads off their trajectory (for reviews see Brestan and Eyberg, 1998; Dumas, 1989; Kazdin, 1993, 1995; Webster-Stratton and Hammond, 1990). Even more compelling is the empirical evidence that, although treatment gains may be evident upon completion of an intervention program, dyads usually return to their old coercive patterns within one to three years (Kazdin, 1993; Lochman, 1992). Thus, aggressive dyads seem to follow a developmental trajectory that exerts a powerful self-stabilizing force.

Conclusion

In the preceding section, I have attempted to apply principles of self organization to one dyadic trajectory – the aggressive parent-child relationship. My objective in doing so was twofold: first, to illustrate the utility of applying a self-organization framework to parent-child relationships, and second, to highlight new questions and theoretical extensions that such an approach suggests. This was a preliminary attempt at such an endeavor, and there are many issues that remain unexplored. For example, a self-organization approach not only explains why treatment efforts with aggressive families may be unsuccessful – perhaps due to dyadic homeorhesis – it also points to some encouraging directions for intervention. Most notably, there may be bifurcation points in the parent-child trajectory (e.g., immediately after the birth of a sibling, the beginning of schooling, puberty) during which interventions may be targeted most productively. These critical periods may represent thresholds of instability at which the parent-child system is more flexible and, thus, more amenable to treatment. Some additional directions for future study include specifying dyadic "typical forms," that is, the various patterns of parent-child coupling that can stabilize. It may also be important to understand whether, in response to normative perturbations, predictable patterns of reorganization of the dyadic state space can be identified for particular types of dyads.

In this chapter, I have suggested that socialization models have evolved from viewing parent-child relations as separate linear contingencies, to viewing them as reciprocal effects, and finally to seeing them as circular, recursive processes. This move from discrete, linear causal processes to complex, nonlinear causes directs us toward a radically different view of dyadic development. To progress further, an integrative theoretical framework based on principles of self-organization seems necessary to ground this emerging perspective.

References

Abramson, L. Y., Seligman, M., and Teasdale, J. (1978). Learned helplessness in humans: Critique and reformulation. *Journal of Abnormal Psychology, 87*, 49–74.

Anderson, K. E., Lytton, H., and Romney, D. M. (1986). Mothers' interactions with normal and conduct-disordered boys: Who affects whom? *Developmental Psychology, 22*, 604–609.

Bates, J. E. (1980). The concept of difficult temperament. *Merrill-Palmer Quarterly, 26*, 299–319.

Bates, J. E., and Bayles, K. (1988). Attachment and the development of behavior problems. In J. Belsky and T. Nezworski (Eds.), *Clinical implications of attachment: Child psychology* (pp. 253–299). Hillsdale, NJ: Erlbaum.

Bateson, G. (1972). *Steps to an ecology of mind: Collected essays in anthropology, psychiatry, evolution and epistemology.* New York: Ballantine Books.

Baumrind, D. (1971). Current patterns of parental authority. *Developmental Psychology Monographs, 4*, 1–103.

Baumrind, D. (1991). The influence of parenting style on adolescent competence and substance use. *Journal of Early Adolescence, 11*, 56–95.

Behar, D., and Stewart, M. A. (1982). Aggressive conduct disorder of children. *Acta Psychiatrica Scandinavica, 65*, 210–220.

Bell, R. Q. (1968). A reinterpretation of the direction of effects in studies of socialization. *Psychological Review, 75*, 81–95.

Bell, R. Q., and Chapman, M. (1986). Child effects in studies using experimental or brief longitudinal approaches to socialization. *Developmental Psychology, 22*, 595–603.

Bell, R. Q., and Harper, L. V. (1977). *Child effects on adults.* Hillsdale, NJ: Erlbaum.

Bowlby, J. (1969). *Attachment.* New York: Basic Books.

Brazelton, T. B., Koslowski, B., and Main, M. (1974). The origins of reciprocity: The early mother-infant interaction. In M. Lewis and L. Rosenblum (Eds.), *The effect of the infant on its caregiver.* New York: Wiley.

Brent, S. B. (1978). Prigogine's model for self-organization in nonequilibrium systems: Its relevance for developmental psychology. *Human Development, 21*, 374–387.

Brestan, E. V., and Eyberg, S. M. (1998). Effective psychosocial treatments of conduct-disordered children and adolescents: 29 years, 82 studies, and 5,272 kids. *Journal of Clinical Child Psychology, 27,* 180–189.

Brody, G. H., and Forehand, R. (1986). Maternal perceptions of child maladjustment as a function of the combined influence of child behavior and maternal depression. *Journal of Consulting and Clinical Psychology, 54,* 237–240.

Bronstein, P. (1984). Differences in mothers' and fathers' behaviors toward children: A cross-cultural comparison. *Developmental Psychology, 20,* 995–1003.

Brooks-Gunn, J., and Reiter, E. O. (1990). The role of pubertal processes. In S. S. Feldman and G. R. Elliot (Eds.), *At the threshold: The developing adolescent* (pp. 16–53). Cambridge, MA: Harvard University Press.

Bruner, J. S. (1975). The ontogenesis of speech acts. *Journal of Child Language, 2,* 1–19.

Brunk, M. A., and Henggeler, S. Q. (1984). Child influences on adult controls: An experimental investigation. *Developmental Psychology, 20,* 1074–1081.

Cairns, R. B (1979). Social interactional methods: An introduction. In R. B. Cairns (Ed.), *The analysis of social interactions: Methods, issues and illustrations.* Hillsdale, NJ: Erlbaum.

Cairns, R. B. (1983). The emergence of a developmental psychology. In P.H. Mussen (series ed.) and W. Kessen (vol. ed.), *Handbook of child psychology: Vol. 1. History, theory, and methods* (4th ed., pp. 41–102). New York: Wiley.

Case, R. (1985). *Intellectual development: Birth to adulthood.* Orlando, FL: Academic Press.

Chamberlain, P., and Patterson, G. R. (1995). Discipline and child compliance in parenting. In M. H. Bornstein (Ed.), *Handbook of parenting: Vol. 4. Applied and practical parenting* (pp. 205–225). Mahwah, NJ: Erlbaum.

Cicchetti, D., and Rogosch, F. (Eds.) (1997). Self-organization [special issue]. *Development and Psychopathology, 9,* 595–929.

Deater-Deckard, K., and Dodge, K. A. (1997). Externalizing behavior problems and discipline revisited: Nonlinear effects and variation by culture, context, and gender: Target article. *Psychological Inquiry, 8,* 161–175.

Demos, V. (1986). Crying in early infancy: An illustration of the motivational function of affect. In T. B. Brazelton and M. W. Yogman (Eds.), *Affective development in infancy* (pp. 39–73). Norwood, NJ: Ablex.

Dishion, T. J., Capaldi, D., Spracklen, K. M., and Li, F. (1995). Peer ecology of male adolescent drug use. *Development and Psychopathology, 7,* 803–824.

Dishion, T. J., Spracklen, K. M., Andrews, D. W., and Patterson, G. R. (1996). Deviancy training in male adolescent friendships. *Behaviour Therapy, 27,* 373–390.

Dix, T. (1991). The affective organization of parenting: Adaptive and maladaptive processes. *Psychological Bulletin, 110,* 3–25.

Dix, T., Rubel, D. N., and Zambarano, R. J. (1989). Mother's implicit theories of discipline: Child effects, parent effects, and the attribution process. *Child Development, 60,* 1373–1391.

Dodge, K. A. (1980). Social cognition and children's aggressive behavior. *Child Development, 51,* 162–170.

Dodge, K. A., Pettit, G. S., McClaskey, C. L., and Brown, M. M. (1986). Social competence in children. *Monographs of the Society for Research in Child Development, 51* (2, serial no. 213).

Dodge, K. A., and Somberg, D. R. (1987). Hostile attributional biases among aggressive boys are exacerbated under conditions of threats to the self. *Child Development, 58,* 213–224.

Dumas, J. E. (1989). Treating antisocial behavior in children: Child and family approaches. *Clinical Psychology Review, 9,* 197–222.

Dumas, J. E., and LaFreniere, P. J. (1993). Mother-child relationships as sources of support or stress: A comparison of competent, average, aggressive and anxious dyads. *Child Development, 64,* 1732–1754.

Dumas, J. E., and LaFreniere, P. J. (1995). Relationships as context: Supportive and coercive interactions in competent, aggressive, and anxious mother-child dyads. In J. McCord (Ed.), *Coercion and punishment in long-term perspectives* (pp. 9–33). New York: Cambridge University Press.

Elder, G., Caspi, A., and Van Nguyen, T. (1986). Resourceful and vulnerable children: Family influence and hard times. In R. Silbereisen, K. Eyferth, and K. G. Rudinger (Eds.), *Developmental action in context: Integrative perspectives on youth development* (pp. 167–186). Berlin: Springer-Verlag.

Elliot, D. S., Huizinga, D., and Ageton, S. S. (1985). *Explaining delinquency and drug use.* Beverly Hills, CA: Sage.

Fogel, A. (1993). *Developing through relationships: Origins of communication, self and culture.* Chicago: University of Chicago Press.

Fogel, A., and Branco, A. U. (1997). Meta-communication as a source of indeterminism in relationship development. In A. Fogel, M. C. Lyra, and J. Valsiner (Eds.), *Dynamics and indeterminism in developmental and social processes* (pp. 65–92). Hillsdale, NJ: Erlbaum.

Fogel, A., Nwokah, E., Dedo, J. Y., Messinger, D., Dickson, K. L., Matusov, E., and Holt, S. A. (1992). Social process theory of emotion: A dynamic systems approach. *Social Development, 1,* 122–142.

Fogel, A., and Thelen, E. (1987). The development of early expressive and communicative action: Re-interpreting the evidence from a dynamic systems perspective. *Developmental Psychology, 23,* 747–761.

Forehand, R., Brody, G., and Smith, K. (1986). Contribution of child behaviour and marital dissatisfaction to maternal perceptions of child maladjustment. *Behaviour Research and Therapy, 24,* 43–48.

Frijda, N. H. (1986). *The emotions.* New York: Cambridge University Press.

Goerner, S. (1995). Chaos, evolution and deep ecology. In R. Robertson and A. Combs (Eds.), *Chaos theory is psychology and the life sciences* (pp. 17–38). Mahwah, NJ: Erlbaum.

Goodwin, B. C. (1987). Developing organisms as self-organizing fields. In F. E. Yates (Ed.), *Self-organizing systems: The emergence of order* (pp. 167–180). New York: Plenum.

Goodwin, B. C. (1994). *How the leopard changed its spots: The evolution of complexity.* New York: Touchstone.

Gottman, J. M. (1993). The roles of conflict engagement, escalation, and avoidance in marital interaction: A longitudinal view of five types of couples. *Journal of Consulting and Clinical Psychology, 61,* 6–15.

Granic, I. (1998). *Hysteresis: An index of treatment progress.* Paper presented at the annual meeting of the Society for Chaos Theory in Psychology and the Life Sciences, Boston, August.

Granic, I., and Butler, S. (1998). The relation between anger and antisocial beliefs in young offenders. *Personality and Individual Differences, 24*, 759–765.

Granic, I., and Lewis, M. D. (1997). *A dynamic systems approach to the study of anger and antisocial beliefs in young offenders.* Paper presented at the meeting of the International Society for Research in Child and Adolescent Psychopathology, Paris, July.

Grusec, J. E., and Kuczynski, L. (1980). Direction of effect on socialization: A comparison of the parent's versus the child's behavior as determinants of disciplinary techniques. *Developmental Psychology, 16*, 1–9.

Grusec, J. E., Rudy, D., and Martini, T. (1997). Parenting cognitions and child outcomes: An overview and implications for children's internalization of values. In J. E. Grusec and L. Kuczynski (Eds.), *Parenting and children's internalization of values: A handbook of contemporary theory* (pp. 259–282). New York: Wiley.

Haken, H. (1977). *Synergetics – An introduction: Nonequilibrium phase transitions and self-organization in physics, chemistry and biology.* Berlin: Springer-Verlag.

Hart, G. H., Ladd, G. W., and Burleson, B. R. (1990). Children's expectations of the outcomes of social strategies: Relations with sociometric status and maternal disciplinary styles. *Child Development, 61*, 127–137.

Izard, C. E. (1977). *Human emotions.* New York: Plenum.

Jantsch, E. (1980). *The self-organizing universe.* Oxford: Pergamon.

Kandel, D. B., and Wu, P. (1995). Disentangling mother-child effects in the development of antisocial behavior. In J. McCord (Ed.), *Coercion and punishment in long-term perspectives* (pp. 106–123). New York: Cambridge University Press.

Kauffman, S. A. (1993). *The origins of order: Self-organization and selection in evolution.* New York: Oxford University Press.

Kazdin, A. E. (1993). Treatment of conduct disorder: Progress and direction in psychotherapy research. *Development and Psychopathology, 5*, 277–310.

Kazdin, A. E. (1995). *Conduct disorders in childhood and adolescence* (2nd ed.). Thousand Oaks, CA: Sage.

Keating, D. P. (1990). Developmental processes in the socialization of cognitive structures. In *Development and learning: Proceedings of a symposium in honor of Wolfgang Edelstein on his sixtieth birthday* (pp. 37–72). Berlin: Max Planck Institute.

Kelso, J. A. (1995). *Dynamic patterns: The self-organization of brain and behavior.* Cambridge, MA: Bradford/MIT Press.

Kochanska, G. (1992). Children's interpersonal influence with mothers and peers. *Developmental Psychology, 28*, 491–499.

LaFreniere, P. J., and Dumas, J. E. (1992). A transactional analysis of early childhood anxiety and social withdrawal. *Development and Psychopathology, 4*, 385–402.

Lay, K., Waters, E., and Park, K. A. (1989). Maternal responsiveness and child compliance: The role of mood as a mediator. *Child Development, 60*, 1405–1411.

Lazarus, R. (1982). Thoughts on the relations between emotion and cognition. *American Psychologist, 37*, 1019–1024.

Lazarus, R. (1984). On the primacy of cognition. *American Psychologist, 39*, 124–129.

Lewis, M. D. (1995). Cognition-emotion feedback and the self-organization of developmental paths. *Human Development, 38*, 71–102.

Lewis, M. D. (1997). Personality self-organization: Cascading constraints on cognition-emotion interaction. In A. Fogel, M. C. Lyra, and J. Valsiner (Eds.), *Dynamics and indeterminism in developmental and social processes* (pp. 193–216). Mahwah, NJ: Erlbaum.

Lewis, M. D., and Granic, I. (1999). Who put the self in self-organization? A clarification of terms and concepts for developmental psychopathology. *Development and Psychopathology, 11*, 365–374.

Lochman, J. E. (1992). Cognitive-behavioral intervention with aggressive boys: Three-year follow-up and preventive effects. *Journal of Consulting and Clinical Psychology, 60*, 426–432.

Loeber, R. (1990). Development and risk factors of juvenile antisocial behavior and delinquency. *Clinical Psychology Review, 10*, 1–41.

Lytton, H. (1990). Child and parent effects in boys' conduct disorder: A reinterpretation. *Developmental Psychology, 26*, 683–692.

Maccoby, E. E. (1984). Socialization and developmental change: Presidential address. *Child Development, 55*, 317–328.

Maccoby, E. E. (1992). The role of parents in the socialization of children: An historical overview. *Developmental Psychology, 28*, 1006–1017.

Maccoby, E. E., and Martin, J. A. (1983). Socialization in the context of the family: Parent-child interaction. In P. H. Mussen (series ed.) and E. M. Hetherington (vol. ed.), *Handbook of child psychology: Vol. 4. Socialization, personality and social development* (4th ed., pp. 1–101). New York: Wiley.

MacKinnon-Lewis, C., Lamb, M. E., Arbuckle, B., Baradaran, L. P., and Volling, B. L. (1992). The relationship between biased maternal and filial attributions and the aggressiveness of their interactions. *Development and Psychopathology, 4*, 403–415.

Magai, C., and McFadden, S. H. (1995). *The role of emotions in social and personality development: History, theory, and research.* New York: Plenum.

Mahler, M. S., Pine, F., and Bergman, A. (1975). *The psychological birth of the human infant: Symbiosis and individuation.* New York: Basic Books.

Malatesta, C. Z., and Wilson, A. (1988). Emotion cognition interaction in personality development: A discrete emotions, functionalist analysis. *British Journal of Social Psychology, 27*, 91–112.

Mash, E. J., and Johnston, C. (1982). A comparison of the mother-child interactions of younger and older hyperactive and normal children. *Child Development, 53*, 1371–1381.

Oatley, K., and Johnson-Laird, P. N. (1987). Towards a cognitive theory of emotions. *Cognition and Emotion, 1*, 29–50.

Olweus, D. (1980). Familial and temperamental determinants of aggressive behavior in adolescent boys: A causal analysis. *Developmental Psychology, 16*, 644–660.

Parke, R. D. (1977). Punishment in children: Effects, side effects, and alternative strategies. In H. L. Hom, Jr. and P. Robinson (Eds.), *Psychological processes in early education* (pp. 71–97). San Diego, CA: Academic Press.

Parpal, M., and Maccoby, E. E. (1985). Maternal responsiveness and subsequent child compliance. *Child Development, 56*, 1326–1334.

Patterson, G. R. (1982). *Coercive family processes.* Eugene, OR: Castalia.

Patterson, G. R. (1995). Coercion as a basis for early age of onset for arrest. In J. McCord (Ed.), *Coercion and punishment in long-term perspectives* (pp. 81–105). New York: Cambridge University Press.

Patterson, G. R., and Bank, L. (1989). Some amplifying mechanisms for pathologic processes in families. In M. R. Gunnar and E. Thelen (Eds.), *Minnesota Symposium on Child Psychology: Vol. 22. Systems and development* (pp. 167–209). Hillsdale, NJ: Erlbaum.

Patterson, G. R., Chamberlain, P., and Reid, J. B. (1982). A comparative evaluation of a parent-training program. *Behavior Therapy, 13,* 638–650.

Patterson, G. R., Reid, J. B., and Dishion, T. J. (1992). *Antisocial boys.* Eugene, OR: Castalia Press.

Prigogine, I., and Stengers, I. (1984). *Order out of chaos.* New York: Bantam.

Rothbaum, F., and Weisz, J. R. (1994). Parental caregiving and child externalizing behavior in nonclinical samples: A meta-analysis. *Psychological Bulletin, 116,* 55–74.

Sameroff, A. J. (1975). Transactional models in early social relations. *Human Development, 18,* 65–79.

Sameroff, A. J. (1983). Developmental systems: Contexts and evolution. In P. H. Mussen (series ed.) and W. Kessen (vol. ed.), *Handbook of child psychology: Vol. 1. History, theory, and methods* (4th ed., pp. 237–294). New York: Wiley.

Sameroff, A. J. (1995). General systems theories and developmental psychopathology. In D. Cicchetti and D. J. Cohen (Eds.), *Developmental psychopathology: Vol. 1. Theory and methods* (pp. 659–695). New York: Wiley.

Sameroff, A. J., and Chandler, M. J. (1975). Reproductive risk and the continuum of caretaking casualty. In F. D. Horowitz, M. Hetherington, S. Scarr-Salapatek, and G. Siegel (Eds.), *Review of child development research* (vol. 4, pp. 187–244). Chicago: University of Chicago Press.

Sameroff, A. J., and Emde, R. N. (Eds.). (1989). *Relationship disturbances in early childhood: A developmental approach.* New York: Basic Books.

Schore, A. N. (1997). Early organization of the nonlinear right brain and development of a predisposition to psychiatric disorders. *Development and Psychopathology, 9,* 595–631.

Snyder, J., Edwards, P., McGraw, K., Kilgore, K., and Holton, A. (1994). Escalation and reinforcement in mother-child conflict: Social processes associated with the development of physical aggression. *Development and Psychopathology, 6,* 305–321.

Sroufe, L. A. (1996). *Emotional development: The organization of emotional life in the early years.* New York: Cambridge University Press.

Steinberg, L. (1990). Autonomy, conflict and harmony in the family relationship. In S. S. Feldman and G. R. Elliot (Eds.), *At the threshold: The developing adolescent* (pp. 255–276). Cambridge, MA: Harvard University Press.

Stern, D. N. (1974). Mother and infant at play: The dyadic interaction involving facial, vocal and gaze behaviors. In M. Lewis and L. A. Rosenblum (Eds.), *The effect of the infant on its caregiver* (pp. 76–94). New York: Wiley.

Stern, D. N., Beebe, B., Jaffe, J., and Bennett, S. L. (1977). The infant's stimulus world during social interaction: A study of caregiver behaviors with particular reference to repetition and timing. In H. R. Schaffer (Ed.), *Studies in mother-infant interaction* (pp. 89–99). London: Academic Press.

Teasdale, J. D. (1983). Negative thinking in depression: Cause, effect or reciprocal relationship? *Advances in Behaviour Research and Therapy, 5,* 3–25.

Teasdale, J. D., and Barnard, P. J. (1993). *Affect, cognition, and change: Re-modelling depressive thought.* Hillsdale, NJ: Erlbaum.

Thelen, E., and Smith, L. B. (1994). *A dynamic systems approach to the development of cognition and action.* Cambridge, MA: Bradford/MIT Press.

Thelen, E., and Ulrich, B. D. (1991). Hidden skills: A dynamic systems analysis of treadmill stepping during the first year. *Monographs of the Society for Research in Child Development, 56* (1, serial no. 223).

Tomkins, S. S. (1987). Script theory. In J. Aronoff, A. I. Rabin, and R. A. Zucker (Eds.), *The emergence of personality* (pp. 147–216). New York: Springer.

Tomkins, S. S. (1991). *Affect, imagery, consciousness. Vol. 3: Anger and fear.* New York: Springer.

Tremblay, R. E., Masse, B., Perron, D., LeBlanc, M., Schwartzman, A. E., and Ledingham, J. E. (1992). Early disruptive behavior, poor school achievement, delinquent behavior, and delinquent personality: Longitudinal analyses. *Journal of Consulting and Clinical Psychology, 60,* 65–72.

Tremblay, R. E., Pihl, R. O., Vitaro, F., and Dobkin, P. L. (1994). Predicting early onset of male antisocial behavior from preschool behavior. *Archives of General Psychiatry, 51,* 732–738.

Trevarthen, C. (1993). The self born in intersubjectivity: The psychology of an infant communicating. In U. Neisser (Ed.), *The perceived self: Ecological and interpersonal sources of self-knowledge* (pp. 121–173). New York: Cambridge University Press.

Tronick, E. Z., Ricks, M., and Cohn, J. F. (1982). Maternal and infant affective exchange: Patterns of adaptation. In T. Field and A. Fogel (Eds.), *Emotion and early interaction* (pp. 83–100). Hillsdale, NJ: Erlbaum.

Vallacher, R. R., and Nowak, A. (Eds.). (1994). *Dynamical systems in social psychology.* San Diego, CA: Academic.

Vallacher, R. R., and Nowak, A. (1997). The emergence of dynamical social psychology: Target article. *Psychological Inquiry, 8,* 73–99.

van Gelder, T., and Port, R. F. (1995). It's about time: An overview of the dynamical approach to cognition. In R. F. Port and T. van Gelder (Eds.), *Mind as motion: Explorations in the dynamics of cognition* (pp. 1–43). Cambridge, MA: MIT Press.

Webster-Stratton, C., and Hammond, M. (1990). Predictors of treatment outcome in parent training for families with conduct problem children. *Behaviour Therapy, 21,* 319–337.

Weiner, B. (1979). A theory of motivation for some classroom experiences. *Journal of Educational Psychology, 71,* 3–25.

Wilson, B. J., and Gottman, J. M. (1995). Marital interaction and parenting. In M. H. Bornstein (Ed.), *Handbook of parenting: Vol. 4. Applied and practical parenting* (pp. 33–55). Mahwah, NJ: Erlbaum.

Zahn-Waxler, C., and Radke-Yarrow, M. (1990). The origins of empathic concern. *Motivation and Emotion, 14,* 107–130.

Zahn-Waxler, C., Radke-Yarrow, M., and King, R. A. (1979). Child-rearing and children's prosocial initiations toward victims of distress. *Child Development, 50,* 319–330.

11   Attachment and Self-Organization

Deborah J. Laible and Ross A. Thompson

The history of the scientific study of human development shows that conventional portrayals of development tend to be maintained until newer, better models emerge to take their place. This paradigmatic shift is much clearer in hindsight than at the time it occurs, during which the potential benefits of new formulations and their heuristic potential are explored, scrutinized, and debated. When this occurs, traditional ideas may be maintained (albeit in altered form) or integrated with new formulations, or more comprehensive changes may occur in how developmentalists fundamentally view familiar phenomena as a result of alternative models.

Are we in the midst of such a shift in thinking because of the emergence of dynamic systems views of development? At present, it is difficult to say. While many of the heuristic possibilities of dynamic systems approaches are becoming apparent, their broader utility for a comprehensive developmental formulation is yet unclear, and their empirical testability is even more obscure. One way of assessing the potential value of a dynamic systems approach as a framework for developmental thinking is to apply it to a well-developed body of research in order to explore whether it offers valuable new insights, enables researchers to ask new questions, and explains perplexing findings in a manner that suggests its broader value for developmental theory.

This chapter is concerned with the relevance of dynamic systems formulations to attachment theory, a field of research that has dominated the study of early sociopersonality development for more than a quarter of a century (Thompson, 1998). Although subject to various critiques over the years, attachment theory remains a dominant perspective on the importance of early infant-parent relationships for later sociopersonality growth, especially as its ideas are being extended to encompass children's social cognition, developmental psychopathology, and adult relationships. Yet the

298

limitations of attachment theory are also becoming apparent in light of the empirical research it has generated, prompting periodic calls for new conceptual approaches to better integrate and interpret emerging findings. Does a dynamic systems approach offer the possibility of complementing the insights of traditional attachment formulations with new explanations and new questions? In this chapter, we briefly summarize the basic and most relevant ideas of a dynamic systems approach to development, and of traditional attachment theory, before offering some tentative thoughts concerning this question.

Dynamic Systems and Self-Organization

Due to perceived failures of traditional theories to account for accumulating developmental research findings, growing numbers of developmental psychologists are borrowing principles from dynamic systems theory to explain developmental processes (e.g., Camras, 1992; Fogel, Lyra, and Valsiner, 1997; Lewis, 1995, 1997; Smith, 1995; Thelen, 1989; van Geert, 1994). Dynamic systems approaches have led to a revolution in scientific thinking by advancing the idea that order emerges from chaos and that pattern, coordination, coherence, and synchronization are the results of the interdependence of systems and system elements (Goerner, 1995; Kelso, Ding, and Schoner, 1993). Dynamic systems perspectives are an attempt to explain the evolution of complex, nonlinear systems, including their ability to self-organize – that is, to form intricate patterns from interactions among simpler parts, without prespecified blueprints (e.g., Kauffman, 1993; Madore and Freedman, 1987; Prigogine, 1980).

In their application to developmental psychology, dynamic systems approaches have several potential advantages over other developmental theories. First, dynamic systems views are better able to account for the processes by which novel behavioral forms emerge developmentally from earlier forms (Thelen, 1992; Thelen and Smith, 1994; van Geert, 1994). Structuralist theories (such as those of Piaget, Kohlberg, and others) have difficulty accounting for the ultimate origins of new behavioral forms, for example, because they assign the plan of ontogenetic change either to forces within the organism (e.g., genetics) or to forces in the environment (Oyama, 1985; Thelen, 1989). The assumption that development is either the result of genetic blueprints or structure internalized from the environment (or some interaction of the two) is inadequate, dynamic systems theorists argue, because it does not explain either what activates the genes in particular ways or how information from the environment is selected

(Oyama, 1985). Moreover, both heredity and environment underspecify the complexity of behavioral organization. Taking an interactionist perspective does not solve the problem either, because it only attributes the outcome to two unexplained causes instead of one (Thelen, 1989, 1992; Thelen and Smith, 1994). By taking such an interactionist perspective, theorists taking a dynamic systems perspective argue, most developmental theories sidestep a fundamental issue in development: the processes and mechanisms that produce developmental change.

In contrast, theorists taking a dynamic systems perspective are interested foremost in explaining the processes that give rise to new behavioral forms. According to dynamic principles, as organisms develop, novel behavioral patterns emerge from the *process* of interaction among multiple, interdependent elements of a particular system (Goerner, 1995; Smith and Thelen, 1993a; Thelen, 1989). The behavioral patterns that emerge are not prescribed by either forces within the individual or those in the context, but instead grow out of the relationship among system elements (Lewis, 1995). Because an organism is part of a living system and is exchanging energy with its surrounding environment (Butterworth, 1993; Thelen, 1989), components within the organism and those within the context are functionally comparable with regard to the emergence of novel behavioral forms, and neither has precedence in driving development. System phase shifts (or reorganizations) that result in qualitatively different patterns of behavior may be driven either by change in contextual elements (e.g., the scaffolding of an adult) or as the result of changes within the organism (e.g., cortical maturation).

Development from a dynamic systems perspective is thus generally not envisioned as progression through a series of invariant structural stages (but see van Geert, 1994, for an alternative view), but as the evolution and subsequent disintegration of these preferred behavioral states, known as attractors (Abraham and Shaw, 1982), which have varying degrees of stability (Thelen and Smith, 1994). Each new reorganization of the system is constrained by the previous pattern (a process described as "cascading constraints" [Lewis, 1997]), and development is heterochronous (that is, elements of a particular behavioral system are developing at different rates; see Camras, 1992; Thelen and Smith, 1994). As the elements of the system change, the organization of existing elements may disintegrate, leading to the reorganization of the system and the emergence of a new, more stable attractor state (Abraham, Abraham, and Shaw, 1990). Each resulting attractor is the preferred state of the system of the individual vis-à-vis a particular task or environment (Thelen, 1992).

Second, dynamic systems approaches are better able to account for the local variability of development. Although most developmental theories emphasize the regularity of behavioral forms, research has revealed the fragility of children's competencies, the inconsistency in performance across contexts and tasks, and the frustrating nonlinearities, regressions, and dissimilarities in developmental outcomes (see Rosser, 1994; Thelen and Smith, 1994). This variability is often described as "noise" or attributed to performance variables (e.g., attention). Theorists from a dynamic systems perspective, by contrast, consider variability to be an inherent part of development. Novel behavior, from a dynamic systems perspective, is not noise but evidence of the system's dynamic nature. Because dynamic systems are nonlinear, flexible, and multicausal, small changes in either the context or the organism can result in qualitatively unique organizations of behavior (Kelso et al., 1993; Thelen, 1992). A particular dynamic system may have many different patterns of behavior (i.e., attractors), and transformations between patterns may appear as abrupt changes in behavior, known as phase transitions. A single element of the system, known as a control parameter, often determines which organization appears. When a control parameter passes a critical threshold, precipitous change is instigated and a sudden reorganization of the system occurs (Abraham, 1995). Control parameters themselves may change with development, adding further variability to the system.

It is important to realize that changes in system organization occur on two different time scales, real time and developmental time, and that the same principles and process apply to system changes at both time scales. Real-time phase shifts involve the immediate, or second-by-second, assemblages of behavior in response to the rich, changing task environment. Developmental-time phase shifts are those occurring across a larger time scale (e.g., days, months, years) and are the result of changes in the organism, task, and environmental supports. Control parameters and phase transitions can be depicted at either time scale, and development is the result of system reorganizations at both time scales. The two time scales are interwoven in the developmental process; for example, as an action is performed in real time, it contributes to the dynamic (and developmental) history of the organism and shapes future actions (Thelen and Smith, 1994).

Despite the real-time variability of dynamic systems (and the messiness of development on a real-time scale), there is global order to development using dynamic principles (Thelen, 1992) for several reasons. First, attractors become increasingly stable across developmental time – with the growing consolidation of skills, for example – and developmental pathways become likewise consolidated as prior patterns of self-organization constrain subsequent reorganizations. Second, although dynamic systems are complex, nonlinear systems, they are strongly constrained both by the phylogenetic and ontogenetic history of the organism and by the typical species-expected environment (Keating, 1990). Therefore, although development has individual variability in a dynamic systems perspective, all normal children essentially develop in a similar manner.

Dynamic systems principles have recently been applied to several areas of development, including emotion and personality (Lewis, 1995, 1997), motor development (Thelen, 1989), communication (Fogel and Thelen, 1987), and language development (Smith, 1995). The value of applying this perspective to developmental processes is perhaps most clearly seen in Thelen's application of dynamic principles to the development of walking (Thelen, 1984, 1985, 1989). Thelen (1989) has argued that the rhythmic leg cycling seen in walking and in early infant kicking is a critical motor structure that becomes entrained into the motor system for walking. Walking does not develop when a "central program" is triggered by maturation, but when the ratio of fat to muscle in the leg changes in such a manner that an infant is capable of lifting her legs against gravity when in an upright position. Thus the ratio of muscle to fat serves as a control parameter that forces the reorganization of previously present behavioral components into a new developmental structure (i.e., walking) when the control parameter passes a critical threshold.

Although the application of dynamic systems principles to motor development has had much success, its direct application to other areas of development may be limited. The application of dynamic systems principles to motor development has been especially appropriate because many of the underlying elements that constrain behavior can be specified (e.g., limb length, gravity, muscle-to-fat ratio) (Aslin, 1993). However, in the majority of developmental domains, where constraints on behavior are not as clear, identifying system elements and the range of control parameters driving system reorganizations may not be possible. In addition, the types of analyses necessary for empirical investigations of dynamic systems often require an extensive database (Smith and Thelen, 1993a), the kind of data that are not available for many developmental domains.

The application of dynamic systems perspectives to developmental psychology is in its infancy, however, and much thoughtful discussion of its applications is needed in order to discover its potential for explaining developmental processes. Moreover, dynamic systems principles may serve as a powerful heuristic, even if all of the potential underlying components cannot be specified (Aslin, 1993; Smith and Thelen, 1993b). By applying general dynamic systems principles to different domains of development, researchers can begin to ask new questions about developmental processes (Smith and Thelen, 1993b).

Attachment Theory

One of the developmental domains to which dynamic systems principles may be applicable is infant-parent attachment. For the last quarter of the twentieth century, attachment theory has guided developmental psychologists' thinking about early parent-child relationships and their consequences for sociopersonality development. Attachment theory, pioneered by Bowlby (1969, 1973), borrows principles from psychoanalytic theory, ethology, evolutionary biology, and control systems theory to argue that a warm, supportive relationship with a caregiver promotes psychological well-being in infancy and throughout life. In collaboration with Ainsworth (1973, 1989), Bowlby suggested that differences in the security of the attachment relationship with the primary caregiver influence a child's subsequent relationships with others, as well as the child's self-esteem, self-understanding, and psychological health.

According to attachment theorists, differences in attachment security derive primarily from differences in sensitivity of the caregiver to the infant. Mothers who attend to their infants' signals, who make accurate interpretations of those signals, and who respond appropriately and responsively are believed to foster a secure attachment (Ainsworth, Bell, and Stayton, 1974). Several decades of research have generally supported the notion that mothers who respond more warmly and consistently to their infants' signals are more likely to have infants deemed securely attached, although a significant number of studies have not found this relationship or report inconsistent findings (De Wolff and van IJzendoorn, 1997; Isabella, 1995; Thompson, 1997). Other influences on developing attachment security require consideration, including the child's characteristics, such as temperament. Research examining the relationship between attachment security and temperament, however, reports mixed findings, with some studies reporting relationships between attachment security and certain temperamental dimensions (e.g., negative reactivity) and others finding no such links (see Thompson, 1998).

Attachment security is believed to influence a child's subsequent sociopersonality development in several ways. First, Bowlby (1969, 1973) and others (e.g., Bretherton, 1993; Crittenden, 1992) have emphasized that young children construct "internal working models" out of their interactions with attachment figures. Thus, if a caregiver has responded warmly to a child, protected her, and respected her need for autonomous exploration with support, a child will construct an internal working model of herself as lovable, protected, and capable and will respond to partners with warmth and affection. Second, children acquire social skills and predispositions from attachment relationships with caregivers (Thompson, 1999). Through their rich exchanges with caregivers, securely attached children are acquiring positive, adaptive social competencies that, when generalized to other relationships, allow for further rich exchanges and social growth. Third, attachment security might be linked to subsequent psychosocial functioning because the continuity in caregiving that initially shaped attachment security subsequently contributes to positive personality and social inclinations (Lamb et al., 1985; Thompson, 1999). Lamb and his colleagues (1985) have argued that the sensitivity and responsiveness of parents that initially led to the formation of a secure attachment will also foster healthy social and emotional development if parental sensitivity is subsequently maintained across the child's development.

Empirical studies examining whether attachment security predicts later sociopersonality development yield mixed results, however (Belsky and Cassidy, 1994; Thompson, 1998, 2000). Research has confirmed, for example, that attachment security in infancy forms the foundation for more harmonious subsequent parent-child relationships. Securely attached children show more affective sharing and compliance during free play (Londerville and Main, 1981; Main, 1983), as well as more enthusiasm and positive affect in mutual tasks with their mothers (Frankel and Bates, 1990; Matas, Arend, and Sroufe, 1978). Research findings support the idea that attachment security fosters social skills with unfamiliar partners in certain situations (e.g., Londerville and Main, 1981; Main, 1983; Main and Weston, 1981) but not in others (e.g., Booth, Rose-Krasnor, and Rubin, 1991; Pastor, 1981). Empirical evidence concerning personality differences between secure and insecure children is also inconsistent. In examining ego resiliency, several studies have found that securely attached toddlers and preschoolers receive higher scores on measures of ego resiliency (Arend, Gove, and Sroufe, 1979; Sroufe, 1983), but others have not found this relationship (e.g., Easterbrooks and Goldberg, 1990; Howes, Matheson, and Hamilton, 1994; Oppenheim, Sagi, and Lamb, 1988). Similarly, research concerning the expected relation between insecure attachments and subsequent behavioral problems has provided only limited support for this association (e.g., Bates and Bayles, 1988; Fagot and Kavanagh, 1990).

These modest and inconsistent associations between attachment security and subsequent sociopersonality development may arise for several reasons. First, young children develop emotionally salient attachments to many partners, not just to the mother, including fathers, grandparents, day care teachers, and siblings. These additional attachment relationships also influence the child's internal representations and social skills, contributing to the weak predictive power of attachment assessments with only one caregiver (Thompson, 1998). Attachment theorists have yet to discover how multiple attachment relationships become integrated into a child's internal working models, especially when experiences with different attachment figures are highly divergent (see Howes, 1999). Second, attachment security is not necessarily consistent over time. Often the security of attachment changes, and as a result its influence might not be as enduring as predicted by attachment theory. Although initial studies examining the stability of attachment from twelve to eighteen months found that a high proportion of infants received the same classification at both assessments, more recent studies have found much lower stability rates (see, e.g., Belsky et al., 1996; see also Thompson, 1998). Overall the evidence suggests that attachment security is not necessarily stable over time but may change, for example, in response to changing family circumstances that cause a renegotiation of parent-child relationships (Owen et al., 1984; Thompson, 1998, 2000; Thompson, Lamb, and Estes, 1982).

Therefore, the empirical research generated by the provocative formulations of attachment theory yields findings that are not entirely consistent with theoretical expectations. The expected strong association between sensitive maternal care and a secure attachment is an empirically modest one, and it is possible that infant temperament assumes a direct or moderating role in the formation of a secure attachment. Likewise, the expected strong relations between attachment security and the child's subsequent sociopersonality development (based on the growth of internal working models, the emergence of social skills and predispositions, or continuity in caregivers' sensitivity) are empirically modest or inconsistent, and depend on the nature of the outcome in question. This may derive from the fact that children are influenced by multiple attachment relationships, and that attachments formed in infancy may or may not endure as secure or insecure, but may instead change over time. Because attachment is unquestionably a crucial feature of early sociopersonality growth, the dissonance between theoretical expectations and empirical findings warrants further exploration of whether traditional theoretical formulations offer an adequate picture of the growth and outcomes of parent-infant attachment.

Dynamic systems approaches may offer alternative formulations that can better explain current research findings, and provoke new questions for future study.

Attachment Theory through a Different Lens: Self-Organization

There has been little consideration of the relevance of dynamic systems approaches to an understanding of attachment relationships and processes, which is surprising for several reasons (see, however, Fogel, 1997). First, the formation of attachment bonds is considered to be a *dynamic* process involving a series of interactions between the caregiver and infant through real time (e.g., separations and reunions) and through distinct developmental phases that easily parallel reorganizations in a dynamic systems perspective. Second, attachment has typically been conceptualized as part of a *system* of behavior (including both the infant and the caregiver and their interactive context), and as a system, attachment lends itself well to dynamic systems analyses. Third, one of the greatest contributions of attachment theory to developmental thinking has been the *organizational* view (Sroufe and Waters, 1977) that, guided by functionalist considerations, portrays attachment patterns as organized constellations of behavior intended to achieve the goal of proximity to mother. Such a view is consistent with the dynamic systems portrayal of the developmental self-organization of behavior. Finally, secure and insecure attachments are believed to result in *distinct patterns* of infant behavior that can easily be equated to the attractor patterns proposed by dynamic systems approaches. As a result, dynamic systems approaches may offer some insight into attachment processes. However, it is important to note that a dynamic systems interpretation would depart from traditional attachment theory in conceptualizing attachment as a flexible process that is open to constant reorganization over both real time and developmental time.

The Self-Organization of Attachment

From a dynamic systems approach, attachment processes in the child should show clear reorganizations (and therefore qualitative differences) with development. The premise that attachment is qualitatively reorganized at different periods in life is also consistent with traditional attachment theory, and with emerging new views in this field.

The newborn infant is not born attached. Bowlby (1969) emphasized that the formation of attachment relationships to parents in infancy occurs in several distinct phases. In the first "preattachment" phase (up to three months), according to Bowlby, an infant is indiscriminately responsive to people in the environment. Different partners are interchangeable, and thus the young infant cannot be described as attached to anyone. However, by the second phase of "attachment-in-the-making" (three to six months), the infant begins preferentially responding to familiar caregivers, directing more frequent smiles, reaches, and other signals to them than to other people in the environment. By seven months of age (the beginning of the third, "clear-cut attachment" phase), infants show attachments to caregivers and display active goal-corrected maintenance of proximity to the caregiver through signaling, locomotion, separation protest, and other behavior. Shortly after this time, moreover, individual differences in the organization of attachment behavior can be observed, with significantly different patterns of behavior toward the caregiver distinguishing securely attached infants from insecurely attached infants.

By the end of the first year, therefore, discrete attachment behaviors have become self-organized into (in Bowlby's term) an attachment "behavioral system" in which specific attachment behaviors (smiling, reaching, following, clinging, protesting separation, etc.) are functionally interchangeable in relation to the overall "set goal" of the attachment system (Sroufe and Waters, 1977). Viewed developmentally, Bowlby believed that the progressive organization of specific attachment behaviors into a behavioral system enabled these behaviors to function more flexibly, by contrast with the inflexible manner (resembling fixed-action patterns) in which smiling, reaching, and other attachment behaviors function in younger infants. Bowlby suggested that the set goal of the attachment behavioral system is the achievement of proximity to the caregiver; however, others (e.g., Sroufe and Waters, 1977) have argued that "felt security" may be a better portrayal of its goal. In either case, it is unimportant whether the infant achieves proximity (or feels secure) by reaching to the caregiver, locomoting toward the caregiver, looking to the caregiver while also smiling and vocalizing, or clinging to the caregiver after having been picked up. Because specific attachment behaviors are functionally and flexibly organized in relation to the set goal of the system, it is achieving the goal rather than how it is achieved that is important.

Bowlby and other attachment theorists have had little to say about how specific attachment behaviors become developmentally organized in such a manner, nor is attachment theory clear about how specific attachment behaviors begin to function in an interchangeable manner to accomplish the system's set goal. Bowlby's (1969) cybernetic control-systems formulations used the metaphor of a thermostat or a servomechanism to describe the attachment behavioral system's programmed capacities for behavioral adjustment using goal-corrected feedback from the consequences of its prior actions. In this manner, he believed, the child's attachment behavior is dynamically adjusted to changes in the caregiver's behavior, the presence of unfamiliar people, and related factors. Thus the attachment behavioral system becomes more highly "activated" (i.e., attachment behaviors occur with greater frequency or intensity) if the caregiver departs, a stranger enters, the child becomes frightened, or other circumstances occur that heighten the child's need (i.e., heighten the set goal) for proximity to the caregiver. As proximity is achieved or these other circumstances change, the set goal becomes progressively readjusted, resulting in a diminishing of attachment behavior as the system becomes less active and the child can turn to other activities (e.g., exploring). In Bowlby's ethologically oriented theory, both the behavioral organization and the nature and functioning of the set goal are biologically deeply rooted in the human species, particularly in terms of the importance of proximity-seeking behavior to an infant's protection, nurturance, and learning from caregivers throughout human evolution.

Dynamic systems theorists would argue that attachment theory relies too much on nativistic explanations like these to account for the developmental organization of attachment behavior, and would offer other heuristics as alternative explanations. For example, early in infancy, specific components of the attachment system are likely becoming progressively coupled, or entrained, through the positive feedback generated by their mutual recurrence within the infant-caregiver system (see Lewis, 1997, for a good discussion of coupling). It is important to remember that from a dynamic systems perspective, both the infant and the caregiver are part of the system, inextricably linked to each other in the context of their interactive activity. Consequently, infant behaviors may become coupled (or functionally related) in relation to the positive feedback generated by the caregiver's responsive behavior, the infant's affective reactions with which they are associated, and other components of the infant-parent system. This progressive organization of attachment behavior occurs in concert with the growing complexity and integration of the interactive activity of the infant-caregiver dyad during the first six months of life (see, e.g., Cohn and Tronick, 1987; Fogel et al., 1992; Fogel and Thelen, 1987). Thus, as infants become capable of a broader variety of social signals and of using them with greater intentionality, these behaviors also become progressively organized into attractor states based on how they function within the infant-caregiver system.

It is likely that this early system of attachment-related behavior becomes reorganized several times during the first six months, and an important challenge is to identify the developmental-time control parameters that are relevant to these phase shifts. Candidates include changing characteristics of the baby (growing alertness; enhanced motor coordination; intellectual capacities relevant to distinguishing familiar from unfamiliar people; emotional growth), of the caregiver (changing parental representations of the baby), and of the interactive qualities they share (the onset and growing sophistication of face-to-face play), as well as changes in the broader context of their interactive activity. Other system elements include the infant's temperamental qualities, the caregiver's sensitivity, and family stresses and support. By the time the infant reaches the third phase of "clear-cut attachment," a wide repertoire of attachment behaviors have thus become entrained into what Bowlby conceived as the attachment behavioral system in relation to a particular social partner. Moreover, distinct patterns of entrainment have already begun to characterize the self-organization of attachment for securely attached and insecurely attached infants, based again on characteristics of the baby, the caregiver, their interactive activity, and the context. This means that interpreted from a dynamic systems perspective, the attachment behavioral system by one year of age has assumed different preferred states, or attractors, that attachment theorists recognize as different patterns of secure or insecure attachment behavior. This progressive self-organization of attachment behavior occurs over developmental time in relation to concurrent changes in other infant capabilities.

A dynamic systems perspective may be helpful toward conceptualizing not only the self-organization of attachment across developmental time, but also the micro-organization of attachment behavior in real time. By contrast with Bowlby's cybernetic control-systems formulation, theorists taking a dynamic systems approach might explain the moment-by-moment dynamics of attachment behavior in a one-year-old in the following manner. In any situation, the organization of attachment behavior is sensitive to a set of real-time control parameters that include the distance between parent and baby, the familiarity of the setting, the presence of unfamiliar people or unusual events, the psychological impact of prior (pleasant or unpleasant) experiences, the mother's immediate behavior (including her behavioral sensitivity to the infant's cues), and other factors. A change in any of these real-time control parameters to which the attachment system is sensitive would result in a reorganization of the system: a child who was previously quietly playing with toys, for example, would now abandon them to crawl toward mother and cling to her legs. Other changes in these real-time control parameters could lead to a return of the attachment system to its preferred state (attractor), which will differ across infants who vary in attachment security. Although the cogency of this dynamic systems analysis of attachment behavior in real time depends on the identification and verification of relevant control parameters, it is noteworthy that some attachment theorists have offered speculation on these issues that provides a basis for future work (see Sroufe, Waters, and Matas, 1974). Importantly, such an approach recognizes that it is not only changes in the parent's behavior that can provoke phase shifts in attachment organization, but that other control parameters exist that are intrinsic to the child, the context, or the interaction of parent and child.

To illustrate, consider the organization of an infant's behavior in the Strange Situation, which is the laboratory procedure used to assess individual differences in infant attachment (Ainsworth et al., 1978). Each infant in this procedure could be characterized by preferred attractor states that describe the organization not only of attachment behavior (conventionally portrayed as secure or insecure) but also of other behavioral systems associated with exploration and play, sociability, fear/wariness, and so forth. The control parameters described above are thus pertinent to the organization not only of attachment but also of competing and complementary behaviors. Consequently, changes in control parameters affect multiple attractor states that organize infant behavior: a stranger's entrance into the room may invoke phase transitions into attractor landscapes that can make a previously playful child abruptly clingy to mother and wary of the stranger, but make another previously playful child avoidant of the mother and receptive to the stranger. Dynamic systems formulations offer, in short, rather powerful conceptual tools for conceptualizing the real-time transitions in the organization of infant behavior.

Attachment Patterns as Attractor Patterns

Attachment theory has emphasized individual differences in the patterning of attachment behavior in infancy. Four distinct patterns of attachment behavior have been observed in the Strange Situation. Securely attached infants explore freely in the presence of the mother and use her as a source of comfort upon reunion after brief separations from her. Insecure-avoidant children explore and play without sharing affect with the mother, and they ignore, rebuff, or avoid the mother upon reunion after separations. Insecure-resistant children show little exploration, much wariness, and anger or resistance to the mother upon reunion. Finally, insecure-disorganized infants display no coherent organization of attachment behavior and instead exhibit unusual, inconsistent, or bizarre behavior (such as freezing; or undirected, incomplete, or interrupted movements; or disoriented behavior; see Main and Solomon, 1990).

From a dynamic systems perspective, these four attachment patterns can be conceptualized as attractor states, or the preferred states of the attachment system in a particular context (i.e., with a particular caregiver). To be sure, the incoherent and inconsistent behavior of insecure-disorganized infants may reveal that their attachment system involves multiple unstable attractor patterns, causing the attachment system to fluctuate widely, rapidly shifting between extremely unstable behavioral patterns as the result of small (even random) perturbations. More generally, however, dynamic systems approaches raise important questions concerning the control parameters that determine the attractor state of the attachment system for each particular infant contributing to secure or insecure patterns. From a dynamic systems perspective, parental sensitivity is one of many, potentially functionally equivalent interacting elements of the attachment system; other elements noted earlier include characteristics of the infant (including temperament and age), of the parent (including the adult's attachment representations), and of their context (e.g., marital quality, parental employment). Consistent with attachment formulations, parental sensitivity is best considered a control parameter with critical thresholds that determine which attachment pattern appears. But there may be others, and especially in light of the limited empirical relations between variations in maternal sensitivity and attachment security, further theoretical and empirical exploration of other control parameters is warranted.

When attachment patterns are conceptualized as attractor patterns, a dynamic systems perspective underscores that they are best viewed as flexible adaptations to particular contexts and partners. There is no reason to expect that attachment organization would be consistent for a child's relationship with the mother and with another caregiver (such as a day-care teacher), because the child and partner are each part of the same dynamic system, and therefore there are different system elements that are organized in potentially different ways for each partner. This view is consistent with research evidence that attachment security is generally relationship-specific (Thompson, 1998). For the same reason, there should be no expectation that attachment organization in relation to the same partner would be consistent across significant changes in context, such as changes in family life upon the birth of a new child, marital disruption, or significant changes in parents' work obligations (see, e.g., Davies and Cummings, 1994; Teti et al., 1996; Thompson, 1998). Although the research evidence on the correlates of stability and change in attachment is limited, further examination of these correlates would help to identify additional control parameters that may be related to the reorganization of attachment in the early years of life in a manner that is either independent of, or contributes to, differences in parental sensitivity.

Attractor patterns have various degrees of stability and instability from a dynamic systems viewpoint (Thelen and Smith, 1994). The stability of a particular attractor state may be influenced by various factors, including the nature of the interrelations among its system elements. When systems are prone to reorganization as the result of changes in the system elements, for example, attractors become more unstable (Thelen, 1989). Unstable systems are necessary in order for system elements to be capable of reorganizing to create a better functional match to a particular context or task (Thelen and Smith, 1994). This has several potential implications for the portrayal of attachment patterns as attractor states. First, it enables researchers to look more incisively at certain attachment patterns, such as the insecure-disorganized classification, that may be characterized by multiple unstable attractors. The incoherent, disorganized behavior of infants in this classification may reflect rapid fluctuations between unstable attractor states. Second, it offers a new interpretive context for understanding research findings that indicate, quite consistently, that secure attachments are more stable over time than are insecure attachments (Thompson, 1998). There may be, as Bowlby (1969) believed, inherently stabilizing qualities to secure attachments that derive, from a dynamic systems view, from the fact that they are organizationally more stable systems (i.e., there is a stronger coupling among system elements owing to the prior history of positive parent-infant interactions). Third, periods of reorganization of attachment processes, such as those to be described here, may result in the formation of different attractor states than those that preceded them. Indeed, there is the potential for rather significant changes in attachment patterns during the reorganization of attachment processes, such as in the transition from behavioral to representational attachment forms to be described later.

Later Organizations of Attachment

The self-organization of attachment is thus consistent with Bowlby's (1969) original theory and with dynamic systems formulations, although distinctly different kinds of explanations are offered in each case. To Bowlby and his followers, attachment continues to be reorganized after infancy, although there is less specificity in the relevant developmental processes. According to Bowlby (1969/1982), the fourth and final phase of attachment, which he called the "goal-corrected partnership," emerges around the child's fourth birthday. This phase involves the mutual regulation of the attachment relationship by the parent and child based on their shared understandings, especially of each partner's goals, plans, and other characteristics.

Bowlby's formulation of the fourth phase clearly anticipates the "move to the level of representation" of contemporary attachment theorists. These theorists have focused on the growth and influence of a child's representations (or "internal working models") of relationships, partners, and self that emerge from attachment processes (e.g., Bretherton, 1993; Crittenden, 1992; Main, Kaplan, and Cassidy, 1985). The emphasis on attachment representations has lifespan relevance because it highlights how attachment relationships continue to be important and to evolve across the life course (e.g., Ainsworth, 1989; Kobak and Sceery, 1988). But there has been little systematic consideration within attachment theory about how the attachment behavioral system of infancy becomes developmentally reorganized to become a representational system of postinfancy, and how that representational system is further reorganized as individuals mature through childhood, adolescence, and the early adult years.

Dynamic systems formulations may prove helpful. As earlier noted, dynamic systems approaches focus on uncovering the factors responsible for reorganizations in dynamic systems (i.e., the control parameters and their critical thresholds) and in the variability in preferred behavioral states (i.e., attractors) and in transitions between attractors over time. If we assume that the life course development of attachment processes involves several reorganizations in the attachment system, it is possible to speculate about when these reorganizations may occur. One such transition certainly occurs during Bowlby's fourth phase of attachment, when attachment processes are guided less by behavioral organization and increasingly by representational organization. In other words, the nature of a person's attachment behavior becomes organized less by immediate behavioral contingencies (such as those described earlier) and more by enduring representations of the partner, oneself, and the relationship. From this time forth, attachment is primarily a representational process, and this is a significant reorganization of behavioral forms.

Reorganizations in the attachment system after infancy may occur through changes in the functional goals of the represented attachment relationship. Whereas in infancy the behavioral function of attachment is primarily to maintain proximity to the caregiver and therefore to ensure that the basic physical needs of the baby are satisfied, it is likely that after attachment becomes a representational system, other functions become more prominent. These may include parent-child attachment representations as a basis for predicting the responsiveness and warmth of the caregiver (early childhood), as a secure base for negotiating issues of achievement and competence (middle childhood), for establishing autonomy while maintaining connectedness to the parent (adolescence), and as a foundation for establishing new attachments to a marital partner and, eventually, to one's own offspring (early adulthood). This portrayal of functional changes is admittedly quite speculative, because although there is increasing empirical work concerning attachment in childhood, adolescence, and adulthood, there has been little attention to changes in the functional goals of attachment relationships and their representations. Thus, considerably more theoretical work is required.

Dynamic systems approaches also raise important questions about how attachment becomes developmentally reorganized with respect to its control parameters. As earlier noted, control parameters can cause system phase shifts or reorganizations to occur when they pass critical thresholds, but control parameters may also change with the organization of new behavioral forms. The control parameters that are relevant for reorganizations in attachment representations likely include factors within the child (e.g., advances in representational capabilities, developing self-understanding, puberty), in the caregiver (e.g., changing caregiving roles in relation to the child, changing representations of the child), in their relationship (and the functional contexts in which the parent and child encounter each other), as well as in the broader context (such as the onset of day care or school). Understanding how these control parameters drive development is complicated for several reasons. First, several of these hypothesized control parameters for the developmental reorganization of attachment are likely to be dynamic systems themselves, which change in a heterochronous manner in relation to different control parameters. As noted by Thompson (1998), for example, representations of attachment relationships are influenced by changes in event representation, autobiographical memory, and theory of mind understanding, each of which may be conceptualized as a dynamic system itself. Second, some of the control parameters pertinent to changing attachment representations are likely to be relationship-specific (e.g., a caregiver's changing role with a particular child) and others relationship-general (e.g., developing theory of mind), adding further complexity to this developmental reorganization. Third, the control parameters responsible for the reorganization of attachment may differ at different periods of development (Thelen and Smith, 1994). Therefore, the factors responsible for provoking reorganization of attachment in infancy (e.g., changing representations of others' beliefs and goals) may not be the same as those contributing to subsequent shifts in the representation of attachment in adolescence (e.g., sexual maturity and changing heterosexual relationships).

There is, therefore, considerable need for theoretical exploration of the control parameters relevant to the organization and functioning of attachment representations at different stages of life. These considerations from a dynamic systems perspective are quite important, however, in light of the tendency within attachment theory to generalize the behavioral and representational forms of attachment organization from infancy and early childhood to attachment at later ages. Indeed, it is common to find researchers conceptualizing attachment representations in adolescents and adults in a manner very similar to the classification of behavioral attachment organization in infancy, with an emphasis on security, reliability, and confidence in the warmth and accessibility of an attachment figure (e.g., Kobak and Sceery, 1988; van IJzendoorn, 1995). In contrast, from a dynamic systems viewpoint, there is no necessary reason to expect behavioral or representational forms to be consistent across periods of developmental reorganization. Although each reorganization of the attachment system is constrained by previous organizations, the resulting form may also be qualitatively different and bear no resemblance to the previous form. Thus, from a dynamic systems perspective, there is no compelling theoretical reason to believe that attachment would be manifested or represented in a consistent way throughout life, or have the same meaning or function at each stage in development.

Continuity and Change in Sociopersonality Development

Although dynamic systems are flexible, they are also constrained both by the elements of the system and by previous organizations of the system. Infant-caregiver interaction and the organization of attachment behavior result from the constraints imposed by each partner on the other, as well as by other contextual and organismic constraints, the represented history of their interactions, and cultural and historical influences (Fogel and Branco, 1997; Lyra and Winegar, 1997). In addition, the organization of attachment is also constrained by its prior organizational patterns. In this concept of "cascading constraints," dynamic systems theorists recognize that prior organizations of system elements guide future self-organizations as development proceeds (Lewis, 1997). In this respect, therefore, each new behavioral form that emerges influences the formation of the next, guiding and narrowing subsequent developmental possibilities by increasingly refining and narrowing possible outcomes.

The concept of cascading constraints is harmonious with other developmental approaches, including those of attachment theory. To attachment theorists, the internal representations (or working models) that derive from attachment relationships are believed to impose interpretive filters on experience, guiding how children perceive others and respond to them. As a consequence, children not only construe subsequent experiences in accord with the expectations deriving from their secure or insecure attachments, but also evoke from others the responses that are consistent with these expectations. Secure children provoke affirmative and supportive responses by their positive, sociable behavior, for example, while insecure children confirm their expectations of others' unreliability through their oppositional or indifferent behavior. Over time, therefore, these working models of others become increasingly consolidated as children's experiences (or their interpretations of them) recurrently confirm their representations of self, others, and relationships in general (Bowlby, 1973, 1980; Bretherton, 1993; Sroufe, 1996). At the same time, these increasingly consolidated internal representations affect other developmental processes, including self-concept, personality growth, and behavioral compliance. In this manner, developmental pathways become increasingly channeled over time in relation to past attachment history.

A dynamic systems theorist would agree that later attachment representations both result from prior organizations of attachment processes in the developing child, and help to constrain subsequent reorganizations of attachment. They may also influence other developmental outcomes (such as personality growth). But this developmental process of reorganization is significantly complicated by several other dynamic theoretical considerations. First, attachment representations are likely only one of several system elements that drive the reorganization of later attachment processes (in developmental time). Other system elements might include contemporary relationship influences, current modes of self-representation, the context of the relationship (including broader family influences), and other relationship representations. These system elements may thus exert influences complementary to or competing with those of prior attachment representations on the forces contributing to the reorganization of attachment at later ages. Change as well as continuity vis-à-vis previous organizational forms may result. Second, as earlier noted, attachment representations are also part of broader representational networks that can themselves be conceptualized as dynamic systems with their own system elements and control parameters. Therefore, how they change and the dynamic processes influencing them are likely to be complex, and this complicates an analysis of consistency and change in attachment representations over time and their influence on other developmental processes. At present, neither attachment theory nor dynamic systems formulations offer sufficiently powerful conceptual tools for this analysis, and equally important, critical empirical data are lacking.

In this light, understanding the expected consequences of a secure or insecure attachment in infancy for later behavior and personality is one of the most difficult theoretical challenges facing both attachment theorists and dynamic systems theorists interested in attachment processes. Elucidating this complex question requires a theoretical framework that specifies how attachment representations are influenced by other relational and representational processes (i.e., their system elements), how they change normatively and individually as the result of conceptual growth and life experience (i.e., their control parameters), and the role they assume in later personality functioning, together with other influences (i.e., their functioning as system elements in other dynamic systems). At present, there is no consistent theoretical framework for conceptualizing the later outcomes of attachment security within attachment theory (Belsky and Cassidy, 1994), and this remains a formidable challenge to dynamic systems theorists also. Nevertheless, the inconsistent empirical picture of the consequences of early attachment, together with enticing findings of a lingering effect of attachment on later behavior (Egeland, Carlson, and Sroufe, 1993; Sroufe, Egeland, and Kreutzer, 1990), warrant tackling this theoretical challenge.

Conclusion

Does a dynamic systems interpretation of the determinants and consequences of attachment security better account for the empirical findings than traditional attachment theory? In many respects, it may, but it is too early to draw firm conclusions. Certainly, consistent with dynamic systems formulations, research seems to suggest that rather than being stable and fixed, attachment patterns are *dynamic* and thus more flexible, adaptive, and context-specific than traditional attachment theory would suggest (see Thompson, 1998). In addition, consistent with dynamic systems formulations, research also supports the idea that attachment relationships and processes are reorganized across the lifespan, not only to accommodate the increasing skills of the child, but also to incorporate the changing roles of parents. Finally, dynamic systems approaches offer a potential resolution to the mixed and inconsistent empirical relations among attachment security, maternal sensitivity, and sociopersonality development. From a dynamic systems perspective, relations between elements of a system and the resulting patterns of behavior are not linear, and as a result, the lack of consistent linear relations among these variables is not unexpected. However, to interpret the lack of expected linear relations in the empirical literature as support for a dynamic systems approach is premature, and to do so would be to invoke mostly post hoc explanations (Bloom, 1992; Thelen, 1989).

In order to truly determine the usefulness of a dynamic systems perspective in explaining attachment-related phenomena, research into attachment needs to be reconceptualized using empirical techniques appropriate for examining dynamic systems (see Thelen, 1989, concerning potential research approaches). Unfortunately, although dynamic systems approaches are appealing at the theoretical level, on a practical and empirical level this perspective is often extremely difficult to test, because many of the elements that constrain developmental systems are not known. This is certainly the case for attachment, because attachment processes are complex and the elements that constrain these systems are not clear.

Therefore, the strength of a dynamic systems interpretation of attachment theory may lie not only in its ability to account for puzzling empirical findings, but also in the useful heuristics it offers in portraying attachment processes as dynamic (thus flexible, adaptive, and context-specific) and in emphasizing the periodic reorganization of attachment across life (involving various control parameters that may themselves change with development). Moreover, in describing attachment-related phenomena as part of multiple dynamic systems with complex system elements, dynamic systems views raise new questions about the development of attachment relationships that, while empirically daunting, are conceptually important.

References

Abraham, F. D. (1995). Introduction to dynamics: A basic language; a basic meta-modeling strategy. In F. D. Abraham and A. R. Gilgen (Eds.), *Chaos theory in psychology* (pp. 31–49). Westport, CT: Praeger.

Abraham, F. D., Abraham, R. H., and Shaw, C. D. (1990). *A visual introduction to dynamical systems theory for psychology.* Santa Cruz, CA: Aerial Press.

Abraham, R. H., and Shaw, C. D. (1982). *Dynamics: The geometry of human behavior.* Santa Cruz, CA: Aerial Press.

Ainsworth, M. D. (1973). The development of infant-mother attachment. In B. Caldwell and H. Riccuti (Eds.), *Review of child development research* (vol. 3, pp. 1–94). Chicago: University of Chicago Press.

Ainsworth, M. D. (1989). Attachments beyond infancy. *American Psychologist, 44,* 709–716.

Ainsworth, M. D., Bell, S. M., and Stayton, D. J. (1974). Infant-mother attachment and social development: Socialization as a product of reciprocal responsiveness to signals. In M. P. Richards (Ed.), *The integration of the child into a social world* (pp. 99–135). Cambridge: Cambridge University Press.

Ainsworth, M. D., Blehar, M. C., Waters, E., and Wall, S. (1978). *Patterns of attachment.* Hillsdale, NJ: Erlbaum.

Arend, R., Gove, F. L., and Sroufe, L. A. (1979). Continuity of individual adaptation from infancy to kindergarten: A predictive study of ego-resiliency and curiosity in preschoolers. *Child Development, 50,* 950–959.

Aslin, R. N. (1993). Commentary: The strange attractiveness of dynamic systems to development. In L. Smith and E. Thelen (Eds.), *A dynamic systems approach to development: Applications* (pp. 385–399). Cambridge, MA: MIT Press.

Bates, J. E., and Bayles, K. (1988). Attachment and the development of behavior problems. In J. Belsky and T. Nezworski (Eds.), *Clinical implications of attachment* (pp. 253–299). Hillsdale, NJ: Erlbaum.

Belsky, J., Campbell, S. B., Cohn, J. F., and Moore, G. (1996). Instability of infant-parent attachment security. *Developmental Psychology, 32,* 921–924.

Belsky, J., and Cassidy, J. (1994). Attachment: Theory and evidence. In M. Rutter and D. Hay (Eds.), *Development through life* (pp. 373–402). Oxford: Blackwell.

Bloom, L. (1992). Commentary on Fogel, A., et al. (1992): Patterns are not enough. *Social Development, 1,* 143–146.

Booth, C. L., Rose-Krasnor, L., and Rubin, K. H. (1991). Relating preschoolers' social competence and their mothers' parenting behaviors to early attachment security and high-risk status. *Journal of Social and Personal Relationships, 8,* 363–382.

Bowlby, J. (1969). *Attachment and loss: Vol. 1. Attachment.* New York: Basic Books.

Bowlby, J. (1973). *Attachment and loss: Vol. 2. Separation: Anxiety and anger.* New York: Basic Books.

Bowlby, J. (1980). *Attachment and loss: Vol. 3. Loss: Sadness and depression.* New York: Basic Books.

Bretherton, I. (1993). From dialogue to internal working models: The co-construction of self in relations. In C. Nelson (Ed.), *Minnesota Symposium on Child Psychology: Vol. 26. Memory and affect in development* (pp. 237–263). Hillsdale, NJ: Erlbaum.

Butterworth, G. (1993). Dynamic approaches to infant perception and action: Old and new theories about the origins of knowledge. In L. Smith and E. Thelen (Eds.), *A dynamic systems approach to development: Applications* (pp. 171–188). Cambridge, MA: MIT Press.

Camras, L. A. (1992). Expressive development and basic emotions. *Cognition and Emotion, 6,* 269–283.

Cohn, J. F., and Tronick, E. Z. (1987). Mother-infant face-to-face interaction: The sequence of dyadic states at 3, 6, and 9 months. *Developmental Psychology, 23,* 68–77.

Crittenden, P. M. (1992). Quality of attachment in the preschool years. *Development and Psychopathology, 4,* 209–241.

Davies, P. T., and Cummings, E. M. (1994). Marital conflict and child adjustment: An emotional security hypothesis. *Psychological Bulletin, 116,* 387–411.

De Wolff, M., and van IJzendoorn, M. H. (1997). Sensitivity and attachment: A meta-analysis on parental antecedents of infant attachment. *Child Development, 68,* 571–591.

Easterbrooks, M. A., and Goldberg, W. A. (1990). Security of toddler-parent attachment: Relation to children's sociopersonality functioning during kindergarten. In M. T. Greenberg, D. Cicchetti, and E. M. Cummings (Eds.), *Attachment in the preschool years* (pp. 221–244). Chicago: University of Chicago Press.

Egeland, B., Carlson, E., and Sroufe, L. A. (1993). Resilience as process. *Development and Psychopathology, 5,* 517–528.

Fagot, B. I., and Kavanagh, K. (1990). The prediction of antisocial behavior from avoidant attachment classifications. *Child Development, 61,* 864–873.

Fogel, A. (1997). A relational perspective on attachment. In W. Koops, J. Hoeksma, and D. van den Boom (Eds.), *Development of interaction and attachment: Traditional and nontraditional approaches* (pp. 219–232). Amsterdam: Elsevier.

Fogel, A., and Branco, A. U. (1997). Metacommunication as a source of indeterminism in relationship development. In A. Fogel, M. C. Lyra, and J. Valsiner (Eds.), *Dynamics and indeterminism in developmental and social processes* (pp. 65–92). Mahwah, NJ: Erlbaum.

Fogel, A., Lyra, M. C., and Valsiner, J. (1997). Introduction: Perspectives on indeterminism and development. In A. Fogel, M. C. Lyra, and J. Valsiner (Eds.), *Dynamics and indeterminism in developmental and social processes* (pp. 1–12). Mahwah, NJ: Erlbaum.

Fogel, A., Nwokah, E., Dedo, J. Y., Messinger, D., Dickson, K. L., Matusov, E., and Holt, S. A. (1992). Social process theory of emotion: A dynamic systems approach. *Social Development, 1,* 122–142.

Fogel, A., and Thelen, E. (1987). Development of early expressive and communicative action: Reinterpreting the evidence from dynamic systems perspective. *Developmental Psychology, 23,* 747–761.

Frankel, K. A., and Bates, J. E. (1990). Mother-toddler problem solving: Antecedents in attachment, home behavior and temperament. *Child Development, 61,* 810–819.

Goerner, S. J. (1995). Chaos and deep ecology. In F. D. Abraham and A. Gilgen (Eds.), *Chaos theory in psychology* (pp. 3–18). Westport, CT: Praeger.

Howes, C. (1999). Attachment relationships in the context of multiple caregivers. In J. Cassidy and P. Shaver (Eds.), *Handbook of attachment* (pp. 671–687). New York: Guilford.

Howes, C., Matheson, C. C., and Hamilton, C. E. (1994). Maternal, teacher, and child care history correlates of children's relationships with peers. *Child Development, 65*, 264–273.

Isabella, R. A. (1995). The origins of infant-mother attachment: Maternal behavior and infant development. In R. Vasta (Ed.), *Annals of child development* (vol. 10, pp. 57–82). London: Kingsley.

Kauffman, S. A. (1993). *The origins of order.* New York: Oxford University Press.

Keating, D. P. (1990). Charting pathways to the development of expertise. *Educational Psychologist, 25*, 243–267.

Kelso, J. A., Ding, M., and Schoner, G. (1993). Dynamic pattern formation: A primer. In L. Smith and E. Thelen (Eds.), *A dynamic systems approach to development: Applications* (pp. 151–170). Cambridge, MA: MIT Press.

Kobak, R. R., and Sceery, A. (1988). Attachment in late adolescence: Working models, affect regulation, and representations of self and others. *Child Development, 59*, 135–146.

Lamb, M. E., Thompson, R. A., Gardner, W., and Charnov, E. L. (1985). *Infant-mother attachment.* Hillsdale, NJ: Erlbaum.

Lewis, M. D. (1995). Cognition-emotion feedback and the self-organization of developmental paths. *Human Development, 38*, 71–102.

Lewis, M. D. (1997). Personality self-organization: Cascading constraints on cognition-emotion interaction. In A. Fogel, M. C. Lyra, and J. Valsiner (Eds.), *Dynamics and indeterminism in developmental and social processes* (pp. 193–216). Mahwah, NJ: Erlbaum.

Londerville, S., and Main, M. (1981). Security of attachment, compliance, and maternal training methods in the second year of life. *Developmental Psychology, 17*, 289–299.

Lyra, M. C., and Winegar, L. T. (1997). Processual dynamics of interaction through time: Adult-child interactions and process of development. In A. Fogel, M. C. Lyra, and J. Valsiner (Eds.), *Dynamics and indeterminism in developmental and social processes* (pp. 93–110). Mahwah, NJ: Erlbaum.

Madore, B. F., and Freedman, W. L. (1987). Self-organizing structures. *American Scientist, 75*, 252–259.

Main, M. (1983). Exploration, play, and cognitive functioning related to infant-mother attachment. *Infant Behavior and Development, 6*, 167–174.

Main, M., Kaplan, N., and Cassidy, J. (1985). Security in infancy, childhood, and adulthood: A move to the level of representation. In I. Bretherton and E. Waters (Eds.), *Growing points of attachment theory and research. Monographs of the Society for Research in Child Development, 50* (1–2, serial no. 209), pp. 66–104.

Main, M., and Solomon, J. (1990). Patterns for identifying infants as disorganized/disoriented during Ainsworth's Strange Situation. In M. Greenberg, D. Cicchetti, and E. M. Cummings (Eds.), *Attachment in the preschool years* (pp. 121–160). Chicago: University of Chicago Press.

Main, M., and Weston, D. R. (1981). The quality of the toddler's relationship to mother and to father: Related to conflict behavior and the readiness to establish new relationships. *Child Development, 52*, 932–940.

Matas, L., Arend, R., and Sroufe, L. A. (1978). Continuity of adaptation in the second year: The relationship between quality of attachment and later competence. *Child Development, 49*, 547–556.

Oppenheim, D., Sagi, A., and Lamb, M. E. (1988). Infant-adult attachment on the kibbutz and their relation to socioemotional development 4 years later. *Developmental Psychology, 24*, 427–433.

Owen, M. T., Easterbrooks, M. A., Chase-Lansdale, L., and Goldberg, W. A. (1984). The relation between maternal employment status and the stability of attachments to mother and father. *Child Development, 55*, 1894–1901.

Oyama, S. (1985). *The ontogeny of information: Developmental systems and evolution*. Cambridge: Cambridge University Press.

Pastor, D. L. (1981). The quality of mother-infant attachment and its relationship to toddlers' initial sociability with peers. *Developmental Psychology, 17*, 326–335.

Prigogine, I. (1980). *From being to becoming*. San Francisco: Freeman.

Rosser, R. (1994). *Cognitive development: Psychological and biological perspectives*. Boston: Allyn and Bacon.

Smith, L. B. (1995). Self-organizing processes in learning to learn new words: Development is not induction. In C. A. Nelson (Ed.), *Minnesota Symposium on Child Psychology: Vol. 28. New perspectives on learning and development* (pp. 1–32). New York: Academic Press.

Smith, L. B., and Thelen, E. (1993a). From the dynamics of motor skill to the dynamics of development. In L. Smith and E. Thelen (Eds.), *A dynamic systems approach to development: Applications* (pp. 1–12). Cambridge, MA: MIT Press.

Smith, L. B., and Thelen, E. (1993b). Can dynamic systems theory be usefully applied in areas other than motor development? In L. Smith and E. Thelen (Eds.), *A dynamic systems approach to development: Applications* (pp. 151–170). Cambridge, MA: MIT Press.

Sroufe, L. A. (1983). Infant-caregiver attachment and patterns of adaptation in preschool: The roots of maladaptation and competence. In M. Perlmutter (Ed.), *Minnesota Symposium on Child Psychology: Vol. 16. Development and policy concerning children with special needs* (pp. 41–83). Hillsdale, NJ: Erlbaum.

Sroufe, L. A. (1996). *Emotional development*. New York: Cambridge University Press.

Sroufe, L. A., Egeland, B., and Kreutzer, T. (1990). The fate of early experience following developmental change: Longitudinal approaches to individual adaptation in childhood. *Child Development, 61*, 1363–1373.

Sroufe, L. A., and Waters, E. (1977). Attachment as an organizational construct. *Child Development, 48*, 1184–1199.

Sroufe, L. A., Waters, E., and Matas, L. (1974). Contextual determinants of infant affective response. In M. Lewis and L. Rosenblum (Eds.), *The origins of fear* (pp. 49–72). New York: Wiley.

Teti, D. M., Salkin, J., Kucera, E., Corns, K. M., and Das Eisen, R. (1996). And baby makes four: Predictors of attachment security among preschool-aged firstborns during the transition to siblinghood. *Child Development, 67*, 579–596.

Thelen, E. (1984). Learning to walk: Ecological demands and phylogenetic constraints. In L. Lipsitt (Ed.), *Advances in infancy research* (vol. 3, pp. 213–250). Norwood, NJ: Ablex.

Thelen, E. (1985). Developmental origins of motor coordination: Leg movements in human infants. *Developmental Psychobiology, 18*, 1–22.

Thelen, E. (1989). Self-organization in developmental processes: Can systems approaches work? In M. R. Gunnar and E. Thelen (Eds.), *Minnesota Symposium on Child Psychology: Vol. 22. Systems and development* (pp. 77–118). Hillsdale, NJ: Erlbaum.

Thelen, E. (1992). Development as a dynamic system. *Current Directions in Psychological Science, 1*, 189–193.

Thelen, E., and Smith, L. B. (1994). *A dynamic approach to the development of cognition and action*. Cambridge, MA: Bradford/MIT Press.

Thompson, R. A. (1997). Sensitivity and security: New questions to ponder. *Child Development, 68*, 595–597.

Thompson, R. A. (1998). Early sociopersonality development. In W. Damon (series ed.) and N. Eisenberg (vol. ed.), *Handbook of child psychology: Vol. 3. Social, emotional, and personality development* (5th ed., pp. 25–104). New York: Wiley.

Thompson, R. A. (1999). Early attachment and later behavior. In J. Cassidy and P. Shaver (Eds.), *Handbook of attachment* (pp. 265–286). New York: Guilford.

Thompson, R. A. (2000). The legacy of early attachments. *Child Development, 71*, 145–152.

Thompson, R. A., Lamb, M. E., and Estes, D. (1982). Stability of infant-mother attachment and its relationship to changing life circumstances in an unselected middle-class sample. *Child Development, 53*, 144–148.

van Geert, P. (1994). *Dynamic systems of development: Change between complexity and chaos*. New York: Harvester Wheatsheaf.

van IJzendoorn, M. H. (1995). The association between adult attachment representations and infant attachment, parental responsiveness, and clinical status: A meta-analysis on the predictive validity of the Adult Attachment Interview. *Psychological Bulletin, 111*, 404–410.

12 The Dynamics of Emotion-Related Behaviors in Infancy

Carolina de Weerth and Paul van Geert

The maintenance, production, and transformation of stable organism-environment systems require an intricate organization of the organism's behavior. In man as in many other species, emotions are an essential part of the behavioral system. They play a crucial role as evaluative classifiers or categorizers of states and events, as signals to oneself or to conspecifics, all in the service of generalized appropriate action on the vagaries of an only partially predictable and manageable environment. Emotions are not just internal states. On the contrary, they should be viewed as internal reactions that an organism has learned to observe or detect within itself and within other organisms, in principle conspecifics and related species. Thus, the outward expression of emotions has important signal value. Especially in social species, where the maintenance of a successful organism-environment system depends on the regulation of action among members of a social group, emotional expressions are vital signals of the internal states of individuals.

A particular and biologically extremely important social bond is that between a young infant and its primary caregivers, simply because most neonates cannot survive without the care of their elders, and – in our own and related species – the care of the mother in particular. The questions one may ask are: to what extent are emotions important in the behavioral system that specifies the way in which neonates and young infants are cared for and nurtured and, second, how do emotions contribute to the establishment and transformation of this behavioral system? Human infants, for instance, must be able to signal that they are either satisfied or feel discomfort, in order for the parent to decide what action should be undertaken. This notion of emotion-related behaviors, such as crying and smiling, as signals of internal states that are interpreted by caregivers as appeals for specific actions, such as feeding and changing diapers, is more

324

or less the core of what one may call the "standard view" of the role of emotions in mother-infant – or parent-infant – interaction. The problem with this standard view is that it implies a high level of stability and organization from the start. That is, it presupposes the functioning of a set of rules, such as "if the infant feels discomfort, he will start fretting and fussing," "if the infant feels great discomfort, he will cry," "if he feels happy, he will smile," and so forth. It is beyond doubt that these rules, whatever their nature, capture a considerable part of the regularities and stabilities behind infant behavior, and consequently, behind mother-infant interaction. The problem is, however, that the relation between the internal state ("feeling discomfort") and the consequent expression of the state ("crying") is not a rigid system. It is a dynamic pattern whose dynamics occur on different time scales.

At the short-term scale of action time, an expression and its corresponding emotion are the result of an on-line assembly process (Camras, this volume). Assume, for example, that a baby has just been fed, is sitting on his mother's lap, has wetted his diapers, and is thus resting on a slowly cooling and increasingly irritating volume of moist cloth. Is he feeling discomfort or not? Will he indeed start crying, and when will he do so? The actual moment at which the infant begins to cry (like the intensity and duration of the crying) will of course depend on person-specific levels of irritability and additional temperamental characteristics, but also on purely accidental factors and variable state factors. Another point that contributes to the variability in the expression of emotions is the fact that, in young infants, the concordance between facial expression and underlying emotion is considerably less fixed than in older subjects (Camras, 1994, this volume). Facial expressions that suggest certain emotions may thus be based on entirely different conditions than the emotion that they are supposed to indicate.

At the long-term scale of developmental time, the dynamics of emotion takes the form of changes in the relationship between emotions and their expression (Camras, 1994, this volume); in the pattern of emotions (Lewis, 1993); in the psychological structure of emotions, for instance, with regard to the importance of cognition (Lewis, 1995; Malatesta et al., 1989; Sroufe, 1979); and in the social functioning of emotions, for instance, in the process of attachment formation (Malatesta et al., 1989).

This long-term dynamics of emotional development has often been interpreted as the socialization of emotions, but the latter notion emphasizes the socially malleable nature of emotions and underestimates the self-organizational and interactive aspects of the process. An important aspect of this long-term process is the differentiation of the emotional repertoire (Lewis, 1995), which thus refers to an increase in terms of qualitative diversity. On the other hand, however, emotional development in infancy shows a decrease in the frequency of intense emotions (Bridges, 1932). In addition, emotional expressivity becomes less frequent and less variable (Malatesta et al., 1989, p. 7). In summary, early emotional development is characterized by three tendencies: first, an increase in qualitative diversity; second, a decrease in quantitative bandwidth; and third, an increase in social uniformity and interpretability.

In our view, these three tendencies are dynamically linked. This dynamical link can be better understood by reckoning with an evolutionary consideration, namely that the early emotional system has a primary survival function, which is to draw and maintain the mother's and conspecifics' care and attention. In view of the relative neurological immaturity of the human infant, we expect to find functional systems in the young infant that are still relatively unstructured (Touwen, 1976). Such systems tend to be highly variable within and between subjects, which also means that they are highly idiosyncratic. In order to be biologically functional, they must be simple. For instance, they must consist of a mixture of basically positive and basically negative emotions (Belsky, Hsieh, and Crnic, 1996). Also, as Camras (1994, this volume) argues, early emotional expressions are more strongly under the influence of accidental contextual factors than those occurring during later infancy. It is thus more likely that such contextual accidents will lead to episodes of emotional expressivity that are difficult for caregivers to ''explain'' or understand and will thus produce uncertainty and evoke a wide range of emotional responses.

In summary, it is likely that the early emotional pattern of infants is a naturally emerging property of their early neurological and biobehavioral state of relative immaturity and that this emergent property is evolutionarily functional. The major property of that early emotional state is that it combines a narrow qualitative bandwidth with a broad quantitative bandwidth. The latter implies not only a broad quantitative range of emotional intensities but also a high degree of variability across time in the same infant. The result of the social interactions that such an emotional system is likely to produce is, in fact, the opposite of this starting point, namely an emotional system with a considerably increased qualitative bandwidth and a considerably decreased quantitative bandwidth that is much more predictable and easier to manipulate. Note, however, that the magnitude of this variability is not similar across all infants. Differences in that magnitude may in fact constitute an important temperamental feature, although it should also be noted that such temperamental features are far less stable than is often assumed (Plomin et al., 1993).

If the outward expression of emotions is indeed variable, how does this affect the effectiveness of the system and the development of the mother-infant relationship? A crucial issue here, and one which will be discussed in following sections of this chapter, is the amount of variability, both within and between infants, that is socially and biologically tolerable or functional. There exist complicated interactions between the infant's and the mother's response styles (van den Boom, 1988); moreover, the good-ness-of-fit model predicts that the developmental outcome will be strongly mediated by the match between the infant's and the mother's emotional and behavioral styles (Lerner and Lerner, 1987). Variability would provide a wide range of emotional and behavioral options that would enable mother and infant to establish a relationship that optimally suits their needs. The process by which such a relational pattern emerges is most likely of a self-organizational nature, as will be seen in the following section.

Variability and Structure from a Dynamic Systems Point of View

The theory of (nonlinear) dynamics provides a general approach to chang-ing and developing systems (Fogel, Lyra, and Valsiner, 1997; Lewis, 1995, 1996; Newell and Molenaar, 1998; Port and van Gelder, 1995; Smith and Thelen, 1993; Thelen and Smith, 1994; Vallacher and Nowak, 1994; van Geert, 1994). It describes the structure and processes of those systems by specifying general formal principles of change and interaction at the most abstract possible level. One of its advantages is that it allows both for a formal, mathematical description of those principles as well as for a meta-phorical and visual description that captures the major properties of the formalisms.

In our own work in the field of dynamic systems modeling (van Geert, 1991, 1994, 1998), we have explored an approach that is highly reminiscent of ecology. Any system of discernible components that constitute a self-maintained structure shows relationships of mutual support or competition based on a principle of limited resources. The nature of those relationships explains the dynamics and stability of the structure at issue. For instance, the notion of facial expressions of emotion as coordinative motor structures (Camras, this volume) can easily be understood in terms of this ecological dynamics approach. Camras shows how early facial expressions self-organize as a result of recruitment relationships: specific motor components recruit other components, based on synergy, and spontaneously establish adaptive and semistable motor patterns that need not be predefined in the system. Similar principles of self-organization can be applied on a different level, namely that of the interaction between infant and mother in the course of early development (see van Geert, 1996, for an application to attachment). If a system starts with a high level of variability and a structure of synergies and antisynergies applies among the components, it rapidly constrains its own degrees of freedom and settles into an attractor state. Which state this will be depends on various factors, more specifically the nature of the synergies and coincidental factors and events, especially those that occur during critical states (van Geert, 1998). Stated in the metaphor of epigenetic landscapes, high variability means that the developmental valley is broad and shallow, which implies that any external force or perturbation will have a large effect on the state of the system that only slowly damps out. The long-term result of synergetic interactions in such a shallow landscape is that the landscape is molded into one or a few deeper valleys, which act as stable attractors. Such stable attractors show considerably less variability than the shallow landscape of the initial state. A more formal approach to the molding of attractor landscapes is offered by catastrophe theory (Gilmore, 1981; Savelsbergh, van der Maas, and van Geert, 1999; van der Maas, 1993; van der Maas and Molenaar, 1992).

One may ask oneself which initial balance between stability and variability is optimal for a developing infant, given conditions that occur in specific, real-life systems. If applied to the domain of emotion-related behaviors, a low amount of variability would be functional because it would make the behavior of the child extremely predictable to the mother. However, under these circumstances the behavior is most likely not significantly affected by environmental influences, which implies that the emotional-behavioral system is a relatively closed system. If such a closed, protected system is functionally adapted to its environment from the beginning, its closed nature prevents it from unwanted drift, due to, for instance, merely coincidental events. However, if such a closed and protected system is not well adapted from the start, it has only little chance to adapt itself in the relatively short time that is required to establish a strong emotional bond between infant and caregiver, which guarantees stable care.

On the other hand, if variability is high, the child's emotion-related behavior is relatively unpredictable, which could result in uncertainty on the side of the mother. Every mother has the intention of controlling the behavior of her infant to a certain extent. A mother wants to know that if an infant has been fed, he's satisfied, if an infant has slept, he's rested, if an infant has been changed, he's comfortable, and so forth, and that all these small things contribute to the infant's normal development. Although unpredictability would produce feelings of uncertainty, it would only be a major problem in cases in which a mother has extreme tendencies to control.

In normal development, the young infant's behavior is basically controlled by a biological pattern of levels of alertness, ranging from deep sleep to a fully alert state (Fogel, 1991). Moreover, the communication channels that the infant has to rely on consist of few "tools" or means of communication, which implies that the infant, in order to communicate efficiently, has to rely on more dramatic quantitative changes in the components of emotion-related behaviors, that is, on high variability. At the same time, the behavioral variability produces a wide range of possible reaction patterns, which are then open to functional selection. In the end, this initial level of high variability will most likely lead to a pattern of mother-infant behavioral regulation that is optimally stable and reasonably adapted to the temperamental, personal, and contextual factors of the particular mother-infant relationship, that is, stable attractors will have developed. Thus, the result of this self-organizational process is most likely a pattern that is considerably more stable than the initial range of variability, but that is also idiosyncratic and different from that of other mother-infant pairs.

Summarizing, the factors that will influence the development of emotion-related behavior in the infant are, first, the enrichment of the repertoire of outward expressions of emotions, based on developments in the cognitive as well as the sensorimotor and language domains. Second, development consists of an increasing fine-tuning of the interactions between mother and infant. Note that the behavioral variability of the infant at the beginning does not necessarily mean that the relation between the infant's behavior and the mother's reaction is also variable and unstable. For example, the fact that the amount of crying can vary from day to day does not imply that the mother's reaction to crying will also vary. Thus, patterns between mother and infant behaviors can be stable while the infant's behaviors are quantitatively variable and unstable. However, due to the rapidly developing nature of the system, it is not far-fetched to expect changes over time in the patterns of relations between infant and mother behaviors. Also, it is possible that at an early age changes occur on a more frequent basis, producing shorter periods of stability in patterns than those occurring later in development.

Based on this, we predict first that intraindividual variability in quantities of emotion-related behaviors will be considerably higher during the first months of life than at a later stage. Second, we predict that the structural pattern of associations between emotion-related behaviors will undergo considerable change during the first fifteen months of life, resulting in individual patterns that reflect the idiosyncratic trajectories of any particular mother-infant dyad.

From Initial High Variability to Later Stabilization

Studies of Stability and Variability

Students of infant emotions and temperament have invested a great deal of effort in the search for stable features in early development that can reliably predict later developmental characteristics of the infant and child. Also, considerable attention has been given to identifying environmental variables that correlate with specific infant behaviors, such as, for example, identifying the influence of maternal strategies on infant crying. However, the results of these studies often indicate the predictive value of early behavioral characteristics to be low or at the most moderate, and too often show important variability in repeated measures. For example, low stability was found between behavioral observations of difficult behavior in infants between days 2 and 5 of life (St. James-Roberts and Wolke, 1988), and between days 2/4 and weeks 4/5 (Worobey, 1986); for infant temperamental characteristics between months 1 and 3 (Crockenberg and Smith, 1982) and from newborn to 9–12 months (Isabella, Ward, and Belsky, 1985; Peters-Martin and Wachs, 1984; Worobey and Blajda, 1989); and, finally, for infant explorative behavior and positive and negative vocalizations between months 2 and 5 (Bornstein and Tamis-LeMonda, 1990).

Instability in these cases refers to discontinuous scores on tests or observations, produced by variability in an infant's behavior. It is generally either not recognized or ignored, or is seen as the result of measurement errors or environmental factors such as caregiving (Fish, Stifter, and Belsky, 1991), and is generally considered in a somewhat negative light. The fact that this instability in scores could be produced by a high and perfectly normal degree of variability in infant behavior has not often been explored or even recognized. Exceptions to this are a number of studies that have found evidence for day-to-day and week-to-week behavioral variability in infants, and have interpreted it as a normal component of infant development. These are studies on motor and mental development (Freedland and Bertenthal, 1994; McCall, Eichorn, and Hogarty, 1977), on crying (Barr, 1990; Rebelsky and Black, 1972; St. James-Roberts and Halil, 1991) and on crying, fretting/fussing, smiling, and time spent in bodily contact with the mother (de Weerth, van Geert, and Hoitjink, 1999).

Further examples of studies that report intraindividual variability in infant behavior are those on temperamental characteristics (Crockenberg and Smith, 1982; Isabella et al., 1985; Peters-Martin and Wachs, 1984; Worobey and Blajda, 1989), on behavior related to emotions (Belsky, Gilstrap, and Rovine, 1984; Bornstein and Tamis-LeMonda, 1990; Fish et al., 1991; St. James-Roberts and Wolke, 1988; Worobey, 1986), on visual behavior (Canfield et al., 1995; Wachs, Morrow, and Slabach, 1990), on play behavior (Tamis-LeMonda and Bornstein, 1991) and on sleeping and waking patterns (Dittrichova et al., 1992).

The aforementioned studies report variability in infant behavior, but we are also interested in the (in)stability shown by the mother in her interactions with the infant. Studies of mothers of older children and adolescents have found evidence of stability in parental practices and attitudes over time (e.g., Hock and Lindamood, 1981; McNally, Eisenberg, and Harris, 1991), although parents naturally adjust to different ages and situations in interactions (Rogoff, Ellis, and Gardner, 1984). However, studies of mothers of young infants show both stability and changes in maternal behavior. For example, both modest stability and instability of maternal behavior were found with respect to different aspects of promptness of response to infant crying across the first nine months (Hubbard and van IJzendoorn, 1991), while no stability was found in maternal responsiveness between the first and last quarter of the first year (Crockenberg and McCluskey, 1986) or in sensitive responsivity and rejection between one and nine months (Isabella, 1993). Moderate stability in responsiveness was found between three and nine months (Fish and Crockenberg, 1981) and between five and ten months of age (Stifter and Braungart, 1992). St. James-Roberts, Conroy, and Wilsher (1998) found substantial changes rather than stabilities in maternal behavior between the infants' ages of six weeks and five months. They interpreted these changes as following declines in infant crying over this age period. Schölmerich and collaborators (1995) found stability in only three out of eight maternal behaviors between seven and ten months of age of the infant. Tamis-LeMonda and Bornstein (1991) observed mother-infant play behavior at thirteen and twenty months of age, and found that although mothers change their overall level of play between these ages, they maintain their relative status in play sophistication. In addition, Fish and Stifter (1995) report modest stability in maternal sensitivity and intrusiveness in play behavior at the infant's ages of five and ten months. Finally, Belsky and his colleagues (1984) found stability of diverse caregiver behaviors between three and nine months, but not between one and three or between one and nine months. These authors attribute the changes to an infant's greatly fluctuating behavioral states in the first months, which can cause him or her to behave very differently from day to day and week to week, thus obliging the parents to respond to these changes and thereby to display instability.

In summary, the present overview of the literature, which consists almost exclusively of studies that have relied on two, three, or four assessment points and not on frequent measurements of behavior, clearly suggests that we should expect considerable intraindividual variability in young infants. The questions that we want to address are, first, does this conclusion also hold for the emotion-related behaviors observed in our own empirical study, and, second, is there any developmentally relevant change in this variability across the first year of life?

The Concept of Dynamic (In)stability

The main question that should be answered before proceeding to the data, however, is: can we provide a statistically valid specification for "significant intraindividual variability" as opposed to "intraindividual stability"? It is trivial that we will never expect to find levels of crying, smiling, fretting or fussing, and bodily contact that are the same from week to week. Emotions and their behavioral expressions are context- and situation-specific, and these contexts and situations are variable. The questions that we want to answer, however, are whether the levels vary substantially (i.e., produce differing developmental pathways with low assessment frequencies) and whether there is any systematic change in the amount of intraindividual variability across the first fifteen months of life. More precisely, we want to know whether emotion-related behaviors evolve from an initial state of considerable instability and fluctuation to a relatively stable state, that is, a more or less stabilized reaction to fluctuating conditions and situations. In principle, there are many different ways to answer this question. Preferably, our answer should involve a method that enables us to categorize data series into a set of unstable patterns and a set of stable patterns and to do so in a statistically reliable way.

The approach used to study intrinsic variability in the data series of observed behaviors (denoted by y) of the present project, was based on the following line of reasoning. Let us assume that each infant, instead of being observed every week, had been observed every other week by two different observers. We can now think of two "possible worlds." In world

O (the "world" of the odd weeks) the infant has been observed in weeks 1, 3, 5, 7.... In world E (the even weeks), the same infant has been observed in weeks 2, 4, 6, 8.... The two possible observers have a limited access to the "real" data series, which we can operationally define as the data series that we have found by making observations during weeks 1, 2, 3, 4, 5.... We shall now define a process that is dynamically stable under sampling frequency *f* as one in which the underlying processes estimated by observers O and E, respectively, are similar. Or, to put it differently, if the behavior at issue is dynamically stable, the developmental trend expressed by the data from the odd weeks should not differ from the trend expressed by the data from the even weeks.

In order to determine this we employed longitudinal data sets from four babies, each consisting of more than sixty weekly observations of behavioral indicators of emotion, namely crying, fretting/fussing, bodily contact, and smiling (de Weerth and van Geert, 1998). For each child, the observations covered an age range between birth and fifteen months.

Changes in the Dynamic Stability of Emotion-Related Behaviors

Hypotheses. In the theoretical introduction we discussed the likelihood of a developmental pattern of high initial variability that gradually stabilizes. With the objective of studying the hypothesized decline in variability and of using data series with a number of data points that more closely resemble those found in the literature, the fifteen-month observation period was divided into three periods of approximately five months. We predicted that, due to intrinsic variability, significant differences would be found between two alternating series of biweekly observations of one and the same infant. These differences would be greater for young infants (first two periods) and tend to disappear with age (last period).

Since "smiling" is not totally established in the first period (i.e., the infants are still in the process of learning to smile), it is not unreasonable to speculate that the intrinsic variability in smiling in the period from birth to five months will be obscured by a strong developmental trend. Therefore, we predicted that only in the second study period would significant differences be found in smiling between two alternating series of biweekly observations of one and the same infant.

Statistical Design. How can we investigate whether the even weeks provide a different trend than the odd weeks, that is, whether the behavior is dynamically unstable? In order to answer this question, we first applied a quadratic regression analysis for each of the observed variables, based only on the odd weeks. We then repeated that analysis with the even weeks added as an additional variable. By doing so we obtained sets of p-values for the regression parameters that enabled us to decide whether or not the addition of the even weeks made a statistically significant contribution to the variance explained by the regression model. If the latter is the case, we may conclude that the developmental trend obtained from the odd weeks alone is significantly different from the developmental trend obtained if the even weeks are added, and thus that the observed behaviors are dynamically unstable. After having obtained the p-values of the regression parameters based on the individual children, we applied a meta-analytic technique (Glass, McGaw, and Smith, 1981) to investigate whether the hypothesis of dynamic instability also held on the population level.

Results and Conclusion. Based on our analyses (de Weerth, 1998), it is possible to conclude that the results support the hypotheses: in the first two periods five out of the seven expected behaviors showed significant differences between the odd/even weeks series, while in the third period, no significant differences were found. This means that at the beginning the behaviors are dynamically unstable and reach dynamic stability beginning around the age of ten months. With regard to bodily contact, for instance, the percentage of variance explained is substantially larger (up to 44 percent) for most of the infants, under the hypothesis of trends that differ for the odd and the even weeks.

The results for the different observed behaviors were the following. As expected, smiling displayed significant differences between the alternating series in the second period and no differences in the first period. The infant's negative vocalizations proved to be variable in the first two periods, that is, from birth to ten months of age. This was true for crying in both periods, and for fretting/fussing in the second period but not, as we had hypothesized, in the first period.

The fact that the infant still shows important variability in negative vocalizations between the ages of five and ten months probably indicates that although the mother has stabilized in her handling of the infant, the infant herself still suffers from a relative lack of sophistication and of variability in the behavioral channels she can make use of in order to communicate with the mother, and furthermore, that she is also relatively immobile. According to Kopp (1989), because the behavioral repertoire is often still inadequate to meet new experiences, infants will become overwhelmed. Crying and fretting/fussing are still the infant's most important means of communication, although at this age she has become more competent by developing expectations on how the caregiver will react to her negative vocalizations.

Bodily contact with the mother was significantly variable from birth to five months, but not from five to ten months. This might be explained by the fact that these mothers, being primiparous, began by trying to reach an equilibrium point in their caregiving practices. Their interactions with the young infant were therefore probably characterized by more experimenting and trial-and-error than were those with the infant at an older age, when she had already reached a certain degree of ''understanding'' and a more stable pattern of daily activities (see also Findji, Pêcheux, and Ruel, 1993).

In the period from ten to fifteen months, we hypothesized that the infant's communication with his mother becomes more complex and sophisticated and therefore does not show such enormous variability in the amount of crying and other expressions of emotion and contact with the mother. Gustafson and Green (1991) found that by the age of twelve months, the total amount of crying had decreased and that by then most infants elaborated their cries with gestures and other communicative behaviors. Also, studies on temperament show that individual differences in emotional components of temperament become stable from the end of the first year on (Denham et al., 1995; Goldsmith, 1993; Matheny, 1986). These studies fit in nicely with our results and support the idea that variability in the number of negative vocalizations and smiles decreases substantially in the period from ten to fifteen months because the infant's behavior stabilizes, he is acquiring independent mobility, and his means of communication with his mother become more sophisticated.

Development of Structural Relationships in Emotion-Related Behavior Patterns

Emotions and Patterns of Behavior

Emotions and the expressions of emotions as they occur in dyadic interaction between a mother and an infant are more likely to be the results of so-called soft assembly processes (Thelen and Smith, 1994) than the direct expression of internally represented, innate patterns that undergo maturational change. They emerge during the interaction process and take part in the construction of consensual frames, that is, dynamic structures that regulate social and emotional interactions between people (Fogel,

1993). The fact that they are created on the spot, so to speak, does not imply that they are entirely coincidental and context-dependent. The literature on emotional development clearly shows that emotions and their expression undergo specific changes, for instance, in the form and diversity of the emotions (Lewis, 1993). Overviews of developmental patterns tend to emphasize the universal or population-specific aspects of change. In addition, developmental models primarily focus on the emergence of particular emotional patterns, such as embarrassment, pride, and shame. These are what we might call microscopic emotional patterns because they unfold – or self-assemble – across a short time span. It is also possible to study emotional development by focusing on macroscopic patterns, that is, patterns that specify how emotions are related to one another and how such relationships change across time. Such relations can be specified for a single person, but it makes far more sense to study these relationships in dyads (or groups, for that matter), because macroscopic emotional patterns refer to recognizable ways in which people react emotionally to one another.

Although it would be very interesting to study the development of such patterns longitudinally, our longitudinal data do not allow us to specify such emotional patterns, simply because we have confined ourselves to ethological registrations of separate behaviors, such as smiling, crying, and bodily contact. However, we think our data can nevertheless be used to study general qualitative aspects of longitudinal change in patterns of emotion-related behaviors. This can be done in the following way.

It is likely that behaviors such as smiling, bodily contact, and so forth, are associated in ways that are characteristic of specific ages or developmental stages. For instance, it is likely that the nature of the overall association between crying and bodily contact in neonates differs from their association in older infants. When neonates cry, they are probably immediately soothed, cuddled, and so forth, whereas when older infants cry it is likely that the caretakers are less inclined to rush immediately to the child, pick her up, and comfort her by physical means. Our data set, with its many assessment points, gives us a good opportunity to study the ways in which such associations changed across developmental time in our four mother-infant dyads. What we expected to find, given our dynamic systems point of view, is that the change trajectories would often be nonlinear in nature and that they would also show considerable variability between infants and between variables. This variability may stem in part from the fact that the initial state of those emotion-related behaviors shows a high level of intra-individual variation, which provides a host of devel-

opmental opportunities in comparison to an alternative starting point where
all infants would be far more predictable and stable at the beginning.

Developmental Changes in Macroscopic Behavioral Patterns

Whereas the mother is an adult who can be assumed to have acquired
relatively stable personality characteristics that have been shown to affect
her interactions with the infant (Kaeller and Roe, 1990), the infant pos-
sesses relatively unstable temperamental characteristics (Crockenberg and
Smith, 1982; Isabella et al., 1985; Peters-Martin and Wachs, 1984; Worobey and Blajda, 1989) that help shape his display of behaviors. At the
same time, the infant is developing at great speed and is being constantly
confronted with new, or newly perceived, stimuli. Changes in the infant
will in turn mean different demands on the mother, and in such a rapidly
developing system it does not seem too far-fetched to assume that important demands will be made on the mother's behavioral plasticity. While a
natural goal for the mother will be to obtain homeostasis (i.e., stability) in
her relationship with the infant, the infant's quick pace of development will
possibly greatly diminish the chances of attaining long-lasting and un-
changing periods of homeostasis, especially during the first year of life. A
likely indicator of such – temporal – homeostasis is the existence of stable
statistical associations between behavioral variables in the mother and
infant that last for a number of weeks at least. Taking into account the
variability found in both individual maternal and infant behavior, is it
possible to find patterns of such statistical relationships between different
behaviors? And also, how stable are these patterns over time? Do they
change as the infant develops?

There are few studies that have investigated changes in mother-infant
patterns of interaction, and these have focused on the microanalysis of
exchanges between mother and infant. Furthermore, the studies described
here consist of analyses of two or three home observations with durations
of forty-five minutes to approximately two hours. Kindermann (1993)
found changes in the interaction patterns of mothers and infants between
the ages of nine and twenty-one months. Schaefer (1989) observed mother-
infant dyads at four and twelve months of age, and found that while the
dimension of positive mother-infant interaction was stable over the two
observations, that of punitiveness and irritability was not. Schölmerich et
al. (1995) found composite measures of mother-infant interaction to be
moderately stable between the ages of seven and ten months; and while
Findji and collaborators (1993) found stability of dyadic activities between

observations performed at five and eight months of age, Bornstein and Tamis-LeMonda (1990) found stability for some maternal activities together with instability of infant behaviors between the ages of two and five months.

That mother-infant interactions are different at the very beginning than they are later, when the infant is around a year of age, should not be surprising. For example, infants in the first three months show increased crying of a reflexive nature, primarily due to poor state regulation and irritability (St. James-Roberts et al., 1998). This fits with the idea that altricial species (e.g., primates, rats, dogs), in contrast to precocial species (e.g., sheep, cattle, guinea pigs), have a prolongation of immature developmental stages that allows the infant to maintain an open homeostatic system, the regulation of which is partially delegated to phenomena within the relationship with the mother (Hofer, 1987). Thus, particularly in the first months of life, the mother plays an essential regulatory role in the internal state of the infant, and the communication between mother and infant is greatly determined by the mutual attempts to reach homeostasis in the infant. Later on, as the infant becomes more adept and independent in his or her state regulation, other aspects of mother-infant communication (social, cognitive, etc.) will gain in relative importance. Such an interpretation would explain the differences in the nature of a behavior such as crying, and in the nature of mother-infant interactions, between early and later developmental stages.

According to Kindermann (1993), the fact that the mother adjusts to her developing child's changing demands might mean that a certain pattern of maternal behaviors could be more adaptive at one age of the child than at another. Similarly, Bornstein (1989) states that caregivers will interact with their children in a different balance of patterns at different developmental periods. He finds that the interactions between the two can vary over time in their prevalence as well as in their predictive validity for developmental outcome.

The opposite of adaptive change, that is, the inability to behaviorally adapt to changes in the developing infant, could even have deleterious effects on the child. Bee and associates (1982) found evidence that one of the features of low-education families that increases the risk of later poor intellectual performance for the infant is a lesser ability of the caregivers to adapt to the child's changing demands.

Our present study, in which changes in emotion-related behaviors in four mother-infant pairs were intensively followed, is ideally suited for an investigation of changes in the relationships among important indicators of mood, such as crying, smiling, and fretting/fussing. The behaviors mentioned are very likely to change in function and form over time. For example, as we have seen, crying is initially largely reflexive in nature, but increasingly becomes a complex social signal as the infant develops and begins to combine it with gazing and gestures (Gustafson and Green, 1991; St. James-Roberts et al., 1998). On the other hand, smiling is a behavior that initially is (almost) nonexistent, gains in frequency and importance over the months (Belsky et al., 1984), and finally plays an increasingly sophisticated and complex role in social interactions. Therefore, because these behaviors change over time, and because mother-infant interactions have been shown to be influenced by each partners' contributions to the relationship (Acebo and Thoman, 1992; Brinker, Baxter, and Butler, 1994; Fish and Stifter, 1995; Tamis-LeMonda and Bornstein, 1991), a logical consequence would be for the patterns of relations between them also to change.

In this study (de Weerth, 1998) we investigated both variability and stability between and within the four mother-infant dyads. First, we wished to establish whether or not, for any given moment in time, there existed (relatively) stable associations between emotion-related behaviors in mother-infant dyads. Provided such patterns were found, we also wanted to know whether they were stable across the whole time interval covered by our observations (approximately fifteen months). If they were not, we wanted to know how they changed. More specifically, did they change in a linear fashion, or was there evidence of nonlinear change? Finally, in view of the dynamic nature of the process and its initial state, we also wished to know whether the patterns and changes found applied to all infants or whether they were characteristic of specific dyads and therefore showed considerable across-dyad differences.

Statistical Method

Multiple regression analyses were used to study *the relations between the observed behaviors* and the changes they underwent over time. Because the data consisted of residuals with the mean equal to 0, the regression for the relation between two variables was:

$$y = \beta * x + e \tag{1}$$

for y and x, two of the variables studied, β the regression parameter, and e an error residual. For instance, we tried to predict crying (the explained variable y) on the basis of smiling (the explaining variable x).

In order to investigate whether these relations changed with time, β was modeled as a function of "time" and "time^2," where time was the observation number and thus varied from 1 to 61, 63, or 64, according to the length of each infant's observation period:

$$\beta = \beta_0 + \beta_1 \text{*time} + \beta_2 \text{*time}^2 + e \qquad (2)$$

Significant results of this dynamic or time-dependent regression indicate that variable y has a significant relation to variable x and that this relation varies linearly and/or quadratically over time. *How* the relation varies can be observed by plotting the β of regression (2). The β plots of the different infants can thus be compared in order to see if the relations between the variables vary in the same way over the observation period of fifteen months.

As an additional test, we also computed moving regressions of pairs of observed variables on twenty-week series in order to examine in more detail how well one variable predicts another at different points in time. Thus, a standard linear regression model of the form

$$y_{t(n-n+19)} = \beta_{0(n-n+19)} + \beta_{1(n-n+19)} xt \qquad (3)$$

was fitted on a moving series consisting of twenty weeks. For an observation set consisting of sixty-three weeks, for example, we obtained forty-four parameter sets, which could then be plotted in order to obtain an indication of the relationship (and the eventual change in that relationship) between the independent variable x (e.g., crying) and the dependent variable y (e.g., smiling). Note that each variable in turn played the role of independent and dependent variable with each other variable. Also, bodily contact was split into the positions: "ventral", "lap," and "next to the mother" (see de Weerth, 1998).

Results and Conclusion

For each separate mother-infant pair, various patterns of association were found between emotion-related behaviors. For instance, not surprisingly, crying (duration and frequency) were positively related to fretting/fussing, and negatively related to smiling. Also, fretting/fussing was negatively related to smiling in two infants.

Although these patterns indicate that (relatively) stable relations exist between the studied variables (up to 41 percent of the explained variance), often only 10 percent of the variance was explained. This points in the direction of flexibility in the behaviors and their associations. It probably indicates that factors such as day-to-day and week-to-week variability in behavior, due to such factors as contextual characteristics and the nature of infant development, also account for an important part of the unexplained variance in the associations (de Weerth et al., 1999; St. James-Roberts and Plewis, 1996).

Most of the patterns showed significant long-term changes. These changes were in the strength of the association or in the nature of the association, and in many cases they even showed several major changes in the nature of the association throughout the fifteen-month period. Two major groups of curves specifying changes in patterns were distinguished: those that were linear or quadratic and those that were U-shaped. Within these groups, trajectories differed with regard to whether or not the sign of the association remained the same (e.g., remained positive or changed from positive to negative). An example of how relationships between behaviors change over time is presented in Figure 12.1.

With respect to the variability between dyads, the analyses carried out in this intensive study show that even when mother-infant pairs are drawn from a normal and narrowly defined population, they can display important

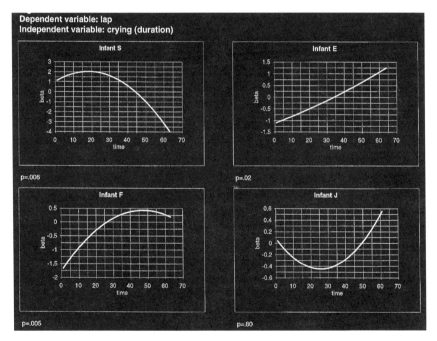

Figure 12.1. The relationship between bodily contact with infant on mother's lap and duration of crying changes over time (in weeks). The nature of the relationship and the change differ among infants.

general differences in amounts of infant crying, fretting/fussing, and smiling, and in the amount and types of bodily contact between mother and infant. The fact that notwithstanding these differences, several similarities were found in the relations between the studied behaviors, in the tendency for these relations to change over time, and in the way the patterns changed over time, make the results all the more interesting. However, we must not forget that both the relations between the behaviors and the way in which they change over time were often highly variable and idiosyncratic to each mother-infant pair.

An interesting point is that the similarities in the relations between behaviors and their changes over time were limited to behaviors of which the infant was the sole author, namely the negative vocalizations and smiling. All the relations that included bodily contact, of which the mother was the most important determining factor, showed much more variability both in the relation per se and in how it changed over time. This finding appears to indicate that while infants possess generalities in development that go beyond their natural differences in temperament, mothers, with their more established personalities and beliefs, show fewer macroscopic generalities in their interactions with their infants. Note, however, that these associations between behaviors say nothing about how these behaviors are organized over shorter time intervals, that is, over the microstructure of mother-infant interactions.

The use of moving regressions on twenty-week data series showed that in half the cases in which the meta-analysis of the time-dependent multiple regression was significant (or approached significance), delimited periods could be determined in which one variable predicted another. These findings support earlier research results in which stability of behavior is found over shorter periods of time (for example, Crockenberg and McCluskey, 1986; Findji et al., 1993; Green, Gustafson, and West, 1980; Schölmerich et al., 1995).

An important point that should not be forgotten is that by studying the relations between pairs of behavioral variables, we have left aside more complex interactions between groups of variables. This approach overly simplifies reality and precludes potentially significant influences and effects between groups of behaviors (Bornstein, 1989). In an exploratory analysis, however, we found that single variables (e.g., crying) could be reasonably well predicted by the additional observed variables (e.g., smiling, fretting/fussing, and contact).

General Conclusion

In this chapter we set out to discuss the long-term dynamics of emotion-related behaviors in infancy. After having presented a dynamic systems view on variability and structure in emotions, behavior, and social interaction, we formulated two predictions. First, we predicted that intra-individual variability in emotion-related behaviors would be considerably higher during the first months of life than at a later stage, thus suggesting a process of increasing stabilization. This prediction was borne out. Second, we predicted that the macroscopic associations between emotion-related behaviors would undergo nonlinear changes during the first fifteen months of life. We found considerable changes in some of the patterns and reasonable stability in others. A few of those changes showed uniformity across our subjects; the majority did not. In short, our empirical findings suggest a rich and complicated landscape of change and dynamic stability of emotion-related behaviors that can only be uncovered by detailed, longitudinal studies with high observation or measurement frequencies.

How do our findings contribute to a nonlinear dynamics theory of emotional development? Since we focused solely on changes in frequencies of emotion-related behaviors, we are not in a position to make claims about the actual, real-time assembly of patterns in emotions and emotion-related behaviors. However, the application of dynamic systems models to behavioral and developmental phenomena is often highly complicated, and it remains difficult to prove directly that a particular developmental process is indeed a form of self-organization. Instead of looking for direct evidence, we have tried to present indirect evidence in the form of general indicators of dynamic processes in emotional development. These indicators – comparable to the so-called catastrophe flags in catastrophe analysis – concerned the process of stabilization of an initially highly variable pattern on the one hand, and the occurrence of nonlinear trajectories of change in associations between emotion-related behaviors on the other hand.

References

Acebo, C., and Thoman, E. B. (1992). Crying as social behavior. *Infant Mental Health Journal, 13,* 67–82.

Barr, R. G. (1990). The normal crying curve: What do we really know? *Developmental Medicine and Child Neurology, 32,* 356–362.

Bee, H. L., Barnard, K. E., Eyres, S. J., Gray, C. A., Hammond, M. A., Spietz, A. L., Snyder, C., and Clark, B. (1982). Prediction of IQ and language skill from perinatal status, child performance, family characteristics, and mother-infant interaction. *Child Development, 53,* 1134–1156.

Belsky, J., Gilstrap, B., and Rovine, M. (1984). The Pennsylvania Infant and Family Development Project: I. Stability and change in mother-infant and father-infant interaction in a family setting at one, three, and nine months. *Child Development, 55,* 692–705.

Belsky, J., Hsieh, K. H., and Crnic, K. (1996). Infant positive and negative emotionality: One dimension or two? *Developmental Psychology, 32,* 289–298.

Bornstein, M. H. (1989). Between caretakers and their young: Two modes of interaction and their consequences for cognitive growth. In M. H. Bornstein and J. S. Bruner (Eds.), *Interaction in human development* (pp. 197–214). Hillsdale, NJ: Erlbaum.

Bornstein, M. H., and Tamis-LeMonda, C. S. (1990). Activities and interactions of mothers and their firstborn infants in the first six months of life: Covariation, stability, continuity, correspondence, and prediction. *Child Development, 61,* 1206–1217.

Bridges, K. M. (1932). Emotional development in early infancy. *Child Development, 3,* 324–341.

Brinker, R. P., Baxter, A., and Butler, L. S. (1994). An ordinal pattern analysis of four hypotheses describing the interactions between drug-addicted, chronically disadvantaged, and middle-class mother-infant dyads. *Child Development, 65,* 361–372.

Camras, L. A. (1994). Two aspects of emotional development: Expression and elicitation. In P. Ekman and R. J. Davidson (Eds.), *The nature of emotion* (pp. 347–351). New York: Oxford University Press.

Canfield, R. L., Wilken, J., Schmerl, L., and Smith, E. G. (1995). Age-related change and stability of individual differences in infant saccade reaction time. *Infant Behavior and Development, 18,* 351–358.

Crockenberg, S. B., and McCluskey, K. (1986). Change in maternal behavior during the baby's first year of life. *Child Development, 57,* 746–753.

Crockenberg, S. B., and Smith, P. (1982). Antecedents of mother-infant interaction and infant irritability in the first three months of life. *Infant Behavior and Development, 5,* 105–119.

Denham, S. A., Lehman, E. B., Moser, M. H., and Reeves, S. L. (1995). Continuity and change in emotional components of infant temperament. *Child Study Journal, 25,* 289–308.

de Weerth, C. (1998). *Emotion-related behaviors in infants: A longitudinal study of patterns and variability.* Unpublished doctoral dissertation, University of Groningen, Groningen.

de Weerth, C., and van Geert, P. (1998). Emotional instability as an indicator of strictly timed infantile developmental transitions. *British Journal of Developmental Psychology, 16,* 15–44.

de Weerth, C., van Geert, P., and Hoijtink, H. (1999). Intraindividual variability in infant behavior. *Developmental Psychology, 35,* 1102–1112.

Dittrichova, J., Paul, K., Tautermannova, M., and Vondracek, J. (1992). Individual variability in infant's early behavior. *Studia Psychologica, 34,* 199–210.

Findji, F., Pêcheux, M. G. and Ruel, J. (1993). Dyadic activities and attention in the infant: A developmental study. *European Journal of Psychology of Education, 8,* 23–33.

Fish, M., and Crockenberg, S. (1981). Correlates and antecedents of nine-month infant behavior and mother-infant interaction. *Infant Behavior and Development, 4,* 69–81.

Fish, M., and Stifter, C. A. (1995). Patterns of mother-infant interaction and attachment: A cluster-analytic approach. *Infant Behavior and Development, 18,* 435–446.

Fish, M., Stifter, C. A., and Belsky, J. (1991). Conditions of continuity and discontinuity in infant negative emotionality: Newborn to five months. *Child Development, 62,* 1525–1537.

Fogel, A. (1991). *Infancy: Infant, family and society* (2nd ed.). St. Paul, MN: West.

Fogel, A. (1993). *Developing through relationships: Origins of communication, self and culture.* New York: Harvester Wheatsheaf.

Fogel, A., Lyra, M. C., and Valsiner, J. (1997). *Dynamics and indeterminism in developmental and social processes.* Mahwah, NJ: Erlbaum.

Freedland, R. L., and Bertenthal, B. I. (1994). Developmental changes in interlimb coordination: Transition to hands-and-knees crawling. *Psychological Science, 5,* 26–32.

Gilmore, R. (1981). *Catastrophe theory for scientists and engineers.* New York: Wiley.

Glass, G. V., McGaw, B., and Smith, M. L. (1981). *Meta-analysis in social research.* London: Sage.

Goldsmith, H. H. (1993). Temperament: Variability in developing emotion systems. In M. Lewis and J. M. Haviland (Eds.), *Handbook of emotions* (pp. 353–364). New York: Guilford.

Green, J. A., Gustafson, G. E., and West, M. J. (1980). Effects of infant development on mother-infant interactions. *Child Development, 51,* 199–207.

Gustafson, G. E., and Green, J. A. (1991). Developmental coordination of cry sounds with visual regard and gestures. *Infant Behavior and Development, 14,* 51–57.

Hock, E., and Lindamood, J. (1981). Continuity of child-rearing attitudes in mothers of young children. *Journal of Genetic Psychology, 138,* 305–306.

Hofer, M. A. (1987). Early social relationships: A psychobiologist's view. *Child Development, 58,* 633–647.

Hubbard, F. O. A., and van IJzendoorn, M. H. (1991). Maternal unresponsiveness and infant crying across the first 9 months: A naturalistic longitudinal study. *Infant Behavior and Development, 14,* 299–312.

Isabella, R. A. (1993). Origins of attachment: Maternal interactive behavior across the first year. *Child Development, 64,* 605–621.

Isabella, R. A., Ward, M. J., and Belsky, J. (1985). Convergence of multiple sources of information on infant individuality: Neonatal behavior, infant behavior, and temperament reports. *Infant Behavior and Development, 8,* 283–291.

Kaeller, M. G., and Roe, K. V. (1990). Personality variables as assessed by the MMPI and their relationship to mother-infant interactional behaviors at age three months. *Psychological Reports, 66,* 899–904.

Kindermann, T. A. (1993). Fostering independence in mother-child interactions: Longitudinal changes in contingency patterns as children grow competent in developmental tasks. *International Journal of Behavioral Development, 16,* 513–535.

Kopp, C. B. (1989). Regulation of distress and negative emotions: A developmental view. *Developmental Psychology, 25,* 343–354.

Lerner, R. M., and Lerner, J. V. (1987). Children in their contexts: A goodness-of-fit model. In J. B. Lancaster, J. Altmann, A. S. Rossi, and L. B. Sherrod (Eds.), *Parenting across the life-span: Biosocial dimensions* (pp. 377–404). Hawthorne, NY: Aldine.

Lewis, M. (1993). The emergence of human emotions. In M. Lewis and J. M. Haviland (Eds.), *Handbook of emotions* (pp. 223–236). New York: Guilford.

Lewis, M. D. (1995). Cognition-emotion feedback and the self-organization of developmental paths. *Human Development, 38,* 71–102.

Lewis, M. D. (1996). Self-organising cognitive appraisals. *Cognition and Emotion, 10,* 1–25.

Malatesta, C. Z., Culver, C., Tesman, J. R., and Shepard, B. (1989). The development of emotion expression during the first two years of life. *Monographs of the Society for Research in Child Development, 54* (1–2, serial no. 219).

Matheny, A. (1986). Stability and change of infant temperament: Contributions from the infant, mother and family environment. In G. A. Kohnstamm (Ed.), *Temperament discussed: Temperament and development in infancy and childhood* (pp. 49–58). Lisse: Swets and Zeitlinger.

McCall, R. B., Eichorn, D. H., and Hogarty, P. S. (1977). Transitions in early mental development. *Monographs of the Society for Research in Child Development, 42* (3, serial no. 171).

McNally, S., Eisenberg, N., and Harris, J. D. (1991). Consistency and change in maternal child-rearing practices and values: A longitudinal study. *Child Development, 62,* 190–198.

Newell, K. M., and Molenaar, P. C. (1998). *Applications of nonlinear dynamics to developmental process modeling.* Mahwah, NJ: Erlbaum.

Peters-Martin, P., and Wachs, T. D. (1984). A longitudinal study of temperament and its correlates in the first 12 months. *Infant Behavior and Development, 7,* 285–298.

Plomin, R., Emde, R. N., Braungart, J. M., Campos, J., Corley, R., Fulker, D. W., Kagan, J., Reznick, J. S., Robinson, J., Zahn-Waxler, C., and DeFries, J. C. (1993). Genetic change and continuity from fourteen to twenty months: The MacArthur Longitudinal Twin Study. *Child Development, 64,* 1354–1376.

Port, R. F., and van Gelder, T. (1995). *Mind as motion: Explorations in the dynamics of cognition.* Cambridge, MA: Bradford/MIT Press.

Rebelsky, F., and Black, R. (1972). Crying in infancy. *Journal of Genetic Psychology, 121,* 49–57.

Rogoff, B., Ellis, S., and Gardner, W. (1984). Adjustment of adult-child instruction according to child's age and task. *Developmental Psychology, 20,* 193–199.

Savelsbergh, G., van der Maas, H., and van Geert, P. (1999). *Nonlinear developmental processes.* New York: Elsevier.

Schaefer, E. S. (1989). Dimensions of mother-infant interaction: Measurement, stability, and predictive validity. *Infant Behavior and Development, 12,* 379–393.

Schölmerich, A., Fracasso, M. P., Lamb, M. E., and Broberg, A. G. (1995). Interactional harmony at 7 and 10 months of age predicts security of attachment as measured by Q-sort ratings. *Social Development, 4,* 62–74.

Smith, L. B., and Thelen, E. (1993). *A dynamic systems approach to development: Applications.* Cambridge, MA: Bradford/MIT Press.

Sroufe, L. A. (1979). Socio-emotional development. In J. D. Osofsky (Ed.), *Handbook of infant development* (pp. 462–516). New York: Wiley.

St. James-Roberts, I., Conroy, S., and Wilsher, K. (1998). Links between maternal care and persistent infant crying in the early months. *Child Care, Health and Development, 24,* 353–376.

St. James-Roberts, I., and Halil, T. (1991). Infant crying patterns in the first year: Normal community and clinical findings. *Journal of Child Psychology and Psychiatry, 32,* 951–968.

St. James-Roberts, I., and Plewis, I. (1996). Individual differences, daily fluctuations, and developmental changes in amounts of infant waking, fussing, crying, feeding, and sleeping. *Child Development, 67,* 2527–2540.

St. James-Roberts, I., and Wolke, D. (1988). Convergences and discrepancies among mothers' and professionals' assessments of difficult neonatal behaviour. *Journal of Child Psychology and Psychiatry, 29,* 21–42.

Stifter, C. A., and Braungart, J. (1992). Infant colic: A transient condition with no apparent effects. *Journal of Applied Developmental Psychology, 13,* 447–462.

Tamis-LeMonda, C. S., and Bornstein, M. H. (1991). Individual variation, correspondence, stability, and change in mother and toddler play. *Infant Behavior and Development, 14,* 143–162.

Thelen, E., and Smith, L. B. (1994). *A dynamic systems approach to the development of cognition and action.* Cambridge, MA: Bradford/MIT Press.

Touwen, B. (1976) *Neurological development in infancy.* London: Heinemann.

Vallacher, R. R., and Nowak, A. (1994). *Dynamical systems in social psychology.* San Diego, CA: Academic Press.

van den Boom, D. C. (1988). *Neonatal irritability and the development of attachment: Observation and intervention.* Unpublished doctoral dissertation, University of Leiden, Leiden.

van der Maas, H. L. (1993). *Catastrophe analysis of stagewise cognitive development: Model, method and applications.* Unpublished doctoral dissertation, University of Amsterdam, Amsterdam.

van der Maas, H. L., and Molenaar, P. C. (1992). Stagewise cognitive development: An application of catastrophe theory. *Psychological Review, 99,* 395–417.

van Geert, P. (1991). A dynamic systems model of cognitive and language growth. *Psychological Review, 98,* 3–53.

van Geert, P. (1994). *Dynamic systems of development: Change between complexity and chaos.* New York: Harvester Wheatsheaf.

van Geert, P. (1996). The development of attachment and attachment-related competences: A dynamic model. In W. Koops, J. Hoeksma, and J. van den Boom (Eds.), *New developments in attachment research* (pp. 181–199). Amsterdam: North-Holland.

van Geert, P. (1998). A dynamic systems model of basic developmental mechanisms: Piaget, Vygotsky and beyond. *Psychological Review, 105,* 634–677.

Wachs, T. D., Morrow, J., and Slabach, E. H. (1990). Intraindividual variability in infant visual recognition memory performance: Temperamental and environmental correlates. *Infant Behavior and Development, 13,* 397–403.

Worobey, J. (1986). Convergence among assessments of temperament in the first month. *Child Development, 57,* 47–55.

Worobey, J., and Blajda, V. M. (1989). Temperament ratings at 2 weeks, 2 months and 1 year: Differential stability of activity and emotionality. *Developmental Psychology, 25,* 257–263.

13 Theoretical and Mathematical Modeling of Marriage

Kimberly D. Ryan, John M. Gottman,
James D. Murray, Sybil Carrère,
and Catherine Swanson

Our work shows the marital relationship to be a complex system in which the movement of marital interaction to predictable points in that system represents the emergence of order. In this chapter we present two methods for describing this system. First we present an empirically based theory, the Sound Marital House theory, which describes the process of function and dysfunction in marriage. Following this, the order of the marital system is depicted in our recently developed mathematical model. These congruent models of marital interaction provide us with a method for delineating the underlying emotional structure, and the developmental trajectory, of the marital system. Furthermore, these models present us with an opportunity to prescribe clinical interventions with the aim of devising effective marital therapies.

The Field of Marital Therapy

Current marital therapies are not primarily based on prior empirical research. This is true even of the most studied marital therapies, the behavioral marital therapies. Instead, most therapies have evolved from the recommendations of respected therapists. Consider the evolution of a form of marital therapy called "contingency contracting," which originated from the writings of Lederer and Jackson (1968). In their book, *The Mirages of Marriage*, these authors suggested that the failure of couples to have equitable exchange agreements was the basic problem of distressed marriages. The idea had never been tested, but it quickly appeared as a new marital therapy in the behavioral literature (Azrin, Naster, and Jones, 1973). Over a decade after its introduction, Murstein, Cerreto, and MacDonald (1977) found that the concept of contingency contracting was flawed; in fact, quid pro quo arrangements in marriage were shown to be characteris-

349

tic of distressed, not nondistressed, couples. Interestingly, though, the health of contingency contracting therapy was unaffected by this discovery. Since that time, contingency contracting and behavior exchange have undergone a slow evolution due to clinical writing. The publication of Richard Stuart's (1980) book, *Helping Couples Change*, and his suggestion of "love days," led to interventions that were noncontingent and oriented toward changing the everyday level of positivity as opposed to conflict. Hence, the intervention evolved, but again these changes were not based on data.

Our Divorce Prediction Research

In our early studies we were particularly interested in predicting which couples would become dissatisfied with their marriages and choose to divorce (Gottman, 1994a; Gottman and Levenson, 1992). Moreover, we wanted to identify what was dysfunctional in these ailing marriages. Our work revealed that the emotional interactions taking place in a marital system were at the root of dysfunctional marital processes (Gottman and Levenson, 1992). Observational coding of these affective patterns (based on the Rapid Couples Interaction Coding System, RCICS) allowed Gottman and Levenson to derive one variable (the slope of a cumulated curve that plotted positive minus negative behaviors) to classify couples into two groups, regulated couples and nonregulated couples (Krokoff, Gottman, and Haas, 1989).

Regulated couples had positive slopes, indicating that both spouses displayed a significantly greater number of positive problem-solving behaviors (e.g., neutral or positive problem description, assent, humor) than negative problem-solving behaviors (e.g., complaining, criticizing, defensiveness, escalating negative affect). Nonregulated couples were those couples showing a curve of any other shape, the result of at least one spouse exhibiting a greater number of negative problem-solving than positive problem-solving behaviors. This distinction between couples made it possible to predict marital dissolution with 75 percent accuracy across a period of four years. It also allowed for the establishment of a developmental trajectory toward divorce. This trajectory, later termed the Cascade Model of Dissolution, delineates a predictable series of stages leading up to marital dissolution. The couples who later divorced initially showed marital unhappiness and dissatisfaction followed by thoughts of separation and divorce. This consideration of separation and divorce eventually led to actual separation and, finally, to divorce. The ability to reliably predict this cascade toward divorce allowed us to quantify improvement in marital interaction in terms of divorce predictors. Moreover, it helped to unify the research on the correlates of marital dissatisfaction with the research on divorce prediction.

In later work, Gottman (1994a) proposed that negative affective behaviors were not all equally corrosive. Moreover, only four were shown to produce deleterious effects in the marriage. These particularly corrosive affective behaviors include criticism, contempt, defensiveness, and stonewalling. Gottman grouped these behaviors together, calling them the Four Horsemen of the Apocalypse. Using these variables, the accurate prediction of dissolution increased to 85 percent. Subsequently, Gottman defined a cascade model, the Distance and Isolation Cascade, which included the following variables: emotional flooding, viewing problems as severe, not wanting to work out problems with the spouse, parallel lives, and loneliness. The addition of these variables increased the accuracy of the prediction of dissolution to more than 90 percent.

Finally, using a semistructured interview called the Oral History Interview (Buehlman, Gottman, and Katz, 1992) that assesses a couple's relationship history and their philosophy of marriage, Buehlman and colleagues were able to code for lasting thoughts and attributions about the marriage. With these variables alone Buehlman and her associates accurately predicted divorce at a rate of 94 percent. In many ways the results were unremarkable, with fondness toward one's partner predicting stability, and contempt in the marital interaction predicting divorce. There were, however, some surprising findings. The first suggested that anger was unrelated to any negative outcome longitudinally – provided that the anger was not blended with defensiveness or contempt, or delivered in a belligerent manner (Buehlman and Gottman, 1996). The second was the discovery that successful marriages were not uniform in structure but could take one of three ordered forms, each having a distinctive communication pattern. The typology of these three forms of stable marriage include validating couples, volatile couples, and conflict-avoiding couples. Validating couples tend to be good listeners, reflecting back their partner's feelings before beginning persuasion attempts. By contrast, volatile couples use persuasion attempts almost immediately, with little direct listening and validation before these attempts begin. Finally, conflict-avoiding couples almost never engage in persuasion attempts (Gottman, 1993a, 1994b). One serendipitous result of this work was the finding that all three types of stable marriages had positive-to-negative ratios not significantly different from 5.0. In the unstable couples headed for divorce the positive-to-negative ratio was .80. This work led to the development of a balance theory of marriage (Gottman, 1993b). This theory suggests that each couple will find a balance between positive and negative affect.

These research data are useful as we begin to consider the possible structure for, and the necessary components of, a successful marital intervention. However, we are also in need of a comprehensive theory of marriage to guide the development of such interventions. A comprehensive theory would offer a mechanism by which marriages either travel the high road of functioning well or travel the low road of decay and dissolution.

The Sound Marital House Theory

The Sound Marital House theory is an empirically based theory that originated from our research on marriage. It is a comprehensive theory that outlines some of the elements we have identified in our laboratory as important in establishing a satisfying marital relationship. Moreover, the theory explains what is "dysfunctional" when a marriage is unstable and dissatisfying, what is "functional" when a marriage is stable and satisfying, and the etiology of dysfunctional patterns. It also provides explanations of mechanisms at work in marital relationships (see Figure 13.1).

The Sound Marital House theory has proven to be pivotal in expanding our understanding of the role of emotion in marriage, including the role of positive affect in well-functioning marriages, the etiology of specific nega-

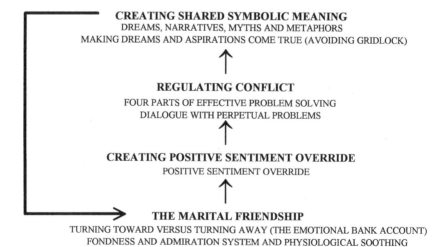

Figure 13.1. The Gottman Sound Marital House.

tive affects predictive of divorce, and the nature of conflict resolution in well-functioning marriages. For instance, our own work indicates that satisfaction in marriage is related to a high level of (or increase in) everyday positive affect, and a low level of (or reduction in) negative affect, especially during conflict resolution. The use of positive affect during a couple's daily interactions appears to be particularly important. Indeed, our research with stable couples indicated that positive affect was predictive of marital stability and marital satisfaction. In these stable relationships, positive affect was used to de-escalate conflict and to physiologically soothe oneself and one's spouse. Surprisingly, it was the absence of positive affect and not the presence of negative affect that predicted the couples who would later divorce (Gottman and Levenson, 1997).

An important question to come out of these findings concerns how couples actually go about building and sustaining positive affect in their marital interactions. Unfortunately, it is difficult to create positive affect, or to recreate it in a distressed marriage that has lost it. The admonition to be positive, or the setting up of behavioral exchanges, is usually doomed (Vincent et al., 1979). Rather than using techniques like contingency contracting to create positive affect in the marriage, we have found that building or rebuilding a couple's friendship is the treatment of choice. In particular, this involves creating positive affect and friendship in nonconflict contexts. The first three levels of the Sound Marital House theory form the foundation needed to establish this friendship. These include the Love Map Level, the Fondness and Admiration Level, and the Turning Toward versus Turning Away Level.

Love Map Level. It is well known that over half of all divorces occur in the first seven years of marriage. Some of this involves a cascade toward divorce that follows the birth of the first child. Indeed, 75 percent of all couples (mainly wives) experience a significant drop in marital satisfaction at this time. Our research indicates that knowledge regarding one's partner and one's relationship history (what Gottman refers to as the ''love map'') is predictive of marital satisfaction. This was particularly true for husbands. Indeed, it was those husbands who were able to describe their wives' world and who continued to know their wives' psychological world who wound up in the 25 percent of couples not showing a drop in marital satisfaction following the birth of their first child.

Fondness and Admiration Level. When members of a couple express fondness and admiration for one another they are more likely to have a satisfying, stable marriage (Buehlman et al., 1992). We have found support for this idea across two separate studies. These studies showed that variables tapping the Fondness and Admiration System were predictive of the longitudinal course of marriage.

Turning Toward versus Turning Away Level. The concept of "turning toward" versus "turning away" has its basis in a couple's everyday, mundane interactions. Turning toward and turning away represent two opposite actions characterized by orienting towards one's partner and responding to one's partner. Across time, these actions are thought to establish a kind of emotional bank account. The idea is that if partners characteristically turn toward one another rather than away, it is "emotional money in the bank." In contrast, too many withdrawals (turning away) will leave the "emotional account" depleted. In research terms, the emotional bank account involves relating the ratio of positivity to negativity in non-conflict discussions to the way people interact when resolving conflict. Over the long run, turning away behaviors are likely to lead to a sense of distance and isolation which, in turn, is predictive of emotional toxicity and divorce.

Positive Sentiment Override. The most consistent discriminator between distressed and nondistressed marriages is negative affect reciprocity. Negative affect reciprocity is a sequential pattern in which negative affect by a spouse becomes more likely than his or her baseline level of negative affect would suggest following negativity from the partner. This suggests that it is very important that a couple be able to repair their emotional interaction, and particularly that they be able to exit a negative affect cycle once they have entered it. We have been studying these repair processes and have discovered that, on average, repair efforts occur about once every three minutes.

Interestingly, efforts at repair occur more frequently in distressed couples, and the success of the repair attempt cannot be predicted from any parameter of its delivery, context, or timing. Instead, our research suggests that successful repair attempts are determined by a concept called positive sentiment override (PSO; Lorber, 1997; Weiss, 1980). In PSO, when a spouse communicates something with negative affect the partner receives it as if it were a neutral message. The opposite is true of negative sentiment override (NSO), with neutral messages being received as if they were negative. Our theory suggests that PSO mediates positive affect in everyday interaction, as well as negative affect during the resolution of conflict.

We believe that PSO has its origins in the positive affect that couples use during nonconflict interaction.

Effective Problem Solving and Dialogue with Perpetual Problems. Our research suggests that couples face two types of problems in regulating conflict within the relationship. The first type is resolvable, while the second type tends not to have any solution. In our laboratory only about 31 percent of the discussions that took place involved a problem that could be considered to have a solution. Thus, in 69 percent of the discussions, couples were talking about problems that could not be resolved, what we now call ''perpetual problems.'' Perpetual problems tend to involve long-standing issues of disagreement, often having to do with fundamental personality differences between spouses.

With regard to resolvable problems, we have found that there are four skills necessary for effective conflict resolution. These skills, which are predictive of the longitudinal course of the marriages, include Softened Startup, Accepting Influence, Repair and De-Escalation, and Compromise (Gottman et al., 1998). The use of positive affect in the service of de-escalation also plays a role. Unfortunately, as we noted earlier, positive affect during conflict resolution is generally not programmable by intervention.

As we stated earlier, the majority of the conflicts occurring between couples are intractable. Our research indicates that it isn't whether a couple solves a perpetual problem that determines the future of the marriage but the accompanying affect with which they work toward a resolution (Gottman, 1980). What seems to be particularly important is whether a couple can establish an emotional dialogue around their perpetual problems that allows them to communicate amusement and affection while seeking change. If a couple's dialogue lacks positive affect, conflict becomes gridlocked. Gridlocked conflict eventually leads to either a high level of negative affect (criticism, defensiveness, contempt, and stonewalling) or a lack of affect and emotional disengagement. These findings on marital interaction and positive affect point to the importance of positive affect within the regulation and resolution of conflict (Carstensen, Gottman, and Levenson, 1995; Levenson, Carstensen, and Gottman, 1994).

It is important to remember that the autonomic nervous system is strongly related to emotional expression and emotional experience. A major task that spouses have during a marital conflict discussion is emotional regulation. Avoiding escalation that feels out of control requires that a couple balance two goals, the expression of emotion and the control of emotion. When heart rate increases (beyond the pacemaker rate), adrenaline secretion begins (Rowell, 1986) and it becomes increasingly difficult to process information, making it more likely that people will rely on over-learned behavior and thought patterns (Gottman, 1990). Indeed, Levenson and Gottman (1983) found that autonomic indices of physiological arousal in both partners were strongly predictive of changes in marital satisfaction, even after controlling for initial levels of satisfaction. This research suggested that a higher level of physiological arousal for both spouses during marital conflict discussions was predictive of marital deterioration.

Recent analyses of our newlywed data showed that positive affect and de-escalation were associated with self-soothing by the husband and physiological soothing of the husband by the wife (Gottman et al., 1998). Physiological soothing (of self and partner) is fundamental to dealing with both solvable and perpetual problems and is hypothesized to be an important ingredient for avoiding relapse following treatment.

Creating Shared Symbolic Meaning and Honoring Life Dreams.
Gottman discovered clinically that it is the construction of shared meaning that prevents or unlocks gridlocked marital conflict. This involves honoring and meshing each spouse's individual life dreams, narratives, myths, and metaphors. When a couple perceives that their marriage supports their dreams and aspirations they maintain a positive emotional connection to one another. This part of the marriage is about a couple's culture. Our approach to culture is not limited to how these processes vary across ethnicity, race, and geography but includes the more subtle variations to be found across family of origin. The union of two people, no matter how similar, will inevitably involve an integration of two families of origin, and thus the creation of a new culture with its own world of meaning. This culture is a couple's own unique blend of meanings, symbol systems, metaphors, narratives, philosophy, goals, roles, and rituals. It is this culture that fuels both intimacy and estrangement.

Potential Contributions of the Sound Marital House Theory

In addressing the potential contributions of the Sound Marital House theory, we must first consider how the theory relates to current thinking about marital therapy. Unlike many of the current marital therapies, the theory does not suggest that intervention be based primarily on how couples resolve conflict. Instead, the theory presents a more holistic model regarding the development and maintenance of intimacy in marriage. Additionally, it proposes that effective resolution of conflict involves the emotional tone of everyday marital interaction, particularly through the action of positive sentiment override. The theory also suggests that, when conflicts have a solution, the conflict resolution skills targeted by most therapies (active listening) are the wrong targets. Finally, it posits that most marital conflicts involve "perpetual problems" that never get resolved. For these intractable problems it is the couple's emotional interaction that matters the most. Either the couple establishes a "dialogue" with the perpetual problem and communicates mutual acceptance, or the conflict becomes gridlocked. Gottman and Levenson's (1997) fourteen-year prospective longitudinal divorce prediction studies suggest that when conflict becomes gridlocked two patterns emerge, depending on the stage of gridlock. One pattern occurs early in the relationship, during the first seven years of marriage (average of 5.2 years), and involves the Four Horsemen. The second pattern is characterized by emotional disengagement and lack of affect, and is predictive of later divorce (average of 16.4 years). These two critical time points for intervention are consistent with other findings in the marital research literature (Anderson, Dimidjan, and Miller, 1995; Cherlin, 1981).

These findings indicate that couples initially higher in overall positive affect and lower in negative affect during conflict will do best in marital therapy. This suggests that the failure of marital therapy and the failure of marriage in some way involve positive and negative processes of interaction. These findings are consistent with the idea that a two-pronged intervention to increase positivity and to reduce negativity is necessary if a couple is to make lasting changes in their marital interaction patterns. The Sound Marital House theory addresses this lack of positivity and/or the presence of negativity in the marital relationship, and proposes a resolution to gridlocked conflict. The theory suggests that the resolution of conflict, like the etiology of conflict, involves a couple's culture – more specifically, a clash in people's life dreams and a clash in the symbolic meaning of people's stands on life issues.

Mathematical Model of Marital Interaction

The mathematical model of marital interaction is an important advance in our own work. We initially set out to model a stable phenomenon in our laboratory, now replicated in three studies, that divorce or marital stability can be predicted longitudinally from marital interaction with over 90 percent accuracy (Gottman, 1993a, 1994a; Gottman and Levenson, 1992). Our work employed the methods of nonlinear dynamic modeling to arrive at a set of nonlinear difference equations. These equations are capable of amazing complexity with relatively few parameters. We have thereby been able to model the ability of process variables describing marital interaction to predict over a period of many years. To date, we have been able to predict over a fourteen-year period (Cook et al., 1995).

The application of applied mathematics to the study of marriage was presaged by von Bertalanffy (1968), who wrote a classic and highly influential book called *General System Theory*. Von Bertalanffy believed that the interaction of complex organizational units could be characterized by a set of values that change over time. These values indexed a particular unit in the "system," such as mother, father, or child. He thought the system was best described by a set of ordinary differential equations, and assumed that the functions of these equations would generally be nonlinear. His equations are very similar to our own, except that we used discrete difference equations rather than differential equations.

The basic logic for modeling the marital system was developed by James Murray (1989) in his classic book *Mathematical Biology*. In contrast to most problems in mathematical biology, however, developing the nonlinear difference equations for the marriage model required that we write down the "laws" governing a marriage's trajectory. Hence we found ourselves using these mathematical techniques in a novel manner. Indeed, our work in creating these equations led to the development of a technical language capable of describing how the marital interaction process unfolds over time, and this language has been pivotal in developing hypotheses regarding why marriages may succeed or fail.

In employing mathematics to model the marital system we also had to determine the relevant phenomena, or effects. There are many effects to choose from in the marital intervention field. We chose to focus on four, the Epidemic Effect, the Decay Effect, the Relapse Effect, and the Delay Effect. The Epidemic Effect refers to the epidemiological finding that 67 percent of all first marriages in the United States ended in divorce within the first forty years (Cherlin, 1981, Martin and Bumpass, 1989). These statistics suggest that divorce has indeed reached epidemic proportions. The Decay Effect refers to the consistent finding that only about 35 percent of couples make clinically significant improvements in marital satisfaction following our best marital therapies (Jacobson and Addis, 1993). Moreover, of those couples showing initial improvements, 30–50 percent relapse within one year; this is the Relapse Effect. Finally, the average delay time for obtaining marital therapy from the time a couple notices that there are serious marital problems is six years (Buongiorno, 1992). We have termed this the Delay Effect.

Like the balance theory of marriage, our mathematical model suggests that each marriage arrives at a core steady state, also termed "attractor" or "null cline," of cognition, affective behavior, and physiology in which negativity is balanced by positivity in each of these domains. It further suggests that each person brings an uninfluenced steady state (a function of enduring characteristics such as personality and the past history of the relationship) to every marital interaction. As a couple interacts, this steady state is changed through an influence process. The influence process can be described by two influence functions and by each person's inertia. The "inertia" parameter in the mathematical model represents each person's tendency to remain in a particular emotional state for some time, in short, his or her resistance to change.

The equations for the mathematical model are presented below,

$$W_{t+1} = I_{H \to W}(H_t) + r_1 W_t + a_1 \tag{1}$$
$$H_{t+1} = I_{W \to H}(W_t) + r_2 H_t + a_2 \tag{2}$$

where t is time, (H_t) is the husband's data at time t, and (W_t) is the wife's data at time t. The Is represent "influence functions," or the influence of one spouse's state at time t on the other spouse's state at the next time point. These functions have distinct shapes and describe the prediction regarding the course of a couple's marriage, or in mathematical terms the influence that one partner has on the other partner across a range of point-graph values after controlling for autocorrelation. The r_1 and r_2 are the "emotional inertia" parameters, reflecting the rate at which each individual tends to return to his or her natural, uninfluenced set point (baseline temperament). The a_1 and a_2 are constants specific to each individual, and represent each individual's initial state in the interaction. Using these equations, it is possible to compute the "uninfluenced set point," the "influenced set point," and the magnitude of discrepancy between influenced and uninfluenced set points.

To calculate the uninfluenced set point, we assume that during more neutral (or less affective) runs in the interaction, the influence function will be zero. When influence functions are zero, the equations can be reduced to include only the uninfluenced components:

$$W_{t+1} = r_1 W_t + a_1 \tag{1a}$$
$$H_{t+1} = r_2 H_t + a_2 \tag{2a}$$

Then r_1 and a_1 can be estimated using a least-squares best fit to the wife's data during times when her husband's influence is assumed to be zero, and r_2 and a_2 can be estimated using a least-squares best fit to the husband's data during times when the wife's influence is assumed to be zero. The uninfluenced set points are the steady states of equations (1a) and (2a) when the influence functions are zero, and are found by setting

$$W_{t+1} = W_t = W_{\text{uninfluenced}}, \text{ and}$$
$$H_{t+1} = H_t = H_{\text{uninfluenced}}, \text{ and so:}$$

$$W_{\text{uninfluenced}} = r_1\, W_{\text{uninfluenced}} + a_1, \text{ and}$$
$$H_{\text{uninfluenced}} = r_2\, H_{\text{uninfluenced}} + a_2$$

which reduces to the uninfluenced set points being:

$$W_{\text{uninfluenced}} = a_1/(1-r_1), \text{ and}$$
$$H_{\text{uninfluenced}} = a_2/(1-r_2)$$

With this estimation procedure, we are able to use actual data from our studies to compute the shape of the influence functions, where H_t and W_t are the data:

$$I_{H \to W}\,(H_t) = W_{t+1} - (r_2\, W_t + a_1), \text{ and}$$
$$I_{W \to H}\,(W_t) = H_{t+1} - (r_2\, H_t + a_2)$$

After the influence functions are determined from the data, we can compute the model's null-clines in a phase plane space (this is simply the plane with the husband's and the wife's scores as coordinates). Null-clines are theoretical curves where things stay the same over time. Mathematically, this is written as:

$$W_{t+1} = W_t = W, \text{ and}$$
$$H_{t+1} = H_t = H$$

Simple algebra in which we substitute W for all the wife's terms and H for all the husband's terms in equations (1) and (2) gives the form of these null clines as:

$$W(H_t) = [I_{H \to W}(H_t) + a_1]/(1-r_1) \qquad\qquad (3)$$
$$H(W_t) = [I_{W \to H}(W_t) + a_2]/(1-r_2) \qquad\qquad (4)$$

If we plot the husband's and wife's null-clines against their corresponding axes in the phase plane space, the influenced set points can be found where the null-clines intersect. In other words, these are points where both

Table 13.1. *Differences in mathematical model parameters as a function of marital stability*

	Husband inertia	Husband uninfl set pt	Husband infl- uninfl	Wife inertia	Wife uninfl set pt	Wife infl- uninfl
Stable	.29	.44	.17	.20	.55	.10
Unstable	.36	−.16	−.08	.49	−.44	−.10

the husband and wife will tend to stay the same over time. Cook and colleagues (1995) showed that if there is more than one influenced set point, some will be stable and some will be unstable. We have shown that the null-clines have the same shape as the influence functions, but they are moved over (translated) by the individual's initial state (a_1 or a_2), and scaled by one minus the individual's inertia (r_1 or r_2).

The uninfluenced and influenced set points are sometimes referred to as uninfluenced and influenced steady states. Steady states allow one to determine where a system will move when perturbed. This information can then be used to describe the marital system's behavior in the phase plane space. Points will drift toward one stable steady state on one side of the Separatrix curve and toward a different steady state on the other side of the curve. In the positive phase plane space (H_t and W_t both positive) stable influenced steady states are called "positive attractors"; conversely, in the negative phase plane space we find "negative attractors." These are the points at which couples will tend to settle when the affective patterns during an interaction move in a positive direction, as in the first case, or in a negative direction, as in the latter case.

As regards the model parameters, an examination of our research data revealed several differences between stable and unstable marriages (see Table 13.1; Cook et al., 1995). In general, stable marriages show lower inertia than unstable marriages, with unstable marriages showing greater husband and wife inertia when resolving conflict. The inertias tell us how much resistance to change there is in the influence process. High inertias tend to be indicative of distress, as they generally relate to continuance in a particular affective state. Another difference between stable and unstable marriages involves the influence functions. The influence functions of stable couples were shown to be matched in shape. By contrast, unstable couples had more negative husband and wife uninfluenced set points (be-

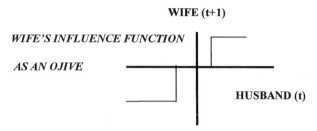

WIFE (t+1)

WIFE'S INFLUENCE FUNCTION

AS AN OJIVE

HUSBAND (t)

Figure 13.2. Influence function of the husband on the wife, where the *x*-axis is the husband's previous score, H_t, and the *y*-axis is the influenced component, $I_{HW}(H_t)$, of the wife's following score, W_{t+1}.

fore influence even begins), and showed a mismatch in shape between husband and wife influence functions. Finally, for couples in stable marriages, the influenced set point was more positive than the uninfluenced set point, while in couples headed for divorce the influenced set point was more negative than the uninfluenced set point.

A closer examination of the three types of stable marriage showed the influence functions to be dramatically different across typology. Validating couples exerted influence throughout the range of values. As such, they had a positive influence for positive values and a negative influence for negative values. Volatile couples exerted influence only when the interaction had negative values, and their influence was negative. Conflict-avoiding couples influenced one another only when the interaction had positive values, and their influence was positive.

While these early studies used actual data to estimate the shape of the influence functions, we have subsequently begun to experiment with a theoretical shape for these functions. That is, we fit a theoretical function to the influenced component of behavior that is calculated for each point in time. This allows us to compute the influenced steady states for these theoretical functions. We are currently assuming that the theoretical shape of the influence function is an ojive (S-shaped curve). Figure 13.2 shows such a function, where the husband has no effect on the wife until he exceeds a certain threshold of positivity, and then he has a constant positive effect on her next behavior. For the negative ranges, he has no effect until he exceeds a threshold of negativity, and then he has a constant negative effect on her next behavior. As the model is modified in subsequent research, individual couples may be shown to have their own thresholds, and the shape of the function could become more complex. For example, we might decide that the more positive the husband's previous behavior, the more positive his impact on the wife's subsequent behavior; so instead of a constant, we would have a straight line with a slope.

Once the theoretical influence functions have been fit to the influenced components of behavior for husband and for wife, it is possible to estimate the influenced set points, or steady states, for this theoretical marital system. We have already shown that the null-clines are the influence functions, translated by a constant and scaled by one minus the inertia. Equations (3) and (4) will be used again, but this time with the fitted values of the theoretical influence functions for each H_t and W_t in the phase plane. The influenced steady states, therefore, are just the intersection of the null-clines. Moreover, these steady states can now be computed, since the functions have a known form, instead of being found graphically (as was the case when the influence functions were simply determined from the data). The null-clines can, of course, still be plotted for each individual couple.

The mathematical model provides a qualitative description of the couple's interactive world. It also allows us to say, for any couple, how the marital interaction will vary as a function of the model parameters. The use of the mathematical model makes it possible to simulate couple cognition, affective behavior, and physiology under conditions different from those in which they were observed. These simulations suggest hypotheses that can be tested in experiments, and the results of these experiments can then be used to test the mathematical model. For example, we can ask what would happen if the husband began a discussion in a much more positive mood (i.e., a_2 is more positive). Then we can do an experiment to see what would happen if we told the husband that he had just won the lab lottery and gave him a fifty-dollar check. When we do our actual experiments, we can test whether the model works in these simulations and, if it does not, perhaps figure out how to modify it. If the model is right, we can use that data to predict how they will interact under entirely different conditions. Then we can test to see if this prediction is correct.

The model also allows for the possibility of catastrophic changes. A catastrophe means that as some model parameter changes continuously, after crossing a threshold, the system becomes qualitatively different. The simplest catastrophic system is called a "cusp" catastrophe, which bifurcates the system into only two possible qualitative steady states. With the S-shaped curve, a marital system can have as many as five steady states. Using our influence functions and the model parameters, which determine the null-clines, we can now model catastrophic qualitative changes in the marriage. For instance, as the parameters of the model undergo gradual continuous change, it is quite possible for a couple to suddenly lose all positive stable steady states and be left with only negative ones. This happens as the initial states (a_1 and a_2) become more negative and the couple's inertia increases (r_1 and r_2). After this point the marriage will be qualitatively different. Depending on where the couple starts, and on the strength of the negative attractors, a marital interaction may begin to drift toward the negative attractor. Gottman (1994a) has termed this process the Distance and Isolation Cascade. Couples in this cascade tend to avoid one another, arrange their lives in parallel, and become increasingly lonely. This process suggests that effective therapy may simply increase the strength of the positive attractor and decrease the strength of the negative attractor.

One problem we have yet to solve is that the cusp catastrophe has symmetrical hysteresis (hysteresis refers to the process by which a system once perturbed returns to its previous state). In symmetrical hysteresis, change is symmetrically possible from positive to negative steady states, meaning that positive catastrophes are as likely as negative ones. If we consider the Epidemic Effect, however, it is clear that marriages are more likely to wind up in negative steady states than in positive ones without the addition of energy into the system. We need to alter the model to suggest that marital systems have asymmetrical hysteresis. It may be possible to model this by computing the "strength" of the positive and negative attractors in each marriage. This can be computed by the sum of the squares of their derivatives, $[W_{t+1} - W_t]^2 + [H_{t+1} - H_t]^2$, near the attractor sites.

An examination of the data collected in our longitudinal study of newlyweds revealed that the negative threshold point on the influence function predicted marital stability. The results suggest that wives showing lower thresholds of negativity during the observations collected in the first few months of marriage were more likely to be members of couples classified as stable at follow-up. In other words, if it took less negativity from the husband to have a negative impact on the wife, the couple showed higher marital satisfaction. Subsequently, we developed the hypothesis that this lowered negative threshold was tapping the wife's greater likelihood to attempt repair of the interaction when it first became negative, rather than waiting or trying to adapt to the negativity. Thus, our model suggests that the Epidemic Effect, the Decay Effect, the Relapse Effect, and the Delay Effect may be conceptualized more accurately as one effect, the Delay Effect. Couples who delay repairing their marriages are those whose marriages deteriorate. Moreover, those couples who delay repair are likely to relapse after marital therapy. We have recently begun work on altering the mathematical model to estimate an added repair function that can jolt the system to a more positive value when a couple exceeds some threshold of negativity.

Developing an Empirically Based Marital Intervention

Using the Sound Marital House theory in combination with our mathematical model we have generated prescriptions for empirically based intervention. We suggest that a more effective marital therapy may be derived from relatively simple social psychological studies in which very specific interventions are designed to produce only proximal change, as opposed to carrying out complex clinical trials that attempt to alter all aspects of the marriage. This makes sense if the goal of the interventions is to target and change specific destructive patterns of marital interaction (e.g., social cognitions, attributions, and physiological patterns). The problem, however, is which predictors to select as targets of change. This problem is solved once we have a mathematical model, since we then have a set of parameters that index the fundamental marital processes related to our prediction of the longitudinal course of a marriage. Moreover, this model is eminently testable and modifiable, allowing us to generate experiments and providing a method for computer simulation of couple behavior across any number of experimental conditions.

The following section contains a series of hypotheses currently under study in our laboratory. Instead of trying to create permanent change in the marriage, the goal of the studies is to improve only the second of two conflict resolution interactions. These interactions involve two conversations in which couples are asked to discuss at least one long-standing area of disagreement. Following these two conversations, we have found that it is possible to determine whether the second conversation is ''better'' than the first, in the sense that the parameters we derive from the second interaction are less characteristic of couples on a trajectory toward divorce than the parameters in the first interaction. Our overall goal is to develop a new empirically based marital therapy, with each hypothesis tapping a different area related to divorce prediction. The eight hypotheses are presented in terms of the parameters of our mathematical model.

Creating Proximal Change by Reducing Emotional Inertia

Negative affect reciprocity has been shown to be the most consistent discriminator in determining whether couples are unhappily or happily married. However, the presence of negative affect reciprocity in and of itself is not sufficient to differentiate between distressed and nondistressed couples. This differentiation requires that we know something about the couple's ability to stop the string of reciprocated negative affect once it has begun. This suggests that it is the duration of negative affect reciprocity that differentiates couples. Finally, the occurrence of positive affect reciprocity does not imply that there is no negative affect reciprocity. In fact, our research indicates that couples who are high in negative affect reciprocity also tend to be high in positive affect reciprocity (Gottman, 1980). The first three hypotheses that we developed target negative affect reciprocity, with the goal of reducing emotional inertia.

Hypothesis 1: Improving the Success of Repair Attempts. An examination of repair attempts, microanalytically, reveals that repair processes include social processes such as feeling probes that explore feelings, information exchange, social comparison, humor, distraction, gossip, finding areas of common ground, and appeals to basic philosophy and expectations in the marriage. While both distressed and nondistressed couples use repair attempts, for some reason these attempts fail in unhappy marriages. The failure of repair processes results in couples being unable to exit the negative affect reciprocity cycle. Indeed, sequential analyses of behavior indicate that the members of dissatisfied couples were more likely to respond to their partners' negative affect by expressing negative affect themselves. These findings argue for an intervention that targets repair attempts. The obvious clinical prescription is to formalize the natural process of repair, driving a wedge into the sequential bond of negativity, and thereby freeing up the repertoire of repair tactics that the couple already possess.

Hypothesis 2: Reducing Defensiveness. The second aspect of emotional inertia involves one of the Four Horsemen of the Apocalypse, defensiveness. Defensiveness tends to fuel the cycle of reciprocated negative affect. We have found that people behave defensively when they feel attacked and believe they are responding to that attack. It is also clear that the way spouses state complaints can make it more or less likely that a defensive response will occur. For instance, when blame is added to a complaint (criticism) or when contempt is used, individuals are more likely to respond defensively. Having each partner state complaints specifically, using nonblaming "XYZ-statements" or "I-statements" instead of "you-statements," and attempting to get the listener to respond to complaints may reduce defensiveness, and in turn reduce emotional inertia.

Hypothesis 3: Increasing Physiological Soothing. We believe that physiological arousal is part of why people reciprocate negative affect in long chains. For instance, defensive behavior seems to involve diffuse physiological arousal and "flooding" in distressed couples (Gottman, 1994b). Each member of the couple may therefore benefit from learning to self-soothe and to soothe the partner during periods of negative affect. The idea of physiological soothing might be considered one of the "nonspecific" components of most treatments. Therapists often perform this task of soothing the couple by modeling a variety of techniques, such as reframing or reinterpreting a comment, encouraging an empathic response, or soothing the receiver of a message that is perceived as an attack. Unfortunately, when the couple leaves the therapist's office and goes home, the therapist is no longer available to do the calming. We suggest that the couple's inability to soothe on their own may be the primary active ingredient in causing relapse after treatment, and thus relapse may be minimized if the couple is taught the skills of physiological soothing.

Making Uninfluenced Set Points More Positive

An additional two hypotheses were developed with the goal of making the uninfluenced set points more positive. The "uninfluenced set points" can be thought of as proportional to the resting affective state regarding marriage. This state encompasses the characteristic cognitions and affects spouses have about the marriage when they are not together (uninfluenced by their partners) or when they are just beginning to interact with their partners.

The reader will recall that a positive-minus-negative index was highly predictive of marital stability and divorce (Gottman and Levenson, 1992). Variables such as positive-minus-negative affect also appear to be remarkably stable across situations (Gottman, 1980). Thus, we suggest that for each couple there exists a "set point" of positivity minus negativity for both husbands and wives. Even when uninfluenced by the partner this set point is more negative in distressed couples than in nondistressed couples. Furthermore, our research indicates that this set point need not be functional. Regardless of its functional or dysfunctional nature, the marital system will defend this set point and resist changing it. The next hypotheses concern this thesis.

Hypothesis 4: Softened Start-Up. We discovered that the manner in which a conflict discussion begins, what we are calling start-up, determines a lot of what happens during the remainder of the conversation. Indeed, what will happen to a marriage in the future can be determined by watching just the first three minutes of a couple's interaction. If a couple's start-up is negative (hardened start-up) the entire conversation is likely to be negative. On the other hand, if a couple's conversation begins in a more positive fashion (softened start-up) the remainder of the conversation is likely to be positive.

Hypothesis 5: Eliminating Contempt. The way people think about their relationships and their partners is predictive of stability and divorce (Booth and White, 1980; Gottman and Levenson, 1992; Holtzworth-Munroe and Jacobson, 1989). In general, distress-maintaining attributions maximize the impact of negativity and minimize the impact of positivity of the partner's behavior. Relationship-enhancing attributions have the opposite effect. This hypothesis suggests that distressed couples may benefit from changing their cognitions and attributions.

An experimental intervention currently under way in our laboratory seeks to do just that by increasing relationship-enhancing cognitions like admiration (the antidote for contempt). We employ a procedure in which couples are required to think about the positive characteristics of their partners and share examples of events in which their partners displayed these positive traits. The hypothesis is that this experience can increase the amount of positive affect with which a couple starts the second interaction. In order to fully understand the action of cognitions and attributions, we are also using negative trait adjectives to engage distress-maintaining cognitions. In this latter case, we expect to see a reduction in the overall amount of positive affect with which couples begin their second discussion. An unexpected finding suggests that this exercise is beneficial, in the short term, for couples who have become emotionally disengaged from one another. By allowing the verbalization of concerns about one's partner, this exercise apparently functions to temporarily reengage the couple in their relationship.

Making the Influenced Set Point More Positive than the Uninfluenced Set Point

The remaining hypotheses seek to establish an influenced set point that is more positive than the uninfluenced set point. The influenced set point is the average value for those times in which a spouse has changed his or her behavior following a partner's behavior. We are interested in measuring the overall direction of this influence, and we approach this issue by asking, how do couples enter the cascade of the Four Horsemen of the Apocalypse? We suggest that it is actually quite easy to enter this behavioral cascade and that, in fact, it requires energy to avoid the cascade during everyday marital interaction. For instance, if we consider criticism, we realize that it is not much different from a complaint, it is simply more global and blaming in nature. In order to avoid these more global, blaming statements, and subsequent entry into the cascade, a couple needs to develop emotional connections across various contexts.

Hypothesis 6: Responding to Anger. Our research suggests that a negative influenced set point is often due to the husband's failure to respond to his wife's anger, leading to an escalation of the negativity (Gottman, 1994a, 1994b). Moreover, this work underscores the importance of making an emotional connection at a lower level of negative affect intensity. This emotional connection need not be an empathetic response or validation; in fact, research indicates that it is rare to find validation in response to anger. The use of role playing and instruction may help to alter the response of both partners to the spouse's anger, thereby reducing the likelihood that an interaction will escalate and become negative.

Hypothesis 7: Responding to Positivity. In marital relationships positive affect, like negative affect, exerts a powerful influence. Indeed, it plays a significant role in determining the developmental course of the marriage. An examination of the Distance and Isolation Cascade provides some insight into the processes involved in building and maintaining positive affect. Couples who enter this cascade ultimately experience loneliness in the marriage. This loneliness often occurs in couples who have ceased to be interested in and excited by one another and their relationship, the result of unrequited interest or excitement. When these unhappily married couples are asked to engage in a discussion of daily events, they often show little response to the events being related to them by their partner. This type of nonresponse is deflating and leads the speaker to withdraw emotionally or to become sad; the process is then usually repeated in identical form, with the partners switching roles. These findings suggest that when spouses fail to respond to one another, they move the set point in a negative direction. We believe that interventions encouraging a couple to "turn toward" each other, through the expression of genuine interest in the partner and the partner's experiences, will strengthen the couple's emotional connections and increase the amount of positive affect expressed during marital inter-actions.

Hypothesis 8: Exploring the Dreams-Within-Conflict. This hypothesis suggests that it is possible to break up the logjam of two uncompromising opposed positions by uncovering the life dreams that underlie each person's entrenchment in his or her position. This involves looking for the symbolic meanings (e.g., metaphors, stories, hopes, and dreams) inherent in each position. For example, discussion and conflict regarding finances often taps into issues of power, freedom, competence, and security. Each spouse's position involves latent images and associations that need to be uncovered and expressed in a safe marital climate.

Even if the couple is not in a state of crisis, they may experience intense pain due to the fact that they are deadlocked on some central issues in their marriage. Typically, a couple experiencing gridlock on an issue will undergo a process that begins with ''dreams in opposition'' and moves to ''entrenchment of positions,'' ''fears of accepting influence,'' and vilification. Exploring the dreams-within-conflict involves having each person, in the conjoint context, express the symbolic meaning of his or her position, as well as the fears around accepting influence on this issue. Behind each person's position, and the resistance to accepting influence, there are usually a set of metaphors, narratives, and mythological stories that can be traced to the individual's past.

Summary

In this chapter we have proposed and outlined both a theoretical model of marriage, the Sound Marital House theory, and a mathematical model of marriage. These models of marital interaction are empirically based and provide us with a more complete topography of the dynamics and complexities inherent in the marital system. We have shown how these advances in our own work have added to the language used to describe marriages and how they have allowed us to simulate marital interaction under new conditions. Finally, we suggested eight hypotheses for marital intervention. The hypothesized studies have two central objectives. First, they are meant to assess whether or not the proposed interventions have changed the variables that are predictive of the cascades toward marital dissolution. Second, we hope to further our understanding of how cognition, affective behavior, and physiology impact on one another and on the marital interaction. Following the attainment of these two broad objectives, a new marital therapy that combines all interventions found to be effective must be created and tested in a real clinical trial. This clinical trial needs to be combined with an epidemiological study so that we can discuss the nature of treatment failures. Analyses of this type will eventually lead to aptitude-by-treatment interaction studies as we learn how to tailor the form and dose of therapy to best suit each individual couple.

References

Anderson, C. M., Dimidjan, S., and Miller, A. (1995). Redefining the past, present, and future: Therapy with long term marriages at mid-life. In N. Jacobson and A. Gurman (Eds.), *Clinical handbook of couple therapy* (pp. 247–260). New York: Guilford.

Azrin, N. H., Naster, B. J., and Jones., R. (1973). Reciprocity counseling: A rapid learning-based procedure for marital counseling. *Behaviour Research and Therapy, 11*, 365–382.

Booth, A., and White, L. (1980). Thinking about divorce. *Journal of Marriage and the Family, 42*, 605–616.

Buehlman, K., and Gottman, J. M. (1996). The oral history coding system. In J. M. Gottman (Ed.), *What predicts divorce? The measures: Questionnaires for the distance and isolation cascade.* Mahwah, NJ: Erlbaum.

Buehlman, K., Gottman, J. M., and Katz, L. (1992). How a couple views their past predicts their future: Predicting divorce from an oral history interview. *Journal of Family Psychology, 5*, 295–318.

Buongiorno, J. (1992). *Wait time until professional treatment in marital therapy.* Unpublished master's thesis, Catholic University of America, Washington, DC.

Carstensen, L. L., Gottman, J. M., and Levenson, R. W. (1995). Emotional behavior in long-term marriage. *Psychology and Aging, 10*, 140–149.

Cherlin, A. (1981). *Marriage, divorce, remarriage.* Cambridge, MA: Harvard University Press.

Cook, J., Tyson, R., White, J., Rushe, R., Gottman, J. M., and Murray, J. (1995). The mathematics of marital conflict: Qualitative dynamic mathematical modeling of marital interaction. *Journal of Family Psychology, 9*, 110–130.

Gottman, J. M. (1980). The consistency of nonverbal affect and affect reciprocity in marital interaction. *Journal of Consulting and Clinical Psychology, 48*, 711–717.

Gottman, J. M. (1990). How marriages change. In G. R. Patterson (Ed.), *Depression and aggression in family interaction* (pp. 75–101). Hillsdale, NJ: Erlbaum.

Gottman, J. M. (1993a). A theory of marital dissolution and stability. *Journal of Family Psychology, 7*, 57–75.

Gottman, J. M. (1993b). The roles of conflict engagement, escalation, or avoidance in marital interaction: A longitudinal view of five types of couples. *Journal of Consulting and Clinical Psychology, 61*, 6–15.

Gottman, J. M. (1994a). *What predicts divorce? The relationship between marital processes and marital outcomes.* Hillsdale, NJ: Erlbaum.

Gottman, J. M. (1994b). *Why marriages succeed or fail.* New York: Simon and Schuster.

Gottman, J. M., Coan, J., Carrère, S., and Swanson, C. (1998). Predicting marital happiness and stability from newlywed interactions. *Journal of Marriage and the Family, 60,* 5–22.

Gottman, J. M., and Levenson, R. W. (1992). Marital processes predictive of later dissolution: Behavior, physiology, and health. *Journal of Personality and Social Psychology, 63,* 221–233.

Gottman, J. M., and Levenson, R. W. (1997). *The role of positive affect in long-term marital stability.* Unpublished manuscript, University of Washington at Seattle.

Holtzworth-Munroe, A., and Jacobson, N. S. (1989). Relationship between behavioral marital therapy outcome and process variables. *Journal of Consulting and Clinical Psychology, 57,* 658–662.

Jacobson, N. S., and Addis, M. E. (1993). Research on couple therapy: What do we know? Where are we going? *Journal of Consulting and Clinical Psychology, 61,* 85–93.

Krokoff, L. J., Gottman, J. M., and Haas, S. D. (1989). Validation of a rapid couples interaction coding system. *Behavioral Assessment, 11,* 65–79.

Lederer, W. J., and Jackson, D. D. (1968). *The mirages of marriage.* New York: Norton.

Levenson, R. W., Carstensen, L. L., and Gottman, J. M. (1994). The influence of age and gender on affect, physiology and their interrelations: A study of long-term marriages. *Journal of Personality and Social Psychology, 67,* 56–68.

Levenson, R. W., and Gottman, J. M. (1983). Marital interaction: Physiological linkage and affective exchange. *Journal of Personality and Social Psychology, 45,* 587–597.

Lorber, M. (1997). *Repair attempts in marital conflict.* Unpublished manuscript, University of Washington at Seattle.

Martin, T. C., and Bumpass, L. (1989). Recent trends in marital disruption. *Demography, 26,* 37–51.

Murray, J. (1989). *Mathematical biology.* New York: Springer-Verlag.

Murstein, B. I., Cerreto, M., and MacDonald, M. G. (1977). A theory of the effect of exchange orientation on marriage and friendship. *Journal of Marriage and the Family, 39,* 543–548.

Rowell, L. (1986). *Human circulation: Regulation during physical stress.* New York: Oxford University Press.

Stuart, R. (1980). *Helping couples change.* New York: Guilford.

von Bertalanffy, L. (1968). *General system theory.* New York: George Braziller.

Vincent, J. P., Friedman, L. C., Nugent, J., and Messerly, L. (1979). Demand characteristics in observations of marital interaction. *Journal of Consulting and Clinical Psychology, 47,* 557–566.

Weiss, R. L. (1980). Strategic behavioral marital therapy: Toward a model for assessment and intervention. In J. P. Vincent (Ed.), *Advances in family intervention, assessment and theory* (vol. 1, pp. 229–271). Greenwich, CT: JAI Press.

COMMENTARY

The Dynamics of Emotional Development: Models, Metaphors, and Methods

Daniel P. Keating and Fiona K. Miller

The editors of this volume have assembled a rich feast for anyone interested in human emotion, its development, and its underlying dynamics. In selecting self-organization (via dynamic systems) as the organizing theme, and in recruiting leading-edge theorists and researchers in the study of emotion and its development to view their own work through the lens of self-organizing dynamic systems, the editors have created an opportunity for coherence to emerge from the complex (perhaps even chaotic) terrain of the science of human emotion and emotional development.

How successful is this attempt at a unifying approach to this field? If, as the editors claim in their introductory chapter and the authors of a number of chapters echo, this approach represents a paradigm shift in the study of emotion and its development, then we will be able to evaluate its success only in the long term. If the ambitious scope – from neurobiology to individual psychology to interpersonal processes – were to be successfully integrated in theory as well as in empirical and practical realization, then this would indeed represent an extraordinary leap forward, analogous perhaps to the modern synthesis of molecular genetics and natural selection in evolutionary biology.

None of the authors lays claim to a modern synthesis on this order of magnitude. More realistically, we may ask whether this approach shows promise of such wide-ranging integration. Clearly, this is an aspiration of some authors. Lewis (this volume), for example, suggests that parallel emotion-cognition processes across emotion episodes (microdevelopment), moods (mesodevelopment), and personality patterns (macrodevelopment) "may express deep principles by which order arises through intentional processes that cause emotion at all scales" (Lewis, p. 64). Although the hope for a major paradigm shift is shared by other authors in this volume, there is also a broadly shared recognition that moving toward this goal will

373

not be easy. As Scherer (this volume) notes, there are a number of "tall orders" to fill before the dynamic systems approach can move from being just another word game toward its realization as a true paradigm shift. Such an effort will "need to (a) study ongoing processes over time, (b) study multiple systems and their interactions (cognition, physiology, expression), (c) adopt experimental approaches using well-controlled manipulations, and (d) formalize predictions" (Scherer, p. 95). Panksepp (this volume) adds a similar cautionary note: "These nonlinear tools are largely descriptive and not necessarily the scalpels we need to probe the ultracomplex *causal* underbelly of nature" (Panksepp, p. 257, emphasis in original).

These and similar observations by other contributors to this volume reflect the diversity of perspectives that one might take toward this emerging enterprise. There is real excitement about the prospects for using principles of self-organizing dynamic systems to unify a wide range of phenomena within a single, coherent explanatory framework. But there is also evident caution about the magnitude of the task, given the constraints it would need to meet (as noted by Scherer) and the tendency for such approaches, at least initially, to increase the complexity that needs to be addressed rather than to reduce it.

Our goal in this chapter is to provide for the nonspecialist reader some sense of both the promise and the current status of the self-organizing dynamic systems approach to the science of emotion and emotional development. Because there are in fact multiple approaches under the dynamic systems banner, it is helpful to view the landscape from several different levels.

A preliminary word on terminology may be of value to the reader not already immersed in the literature. Not all dynamic systems are self-organizing, nor do principles of self-organization always require dynamic systems modeling. As the name suggests, "dynamic systems" refers both to the nature of systems which integrate a variety of change mechanisms and to methods (often mathematical) designed to describe them. Self-organization refers to the principle by which some dynamic systems generate emergent order from previously disorganized or chaotic states, whether or not such emergence is described mathematically. The thrust of this volume is to explore the potential for understanding self-organization using dynamic systems approaches (from the metaphoric to the mathematical, as we will discuss below). In general, we have used "self-organization" to refer to the developmental principle of emergent order and "dynamic systems" to refer to a wide range of approaches to understanding how emergent order actually arises. One goal of this volume and similar efforts is to further clarify the conceptual range of the currently rather loose useage in the field.

We first consider the most general level of the dynamic systems landscape. Do dynamic systems approaches point toward a different overarching model of emotion and its development? If so, can we identify the general outlines of this new paradigm? Next, we consider these approaches as providers of helpful metaphors for thinking about emotion and its development. At present, this is the most widely used aspect of dynamic systems approaches, not only in emotional development but for most other areas of developmental science. The metaphoric uses of dynamic systems approaches are many and varied, and are employed to considerable advantage by the contributors to this volume. We then take up the most specific and stringent use of dynamic systems approaches in the next section: analytic methods for the design of experiments and observation and for the analysis of data to reveal the operation of developing dynamic systems. Again, the diversity of approaches by different contributors to this volume is reflective of the numerous instantiations of dynamic systems ideas in contemporary developmental science. This is akin to the early stages of development of the general linear model, and analogies to that history may afford some perspective on the current growth of dynamic systems methods in developmental science. Finally, we conclude by considering some of the promising directions and potential barriers to dynamic systems approaches to emotion and its development, as it traverses the path from fascinating complexity toward the possibility of a coherent, unified theory.

Dynamic Systems Models

As the chapters in this volume make clear, models of nonlinear dynamic systems seek to capture the self-organizing history of any system, and to identify its core processes (or dynamics). The diversity of uses of dynamic systems approaches evident in the chapters in this volume makes it clear, however, that the applications of these approaches are sufficiently different that coherence across the models is not self-evident. At the risk of oversimplification, some sense of the commonalities may emerge by focusing on some of the basic features that cut across these diverse models.

We begin with the theme of this volume and a first principle of all complex, living dynamic systems: they are self-organizing. Such dynamic systems display the capacity to become organized over time, even from ill-formed or chaotic origins. An important corollary is that infinitely elaborate and formally elegant structures can arise from simple processes operating over time. In simplest terms, there appear to be four central features of self-organizing dynamic systems. The first two features describe their operation: (1) the process must iterate routinely; (2) the process must have a feedback loop. The next two features describe the context within which the system operates: (3) the context includes internal constraints that have historically shaped the system, which, for organisms, means their phylogenetic and ontogenetic history to date; and (4) the context also sets external constraints that limit and shape the actual self-organization that takes place.

We can see that, taken together, these principles define a general developmental function. Process and context interact over time, and the history of those interactions is incorporated into organismic structures. As in the evolution of species, an individual's future is never fully determined by the past, but it is always constrained by it. The nonlinear nature of self-organizing dynamic systems leads to many important consequences, which can be regarded as necessary corollary principles to their operation. Many of these are well illustrated in the chapters of this volume, as new models, metaphors, or methods. In the balance of this section, we take note of three overarching ideas that capture essential features of the potential paradigm shift.

Integration across Systems and Levels

One of the great limitations of linear modeling, as noted by a number of the authors of this volume, is the difficulty of integrating across the operations of different levels of a system, taking into account the variety of its component processes. There are at least two major reasons for this difficulty. The first is that, as the number of components or subsystems – treated, necessarily, as variables in linear models – increases beyond a small number, the resolving capacity of even sophisticated analyses becomes strained. At the simplest level, for example, is the rarity of accurate predictions of 3-way interactions in analysis of variance. For interactions of even higher order, the difficulty increases exponentially. Thus, the problem of modeling person and context variables becomes intractable early in the game, compared to the likely complexity that the study of emotion and its development requires.

More sophisticated linear models afford more scope for complexity, including a rapidly emerging array of structural equation models, hierarchical linear models, and individual growth curve analyses. Even in these cases, however, some a priori carving up of the focal dimensions is required, and decisions about how well a "good fit" or "best fit" model actually fits the data remains somewhat arbitrary. This last point identifies the second difficulty, namely that the interpretation of higher-order interactions, structural models, and multilevel models is too easily "in the eye of the beholder." Many of the key decisions in a lengthy string of contingent choice points are not transparent even to the sophisticated, critical reader – even when findings are presented conscientiously.

This should not be construed as a blanket criticism of the general linear model. Indeed, one of the issues we take up later is the misguided propensity of some advocates of "nonlinearity" to dismiss the important contributions of linear analyses. But it does seem clear that the strength of linear models lies in their ability to analyze (or to break apart, from the original Greek), rather than in their ability to integrate or synthesize (to make whole). A number of authors in this volume point to the potential of dynamic systems models to address directly the problem of integration or synthesis, by creating multilevel, multicomponent, and multisystem models with testable predictions.

Several authors in this volume make this issue a central theme. A compelling example is offered by Freeman (this volume) in his discussion of the dynamics of the preafference loop, where he argues that "[w]hen internally organized action patterns radiate from the limbic system, they are not packets of information. . . . They are solicitations to other parts of the brain to enter into cooperative activity. . . . The linking together in a global pattern is not a directive, . . . [rather] it is a process of evolution by consensus. . . . For the limbic system the contributions are the spacetime field, the feedback regulation of the neuromodulator nuclei in the reticular core, and the simultaneous integration of the input from all of the sensory areas that establishes the unity of perception. That integration provides the basis for the synthesis of intent" (Freeman, this volume, p. 228). Similarly, Scherer (this volume, p. 86) describes a theory of subsystem synchronization as the core dynamic of emotions: "I have proposed to limit the use of the term *emotion* to episodes in time during which the degree of coupling or synchronization of *all* organismic subsystems exceeds a normal threshold of normal covariation. . . . Thus a certain degree of entrainment is the *conditio sine qua non* to speak of emotion in the sense defined here."

Efforts to understand the dynamics of "on-line" emotion characterize one type of integrative model. A second type of integrative model incorporates extra-organismic processes, and their impact on the organism across time. Schore (this volume, p. 158), for example, proposes a dynamic systems model that incorporates "attachment dynamics, . . . the role of bioamines in self-organizational processes of synaptic connectivity, and . . . the energy-dependent imprinting of neural circuitry in the infant brain.'' As noted above, Lewis (this volume) proposes that different levels of emotional activity – episodes, moods, and personality patterns – become integrated across ''real'' and ''developmental'' time.

Space does not permit a careful analysis of how each author deals with this issue, but virtually all chapters touch on it either centrally or peripherally. Thus, it seems safe to conclude that a key aspect of dynamic systems models is the goal of achieving a coherent integration across numerous levels, subsystems, or components. Strides toward this goal are evident in this volume, but the challenges to achieving it are also abundantly reflected.

Narratives and Paradigms

A striking observation arises from consideration of the above examples, and of similar examples in other chapters in this volume. Although couched as sensible scientific theories designed to integrate across different levels, components, or subsystems, much of their power is that they appeal to us as meaningful stories. Before considering the basis for this appealing quality, and its potential consequences, a particularly salient example, abridged from Harkness and Tucker (this volume, p. 199), serves to illustrate the point: ''Repeated experiences of loss, neglect, or abuse continually activate cognitive themes of abandonment and worthlessness, coupled with feelings of hopelessness and guilt. The experience of many such situations leads to the spreading of activation to an increasingly articulated and broad set of appraisals and emotions. As a result, these depressive elements become strengthened, to the detriment of more positive and adaptive cognitive and emotional elements . . . [A]ctivating one part of the network will serve to activate other parts, making negative memories more salient and increasing the probability of forming a negative appraisal of current events. This initial activation serves to magnify depressed mood, which in turn further activates the cognitive network. The end result of this process is a 'downward spiral' of mood and cognition in which minor dysphoria evolves into persistent and more severe depression.''

What is noteworthy about this extended hypothesis, involving over a dozen linked elements from initial experience to the end result of a ''downward spiral,'' is that it is so easily comprehended and encoded (though, obviously, not as easily tested as a traditional univariate, bivariate, or even multivariate model). Multiple feedback and feedforward loops pose no particular problem for our understanding the thrust of the argument. This comprehensibility may be due to the time-linked nature of the hypothesis, which affords easy ordering of events. More fundamental, however, is the possibility that narrative taps into a more fundamental cognitive apparatus than does paradigmatic thinking (Bruner, 1990), which may be more derivative.

In this sense, then, dynamic systems models of self-organization in development may offer a bridge between paradigmatic research designs, which are typically quantitative, and more narrative, typically qualitative, approaches to understanding developmental phenomena. The advantage here is not only ease of understanding, but also the ability to construct theoretical models that can encompass the complexity that is likely to be inherent in the phenomena. Construction of complex theoretical models is, of course, just the first step. We can now turn to the next step – constructing models capable of resolving the envisioned complexity.

Resolving Complexity

If the contributions of such dynamic systems models were merely to highlight the need for integration while allowing the proposition of more complex hypotheses, the future prospects would be dim. The wariness of researchers who favor tight analytic models of small pieces of reality would be justified in such a case, in the sense that the output of dynamic systems models would always be some version of "everything matters, more or less." Advancing the scientific discourse requires the invention of methods to resolve the complexity that dynamic systems models are so capable of introducing.

In a later section we consider a number of specific methods that help to address various aspects of this desideratum. Here, we consider three proposals in this volume that seek to incorporate complexity directly into the model, so as to increase model coherence and thereby reduce the overall complexity.

Ryan and colleagues (this volume) propose a mathematical model of marriage, in which they provide "a more complete topography of the dynamics and complexities inherent in the marital system" and describe how such advances have "allowed us to simulate marital interaction under new conditions" (Ryan et al., this volume, p. 370). In an ingenious use of time-series data on marital interactions, the authors were able to construct seemingly interpretable functions combining the wife's behavior, the husband's behavior, their interaction, and time. They characterize these functions by their locations in phase space, and derive quantitative parameters of the main functions. Using such functions, they are able to explore through simulation various aspects of ''theoretical'' marital relationships. This approach has much to recommend it, particularly the reduction of massive data arrays into comprehensible theoretical accounts. But several caveats remain. Using terms from the more traditional linear model, we may ask: How reliable are the derived parameters of individual and couple functioning, and against what distributional model can we test the claim of ''differences between stable and unstable marriages'' (Ryan et al., this volume, p. 361). How generalizable are the functions, given that they appear to be simultaneously derived from and applied to the same database? These are more than quibbles and less than criticisms. They reflect instead the novelty of the models and the methods invented to test them, a point to which we return later.

Lewis (this volume) uses a different feature of dynamic systems as a method of inducing coherence from complexity. In an effort to integrate across the vastly different time courses of emotional life (episodes, moods, and personality), he proposes a scheme by which an integration of neural and psychological processes might proceed: ''Self-organizing EIs [emotional interpretations, or emotion-appraisal amalgams] . . . emerge in microdevelopment through the coupling of cognitive and affective constituents. . . . [T]he coupling . . . enhance[s] their connectedness on future occasions. . . . [A]t the psychological level, . . . making sense of a situation on one occasion facilitates a similar interpretation on the next occasion. At the neural level, the activation of cortical synapses within an appraisal increases the probability of their coparticipation in a similar appraisal in the future. Thus, coupling within EIs strengthens interpretive habits, laying down characteristic appraisals . . . over macrodevelopment [personality]. It also predisposes an individual toward interpretive biases that forge moods in mesodevelopment'' (Lewis, this volume, p. 60). The self-similarity of these processes is demonstrated through four main parallels in form and function: the role of perturbation; emergence of new patterns following perturbation; cascading constraints, which crystallize present stability and reduce future variability; and circular causality in the interaction of higher-order form with lower-order constituents.

Self-similarity in the senses noted above, which capitalize on the fractal nature of dynamic systems, is a promising avenue for integration across vastly different (superficially, by this account) processes. But one may wonder how to demonstrate such self-similarity convincingly; in other words, how parallel do form and function need to be in order to show that the similarities of form and function (as opposed to the differences) are more than superficial? Alternately, would all dynamic systems that show such parallels be candidates for integration based on self-similarity? If not, what additional criteria (such as content) are needed? Again, this is not a criticism, but rather a challenge. The proposals make intuitive sense (at least to us), but the task of weeding out "false" from "true" self-similarity seems to depend on criteria yet to be defined.

Freeman (this volume) addresses the complexities of awareness, intention, and consciousness by positing a global brain phenomenon that draws on virtually all neural circuits in order to impose a general constraint on localized activity: "Consciousness as a sequence of global states is not an agent that initiates action. Nor is it an epiphenomenon. It is a state variable that constrains erratic activity by quenching local fluctuations. It is an order parameter and operator that comes into play in the action-perception cycle after an action has been taken, and during the learning phase of perception . . . a higher and more inclusive form of self-organization" (Freeman, this volume, pp. 232–233). This is an elegant proposal that identifies the nature of global order as a control parameter governing (in a self-organizing fashion) otherwise chaotic local activity. It is thus an emergent property of the system, not reducible to any particular location or circuit. Furthermore, it is possible to imagine ways in which such a claim might be tested using existing (or soon to be available) techniques of neuroscience, in that specific predictions about energy, coordination, perturbation, and other features could readily be generated.

Taken together, these and other contributions to this volume identify major features of the paradigm shift to new models of emotion and its development: they focus on integration and synthesis across subsystems, components, and time; they can easily entertain hypotheses of a level of complexity more attuned to the reality of emotion and emotional development; and they propose a variety of ways in which the complexity can be resolved into a coherent framework. Yet to be fully worked out, however, is a set of methods that affords meaningful, reliable tests of the validity of the dynamic systems propositions. Before returning to this question, we first consider a use of dynamic systems ideas with which many developmentalists are more familiar and more comfortable: the metaphors that they generate.

Dynamic Systems Metaphors

For many researchers of emotion and emotional development, the most immediate benefit of the new approach that is the focus of this volume lies in "opening up" theorizing about development. Although some of the new ideas have parallels in more conventional forms of theoretical endeavor, and some can be understood mathematically, there are many that are genuinely novel and valuable as metaphors. Lewis and Granic (this volume) offer a glossary of some of these key ideas, which we need not duplicate. Here we are concerned with their potential usefulness *as* metaphors, or engines for developmental thought and enquiry.

Multidimensionality and Reciprocal Causality

One of the troubling aspects of developmental theorizing within a linear model is the question of what constitutes a cause or an effect, especially when time is involved. We know that early developments arise from the concatenation of prior states and events (thus, they are effects), and that those effects can also become causal for future developmental pathways.

Clearly, we should expect causes and effects to be multidimensional, and often mutually causal. More advanced techniques within the general linear model can handle some, but not all, of the complexity this introduces (at least to date). Pathway or trajectory analyses come closest, but they still require a priori identification of core constructs or variables as the basis for aggregation. There are two potential limitations of a priori identification: (1) if construct validity is weak, confusing or spurious patterns may emerge; (2) novel patterns or constructs may go unrecognized. (Such assertions should be read with caution. Statistical modeling is a fast-moving field, and techniques to overcome these limitations may be just over the horizon.)

As noted, many nonlinear enthusiasts emphasize the limited value of strictly linear models. For them, metaphors of multidimensionality and reciprocal causality enhance the range of options for developmental theory, avoiding preassignment to causes or effects. It should be noted, though, that arguing from limitations is a default position. Opening up the possibilities is important, but it does not complete the task of developing suitable and workable alternatives.

Incommensurability and Developmental Timing

The magnitudes of causes and effects will not always be commensurate, and dynamic systems approaches do not require that they should be. Indeed, as noted by a number of authors, the timing of even a minor event may lead to a cascade of constraints and other events the magnitude of whose outcome for the individual is far greater than the seeming magnitude of its origin. The conventional rule of thumb that causes and effects should be of roughly the same magnitude allowed the inappropriate dismissal of significant events or interactions. In contrast, due to the nature of critical or sensitive periods in development, it is entirely likely that numerous features of development, especially early development, may become "biologically embedded" (Keating and Hertzman, 1999), leading to cascading effects on later development. Thus, the cascading metaphor is a useful one.

Discontinuities, Catastrophes, and Qualitative Change

A long-standing controversy in developmental science has been the nature of growth in many domains. Is it gradual and continuous, or abrupt and discontinuous? Learning theories have traditionally opted for the former, whereas developmentalists have tended to prefer the latter. A further issue is whether qualitative shifts are fairly regular (the Piagetian position) or highly idiosyncratic (the Vygotskian position). Even posing the question in this form implies its own answer: it depends on the system and its point in development (Keating, 1990). Dynamic systems approaches take this a step further, by laying out criteria for determining – once we have defined the system parameters – what constitutes hysteresis in a particular state space, and thus what constitutes a phase shift. In other words, metaphors of discontinuity lead, under the right circumstances, to appropriate empirical questions.

Attractors, Repellors, and Basins

These dynamic systems concepts can be used as metaphors that permit a major potential advance for theoretical models of development. Once we begin to imagine the topography of continuity, change, and development in these terms, many durable controversies in the field are reduced to disagreements about what part of the map one has chosen to explore. Attractors represent relatively steady states that the system gravitates toward. They are, however, not black holes from which the system can never escape; perturbations can move the system out of its current attractor, and it may settle into a new attractor. Basins are easy to visualize as the general field within which a system tends to operate, and are capable of "capturing" a system in operation and funneling it in a particular direction. Repellors are places on the map where a system is unlikely to go, and it would take a major perturbation and considerable force to produce movement in that direction. These metaphors, of course, are not the same as the methods available to test them, but they can be useful in thinking outside conventional constraints, as many of this volume's contributors attest.

Clinical Metaphors

Another class of important metaphors emerges from the contributions to this volume that derive potentially important and novel approaches to intervention and prevention from dynamic systems ideas. Ryan and colleagues (this volume), for example, argue that specific predictions about the most likely successful marital interventions can be derived from their mathematical model of successful and unsuccessful marital relationships. These interventions derive from specific parameters of the mathematical model, and their success in effecting change can be tested as changes within the model; they include goals such as improving the success of repair attempts, increasing physiological soothing, and responding to positivity. If such an approach were to prove successful, the power of the metaphors and models would be substantially enhanced.

Harkness and Tucker (this volume) derive ideas for interventions aimed at depression, not from a mathematical model, but rather from a theoretical analysis of the self-organizing dynamic system of neural development. They ask, ''Why are maladaptive patterns maintained when healthier, more rewarding ways of coping with life seem easily available? A possible answer is suggested by the cumulative nature of representations within a massively interconnected network, such as found in the human brain. . . . Because plasticity and change occur only at the expense of stability, the adult depressive may continue to suffer emotionally in order to maintain the continuity of the self. . . . If so, treatments for depression that work at the overt symptom level . . . may not result in enduring changes . . .'' (Harkness and Tucker, this volume, pp. 202–203). This implies, in their view, the necessity for perturbing the historical self sufficiently, by focusing on maladaptive patterns so as to induce schema change. Such interventions are not without risk, as they acknowledge, but their arguments, derived from self-organization metaphors, provide a sharp contrast to some conventional approaches to intervention, such as short-term symptom relief.

Granic (this volume) uses metaphors based on self-organization principles to hypothesize the reasons for the dramatic lack of success of interventions aimed at the aggressive child. Tracing a theoretical history from univariate to dyadic to circular and recursive interactions, she argues that the aggressive trajectory is effectively locked into a self-stabilizing set of interactions within the parent-child dyad and within the peer group setting. This implies that interventions will require greater sensitivity to developmental timing, to focus intervention efforts on "critical periods [that] may represent thresholds of instability at which the . . . system is more flexible and . . . amenable to treatment" (Granic, this volume, p. 290). Moving in this desirable direction presumes, of course, that we can generate a strong understanding of the underlying dynamics, including the control parameters.

In broader terms, the more that dynamic systems models and metaphors enable the identification of key control parameters in the underlying processes, and the state spaces and phases within which they operate, the more likely we will be to devise effective prevention and intervention strategies. Such approaches would also help to explain the lack of success of seemingly "obvious" interventions, which we may otherwise continue to believe would work if only we could apply them more effectively.

Dynamic Systems Methods

The pathway from models and metaphors to methods is perhaps the hardest step in validating the dynamic systems approach. Clearly, this is an evolutionary process, but as a number of the contributors acknowledge, there is a serious need for work to advance this approach. These are issues with which scientists operating within the general linear model (GLM) have been grappling. Too often, dynamic systems proponents have viewed the GLM as a straw man, rather than as a complementary form of analysis. It is important to remember that the mere presence of noise or residuals in the GLM does not validate dynamic systems models by default. Indeed, the potential complementarity of GLM and dynamic systems approaches should become an important focus of future work.

Both GLM and dynamic systems theorists have recognized for some time that the only truly causal pathways are embedded in the transactions between the organism and the environment over time.

> Both [correlational and experimental] methods favor main effects over interactions, whereas the development of all aspects of life . . . involves an interaction of heredity with environment. But dissecting that interaction will require a level of detail and precision not now available. (Green, 1992, p. 331)

As noted earlier, one major problem in pursuing this research agenda is its seemingly overwhelming complexity. The number of potentially important factors and their interactions expands exponentially as we take into account higher-order interactions, and even more when we examine the multiplicative interactions of those factors across time. Beginning with even a small set of factors, we quickly approach an effectively infinite set of possible causal arrangements, at least some of which will be indistinguishable on the basis of statistical fit to a model (Glymour et al., 1987).

The history of methodological developments that have contributed to our ability to make sound developmental inferences is continuously being rewritten. Certainly, the development and sophistication of multivariate analytic techniques represents a major step forward within the correlational approach. Campbell and Stanley's (1963) famous treatment of experimental and quasi-experimental designs expanded dramatically the ways that rigorous research on real, fully contextualized phenomena could be done. Cook and Campbell's (1979) extensions of this work on construct validity, identifying the underlying sources of observed covariance, introduced these important notions to a wide audience. In addition, Cole and Means (1981) have identified critical research methods for comparative studies, especially when differences between populations are the focus.

We need to recognize the tension between tightly controlled studies, which reduce or eliminate complexity by removing context, and studies that embrace a wide range of processes and contexts, but at the risk of being uninterpretable. How might we go about this integration of linear and nonlinear approaches? At the simplest level, it requires the incorporation of experimental, correlational, and developmental methods (including a narrative, historical mode). Darwin's work on evolution provides an interesting case study of this kind of integration, on an equally complex problem (Gould, 1986). A key part of this approach is the recognition that historical observation can be as robust a method as experimental intervention, depending on the question. Indeed, Gould (1986) argues cogently that Darwin's breakthrough was as much methodological as theoretical, and that the two were inseparable in establishing the reality of evolution.

Several areas of progress within the general linear model appear to hold particular promise for contemporary developmentalists. Structural equation modeling of longitudinal data of many different kinds, based on a variety of new techniques, is rapidly becoming quite accessible even to nonspecialists. Given the expanding opportunities for the secondary analyses of longitudinal data archives (Brooks-Gunn, Phelps, and Elder, 1991), it is possible to imagine multiple waves of analyses conducted through a variety of different lenses, to yield a coherent picture with increasing resolution.

Another pair of lenses that require better integration are what we can call marker and process analyses. The former can offer a clear picture of the distribution of various outcomes in the population, and the life courses and consequences that ensue. The latter, which incorporates information on developmental processes, offers the opportunity to interpret those patterns taking the several levels of history into account (Keating, 1999).

Previously, we have proposed (Keating, 1996) that the combination of these approaches might be viewed as a form of developmental integration, and have sought to apply that method to an integrated view of developmental diversity that we have termed "habits of mind" (Keating & Miller, 1999). Developmental integration is in this sense both a theory and a method. The theoretical goal is to describe the causal pathways linking the person, the social and physical environment, and time. In other words, context does not stand aside and operate independently as a modifier of underlying design, but, rather, is incorporated into the organism over time and becomes part of the internal structure of the person. It seems likely that the full realization of such an approach to developmental integration will need to incorporate both linear and nonlinear approaches, which may line up approximately as marker versus process analyses.

From Linear to Nonlinear Modeling: Innovative Methods

As noted previously, such integration across types of analytic approaches is both an opportunity and a challenge for dynamic systems approaches. A number of promising avenues have been opened up by various chapters in this volume. An exhaustive summary is not feasible due to space constraints, but some examples capture the range of approaches, as well as some issues that seem to require further development and resolution.

Just as in the case of the GLM, the development of a standardized "tool box" of dynamic systems methods for the study of emotion and its development, and of human development more broadly, will take some time. It is easy to forget, given the way in which it has become "second nature" to behavioral scientists, that the standard equipment of statistical analysis was invented and refined over many years.

State Space Mapping. State space maps can take many forms, and allow researchers to focus on a range of operators within the space. The incorporation of time as an essential feature of such maps is particularly desirable for developmental scientists. A key question arises regarding the numerous parameters that can be derived from such state space analyses:

How are they to be validated? This includes subsidiary questions, some of which have already been noted, about the reliability, replicability, and distributional qualities of such parameters. It seems likely that there will need to be some hard slogging in order to realize fully the potential of this methodology. A secondary, but important, question is the transparency of parameter derivation. Because such parameters emerge from complex mathematical formulae, such parameters run the risk of arbitrariness and ambiguity that has plagued many aspects of the GLM, from factor analysis to structural equation modeling.

Mathematical Models of Iterative Feedback. We have already discussed the work by Ryan and collaborators (this volume) that employed formal modeling procedures. It is clear that these are rich in interpretable parameters and in the capacity for system simulations. It will be important to consider and define the limitations of such approaches, some of which were also noted earlier. As we move from the sample upon which we derived the parameters to a new sample, for example, would we expect the same parameter estimates, or might we expect a poorer fit, not unlike shrinkage in regression estimates? Against what model should we compare the degree of difference in parameter estimates across different groups? These and related issues are likely to be highlighted in the validation process anticipated by these authors, but we emphasize the general point that moving from demonstration to validity is unlikely to be easy.

Catastrophe Flags and Other Dynamic Systems Indicators. The use of various indicators of the presence of nonlinearity or fluctuation, and estimates of its effects, has been around for some time (van der Maas and Molenaar, 1992). The contribution of de Weerth and van Geert (this volume) is a sound representative of this pioneering method, in which known features of dynamic systems (such as hysteresis or fluctuation) are estimated and identified both in real data sets and in simulations. A key question here is whether all ''flags'' of dynamic systems point in fact toward an underlying dynamic process. Or, to paraphrase Freud's famous observation, is noise sometimes just noise? More precisely, by what principles will we be able to sort out true positives from false alarms among dynamic systems indicators?

A number of further examples could be elaborated, but space constrains such indulgence. Two that should at least be noted are the use of dynamic systems models to resolve paradoxes arising from linear model analyses, such as the role of surprise as a coordinating structure (Camras, this volume), and the use of dynamic systems to shed new light on long-standing theories that appear to have implicit dynamic structure, such as the theory of discrete emotions (Izard et al., this volume) or attachment theory (Laible and Thompson, this volume). It is perhaps noteworthy that, in the latter cases, the idea that new light has been shed on existing theories is viewed more cautiously by those associated with them.

Future Directions

In this overview, we have looked at a number of key issues for the models, metaphors, and methods arising from the application of self-organizing dynamic systems principles to the study of emotion and its development. It is worth restating that, independent of the eventual outcome of dynamic systems approaches to this topic, the theoretical and empirical work in this volume clearly advances the field in dramatic ways, some of which we have attempted to summarize. As noted earlier, there is a real tension between excitement and caution regarding the application of dynamic systems analyses to these questions. Their potential seems unlimited – even to the anticipation of a "modern synthesis" – but the pathway to that outcome is challenging indeed. We conclude by first taking note of some of the caveats articulated throughout the volume and in our overview, and then by noting some additional issues that only add to our sense of the potential of this approach.

Some Caveats

Because the dynamic systems metaphors are so seductive, there is a danger that they will override methods and empirical analysis. Because we can imagine dynamic interactions at infinite levels, there is a corollary risk that we will attempt to model the "universe" of emotion and its development, integrating all processes into a "theory of everything." Experience tells us that this is not likely to be a successful scientific strategy. Expansion to new levels and integration across them is indeed desirable, but translation to fruitful research questions needs to be the primary goal and should set some significant constraints on how to proceed.

In moving along this pathway, it will take much time and effort to develop a standard "tool box" of dynamic systems methods, such that "normal science" can make use of them. Perhaps even more challenging will be efforts to create linkages among methods. At the moment, it is not obvious how the various methods described in this volume, some but not all of which we have summarized in this chapter, relate to each other. No doubt such linkages exist, but they will need to become more transparent if they are to be of more routine use. But as noted earlier, this evolution also characterized the emergence of the general linear model, which after all was invented, not delivered as divine revelation, despite its occasional mode of presentation in undergraduate methods courses. In the interim, it will be important not to overinterpret the outputs of dynamic systems methods, until we have a clearer track record on such mundane issues as reliability, generalizability, and validity. This is particularly true for many of the phenomena under consideration in this volume, where the low density of the data may render initial interpretations somewhat tenuous.

In this process, it is important to recognize the complementary strengths of the general linear model, which identifies candidate systems of interest with increasing resolution. This is of course in addition to its value as a practical tool – Newtonian mechanics is still crucial to engineering, for example, despite the paradigm shift to Einsteinian relativity in physics. Breakthroughs at the edge of the GLM, such as iterative structural equation modeling, may further blur the distinction, and exploring the boundaries of linear/nonlinear methods may well hold promise in the future.

Resolving Dualities (and Avoiding New Ones)

In focusing first on the caveats, we do not intend to place constraints above potential. Readers of this volume will have encountered various levels of excitement about the potential integrative capacity of this approach to emotion and emotional development. The potential for a unified theory does not strike us as unrealistic, but neither does it seem imminent. Perhaps the most crucial insight that cuts across this volume is that our fundamental categorizations of emotion may have sliced reality the wrong way. The analytic divisions between emotion and cognition; between episodes, moods, and personality; between neurobiological, psychological, and interpersonal, may have in their various ways conspired to obscure the core dynamics underlying emotion and its development. If this is so, then the categories of convenience to which we have become accustomed will need to yield to the more comprehensive models more accurately rooted in the complexities of mutually causal dynamic systems. In so doing, they may well resolve a number of damaging dualities that have plagued the study of development, including nature versus nurture, cooperation versus competition, continuity versus change, and continuous versus discontinuous development (Keating, 1999). From the perspective of self-organizing dynamic systems, these polarities are in creative tension with each other, and are thus necessarily resolved in any developing system.

In resolving these dualities, it is important not to introduce new ones in unproductive ways. One that has this potential should be noted. In making the case for emergent self-organization and novelty, it is sometimes too easy to eschew reductionism and constraints. As many of the contributors to this volume have noted, constraints are a key part of self-organizing systems. Sometimes those constraints arise from levels not in our purview, and we might prefer not to include them. One pertinent example is the relative absence in this volume of consideration of genetic influences on emotion and its development, or of macroenvironments that have their impacts at population levels. This is not a criticism, of course, because all treatments necessarily have boundaries. It is rather by way of observing that, as in the case of the other dualities, a bias toward either end of the polarity – emergence of novel forms versus reduction to constraints and external causes – can result in distorted perspectives. By focusing on the dynamic system as a whole and actualizing our conceptions using reliable methods for exploring real phenomena, we can avoid both the old dualities and the newly emerging ones. This volume suggests the promise and the challenge of choosing that path.

References

Brooks-Gunn, J., Phelps, E., and Elder, G. H. (1991). Studying lives through time: Secondary data analyses in developmental psychology. *Developmental Psychology, 27*, 899–910.

Bruner, J. (1990). *Acts of meaning*. Cambridge, MA: Harvard University Press.

Campbell, D. T., and Stanley, J. C. (1963). Experimental and quasi-experimental designs for research on teaching. In N. L. Gage (Ed.), *Handbook of research on teaching* (pp. 171–246). Chicago: Rand McNally.

Cole, M., and Means, B. (1981). *Comparative studies of how people think*. Cambridge, MA: Harvard University Press.

Cook, T. D., and Campbell, D. T. (1979). *Quasi-experimentation*. Boston: Houghton Mifflin.

Glymour, C., Scheines, R., Spirtes, P., and Kelly, K. (1987). *Discovering causal structure*. Orlando, FL: Academic Press.

Gould, S. J. (1986). Evolution and the triumph of homology, or why history matters. *American Scientist, 74*, 60–69.

Green, B. F. (1992). Exposé or smear? The Burt affair. *Psychological Science, 3,* 328–331.

Keating, D. P. (1990). Structuralism, deconstruction, reconstruction: The limits of reasoning. In W. F. Overton (Ed.), *Reasoning, necessity, and logic: Developmental perspectives* (pp. 299–319). Hillsdale, NJ: Erlbaum.

Keating, D. P. (1996). Habits of mind for a learning society: Educating for human development. In D. R. Olson and N. Torrance (Eds.), *Handbook of education and human development: New models of learning, teaching and schooling* (pp. 461–481). Oxford: Blackwell.

Keating, D. P. (1999). Developmental health as the wealth of nations. In D. P. Keating and C. Hertzman (Eds.), *Developmental health and the wealth of nations: Social, biological, and educational dynamics* (pp. 337–347). New York: Guilford.

Keating, D. P., and Hertzman, C. (1999). Modernity's paradox. In D. P. Keating and C. Hertzman (Eds.), *Developmental health and the wealth of nations: Social, biological, and educational dynamics* (pp. 1–17). New York: Guilford.

Keating, D. P., and Miller, F. K. (1999). Individual pathways in competence and coping: From regulatory systems to habits of mind. In D. P. Keating and C. Hertzman (Eds.), *Developmental health and the wealth of nations: Social, biological, and educational dynamics* (pp. 220–233). New York: Guilford.

van der Mass, H., and Molenaar, P. C. (1992). Stagewise cognitive development: An application of catastrophe theory. *Psychological Review, 99*, 395–417.

Name Index

Subject Index

abstract tier, and anger, 146t
accidie, 127
acetylcholine, 227
action readiness, 44
action units (Aus), 111
adaptation: and concurrent activation of emotions, 19; and discrete emotion systems, 17–18; and personality habits, 52; and shame, 25
admiration, and marital therapy, 368
adolescents, and sense of self, 57; *see also* development; parents and parent-child relations
affective-cognitive structures: and discrete emotion systems, 20–21; and dynamic systems theory, 32; and emotional interpretations, 43; *see also* cognitive systems and cognition
affects and affective states: and definition of mood, 51; and feeling tone, 128; and individual differences in discrete emotions, 23
AFFEX coding system, 108, 111, 112
aggression and aggressive behavior: and shame-anger patterns, 28, 29; socialization and parent-child relations, 270, 286–90
amygdala, and expression of emotion, 219
anger: and discrete emotion systems, 19–20; and emotional experience, 128, 130; and hysteresis, 89; and marital therapy, 369; and patterns of shame, 28–9; and self-organization, 136–48; use of term, 72; *see also* hostility
animal models: and EEG recordings of

emotional systems, 247; of neurological sequelae of early trauma, 194–5
appraisal and appraisal theory: and anger, 147; and catastrophe theory, 92–4; and component systems approach to emotional development, 128, 134; and definition of emotion, 126; and individual differences, 37; and mutual regulation, 130–2; parent-child relations and cognitive, 278; and relationship between cognition and emotion, 41–2; and subsystem synchronization, 86–7, 88; and theoretical progress in emotion theory, 3
arousal: and development of brain, 187–90; and histamine, 227; marital conflict and physiological, 356, 367
attachment and attachment theory: and developmental psychology, 303–6; and nonlinear state changes, 162–5; and personality, 52; and right hemisphere of brain, 178–9; and self-organization, 306–17; *see also* parents and parent-child relations
attention-deficit hyperactivity disorder (ADHD), 251–2
attractors: architecture of brain and intentional action, 223, 231; and attachment, 310–12; coercive, 287–8; and component systems approach, 134; definition of, 9; and dynamic systems metaphors, 383–4; and marriage, 359; and parent-child relations, 277–81, 283–4; and self-organization, 40, 45, 134; and stabilization, 273–4; and time scales, 301–2